MACROMEDIA DIRECTOR® 4 FOR MACS® FOR DUMMIES®

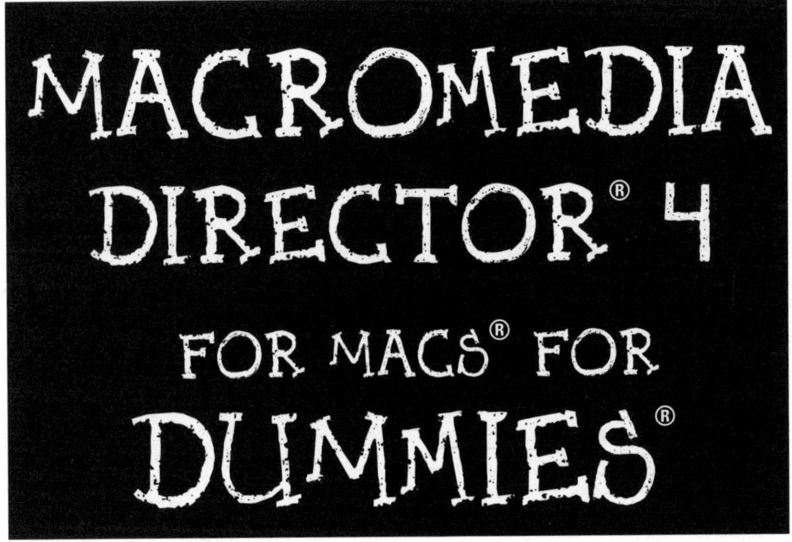

by Lauren Steinhauer

IDG Books Worldwide, Inc.
An International Data Group Company

Foster City, CA ♦ Chicago, IL ♦ Indianapolis, IN ♦ Braintree, MA ♦ Dallas, TX

Macromedia Director® 4 For Macs® For Dummies®

Published by
IDG Books Worldwide, Inc.
An International Data Group Company
919 E. Hillsdale Blvd.
Suite 400
Foster City, CA 94404

Library of Congress Catalog Card No.: 95-78406

ISBN: 1-56884-916-8

Printed in the United States of America

10 9 8 7 6 5 4 3 2 1

1E/SY/QX/ZV

Distributed in the United States by IDG Books Worldwide, Inc.

Distributed by Macmillan Canada for Canada; by Computer and Technical Books for the Caribbean Basin; by Contemporanea de Ediciones for Venezuela; by Distribuidora Cuspide for Argentina; by CITEC for Brazil; by Ediciones ZETA S.C.R. Ltda. for Peru; by Editorial Limusa SA for Mexico; by Transworld Publishers Limited in the United Kingdom and Europe; by Al-Maiman Publishers & Distributors for Saudi Arabia; by Simron Pty. Ltd. for South Africa; by IDG Communications (HK) Ltd. for Hong Kong; by Toppan Company Ltd. for Japan; by Addison Wesley Publishing Company for Korea; by Longman Singapore Publishers Ltd. for Singapore, Malaysia, Thailand, and Indonesia; by Unalis Corporation for Taiwan; by WS Computer Publishing Company, Inc. for the Philippines; by WoodsLane Pty. Ltd. for Australia; by WoodsLane Enterprises Ltd. for New Zealand.

For general information on IDG Books Worldwide's books in the U.S., please call our Consumer Customer Service department at 800-762-2974. For reseller information, including discounts and premium sales, please call our Reseller Customer Service department at 800-434-3422.

For information on where to purchase IDG Books Worldwide's books outside the U.S., contact IDG Books Worldwide at 415-655-3021 or fax 415-655-3295.

For information on translations, contact Marc Jeffrey Mikulich, Director, Foreign & Subsidiary Rights, at IDG Books Worldwide, 415-655-3018 or fax 415-655-3295.

For sales inquiries and special prices for bulk quantities, write to the address above or call IDG Books Worldwide at 415-655-3000.

For information on using IDG Books Worldwide's books in the classroom, or ordering examination copies, contact Jim Kelly at 800-434-2086.

About the Author

Lauren Steinhauer began his design career when dinosaurs roamed the earth and his computer career in 1983 in San Francisco with the Lisa, just before Apple introduced the first Macintosh. Lauren has provided multimedia creative services to clients such as Apple, Claris, Novell, and Sprint, authored numerous books on Macintosh technique, and led countless Macintosh workshops as a sought-after instructor. Lauren is a faculty member of San Francisco State's prestigious Multimedia Studies Department and offers multimedia creative services through Steinhauer & Associates in the City by the Bay.

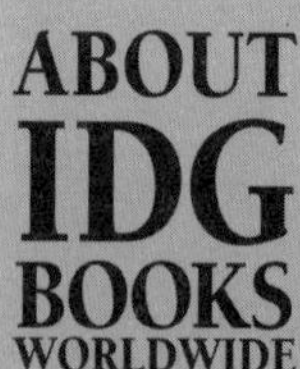

Welcome to the world of IDG Books Worldwide.

IDG Books Worldwide, Inc., is a subsidiary of International Data Group, the world's largest publisher of computer-related information and the leading global provider of information services on information technology. IDG was founded more than 25 years ago and now employs more than 7,500 people worldwide. IDG publishes more than 235 computer publications in 67 countries (see listing below). More than 60 million people read one or more IDG publications each month.

Launched in 1990, IDG Books Worldwide is today the #1 publisher of best-selling computer books in the United States. We are proud to have received 8 awards from the Computer Press Association in recognition of editorial excellence, and our best-selling *...For Dummies™* series has more than 17 million copies in print with translations in 25 languages. IDG Books Worldwide, through a recent joint venture with IDG's Hi-Tech Beijing, became the first U.S. publisher to publish a computer book in the People's Republic of China. In record time, IDG Books Worldwide has become the first choice for millions of readers around the world who want to learn how to better manage their businesses.

VIII

WINNER
Eighth Annual Computer Press Awards 1992

Our mission is simple: Every one of our books is designed to bring extra value and skill-building instructions to the reader. Our books are written by experts who understand and care about our readers. The knowledge base of our editorial staff comes from years of experience in publishing, education, and journalism — experience which we use to produce books for the '90s. In short, we care about books, so we attract the best people. We devote special attention to details such as audience, interior design, use of icons, and illustrations. And because we use an efficient process of authoring, editing, and desktop publishing our books electronically, we can spend more time ensuring superior content and spend less time on the technicalities of making books.

You can count on our commitment to deliver high-quality books at competitive prices on topics consumers want to read about. At IDG Books Worldwide, we value quality, and we have been delivering quality for more than 25 years. You'll find no better book on a subject than an IDG book.

John Kilcullen
President and CEO
IDG Books Worldwide, Inc.

IDG Books Worldwide, Inc., is a subsidiary of International Data Group, the world's largest publisher of computer-related information and the leading global provider of information services on information technology. International Data Group publishes over 235 computer publications in 67 countries. More than sixty million people read one or more International Data Group publications each month. The officers are Patrick J. McGovern, Founder and Board Chairman; Kelly Conlin, President; Jim Casella, Chief Operating Officer. International Data Group's publications include: **ARGENTINA'S** Computerworld Argentina, Infoworld Argentina; **AUSTRALIA'S** Computerworld Australia, Computer Living, Australian PC World, Australian Macworld, Network World, Mobile Business Australia, Publish!, Reseller, IDG Sources; **AUSTRIA'S** Computerwelt Oesterreich, PC Test; **BELGIUM'S** Data News (CW); **BOLIVIA'S** Computerworld; **BRAZIL'S** Computerworld, Connections, Game Power, Mundo Unix, PC World, Publish, Super Game; **BULGARIA'S** Computerworld Bulgaria, PC & Mac World Bulgaria, Network World Bulgaria; **CANADA'S** CIO Canada, Computerworld Canada, InfoCanada, Network World Canada, Reseller; **CHILE'S** Computerworld Chile, Informatica; **COLOMBIA'S** Computerworld Colombia, PC World; **COSTA RICA'S** PC World; **CZECH REPUBLIC'S** Computerworld, Elektronika, PC World; **DENMARK'S** Communications World, Computerworld Danmark, Computerworld Focus, Macintosh Produktkatalog, Macworld Danmark, PC World Danmark, PC Produktguide, Tech World, Windows World; **ECUADOR'S** PC World Ecuador; **EGYPT'S** Computerworld (CW) Middle East, PC World Middle East; **FINLAND'S** MikroPC, Tietoviikko, Tietoverkko; **FRANCE'S** Distributique, GOLDEN MAC, InfoPC, Le Guide du Monde Informatique, Le Monde Informatique, Telecoms & Reseaux; **GERMANY'S** Computerwoche, Computerwoche Focus, Computerwoche Extra, Electronic Entertainment, Gamepro, Information Management, Macwelt, Netzwelt, PC Welt, Publish, Publish; **GREECE'S** Publish & Macworld; **HONG KONG'S** Computerworld Hong Kong, PC World Hong Kong; **HUNGARY'S** Computerworld SZT, PC World; **INDIA'S** Computers & Communications; **INDONESIA'S** Info Komputer; **IRELAND'S** ComputerScope; **ISRAEL'S** Beyond Windows, Computerworld Israel, Multimedia, PC World Israel; **ITALY'S** Computerworld Italia, Lotus Magazine, Macworld Italia, Networking Italia, PC Shopping Italy, PC World Italia; **JAPAN'S** Computerworld Today, Information Systems World, Macworld Japan, Nikkei Personal Computing, SunWorld Japan, Windows World; **KENYA'S** East African Computer News; **KOREA'S** Computerworld Korea, Macworld Korea, PC World Korea; **LATIN AMERICA'S** GamePro; **MALAYSIA'S** Computerworld Malaysia, PC World Malaysia; **MEXICO'S** Compu Edicion, Compu Manufactura, Computacion/Punto de Venta, Computerworld Mexico, MacWorld, Mundo Unix, PC World, Windows; **THE NETHERLANDS'** Computer! Totaal, Computable (CW), LAN Magazine, Lotus Magazine, MacWorld; **NEW ZEALAND'S** Computer Buyer, Computerworld New Zealand, Network World, New Zealand PC World; **NIGERIA'S** PC World Africa; **NORWAY'S** Computerworld Norge, Lotusworld Norge, Macworld Norge, Maxi Data, Networld, PC World Ekspress, PC World Nettverk, PC World Norge, PC World's Produktguide, Publish& Multimedia World, Student Data, Unix World, Windowsworld; **PAKISTAN'S** PC World Pakistan; **PANAMA'S** PC World Panama; **PERU'S** Computerworld Peru, PC World; **PEOPLE'S REPUBLIC OF CHINA'S** China Computerworld, China Infoworld, China PC Info Magazine, Computer Fan, PC World China, Electronics International, Electronics Today/Multimedia World, Electronic Product World, China Network World, Software World Magazine, Telecom Product World; **PHILIPPINES'** Computerworld Philippines, PC Digest (PCW); **POLAND'S** Computerworld Poland, Computerworld Special Report, Networld, PC World/Komputer, Sunworld; **PORTUGAL'S** Cerebro/PC World, Correio Informatico/Computerworld, MacIn; **ROMANIA'S** Computerworld, PC World, Telecom Romania; **RUSSIA'S** Computerworld-Moscow, Mir - PK (PCW), Sety (Networks); **SINGAPORE'S** Computerworld Southeast Asia, PC World Singapore; **SLOVENIA'S** Monitor Magazine; **SOUTH AFRICA'S** Computer Mail (CIO),Computing S.A.,Network World S.A., Software World; **SPAIN'S** Advanced Systems, Amiga World, Computerworld Espana, Communicaciones World, Macworld Espana, NeXTWORLD, Super Juegos Magazine (GamePro), PC World Espana, Publish; **SWEDEN'S** Attack, ComputerSweden, Corporate Computing, Macworld, Mikrodatorn, Natverk & Kommunikation, PC World, CAP & Design, Datalngenjoren, Maxi Data,Windows World; **SWITZERLAND'S** Computerworld Schweiz, Macworld Schweiz, PC Tip; **TAIWAN'S** Computerworld Taiwan, PC World Taiwan; **THAILAND'S** Thai Computerworld; **TURKEY'S** Computerworld Monitor, Macworld Turkiye, PC World Turkiye; **UKRAINE'S** Computerworld, Computers+Software Magazine; **UNITED KINGDOM'S** Computing /Computerworld, Connexion/Network World, Lotus Magazine, Macworld, Open Computing/Sunworld; **UNITED STATES'** Advanced Systems, AmigaWorld, Cable in the Classroom, CD Review, CIO, Computerworld, Computerworld Client/Server Journal, Digital Video, DOS World, Electronic Entertainment Magazine (E2), Federal Computer Week, Game Hits, GamePro, IDG Books Worldwide, Infoworld, Laser Event, Macworld, Maximize, Multimedia World, Network World, PC Letter, PC World, Publish, SWATPro, Video Event; **URUGUAY'S** PC World Uruguay; **VENEZUELA'S** Computerworld Venezuela, PC World; **VIETNAM'S** PC World Vietnam.

05/17/95

Dedication

To the special people in my life, including Rudi, Dorian, my Mother and the rest of my family, and especially to my Big Brother, Rene, who is the real writer among us.

Acknowledgments

Many thanks to Mike Kelly for all of his great suggestions and to the rest of the hardworking people at IDG Books for putting this all together. Jay Lee provided invaluable advice and assistance with his technical review. Also, thanks to Megg Bonar at IDG Books and to Belinda Catalona and Carol McKlendon at Waterside for giving me the opportunity of putting this book together.

(The publisher would like to give special thanks to Patrick J. McGovern, without whom this book would not have been possible.)

Credits

Senior Vice President and Publisher
Milissa L. Koloski

Editorial Director
Diane Graves Steele

Acquisitions Editor
Megg Bonar

Brand Manager
Judith A. Taylor

Editorial Manager
Kristin A. Cocks

Editorial Executive Assistant
Richard Graves

Editorial Assistants
Stacey Holden Prince
Kevin Spencer

Acquisitions Assistant
Suki Gear

Production Director
Beth Jenkins

Supervisor of Project Coordination
Cindy L. Phipps

Pre-Press Coordinator
Steve Peake

AssociatePre-Press Coordinator
Tony Augsburger

Media/Archive Coordinator
Paul Belcastro

Project Editor
Michael Kelly

Copy Editor
Michael Simsic

Technical Reviewer
Jay Lee

Associate Project Coordinator
Sherry Gomoll

Production Staff
Gina Scott
Carla C. Radzikinas
Patricia R. Reynolds
Melissa D. Buddendeck
Dwight Ramsey
Robert Springer
Theresa Sánchez-Baker
Kathie S. Schnorr
Linda Boyer
Megan Briscoe
Brandt Carter
Jae Cho
Angie Hunckler
Brad Johnson
Mark Owens
Laura Puranen
Tim Sturgeon

Proofreader
Kathleen Prata

Indexer
David Heiret

Book Design
University Graphics

Cover Design
Kavish + Kavish

Contents at a Glance

Cartoons at a Glance

By Rich Tennant

"ALL RIGHT, NOW, WE NEED SOMEONE TO PLAY THE PART OF THE GEEK."

Page 289

"How's that for live animation?"

Page 51

"FOR ADDITIONAL SOFTWARE SUPPORT, DIAL "9", "POUND" THE EXTENSION NUMBER DIVIDED BY YOUR ACCOUNT NUMBER, HIT "STAR", YOUR DOG, BLOW INTO THE RECEIVER TWICE, PUNCH IN YOUR HAT SIZE, PUNCH OUT YOUR LANDLORD,..."

Page 342

"No, they're not really a gang, just the new multimedia division."

Page 137

"Let me guess. Another example of interactivity gone awry."

Page 227

Page 333

"It's amazing how much more some people can get out of Director than others."

Page 291

"THERE YOU ARE, SIR. ONE MACPAINT, A MACWRITE, A MAC-ACCOUNTANT, TWO MACSLOTS, A MACPHONE, AND A MACDRAW. WOULD YOU LIKE FRIES WITH THAT?"

Page 9

Page 17

"The error messages on these multimedia applications are getting more interactive all the time."

Page 264

Table of Contents

Introduction

I know, like everyone else, you want to be in the movies. And since Hollywood hasn't been ringing your phone off the hook the last couple of weeks — or years, for that matter — what better than multimedia with Macromedia Director? But wait — just the mention of the name, Director, and, like a .45 caliber Magnum at your temple in a dark alley on Friday the 13th, your palms begin to sweat, your heart rate triples, and you get acne for the first time in 31 years. Director? Me?

You've heard all the stories. Director's hard, like a shot of cheap bourbon at 2 a.m. after a tough case. It's impossible, like the woman who wouldn't forgive you for turning her in — your mother yet. It's rough, like three-day old stubble. (No, I'm not still talking about your mother.)

We've all heard these stories. And they're true.

Unless you have this book. And you have this book, haven't you? At least it's in your hands. Whether you pay for it is between you, your conscience, and the brawny security guard breathing down your neck. Director has a high learning curve; it doesn't hurt to be a rocket scientist with neurosurgery as a side hobby. But ordinary people like you and me can learn to use Director and make smart looking, successful multimedia productions with it.

Who You Are

What I'm trying to say is, this writer's making some basic assumptions about someone who won't ante up more than $19.99 for a book, er, I mean, about someone who buys a book from the . . . *For Dummies* series of computer books. I'm assuming one or more of the following about you:

- You're new to Macintosh computing.
- You're new to animation.
- You're new to multimedia.
- You're new to computing, period.
- You're intimidated by technical jargon.

- You're not interested in technical jargon.
- You're the owner of a 68030 Mac or better.
- You're running the Mac on some version of System 7 (or at least System 6).
- You've had flashbacks of alien abduction lately.

What This Book Offers You

I've done everything possible to make this book on Macromedia Director friendly and accessible. Don't be surprised if you begin feeling like dating it after a couple of reads. I'm not going to make all the assumptions those other books make, as if you're born knowing the difference between a bit and a byte, or what a script is all about (in DirectorSpeak).

This book breaks down seemingly impossible tasks into easy, doable steps, making the essential features of Director windows crystal clear. Director has 13 basic windows, but this book concentrates heavily on the most important windows, including

- The Stage window
- The Cast window
- The Score window
- The Paint window

This book is going to give you plenty of pictures for reference (and to color if you like), and lots of Director tips and tricks. The last chapter of this historic book virtually brims with stuff that'll help make your life more carefree as you learn Director. It may even pay off your mortgage and make your kids behave in public.

Icons Used in This Book

Some of the aids included for you are marked with distinctive icons. In fact, if you cut them out real carefully and paste them neatly on acid-free card stock, they make real nifty holiday gifts.

Optional reading to ease you into a few technical areas for budding propeller-heads and help prepare you for re-reading the manual (you have read the manual, haven't you?) and help prepare you for advanced Macromedia Director topics.

Your Mac is very hale and hardy (I actually knew a person who was hale but not necessarily hardy), which is not to say you should occasionally drop your Mac from a twelve-story building. Physically, you can only break your Mac a couple of ways, and even then, only with determination: plugging or unplugging computer cables while the Mac's on and the ever popular moving-your-Mac-while-it's-running trick, a great way to learn what hard disk head crashes and peptic ulcers are all about. Software-wise, you may try something during the course of exploring Director that makes your Mac freeze up, display an error message, or behave in some other unusual way, but it's just software. As long as you have good backups — you do back up all your software, don't you? — the worst that can happen is having to reinstall Director or your system file. So the Warning icon is meant to alert you to potentially risky or foolhardy detours and acrobatics while working with Director and your Mac. And doting father figure that I am, I'll remind you occasionally to save your work and be sure to eat plenty of leafy, green vegetables.

Throughout the book, you'll find many suggestions to make working with Director more productive, creative, or just generally more successful, such as storing avocados in a brown bag helps them ripen real fast.

This book is also liberally sprinkled with notes or asides that either clarify a point made or seem related, however feebly, to the current topic.

This book is produced with remarkable state-of-the-art scratch-and-hear technology. When you come to one of these, scratch the icon so you can read while listening to Ed Ames sing, "Try to remember. . . ." Hah, caught you scratching.

Conventions Used in This Book

This book tries to be more helpful than those other books on Director. On the off chance you need some information from another computer book, you're sure to run into some descriptions that seem puzzling to you because they won't bother explaining what they mean. However, because I love each and every one of you dearly, I will. You're welcome. It's not that I won't have some standard ways of saying things; it's just that this section helps you know how to interpret them when the time comes. Everyone, put on your decoder rings.

The conventions used in this book include the following two generic forms:

- *Menu Name⇨Command Name:* An example of this convention is "Choose Edit⇨Paste," which means, "Press the mouse on the Edit menu and choose the Paste command." Sometimes I'll say, "Go to the Paste command from the Edit menu," or "Choose Paste from the Edit menu." You'll run into the generic form frequently when you read more technical books.
- *Modifier Key+Other Key:* The Command key, Shift key, Option key, and occasionally the Control key are the Mac modifier keys. With one or more of them pressed in combination with a standard key, you can use keyboard shortcuts for various menu commands or apply a specific Mac technique to a selection. An example is, "Pressing Command+1 alternately hides and shows the menu bar," to mean, "Hold down the Command key and press the 1 key." Occasionally, you may have to use two modifier keys with a keyboard shortcut.

The Command key also has its own symbol, which looks like this: ô. You may find this symbol in this book, in a line referring to pressing the Command key. By the way, some of the newer keyboards emboss both the Apple icon and the "daisy" icon on the Command key. Either icon means the same thing: the Command key.

The Indubitable Rules of Keystrokes

When using modifier keys for keyboard shortcuts, be sure to follow "The Indubitable Rules of Keystrokes," as follows:

1. Press the Command key first.
2. Press other modifier keys next.
3. Press the standard key or keys last.
4. After pressing the complete sequence, release the keys unless specifically instructed not to.

Does This Book Cover Everything?

Now that we've become close, personal friends, you have the gall to ask me, "Does this book have everything anyone ever wanted to know about Director?"

Well, no way. What won't you find in this book? Laughs for one, as you have already found out. You won't find an explanation for every command of every window, either. You won't find detailed pontificating on every Lingo command. (Lingo is Director's name for its built-in computer language.) You won't find many advanced techniques covered, although I do mention some in passing for you prospective propeller-heads out there.

But this book does get you started in a big way. I sincerely think that what this book doesn't cover is more than made up for with clear, concise information about Macromedia Director essentials for the budding computer user and multimedia wannabe, plus nice wide margins to doodle on.

How This Book Is Organized

This book contains three major parts, each part containing several chapters, each chapter made up of billions upon billions of molecules. Makes you think, huh. This is not a book you need to read from cover to cover. I've read it cover to cover for you. I've written the book from the perspective of a comfy reference; this book should summon up images of overstuffed chairs, a crackling fireplace, a Rockwellesque white-haired grandpa tenderly hugging his grandchild as they peruse a fine, weathered, leather-bound classic together. Okay, so this is a softcover printed on paper one notch up from newsprint; use your God-given imagination, won't you? What I'm trying to convey is each topic and exercise is relatively self-contained. Using the Table of Contents or the Index, you can go to any topic and find usable, accessible information on the subject in question and plenty of fine, fire-kindling material to boot.

Part I: The Big Picture

In Part I, I ask you to think big. Bigger. That's it. Now you're set to tackle cosmic questions like, "What is the meaning of life?," "Is there absolute good and evil?" and "How do I install this darn software, anyway?" Part I covers all that existential stuff with illustrations and references numerous enough to cut out and use as designer wallpaper. Along the way, you make incredible discoveries, including the fact that *multimedia* really means something. And that that blank screen you first come to in Director actually has a purpose. And a name.

Part II: Director's Windows of Opportunity

After Part I, the book rapidly focuses on unimportant stuff, such as how to use Director's Cast, Score, Paint, and Text windows. Just learning about the Cast window will make you want to go out and buy a couch. After discovering secrets of the Score window, you'll be swept up in an overpowering urge to pull on riding britches and long boots, and watch creaky, old Erich Von Stroheim movies all night. And I deliberately toned down the Paint window stuff so that you're not tempted to decide you were born with one ear too many. Finally, if the Text window info doesn't bring out the Hemingway in you, I don't know what will.

Part III: Manipulating Director with More Windows

The richness of Director's windows and commands contributes to the program's reputation for being the premiere multimedia-making application. Part III covers Director's remaining windows with thorough but humorous abandon. In fact, I dare you not to laugh yourself silly as you learn about the whimsical Tools window for creating QuickDraw shapes in Director, the belly laugh-inducing Digital Video window for incorporating QuickTime movies into your Director productions, and the side-splitting Color Palettes window for color coordinating Director movies to your underwear.

Part IV: More Interaction, Please!

Here's the Part where you ease into Director's talents for lifting a presentation beyond a glorified slideshow by taking advantage of your Mac's unique computing powers. You learn how to add special effects to your movies with push-button ease and how to use Director's computer language, Lingo, to open up a whole new world of interactivity and excess stomach acid.

Part IV is kind of like riding the bobsleds at Disneyland. Something both thrilling and terrifying draws you to the Matterhorn. Except this ride is more thrilling than terrifying, even if you've never thought of using a computer language in your life. For one thing, Lingo is very conversational in tone. In fact, Lingo's simpler than ever, and believe it or not, you'll be writing Lingo scripts before you know it. I wind up Part IV discussing what multimedia is like in the real world and leave with the burning question, "Do you really want to wear all those hats, and wouldn't that attract a lot of unwanted attention?"

Part V: The Part of Tens

I don't know why, but whenever I think of Part V's name, I can't help picturing Charlton Heston saying it as a line from one of his biblical epics. Can't you just picture him exclaiming, "The Part of Tens," his mouth and chin making those distinctively "Hestonian" gestures? Anyway, Part V includes ten frequently asked questions. For example, perfect strangers come up to me all the time asking, "What's so great about using film loops?" That's the kind of life I lead. And so may you all, if only you can draw the following picture.

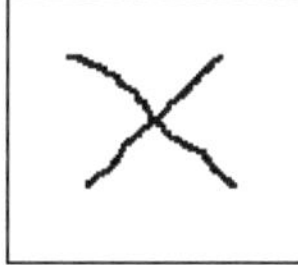

Figure I-1: You, too, can be a multimedia professional.

Seriously, Part V also reviews the ten most important ways to add animation to your Director movies and the ten most essential Lingo commands and concepts to become comfortable with.

What's Next?

Aside from paying for the book, the next step is to turn the page and dive right into the task of tackling Director. Don't forget that burly security guard.

Part I

The Big Picture

The 5th Wave **By Rich Tennant**

"THERE YOU ARE, SIR. ONE MACPAINT, A MACWRITE, A MAC-ACCOUNTANT, TWO MACSLOTS, A MACPHONE, AND A MACDRAW. WOULD YOU LIKE FRIES WITH THAT?"

In this part...

If you've ever dreamed of creating multimedia of your very own, there's no better time to dive in with Macromedia Director 4, by far the easiest version of this program to work with since its humble beginning back in 1985.

Even if you just began your Mac career, this part will prep you for your adventure with introductory chapters where you'll learn why Director is the program of choice for so many multimedia developers, why you should be nutty enough to join their growing ranks, and what multimedia is all about in the first place.

Chapter 1

Stars of Director: Graphics, Sound, Movement, and Old Smiley Face

In This Chapter

- Exploring uses for Director
- Defining multimedia

At one time, multimedia meant setting up a bank of slide projectors, saying your best prayer, and hoping against hope everything would work, without the benefit of anything approaching a personal computer. In 1984, Apple Computer introduced its first Macintosh model, the 128K, with a whopping two programs to explore, MacPaint and MacWrite; few people then were astute enough to anticipate how dramatically this "toy" was to change our personal and professional lives in the years to come.

I wasn't one of them.

My boss dragged me kicking and screaming toward the opposite direction before I wound up, exhausted, by the 128K, my first computer. I think the carpeting still shows heel marks like a jagged scar, leading from traditional drafting table to computer desk. However, I learned to love my Mac; the following year, I was rewarded for this change of heart by being among the first to play with a fascinating new program as part of my job description. The program was VideoWorks, among the major catalysts for today's multimedia industry and destined to evolve into Macromedia Director 4, the current version upon which this book is based.

For those of you new to computing, this book uses the terms *application, program,* and *software* interchangeably. It's what makes you break open your wallet at the computer store; what you take home on one or more floppy disks, copy to your hard drive, and use to accomplish various tasks. Perhaps you're using Microsoft Word for word processing and Excel for creating spreadsheets; they're applications, programs, software — same thing.

As the name of this book implies, I'll be referring to the Macintosh when discussing Director in all its intricacies. However, much of the information within these pages applies to Macromedia's new Director for Windows, too. The programs are nearly mirror images of each other, and in fact, one can open movies of the other with ease, if not downright abandon. For those so inclined, or if you anticipate the need to "port," as we multimedia types like to say, your Director movies to the PC, check out the last section in Chapter 21, "Can I Play My Mac Movies on a PC?", where I review common pitfalls to avoid in the process.

What Do We Use Director For?

Some of you in ReaderLand may desperately want to learn Macromedia Director without the slightest notion why. OK, I'm going to give you some great ammo to fight back with when your spouse finds out you just plunked down nearly a grand for a handful of $3^1/_2$-inch plastic squares you insist are called floppies, along with a couple of beads and a Captain Zork decoder ring you threw in to make the deal look more impressive.

Following in Walt what's-his-name's footprints

First, you'll be able to tell your friends and relatives you're an animator, just like Walt what's-his-name, because Director's an *animation program,* first and foremost. In other words, Director gives you the tools to make presentations that don't just sit there, but actually get up and move. From its humble beginnings in a log cabin — introduced in 1985 as VideoWorks — Director was built to create a unique type of presentation — eye candy that changes over time.

As you explore the successor of VideoWorks, you'll see that Director offers special windows to help build this kind of presentation. For example, you'll run into the Score window, aptly named because it's very much like a musical score, with its distinctive shorthand recording changes in the presentation from moment to moment. In Director's Score window, you can follow the flow of visual information of your presentation, as well as rearrange and modify this information. In another special window, the Stage window, you'll be able to play back your masterpiece. And when your spouse comes up and asks, "Honey, what do you want to do now?" you can say, "I'm going to Disneyland!"

Becoming another Lincoln

How'd you like to have your kids smile up at you and boast to their friends, "My dad's just like Lincoln." Aside from the distinctive facial features, maybe they recognize that you take advantage of Director's *interactive* features to give The People the freedom to navigate through tons of information by choosing what they want to find out about, and having darn good fun at the same time.

Director offers this interactivity by allowing you to integrate graphics, music, narration, sound effects, and movies, as well as buttons to choose what comes up next. Normally, this type of production is reserved for programmers — you know, those people who look like Bill Gates — but Director allows all of us interested in this sort of thing to actually realize our ideas and present them to others.

In other books, you may hear Director described as a program that changes data over time. Which begs the question, "What is data?" I had to look through 12 or 13 glossaries from technical books in my library before I found one definition for data. We're supposed to be born knowing what data is. Well, data is information, plain and simple. When combining information with computers, our definition comes to include some kind of translation process so that information becomes a set of signals recognized by your computer. Only then can a computer like the Mac handle the information; moving, modifying, or manipulating it according to your wishes.

When talking about information "changing over time," I don't mean time from a geological or cosmic perspective, but time measured in very small units, 30ths or 60ths of a second, units so small you're not aware of moving from one to the next. A working definition of animation is visual information changing in units of $^1/_{30}$ of a second. VideoWorks's windows and commands were designed to handle this kind of information, very different from data that a program such as Microsoft Word manipulates. When you type a letter in Word, save the file, and look it over for typos, the letter doesn't change; it's static information. If it does, I've got the number of a great exorcist for you.

By the Way, What the Heck is Multimedia?

Even if you already know that you want to create animation with Director, I'll just bet you probably have a pretty murky concept of what Director's other forte, multimedia, is all about. And "I know it when I see it" just doesn't cut it with those Fortune 500 clients. Trust me.

Defining multimedia is a real challenge; I haven't seen the same definition for multimedia in any two books. It's one of those slippery things to define, like art, truth, and Aunt Edna's holiday fruitcake.

But let's try to agree on a working definition and to stay away from Aunt Edna's holiday fruitcake.

Working definition of multimedia: Multimedia is the presentation of information by combining images, sounds, and movement with the power of the computer.

Now, on to explore this definition one chunk at a time.

Multimedia is image

Multimedia has something to do with images. It's hard to imagine multimedia without graphics, movies, artwork, or photographs. Actually, images represent the strongest component of multimedia.

As it turns out, we're visually oriented creatures getting about 80 percent of the information around us through our sense of sight; compare the richness of our visual life with our sense of smell, taste, or even touch. The other senses are all exquisite, but slip a blindfold over us, and we're lost. You've all seen those figures about how many advertising messages bombard us each day and how much TV we watch (or endure). So commanding visuals is certainly a dominant constituent of multimedia.

Multimedia is sound

But what would multimedia be without sound? Did you know "silent" movies were never silent? A pianist or organist accompanied each screening, and sometimes a sound-effects man was there in the dark, too, adding thunder, clattering horse hooves, and, of course, gunshots to the drama.

Have you ever turned the sound off your TV and watched a movie or commercial without sound? Think of some of your favorite movie scenes and then imagine them without sound. Try to conceive the climactic scene in *Close Encounters of the Third Kind* when the great mother ship appears over Devil's Tower, hovering jewel-like over the gaping scientists. Imagine the stargate sequence in *2001: A Space Odyssey* without sound. Very different experiences — and not for the better.

So sound, including sound effects, music, and narration, is also a major player, no pun intended, in the multimedia game.

Multimedia is movement

In this age of MTV, with its overpowering imagery and movement, color and movement, and creative abandon . . . and movement, movement is an integral extension of the force of imagery that plays such an important part in defining multimedia. And movement.

In an attempt to stretch the definition of movement, pioneers of multimedia, ahem , myself included, tried incorporating video into productions with clumsy workarounds, multiple monitors, separate VCRs, laser disc players, controllers, and wires, wires, and more wires. Then, a couple of years ago, Apple Computer turned the world upside-down with something called *QuickTime,* allowing multimedia types to add video directly within Director with all the Hollywood claptrap — dissolves, fade-ins, fade-outs, really wild special effects, and, oh yes, some content.

QuickTime is what's known as a system extension, meaning an addition to the system. By itself, QuickTime does nothing. Find it in the Extensions folder and try double-clicking its icon. Your Mac gets ticked off and sends you a stern warning. Look how serious the little face looks in the upper left corner — definitely an A-type personality.

Then what does QuickTime do? QuickTime allows your Mac to handle the kind of information discussed earlier in this chapter, information that changes over time, in the form of a special file type called a QuickTime movie or, as this file type has come to be known, *mooV* (pronounced moo-vee).

But TV offers photos, graphics, movies, movement, and sounds of every description — and more than a few that are beyond description. If you've ever caught the "Geraldo" show, you know what I mean. Why isn't TV multimedia? Or movies, for that matter? One other element completes our working definition of multimedia.

Multimedia is your Mac

The power of the computer is the digital glue that binds the other elements of multimedia together and adds the final touches: *interactivity* and *hypertext.* Multimedia has something to do with using the computer to give the user, the person in front of the computer, the freedom to explore information with interactive and hypertext techniques.

Historically, most information has been linear, meaning you start on page one, march in step through subsequent pages, and on the last page, you stop. If you graphed the content, you'd wind up with a straight line — that's linear. What do you get when you graph interactive multimedia? A graph that looks more like a tree with hundreds or thousands of branches. In fact, many multimedia products feature such a map to help the user navigate.

Interactive multimedia

Defining interactivity and hypertext is as slippery as defining multimedia. Thanks a lot. When you use the power of the computer to give the user the ability to decide where to start and which direction to go, you add *interactivity* to multimedia.

As you build your presentation in Director, you add interactivity by presenting the user with options in the form of buttons, sliders, and other controls that look like familiar objects in the real world. Here's where it helps to know at least a little Lingo scripting and when it might be a good idea to check out Chapter 23 on Lingo tips and tricks.

Hypertext

When you use the power of the computer to add conceptual links to text the user can explore, you create *hypertext,* allowing the user to delve into deeper and deeper layers of information at will. The user is unaware of how these links work, that is, they are transparent to the user. Ironically, how you go about creating these links is basically with transparent buttons on the screen that take the user to different sections of the presentation.

Interesting but moldy history of ye olde attempts at interactivity and hypertext

Early insightful experiments in interactivity and hypertext cry out to be cited here. Many illuminated manuscripts, those beautifully gilded pages of hand-drawn text and wondrous illustration from bygone days, feature hyper-text in their structure. As you inspect them carefully — please, put those white gloves on and no sneezing — note the large central block of text, and the smaller text to its left, and yet another, smaller block of text to the left. This is hyper text, 12th-century style. In other words, this kind of layout allows the reader to break away from the main text and delve into deeper levels of content on an intellectual whim. Power is transferred to the reader — that's nearly interactive multimedia; just add a gerbil-powered Mac and you're off and running.

I've got to include the magical *Tristram Shandy,* the novel by Laurence Sterne published in 1760, in this stopover into antiquity. If you've never read it, do yourself a favor. Beg, borrow, or steal a copy. *Tristram Shandy* is not your ordinary book; describing it makes defining multimedia look like a picnic with no ants. There are suddenly blank pages, there are pages with one word on them, there are weird pages. In this inverted Tom Jonesian world, the author tells his story not only with text but with the words themselves, the very pages of the book and how they are or are not laid out. *Tristram Shandy* is certainly an impressive experiment in multimedia, hypertext, interactivity, the whole shebang, worthy of reading and studying.

The 5th Wave
By Rich Tennant
©RICH TENNANT
AND TO COMPLETE THE MULTIMEDIA EXPERIENCE, WE WANT TO SHIP EACH WORKSTATION WITH THIS SCRATCH 'N SNIFF MOUSE PAD AND A SCENT-RESIDENT RAM CARD.

Chapter 2

Launching Director: An Application by Any Other Name

In This Chapter

- Reviewing the Mac, Director's executive producer
- Looking around Director
- Exploring Director's About box
- Purging Director's memory
- Calling S.O.S. with D.O.L.H. (Director's on-line Help)
- Help Pointer? Thought I just pointed to Help
- Using Director's File menu
- Touring Director's other menus

Why has the Mac been such a success, making its founders Steve Jobs and Steve Wozniak instant holders of savings accounts in excess of $1,000 each and revolutionizing the way we work with and think about computers and software? Most computer pundits agree: Chili is better with a big topping of cheddar cheese. Also, the Mac owes much of its success to an innovative graphical user interface, integral to the Mac since the introduction of the Mac 128K in 1984.

I lied. Before 1984, before the Mac 128K, the Apple Lisa was around, which was also my first computer. It stood in all its magnificence like a Mac 128K on steroids, with a 12-inch built-in monitor for the 128K's 9-inch screen. If the Lisa and Mac had met on the beach, Lisa would've kicked sand in Mac's little Smiley Face. It cost $10,000 in pre-1984 dollars, which was a big reason for its demise; we who could afford the Lisa loved it and got a preview of the Mac's Desktop, trash can, menu bar, and icons to boot. And they say money can't buy happiness.

The graphical user interface, or *GUI* (pronounced goo-ee), is the set of mostly visual cues used to work with the Mac in contrast to the old-style *CLI,* or command line interface, which is like *DOS* (Disk Operating System) for PCs where the user faces a featureless screen, reads lines of generic text generated by the computer program, and types in code words from memory or a chart to go to the next step in the program. The Mac's GUI includes the following:

- The Desktop, where you find application and file icons, folder icons, the menu bar at the top of the screen, the hard drive icon, and the trash can, all visual representations or symbols for information coming either from chips in the Mac or from the hard drive.
- The menus and windows of programs you open, and the visual similarity of one program to another.
- The general "look and feel" of the Mac, its friendliness and patience with users — all built-in, of course.

Reviewing the Mac, Director's Executive Producer

One of the Mac's most endearing features is its cozy familiarity. After you learn one Macintosh program, you probably know 30 to 40 percent of every well-written Mac program out there in Marketdom. So opening or launching a heavy-duty program like Macromedia Director is as simple as opening the simplest program you can find. But if you need a quick refresher course in Macology 101, use the following section to get some basic Mac skills up and running first.

Starting your Mac

One way of sorting Mac models apart is how you start them, which gives you two very high stacks of chips, plastic, frosty glass monitors, and model names. You start one set of Macs with a switch; in compact-type Macs with built-in monitors such as the Mac SE and Classic and with some Performas and Mac LCs, chances are a rocker switch is in back and to the left with the Mac facing you. Some oddball Macs like the 660AV and some Power Macs have round button-like switches located in the front right panel rather than rocker switches. Either way, turn on your Mac with the switch.

You start the other type of Mac — Mac II types, some Quadras, some Power Macs, and assorted Performas — from the Power key on the keyboard. The

System 7 alert

I'm assuming you have some version of System 7.0 running your Mac. The descriptions of menus, menu bars, and windows, as well as the illustrations in this book, are based on System 7.5, the latest version of what is now known as the Mac OS (Macintosh Operating System). If you're running the original release of System 7.0, your screen may differ slightly from the illustrations. If you're running the previous system, System 6.0, your screen will differ a little more dramatically, but, once in Director, much of what you see will be very similar if not the same. If you're running an earlier system, shame on you!

Power key is the wide key at the top left of your keyboard, unless you have a really old keyboard where you'll probably find the Power key at the top center. Embossed on the Power key is an off-center icon of a simple pointer, as shown in Figure 2-1.

Simply give the Power key one good press. Then listen for the bong, somewhere around a C-chord for the musically inclined, and soon you see Mr. Smiley Face

Figure 2-1: Power on your Mac!

beaming back at you, the ever popular "Welcome to Macintosh" greeting, and finally the comfy Desktop with trash can and icons. What a trash can is doing on *top* of the Desktop I don't know.

Your pal, the mouse

The humble mouse has actually been around quite a while, long before 1984 when Apple Computer introduced the Macintosh 128K. The late '60s saw a growing interest for a personal computer, although few people could articulate why they wanted a computer and what they'd do with one. While one far-thinking individual, Ivan Sutherland, was working with an early type of graphical user interface astonishingly like what you see today when you a open high-powered graphics program such as Adobe Illustrator, a gentleman named Doug Englebart was developing an odd-looking device he called a mouse for working with his computer. Englebart's mouse looked like a giant bar of Ivory soap. Similar devices appeared at Xerox's Palo Alto Research Center in the '70s, where advanced studies on how people use computers were underway; many of their innovative concepts, including the mouse, wound up reflected in the Macintosh.

Double-clicking

At any rate, double-clicking the mouse is an essential technique when working with the Mac but some of us have trouble getting the hang of it. If you click too slowly, the Mac doesn't recognize the maneuver as a double-click of the mouse, but as two separate clicks, which won't give you the desired results.

One way to make double-clicking easier is to adjust the mouse with the Mouse control panel. You'll find it under the Apple menu at the top left of your screen. From the Apple menu, select Control Panels and look for the Mouse control panel icon, as shown in Figure 2-2.

Figure 2-2: The Mouse control panel icon.

Select the Mouse control panel and choose Open from the File menu, which takes you to the window in Figure 2-3.

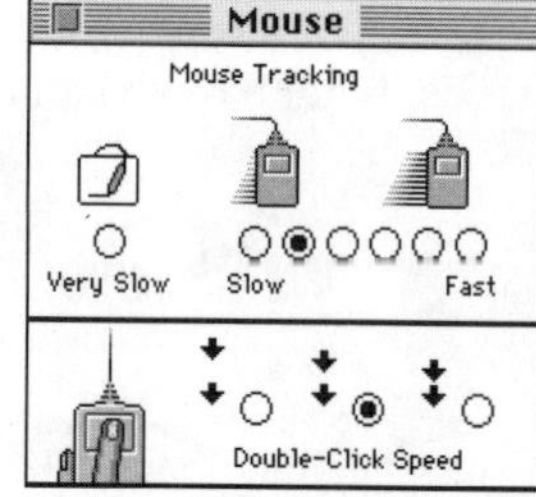

Figure 2-3: The Mouse control panel.

In the bottom panel, you can adjust the mouse's sensitivity to double-clicking. The small round radio buttons give you three levels of Double-Click Speed, from slow on the left to medium in the center to fast on the right. If you're a fast clicker, click the right radio button — hey, no need to brag. The other two radio buttons are for us slower clickers.

Adjusting mouse tracking

By the way, the Mouse control panel allows you to change how fast your mouse moves around the screen, or *tracks*. If the mouse seems too slow, click one of the upper radio buttons to the right. If you're working with a tablet and pen-type device instead of the standard mouse, click the upper left radio button.

Sometimes the Mac resets itself to settings direct from the assembly line, so-called default settings. The default setting for mouse speed or tracking is the slowest setting, intended for using a drawing tablet in place of the mouse. If your mouse seems suddenly sluggish, check the Mouse control panel and reset it, if needed, to your favorite speed.

One thing that really irks this writer is irk. It's so bland. But on a cold, wintry morning there's nothing like a big, steaming bowl of irk; try it with raisins and brown sugar — mmm. Another thing that irks me is all those manuals and computer books that tell you to "click the mouse" when they mean "press." Two completely different techniques. In this book, marvel that it is, I'll say, "Press the mouse" to mean exactly that, pressing the large, mouse button on the standard mouse and *keeping* it pressed. Clicking is pressing and *releasing* the mouse button quickly one time. After all, knowing the difference between pressing and clicking is the kind of stuff that keeps us at the top of the food chain.

Opening Macromedia Director

OK, you're at the Desktop. Many Mac users have an Applications folder where they store all their programs. That's probably where you installed Director. If the word, "install," doesn't ring a bell at all, check out Appendix A, where I walk you through a typical installation procedure. Anyway, find the Director folder. Inside, you'll find Director's custom icon, hand-crafted by Italian artisans for untold generations. (See Figure 2-4.)

Figure 2-4: Ready to start up Director.

From here, you have two ways of opening Director or any other program on the Mac. For the technically challenged, click once on Director's icon to change the icon's appearance (reverses it if you have a black and white screen or darkens it on gray scale and color monitors); this is the Mac's endearing way of showing that the icon is selected. Go to the File menu and choose the Open command to start Director.

But for the truly rugged, high-spirited, and adventurous out there, the kind of Mac user who grew up playing with G.I. Joe and who eats splinters for breakfast, rev up your engines. Point to Director's icon with the mouse and double-click the icon to open Director. And you thought sky-diving without a parachute was macho.

With either method, the Desktop disappears as Director begins to launch. The screen goes blank for a moment, your mouse pointer becomes the infamous watch cursor to show you that your Mac is busily at work, and then Director's first window comes into view. We multimedia types call this window the "splash screen." Just knowing this and saying "splash screen" often and in a loud, boisterous voice puts you leagues ahead of multimedia wannabes who actually think hard work and studying will someday pay off.

Finally, with hearts pounding and arms akimbo (I've always wanted to use that phrase), you arrive at Director to find . . . a blank screen?

This is going to change my life? This blank screen is the beginning of a new career for me? This is why I paid $19.99 for this book, a blank screen? All typical reactions; if I've heard them once, I've heard them two or three times. Trust me; there's more to Director than a blank screen. By the way, this so-called blank screen just happens to be Director's most important window, the Stage, where all the action takes place. More on the Stage to come.

Looking Around Director

Launching Director brings you to a blank screen that is Director's most important window, the Stage. But it's not that blank, is it? Check out what's familiar about Director's interface before you dive into ... the unknown.

There's a menu bar with nine menus at the top of the screen. At the far right, is the Application menu. This menu is in every application you open, which is exactly the idea. It's always available, allowing you to move rapidly from program to program and a way to return to the Desktop at will. Press the Application menu with the mouse and you'll find the Finder listed (see Figure 2-5), which is just another name for the Desktop.

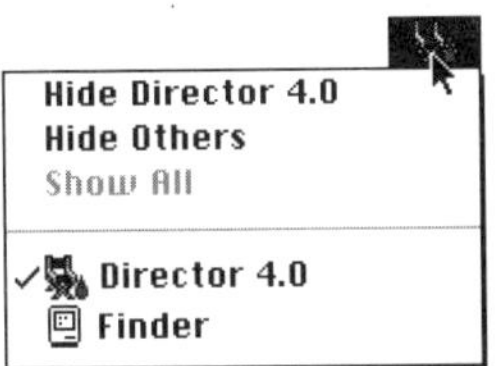

Figure 2-5: Director's Application menu.

I lied. The Finder and Desktop are related but not the same thing. The Finder is a mini-application itself and worthy, therefore, of being listed under the Application menu. Its sole job in life is to create the Desktop (if only we had it that easy), remembering icons in view, what they should look like, where each icon is located, and whether the Trash is empty or is bloated with files waiting to be shredded. The Finder works with the Mac OS, the latest name for the Mac's operating system, but it's not the system itself. In real life, people — those non-computer things you bump into occasionally — use the words Finder and Desktop interchangeably.

Also listed in the Application menu is Director, along with any other applications you may have opened up. Sometimes you forget you opened SimpleText to view a Read Me file, for example, then go to another application without quitting SimpleText only to surprise yourself and see it listed under the Application menu.

To the left of the Application menu is the Guide menu, where you find old Balloon Help and System 7.5's Guide, your Mac's shiny, new, built-in help system. Jumping to the other side of the screen, you find the ubiquitous Apple menu, as in Figure 2-6, ever present wherever you go, as with the Application menu, Guide menu, and the Northern Star.

As you know, then again maybe not, the Apple menu features an About command reflecting the current application. When at the Desktop, you see About This Macintosh as the first command; when in Director, you expect to see About Director. And under the About area is the list of Apple menu items you also expect to see. So far, so good. It's when you look more carefully at Director's About area that things get weird.

About Director...
Help...
Help Pointer ⌘?
Calculator
Chooser
Control Panels
Find File
Key Caps
Scrapbook

Figure 2-6: The Apple menu.

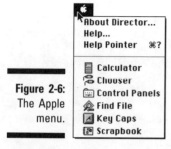

Exploring Director's About Box

Usually seeing a program's About window or box is no big thrill. But then, Director is no ordinary program. Choose About Director from the Apple menu to see what I mean.

Stepping up to the bar (graph)

The bar graph in the center of the about Director window (Figure 2-7) gives a quick overview of how Director is managing memory as you work on an animation. The elements in the bar graph area include the following:

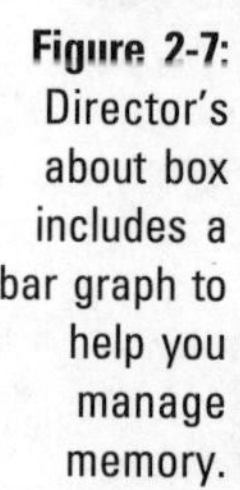
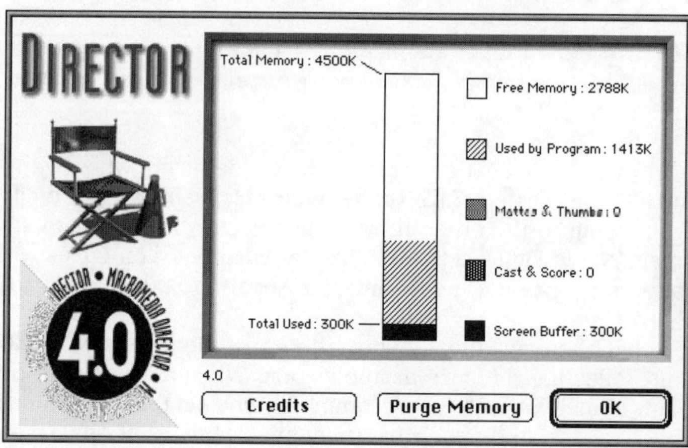

Figure 2-7: Director's about box includes a bar graph to help you manage memory.

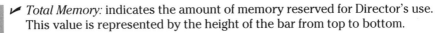

- *Total Memory:* indicates the amount of memory reserved for Director's use. This value is represented by the height of the bar from top to bottom.

  On opening, Director reserves a specific amount of memory for its exclusive use, piggy that it is. Once launched, as long as Director runs — even in the background — the reserved memory remains unavailable to any other program, the system, or any other component of your Mac. The reserved memory is called the program's *application partition.* Out of the box, the initial or default value of the partition is set to the suggested value, but you can change the value to increase the application's performance. (See the sidebar, "Changing Director's application partition," later in this chapter.) More memory, better performance, kind of like presidents.

- *Free Memory:* the white section of the bar. Indicates the current amount of unused memory reserved for Director.

  What's this memory for? Well, it's used when you make your Director file larger by adding more graphics, or when the Mac needs to copy more information from Director into memory. You see, only part of an application's code is copied into memory when you open the program from the Desktop. As you develop an animation, your Mac finds it necessary to go back to the hard drive where the program's stored, find new bits of needed Director code, and copy the code to part of Director's reserved memory, the application partition previously discussed.

- *Used by Program:* Represented on the bar with the light gray section. Indicates how much of Director's program code is currently copied to Director's reserved memory or application partition. When launched, only a portion of Director's code is copied into memory.

- *Mattes & Thumbs:* Currently 0, begins to take some of Director's reserved memory as you create an animation sequence. This value shows in the bar as a medium gray section. Matte refers to a special *ink type* you can give graphics in Director. Thumbs refer to the collection of miniature images you see in the Cast window as you develop an animation. Each matte and thumb, or thumbnail image, takes up a small amount of Director's reserve of memory.

- *Cast & Score:* This is 0 for a blank Director file, too, but grows as you develop your animation sequence. This value is represented in the bar as a dark gray section. Cast refers to the actual set of graphics and text represented in the Cast window by thumbnail images. Score refers to one of Director's main windows, the Score window, which increasingly takes up Director's reserved memory as you build your animation.

- *Screen Buffer:* Represented on the bar as a black section, refers to the amount of Director's reserved memory used to display graphics on the Stage. Screen Buffer size is directly related to the height and width of the Stage window, which you can set and modify in Director at any time.

Beneath the bar area is a row of three buttons: Credits, Purge Memory, and OK. To view a list of credits for developing Director, click the Credits button. To close the About Director window and return to Director, click the OK button. The Purge button will … well, that's what the next section's for.

Purging Director's memory

The About Director window is a very unusual About box. In most programs, the About box doesn't do much more than credit the developers of the program and give the version number. Whoopee.

In the previous section, you saw that Director's About box gives you critical information about Director's management of memory. Even more unique is the Purge Memory button at the bottom of the window. When you click Purge Memory, Director tosses out any unused data and cleans up memory to maximize the amount of available memory. One thing every animation or multimedia program cries out for when it comes to memory is, "More, more, more!" This is one of Director's simplest, built-in ways of freeing up memory.

To use this simple purging feature, follow these steps:

1. **Choose Quit from the File menu.**

   If you're following along on your Mac, what you see on your screen will come closer to matching the following steps by quitting Director first and returning to the Desktop.

2. **Double-click Director's application icon to open Director.**

   You arrive at Director's Stage window.

3. **Choose About Director from the Apple menu.**

   Note the light gray section in the bar chart and the number to the right of Used by Program. The value will be around 1,400K.

Changing Director's application partition

1. Close Director by choosing Quit from the File menu.

   If this step takes you to another program, choose Finder from the Application menu to return to the Desktop.

2. Choose About This Macintosh from the Apple menu.

   Note the number to the right of Largest Unused Block. This number represents the memory you have left to play with measured in Kilobytes. If the number is 4,500K or less, run to the store and buy more memory. You shouldn't even try to run Director; really, you don't have enough memory. If the number is at least 5,000K, click the Close box in the upper-left corner of the About window and go to the next step.

3. Find Director's icon in the Director folder and select it with the mouse.

4. Choose Get Info from the File menu.

   The Director 4.0 Info window appears, as in the following figure.

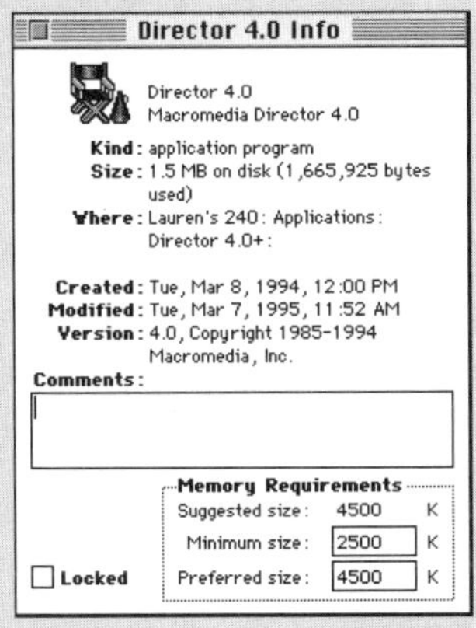

The Minimum size is the smallest application partition you should set for Director. The Suggested size is a better application partition size. The number in the Preferred size entry box is exactly what it says; provided you have enough memory, Director's application partition should be set to *at least* the Preferred size. What you want to do is enter a value higher than the Preferred size for better performance. At this point, I'm going to make two of those assumptions I pooh-poohed earlier. One, if you've come this far you have at least 5,000K of available memory (as indicated in the About box you checked in Step 2). And two, the Preferred size value is currently set to the default, 4500K. Come on, stretch your imagination.

5. Double-click the entry box labeled Preferred size at the bottom of the Director 4.0 Info window to highlight the current value.

6. Enter 4750. You don't even have to include the comma or the *K* (wow, what a computer).

7. Click the Close box in the upper-left corner of the Director 4.0 Info window.

You just upped Director's application partition by 250K, which is fine for the sake of this example, but . . . . Remember real life? When you're not watching TV? In real life, you'd want to set Director's application partition much higher. For a modest animation production, you'd want to see the Preferred size set to at least 8,000K.

4. **Click the Purge Memory button.**

   Note the change in the Used by Program value and the height of the light gray section of the bar. Figure 2-8 shows a drop in value from about 1,400K to 900K, freeing up about 500K of memory. Congratulations!

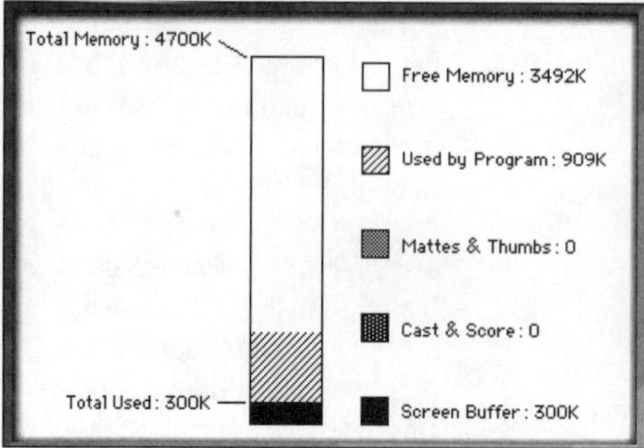

Figure 2-8: Well done — you've freed up some memory.

K stands for kilobytes; each kilobyte equals 1,024 bytes of memory. Don't ask why. The number in Figure 2-7 tells you that 1,400K of Director's programming code was loaded into memory when you opened the application, only a portion of Director's total code.

After clicking Purge Memory, various built-in routines clean up Director's application partition, the amount of memory reserved for the program's exclusive use, and free up memory.

Calling S.O.S. with D.O.L.H. (Director's On-Line Help)

One of Director's marvels is its built-in help system, what we multimedia types call on-line help. Saying "on-line help" and "splash screen" loud and often assure you a place in multimedia history. Or maybe psychiatric history.

You eagle-eyed readers out there may have noticed two other Director commands under the Apple menu, Help and Help Pointer. This section first checks out Help, Director's basic on-line help system. Choose Help from the Apple ure 2-9.

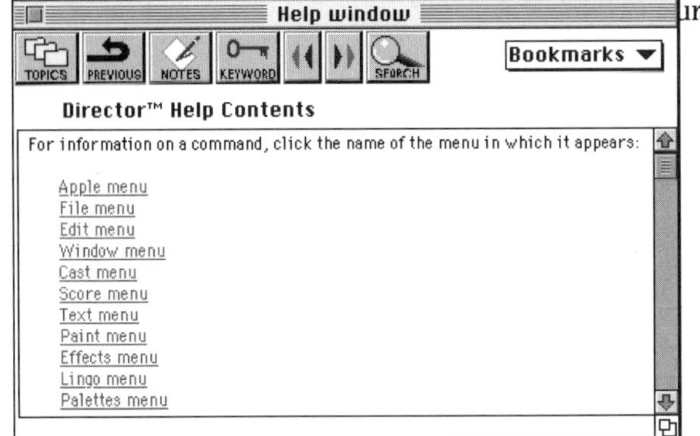

Figure 2-9: Director's Help window.

Table 2-1 explores the appearance, or interface, of this window, summarizing the function of each of the seven buttons at the top of the window.

Table 2-1 Help Window Buttons

Button	***What It Does***
TOPICS	Takes you to Director Help Contents, a complete list of Director topics. Click a topic.
PREVIOUS	For nostalgia buffs. Takes you to the previous topic with a click of the mouse.
NOTES	Takes you to an entry box to type in notes on the topic. A pencil icon marks a topic with notes.
KEYWORD	Takes you to Keywords, an extended index of topics. Click a Keyword and then any subtopic to the right.
	The Backward button steps back one page. Click to browse through topics in reverse order.
	The Forward button steps forward one page. Click to browse through topics.
SEARCH	Takes you to a Search For window where you type a topic and click check boxes for search options.

There's one more intriguing command under Director's Apple menu: Help Pointer.

Help Pointer? Thought I Just Pointed to Help

Ah yes, I've heard these reactions a thousand times before. Trust me, you'll love this feature. Director's help is not only on-line but also what we multimedia types call "context-sensitive." Believe me, if you go around exclaiming, "On-line … splash screen ... context-sensitive," you won't believe where you'll wind up. And I promise to visit every other weekend.

The following steps show you how context-sensitive help works:

1. **With Director up and running, check that you're at the blank Stage window.**
2. **Press the Command key and then the *?* key.**

Figure 2-10: Ahh, the Help cursor.

Notice that the plain-vanilla mouse pointer turns into the Help cursor, as in Figure 2-10. You're ready to try out context-sensitive help. Hold hands, everyone.

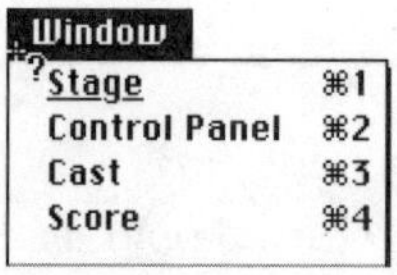

Figure 2-11: Seeking Stage help with the Help cursor.

Window	
Stage	⌘1
Control Panel	⌘2
Cast	⌘3
Score	⌘4

3. **From the menu bar, choose the menu item and command that you want help on with the special Help cursor.**

   Figure 2-11 shows the cursor ready to seek out help on the Stage window.

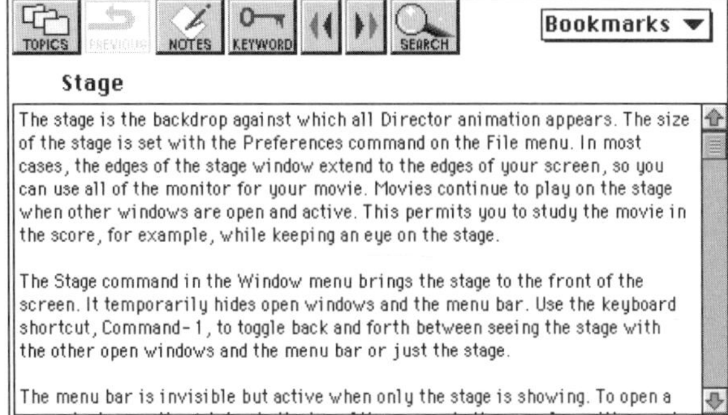

Figure 2-12: Need a hand on Stage? Try the Help window.

Director's context-sensitive help takes you directly to the topic that you indicated using the Help cursor. For example, Figure 2-12 shows the Stage Help window, where you can access information about the Stage, choose another topic, or exit Help by clicking the Close box in the upper-left corner.

4. **Click the Help window's Close box to return to the Stage.**

Should you press the Command+? keys or the Command+Shift+? keys? Don't you type a question mark by pressing the Shift key first? Doesn't the Apple menu show Command+? as the keyboard shortcut for Help Pointer? (See Figure 2-6.)

You know what? In real life, it doesn't matter. I just mentioned it to pad this section; it was looking a little lean.

Director's File Menu

Back at Director's blank Stage window, you're ready to dive into Director's menu bar. Personally, I'm dying for a Pastrami sandwich, but that's another

File
New ⌘N
Open... ⌘O
Close Window ⌘W
Save ⌘S
Save and Compact
Save As...
Revert

Import... ⌘J
Export...
Update Movies...
Create Projector...

Movie Info... ⌘U
Preferences...

Page Setup...
Print...
Quit ⌘Q

Figure 2-13: Director's File menu.

TIP

Hey, They Cheated Me Out of Revert! It's Grayed Out!

Whoa, pardner. Let's review a basic part of the Mac interface. You've got a new Director file, right? You haven't added a blessed dot to it, right again? So you haven't saved anything to the hard drive, "to disk" as we multimedia types say.

Now, Revert takes you to the last *saved* version of your file. If you've got no last saved version, you've got no Revert. You've got no bananas, either, but that's another story. Director is smart enough to know all this even if the rest of us don't, which is why the Revert command is grayed out. The technical name for this condition is *disabled.* And yes, last time I looked it's politically correct. Commands that are available to you, not grayed out, are said to be *enabled.* Enabled, disabled. Add these words to your growing vocabulary, and your future's set. Just remember, Hoffa's future was set, too. Or was it his feet?

matter.

To take a look at Director's File menu, press the mouse on File. The File menu drops down, as in Figure 2-13.

Table 2-2 shows you what to expect from each of the File menu's commands.

Table 2-2 File Menu Commands

Command	***What It Does***
New	Asks you to save any changes to the current file, closes the current file, and creates a new file.
Open	Takes you to the Open dialog box to find an existing Director animation file.
Close Window	Closes any window other than the Stage window, which is always visible.
Save	Updates a file that you've already named and saved to the hard drive.
Save and Compact	Like the Save command, but it compresses the file and removes unneeded data for speed-up.
Save As	Opens Save As dialog box to save a new file to the hard drive.
Revert	Returns the current file to the last saved version stored on the hard drive.
Import	Allows you to add six graphics file types and sound file types to your Director movie.
Export	Allows you to turn a Director file into one of four different external file types.
Update Movies	Turns older files into Director files; also protects custom programming.
Create Projector	Creates a stand-alone version of selected movies for distribution.
Movie Info	Presents the Movie Info dialog box for file-level settings such as using dated code.
Preferences	Allows you to change size, location, and other aspects of a current Director file.
Page Setup	Sets up a current file to print with Page Size, Scaling, and Orientation settings.

Print	Allows you to print all or a portion of the current file, including different windows.
Quit	Closes Director and takes you to an open program or to the Desktop.

All Mac programs are supposed to behave the same way, but even the best of them have individual quirks. For example, here's a collection of some of Director's unique idiosyncrasies reflected in the File menu:

- Director allows only one open file at a time. When you choose the New command, Director asks you whether you'd like to save changes to the current movie, closes the current movie, then presents you with the new blank Director file. In most other programs, you can open as many files as available memory can handle.
- You can't close the current file's Stage window. If the only window visible is the Stage window, choosing Close Window from the File menu does nothing, kind of like politicians. Your only options are to switch to another file with the Open command or Quit to the Desktop.
- Director has always had trouble managing its memory. Built-in commands like Save and Compact in the File menu concede that memory is still a problem area. At least you have this command to fall back on when you've neared completion of your animation to bring the size of the file down and to help it copy into memory faster.

By the way, many of the File commands take you to a window or dialog box featuring a Help button, one more way to access Director's on-line help, only one step better. For example, if you choose File⇨Import and then click the Help button from the Import dialog box, lo and behold, you come to the Help window for the Import command. No looking up topics or keywords! File commands from Import to Print provide Help buttons in their dialog boxes for you.

Touring Director's Other Menus

Director's other menus are no slouches, either. They include:

- Edit
- Window
- Cast
- Score
- Text

Other menus are hidden until an appropriate window is open or until you take a certain action. For example, the Lingo menu, which lists all of Director's special commands, appears when you work with handlers, Macromedia's name for bits of programming code — and yes, you'll be writing code before the day is over. Well, maybe the week. Make that a month.

To make the Lingo menu appear, follow these steps:

1. **Choose Script from the Window menu.**

   The Script window appears with the Lingo menu in Director's menu bar. The Message window will also bring up Director's Lingo menu.

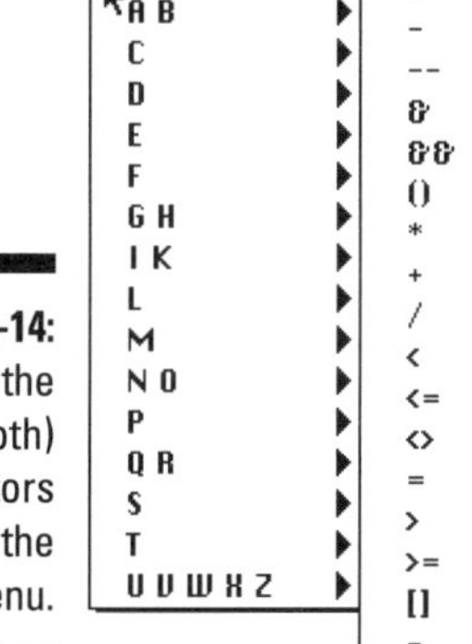

Figure 2-14: Find the (smooth) operators under the Lingo menu.

2. **Press the Lingo menu with the mouse.**

   You'll see an impressive list of Lingo stuff (see Figure 2-14) beginning with operators, then Lingo commands in alphabetical order and with submenus.

   Believe it or not, you'll be able to make heads or tails of this stuff before long.

3. **Click the Close box in the upper left corner of the Script window.**

   The Lingo menu disappears.

Choosing Paint from the Window menu brings up the Paint menu; choosing Color Palettes from the Window menu brings up the Palette menu. I'll get into details of essential commands for the Paint menu in Chapter 7 and for the Palette menu in Chapter 10.

Chapter 3

Lights, Camera, Action!

In This Chapter

- Introducing the Stage
- Traversing the Stage
- Sizing up the Stage
- Channel surfing with the Control Panel
- These buttons aren't on *my* remote control!

If you haven't had the pleasure — ha — of working in the movie industry, have you ever been to Hollywood and wound up at a free taping of a TV show? Wires, cameras, mikes, more wires, more cameras. And where are they pointing? Sure, at the actors or game show host or talk show host; but more important, the cameras point at the stage. If it weren't for the stage there'd be no show. I know, those of you who may have grown up with those grainy, old Mickey Rooney films may be thinking, there's always a barn nearby. But no, the world's grown complicated, and you probably couldn't get fire insurance for the barn, anyway.

All the World's a Stage: Director's Opening Window

As you've seen when you open Director, the introductory window or splash screen greets you momentarily, then you finally come to the Stage. Just as a stage is vital for TV shows, and sound stages, despite all the location shooting going on, are still crucial for moviemaking, Director's Stage window is *the* window. It's your canvas, where all the action occurs, where your special type of information, moving and changing over time, plays across your eyes.

Wait a Minute! The Darn Stage Is Blank as a Polar Bear in a Snow Storm!

If you think it's bad now, just watch this:

1. **Find the Command key.**

   These days the Command key, one of the so-called modifier keys on your keyboard, has both Apple and "daisy" icons embossed on it and usually rests just to the left of the spacebar.

2. **Press the Command key.**

   Continue pressing the Command key. You're about to perform a keyboard shortcut for selecting the Stage command under the Window menu. I know, you're already at the Stage, but watch. . .

3. **Press** 1.

   (That's the number *1.*) Ah, the menu bar disappears. Now, *that's* blank!

Command+1, which is a shortcut way of saying Steps 1 to 3 above, is what we multimedia types call a *toggle* command. Choosing Stage from the Window menu or pressing Command+1 alternately hides and shows the menu bar. After all, a menu bar at the top of your animation would be pretty distracting, not to mention unhygienic. Notice that the Stage window never disappears; it's the one window you can't choose to hide or show.

Bring up the menu bar again, by pressing Command+1, and peek at the Window menu. Notice the line under the Stage window, which is Director's coy way of telling you that the Stage is the currently active window.

In the Mac world, only one window at a time may be in front, or *active.* Active also implies that this is the window you're currently working in. Your Mac gives you other clues, as well. The active window's title bar at the top displays decorative horizontal lines; the window name centered in the title bar is black. Typically, you see a Close box in the upper-left corner of the window and the Zoom box in the upper-right corner. (See Figure 3-1.)

Color Palettes

Figure 3-1: The title bar of an active Color Palettes window.

Not counting the Stage window, which doesn't have a title bar, inactive windows lose their horizontal stripes, and the window name becomes grayed out or disabled. The Close box in the upper-left corner and the Zoom box in the upper-right corner also disappear. (See Figure 3-2.)

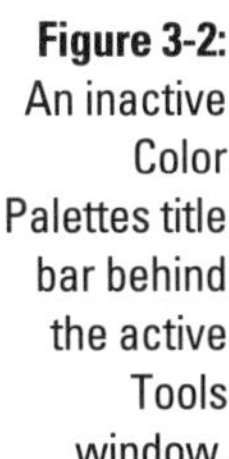

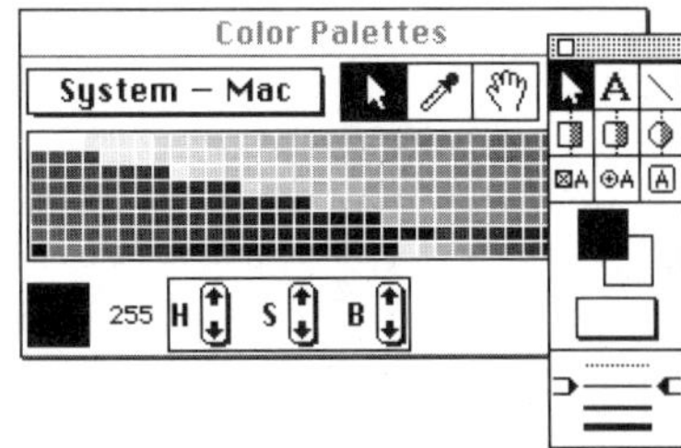

Figure 3-2: An inactive Color Palettes title bar behind the active Tools window.

How Do I Know It's the Stage I'm Staring at?

The Stage window doesn't have a title bar. Great, how do I know it's the Stage? For that matter, how do I know which file I'm in?

Vexing questions to be sure. Not to worry, I have answers for you. It's not unheard of to open a file and three hours later forget which file you've been working on, especially after you purge your memory in Director's About box.

OK, two vexing questions, to be sure. As for knowing which window you're staring at, separate the Stage from Director's other windows. Remember, the Stage window never disappears. It may be hidden under Director's twelve or so other windows, but it's always there. Here are some possible scenarios you may see:

- *The Stage window only, with the menu bar showing:* In the Window menu, Stage is underlined.
- *The Stage window only, with the menu bar hidden:* In the Window menu, Stage is underlined and checked. Actually, the menu bar isn't so much hidden as invisible, you know, like Claude Rains in *The Invisible Man.* When you press where a menu should be, it appears, and you can still choose commands with the mouse. (By the way, keyboard shortcuts still work, too.)
- *The Stage window with another window open:* In the Window menu, Stage is neither underlined or checked; the other window is underlined and checked and remains the active window even if you click on the Stage.
- *The Stage window with two or more other windows open:* In the Window menu, Stage is neither underlined or checked; the active window is underlined and checked, and any inactive windows are only checked.

The reason I've gone into such detail with "this Stage thing," as a former president would say, is that it's not logical and may have you scratching your head and wondering who's wrong, you or Director. It's Director, trust me. From the preceding scenario, clearly a check mark by a command in the Window menu means the window is visible; an underlined command means it's the currently active window. But all the rules go out the window when you try this same logic on the Stage window. So trust your instincts, confused one. May the force be with you.

The Stage and Preferences: Like Bread and Butter or Laurel and Hardy

If you look at the Preferences command under the File menu, you see many options that relate directly to the Stage window. The Preferences dialog box is an important window anyway, so why not take a good look at it? Choose File⇨Preferences, and the Preferences dialog box appears, as in Figure 3-3.

Preferences
Stage Size:
Current monitor
Width: 640 pixels
Height: 480 pixels
Stage Location:
Centered
Left: 0 pixels
Top: 0 pixels
OK
Cancel
When Opening a Movie:
Use Movie's Size/Location
Always Center
Don't Change Size/Location
Switch Monitor's Color Depth to Match Movie's
Save Settings:
Now
When Quitting
Black and White User Interface
Dialogs Appear at Mouse Position
Animate in Background
Using Message Window Recompiles Scripts
Help

Figure 3-3: Choose your preferences in the Preferences dialog box.

You see four main panels in the window:

- *Stage Size:* Allows you to choose from a number of preset sizes with a pop-up menu.
- *Stage Location:* Allows you to decide where you see the Stage on your screen.
- *When Opening a Movie:* Allows you to set the size and location of a QuickTime movie playing within Director.
- *Save Settings:* Allows you to choose when new preferences take effect.

Sizing up the Stage

To select a Stage Size, follow these steps:

1. **Press the Stage Size pop-up button.**

   A pop-up menu appears, as in Figure 3-4. Notice that the set of standard monitor sizes ranges from 9- to 15-inch monitors. Also note the default QuickTime movie Stage size, 160 x 120, measured in pixels.

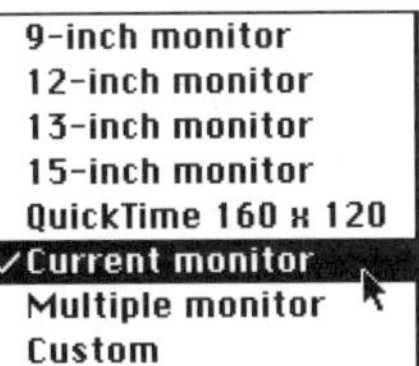

Figure 3-4: The Stage Size pop-up menu lets you change your Stage size on a whim.

2. **Select the desired size.**

If you type in width and height values in the Stage Size area, rather than the standard values in the Stage Size pop-up menu, the Stage Size type changes to Custom in the Stage Size pop-up menu.

We multimedia types often measure things with the pixel, short for picture element, which makes sense. A pixel is the unit that makes up the pictures you see on your monitor. A standard for Mac computers is a 13-inch monitor measuring 640 pixels wide × 480 pixels deep. By the way, the resolution of your screen is 72 pixels per inch (ppi).

Double your pleasure, double your fun

Running two monitors is great for developing Director animation and multimedia with its 13-plus windows. The idea is to drag all those gorgeous windows to an extra monitor and keep a nice, uncluttered view of the Stage on the main monitor. Makes life nice, easy, and expensive.

You can also use multiple monitors as part of the presentation itself. The monitors become one giant "virtual" screen with each monitor serving as ports into this magical world.

Many Power Mac models have built-in multiple monitor capabilities. Otherwise, you'll need an extra video card to run each additional monitor for multimedia extravaganzas.

By the way, when you're running two or more monitors, let Director know by choosing Multiple Monitor from the Stage Size pop-up menu in the Preferences dialog box.

Making other preferences

Beneath the panels in the Preferences dialog box is a column of four miscellaneous options to choose from:

- *Black and White User Interface:* Allows you to display icons, windows, and dialog boxes in simple black and white instead of gray scale or full color. This option saves memory and increases performance, especially with low-powered Macs. I won't ask to see a show of hands.
- *Dialogs Appear at Mouse Position:* Allows you to decide whether dialog boxes appear where Director developers decided at the dialog box factory or in the general location of your mouse pointer.
- *Animate in Background:* Allows you to decide whether the Stage appears in the background when you switch to another program or disappears until you return to Director from the Application menu in the upper-right corner of the screen. With this option checked, an animation playing in the Stage continues playing after you switch to another application.
- *Using Message Window Recompiles Scripts:* The Message window and the term *recompile* are both allied to Lingo, Director's built-in language. You can experiment with Lingo in the Message window and then place the Lingo language that works in various parts of your animation to add interactivity to your movie. The Recompile command turns Lingo into data that your Mac understands; choosing this option recompiles Lingo while you're playing with the Message window.

Director's built-in language, Lingo, is referred to as a high-level language, meaning it's relatively conversational in tone. An example of Lingo's comfortable familiarity would be `Go to frame 1`, using Lingo's Go command and phrased in such a way to take you to the first frame of an animation. It's the job of the compiler, another part of Director, to translate Lingo into so-called assembly code, a low-level language that the Mac understands but looks like a doctor's hand-written prescription to us human beans. The Recompile command is simply another way of saying, "Compile my Lingo code now. And be quick about it, nave."

Round versus square: the politics of selection buttons

Apple's official interface guidelines make the distinction Lucite clear.

Radio buttons look like this: ◉

When you face a set of options from which you may choose only one to the exclusion of the others — whoo, maybe I should have been a lawyer — a well designed program presents you with a set of radio buttons. So the When Opening a Movie panel in the Preferences dialog box gives you one of three choices: Use Movie's Size/Location, Always Center, or Don't Change Size/Location. Logically, only one option can prevail. When you click the option of choice to the exclusion of the others, its radio button adopts the "bull's-eye" style to indicate its standing in the Macintosh community of selection buttons.

Check boxes look like this: ☒

Check boxes are for a set of options that you may choose individually; these options aren't mutually exclusive. A checked check box means you've selected its option.

A selected check box isn't really checked. It's "Xed." I think of something checked looking like, well, a check. Anyway, I don't know of anyone who goes around saying, "I Xed the check box." Maybe it sounds too much like a naughty word. But if you want to instantly establish yourself as a free thinker and all-around character, here's your golden opportunity.

Channel Surfing with the Control Panel

Borrowing metaphors from TV has become very popular in MultimediaLand, especially the VCR metaphor. You see a lot of interfaces that look familiar because the buttons look amazingly like the controls on your VCR and your remote as you channel surf the day and night away. Actually, using the familiar isn't a bad idea in developing animation and multimedia, where communicating quickly and presenting intuitive interfaces present crucial challenges.

The next Director window in order under the Window menu is the Control Panel, which duplicates commands under the Edit menu, but with a familiar VCR interface. These commands include the familiar (Play, Stop, and Rewind) and the new (Lock Frame Durations). Figure 3-5 shows the Edit menu in all its glory.

Edit
Undo Cast ⌘Z
Cut Cast Members ⌘X
Copy Cast Members ⌘C
Paste ⌘V
Clear Cast Members
Select All ⌘A
Play ⌘P
Stop ⌘.
Rewind ⌘R
Step Backward
Step Forward
Disable Sounds ⌘~
✓Loop ⌘L
Selected Frames Only ⌘\
Disable Lingo
Lock Frame Durations

Figure 3-5: Director's Edit menu offers the same options as the Control Panel.

The Control Panel also allows you to

- Zoom forward and backward through the frames of your animation with a special control.
- Set the pace or tempo of your animation.
- Select the way you time your animation.
- Set displayed time values to real times for the specific Mac model running the animation.
- Change the color of the Stage window.

These Buttons Aren't on My Remote Control!

The Control Panel is chock full of buttons and icons and more buttons. (See Figure 3-6.) The first five buttons in the top row are pretty intuitive, as we multimedia types like to say. In other words, you should have an easy time guessing the buttons' functions because they resemble familiar controls on your VCR(s)(s)(s) and remote(s)(s)(s)(s)(s).

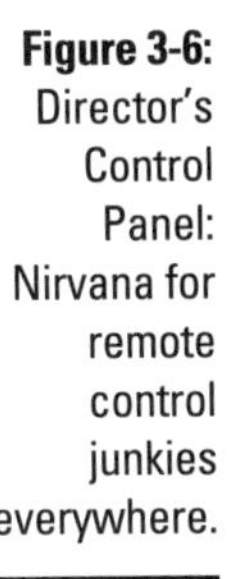

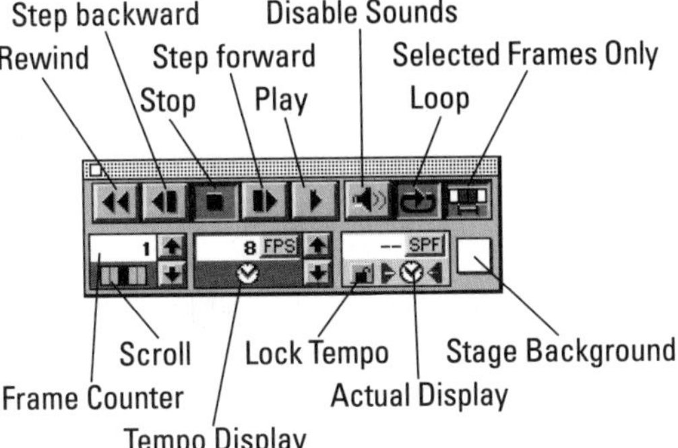

Figure 3-6: Director's Control Panel: Nirvana for remote control junkies everywhere.

Director's Control Panel and other windows have a three-dimensional look when you set your screen to display 256 gray scale or color; the selected button looks depressed — no, silly goose, not sad, depressed as in pressed in. If your monitor's set to black and white, the selected button looks reversed.

Now let's go over the last three buttons in the top row that aren't so intuitive:

- *Disable Sounds:* The Disable Sounds button acts like a toggle command, that is, a command that switches between turning an action on or off, in this case alternately turning sound on and off. The Disable Sounds button as seen in Figure 3-6 is set to play sounds. Note the little sound waves emanating from the speaker icon Click the button again to turn sounds off; the button looks the same except there are no emanating sound waves.

- *Loop:* The Loop button also acts like a toggle command. As shown in Figure 3-6, the Loop button sets your animation to, well, loop, that is, play your animation over and over, forever — you'd better like this animation a lot. Actually, you have many outs, such as clicking the Stop button or pressing Command+. (that's a period, folks). If you want your movie to play once, click Loop again; the button becomes a straight line icon.
- *Selected Frames Only:* Refers to Director's Score window, where you can select a range of frames from the entire animation, click the Selected Frames Only button and play only the selection. The button's on when it looks pressed in as in Figure 3-6. Click again to turn off this feature.

Now turn your attention to the Control Panel's bottom row of controls:

- *Frame Counter:* Tells you where the *playback head* is in the Score window. The playback head is that black rectangle to the right of the word, "Frame," in the Score; it indicates the current frame playing in the movie. Note the small up and down arrows that allow you to move forward or backward one frame at a time.
- *Scroll:* Like a fast forward or fast rewind on a VCR, allows you to move rapidly back and forth through the frames of your animation by pressing the icon and moving the mouse left for fast rewinding or right for fast forwarding.
- *Tempo Display:* Allows you to set the pace or tempo of your animation and how it's measured — in frames per second (fps) or seconds per frame (spf) — in thousandths of a second. Click once to set the tempo to fps, again to set it to spf. Note the small up and down arrows that allow you to step the tempo up and down one unit.
- *Lock Tempo:* Allows you to keep the last tempo setting and forces Director to try to play the movie on a different Mac model at the same rate it played on your computer. Click the button to display the Closed Lock icon; click again to unlock the tempo.
- *Actual Display:* Allows you to see how fast your animation is playing in real or "actual" time and to set how the actual time is displayed — frames per second (fps) or seconds per frame (spf) — in thousandths of a second. Clicking the Actual Display button, cycles you through fps, spf, Sum, and Est. The Sum setting gives you the total actual time an animation plays. The Est setting is considered more accurate for sequences that play longer than a few seconds.
- *Stage Background:* Allows you to set the color of the Stage window as a background for animated graphics. Press the Stage Background button to reveal a pop-up menu of color chips and drag the mouse pointer to the preferred color. Using this button allows you to color the background without adding a new Bitmap or QuickDraw Cast Member to the Cast

window. The only caveat is that once you set the background to anything but white, you'll need to give Cast Members a special ink effect in the Score, which may slow down the animation significantly. The default ink is Copy, and it surrounds a Cast Member on the Stage in a white box; when the background is white, you can stay with Copy ink, Director's fastest ink type. For more info on ink types, jump to Chapter 5 and the section, "All This Ink and Not a Drop on Me — Oops."

Part II

Director's Windows of Opportunity

"How's that for live animation?"

In this part...

One reason why Director is such a wonderful program to work with is its richness of windows and options therein. In this part, I focus on the major players in the Window Department, where you get to become close, personal friends with Mr. Cast, Mr. Score, Ms. Paint, and that ever popular gad-about, Text window.

By the way, if you think the name of this part's a pun, Director really does Windows now, with Director for Windows.

Chapter 4

Casting Coach or Couch? The Cast Window

In This Chapter

- Casting your movie with the Cast window
- Adding Cast Members to your movie
- A brief tour of the Cast menu

Director's Cast window is how we Director types make a casting call in the world of Macintosh moviemaking. All the right file types on your hard drive get all excited, slap down their copies of *Variety*, and come running to queue up with hearts thumping, hoping against hope to find themselves among the chosen, on their way to stardom, wealth, and interviews with Robin Leach.

Calling All Cast Members

Now that you realize how exciting the Cast window is, take a look at it by choosing Cast from the Window menu.

Your Cast window appears like a blinding bank of klieg lights streaming into the crisp, Hollywood night sky! Pretty exciting, huh?

Can I believe my ears? Did I hear someone say, "Not exactly"? Well, maybe you're not the right file type. Director's pretty temperamental about the type of file it accepts in the Cast window as a Cast Member, you know.

Defining the Cast

First, let's define the Cast as anyone working in the food industry in L.A. No. Rewind. A Cast Member is any part of your movie that changes location, shape, or size, including

- Still images of PICT file types
- Sets of still images in a special file type called *PICS*
- Items in the Scrapbook under the Apple menu
- Text
- Sounds
- Collections of colors called *palettes*
- Special animations that Director calls *film loops*
- QuickTime mooVs
- Other Director movies
- Scripts that automate parts of your movie and add interactive features

Of PICTs and PICS

A PICT is an all-purpose file type that may contain a drawing, bitmapped graphic, and/or PostScript code. PICT drawings come from programs such as ClarisDraw, using routines from your Mac called QuickDraw (also used to build the display on your monitor); you'll hear this type of graphics program called object-oriented or vector-based programs, too. Bitmapped graphics come from Paint programs such as the built-in Paint window in Director. PostScript code comes from programs such as Adobe Illustrator and FreeHand. QuickDraw drawings and PostScript code in PICTs are used by printers; PICT bitmaps are used for displaying a preview on-screen.

A PICS file contains a set of individual PICTs, each PICT a "resource" in the file. Mac files have structures called data and resource forks. When you type a letter, the text of the letter goes in the data fork; when you create a PICS file, each PICT you include in the PICS file becomes a resource in the file. Only a few programs including Director offer PICS as a file type. When you import a PICS file, each PICT resource becomes a Cast Member in the Cast window.

You can export a movie as an external PICS file with the Export command under the File menu, turning each frame of your animation into a PICT resource in the PICS file's resource fork. Such power is truly frightening. Mad scientists need not apply.

Adding Cast Members to the Cast window

You can't wait to add a Cast Member to the Cast. I know the feeling, far stronger than a Big Mac attack. That's what the Import command has been waiting so patiently to do for you.

Import is a pretty common command in most Mac programs and does pretty much the same thing in each program: brings in the contents of an external file to a place on your hard drive. Some programs, such as PageMaker, call it the Place command. Same thing.

To add a Cast Member, just follow the Yellow Brick Road, er, these steps:

1. **Choose File⇨Import.**

   The Import dialog box appears where you can set your import preferences. Notice that PICT is the first option in the Type pop-up menu shown in Figure 4-1. PICT is the workhorse file type for the Macintosh. Most of the Cast Members you'll add to Director will be PICTs, so you're all set to find the PICT file of choice.

   Notice the two check boxes under the Type pop-up menu. Clicking the Show Preview check box adds an extra area to the left of the Import dialog box and a Create button so that you can view the selected file before importing it. You'll find more on the Link To File check box in the very next section.

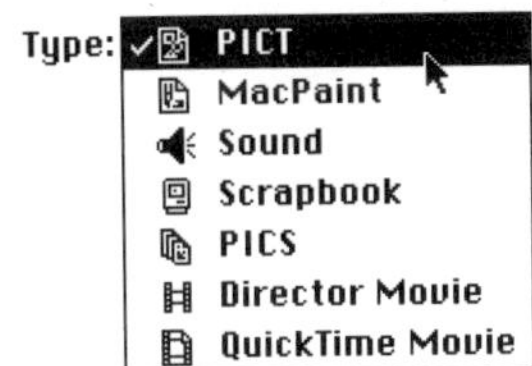

Figure 4-1: Selecting a file type in the Import dialog box.

Only files matching the current type shown in the Type pop-up menu appear in the scrolling field (called the directory in MacSpeak) of the Import dialog box. Be sure to choose the right file type before searching for the desired file. If you're looking for a sound, and you've got PICT displayed in the Type pop-up menu, you're going to wind up being one frustrated camper by day's end.

2. **Find the desired PICT file in the directory.**

   You can avoid scrolling through long lists in the directory and come close to a file by pressing its initial letter on the keyboard. If you're looking for a document named Picture 1, press **p** to select the first file in the directory that begins with the letter *p*. You can get even closer to your file, if not right on, by quickly typing **pi** or **pic**. The trick is to type two or more characters quickly enough so that your Mac recognizes the keys as part of a word. By the way, this technique works with other scrolling lists, including windows on the Desktop and in Director's Help windows.

3. **Highlight the PICT you want.**
4. **Press the Create button to make a preview.**
5. **Click the Import button.**

   Director returns you to the Cast window to find a thumbnail-size preview of the PICT in the Cast.

Director has a few more ways to add Cast Members to the Cast window, including

- Painting a new Cast Member in Director with the Paint window tools
- Entering text in the Text window
- Choosing a set of colors in the Palette window

Another way of thinking of Cast Members in the Cast window is as style sheets in a word-processing program such as Microsoft Word. Think of a Cast Member as a special "style" that you can call up again and again in different parts of your movie. For example, if you're going to build an animation with a screen shot, you might use a PICT-type Cast Member in several places in your animation and then decide to change the color of the Cast Member's background to a beautiful aquamarine. The color change ripples through all instances of the PICT Cast Member in your animation. Pretty clever, huh?

What are style sheets?

I'm glad you asked. A style sheet is a very powerful feature that most word processing programs offer. A style sheet is nothing more than a list describing the appearance of a paragraph of text. Say you're typing a ten-page proposal to Widgets, Inc. and want to take advantage of style sheets. You type your heading in Times Bold with 14-point type, double-spaced. You click on the Styles box, enter Heading, and press Return to create a new style. You repeat this process for subheads, making a style (called *Subhead*) that records Times Bold with 12-point type, double-spaced. Then you save a third style sheet for your main text that you cleverly name *Main Text,* which records Times Regular with 12-point type, single-spaced. Now you start typing the rest of your proposal. When you're about to type another subhead you go to your list of style sheets, choose Subhead, and type away. The text you type mirrors the description you saved in the Subhead style sheet. Better yet, if you decide to change the font or size of your subheads, you don't have to find every instance of it in your proposal. All you do is head straight for the Subhead style and modify it. Any changes ripple through all subheads in your document automatically. Now you *love* style sheets, right? I thought so.

Linking your imported file

In the Import dialog box, you'll find the Link To File check box below the Type pop-up button. (See Figure 4-2.)

Figure 4-2: Select import preferences in the Import dialog box.

If you leave the Link To File check box unchecked, the imported file will become part of your movie, increasing the movie's size. Benefits? You don't have to keep track of the imported file now that it's part of your movie. On the other hand — no, the other hand — checking Link To File gives you a bouquet of advantages, including the following:

- Creating a kind of interactive relationship with the imported file so that you can view the file without physically adding it to your movie, keeping file size down.
- Director updates a linked file after you make changes to the file from another application. For example, if you import a PICT to Director as a linked file and you later open, modify, and save the PICT in Photoshop, Director automatically updates the file the next time you open the movie.
- As an external, linked file, you can share it with several movies without increasing the size of each movie.
- To modify a linked file, you can open the file's parent application from Director with the Launch External Editor command under the Cast menu, as in Figure 4-3.

Figure 4-3: Choose Cast⇨Launch External Editor to modify a linked file.

When choosing Link To File, you must do a good job of keeping track of all linked files. If a file's location changes after you import it as a linked Cast Member, the next time you open the movie Director will ask where the heck the file is, spoiling your presentation with catcalls and boos from the disappointed audience. The safest way to ensure that Director never loses track of linked files is to create a folder for each presentation and to keep all linked files and movies in that one folder. If a file must be moved, move the entire folder. Or, using System 7's Alias feature, make an alias of the file in question and move the alias to a new location.

Whenever you import a QuickTime movie, Director automatically links it to the current movie.

Editing Cast Members 101

Considering how many file types you can bring into Director as part of your movie, you may be wondering which Cast Members can be edited directly in Director. Here's the list; it goes by real fast, so don't blink:

- Imported PICT type Cast Members
- Bitmap Cast Members created in the Paint window

In other words, bitmaps.

Ah, you're wondering how come QuickTime isn't in the nifty list above. You've heard QuickTime movies are nothing more than a collection of PICT images. Almost win the turkey, but not close enough. QuickTime frames may start out as PICTs, but once in a QuickTime movie, they adopt a special format that Director's built-in Paint tools can't currently modify.

Director recognizes PICTs in the Import dialog box. Once you click Import, Director changes imported PICT graphics information into a bitmap.

To add a real PICT to the Cast, bring it into Director with the Clipboard, select an empty cell in the Cast window, and choose Paste as PICT under the Cast menu.

Exploring the Cast window

Happy now? Now that that's out of your system and you've imported a Cast Member, you can go back to exploring the Cast window itself. Notice the custom features of the Cast window.

Custom features

In the upper left of the window is a row of five buttons and two text areas. This section reviews those buttons one by one:

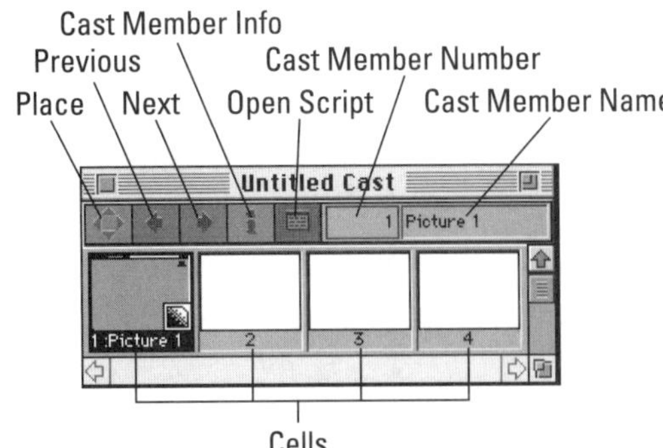

Figure 4-4: The Cast window.

- *Place:* Allows you to position or place selected actors from the Cast window on the Stage by pressing the button and dragging the mouse into the Stage area.
- *Previous:* Each click of the Previous button cycles you back one Cast Member at a time. When you get to the first Cast Member in the Cast window, another click loops you back to the last Cast Member as you continue the backward cycle with each click.
- *Next:* Cycles you forward one Cast Member at a time to the last Cast Member in the Cast. Another click loops you back to the first Cast Member, where you continue the forward cycle.
- *Cast Member Info:* Takes you to the Cast Member Info dialog box, where you learn a lot about the selected Cast Member and can set several options. Find out more in the very next section.
- *Script:* Takes you to the Script window for the currently highlighted Cast Member in the Cast window. It's in the Script window for a particular Cast Member where you play with Lingo, Director's easy-to-use, built-in language.

To the right of this group of buttons is a Cast Member Number field that displays the number of the selected Cast Member in the Cast window. Lastly, you see the Cast Member Name field that displays the name of the file that was imported into the Cast window with the Import command.

Cast Member Info button

You can get to the Cast Member Info window a number of ways:

- Choose Cast Member Info from the Cast menu.
- Press Command+I.
- Click the Cast Member Info button in the Cast window.

Because the Cast Member Info button is so essential, the following steps show you how to use it:

1. **Make sure that a Cast Member is selected in the Cast window.**
2. **Click the Cast Member Info button.**

   Director takes you to a Cast Member Info dialog box similar to Figure 4-5. First of all, notice that the name of the window is actually Bitmap Cast Member Info, which in this case indicates a Cast Member that started out as a PICT file but was transformed into a bitmap when it was imported.

Bitmap Cast Member Info
Cast Member: 1 Picture 1
Palette: System – Mac
Purge Priority: 3 – Normal
Colors: 8 bits
Size: 300.0 K
File Name: Lauren's 240:Picture 1
☒ Auto Hilite
OK
Cancel
Script...
Help

Figure 4-5: This Cast Member Info dialog box is for a bitmap.

   To the right of Cast Member is the Cast Member's position in the Cast window, which in this case is position 1. To the right of that is an entry box with the Cast Member's default name, the name of the file you imported. Notice that Director has highlighted the name for you so that you can change the name of the Cast Member on a whim. Such decadence.

3. **If you're so inclined, type a new name for your Cast Member.**

   The text that Director preselected for you is replaced with the new name you just entered.

   When you enter a name for a Cast Member, be sure to enter a meaningful name. Naming a Cast Member "#1," for example, isn't going to be very significant a week or a month later.

4. **Press the Palette pop-up menu to view Director's built-in palettes.**

   System — Mac is the default palette for you Mac-type developers, but there may come a time when you need to switch palettes, depending on the type of movie you're producing. You can switch palettes with the help of the Palette pop-up menu, shown in Figure 4-6.

Figure 4-6: A sparkling array of colors available in the Palette pop-up menu.

5. **Select the desired palette from the Palette pop-up menu.**

   Be prepared for a potentially startling color change on your screen. As soon as you move away from the default System palette, colors on the screen reflect the set of colors in the new current palette. For example, if you switch from the System palette to NTSC, you're going to see a big difference in colors. NTSC stands for National Television Systems Committee, which created a set of standards for American television broadcasting. These standards include "legal" colors that your color TV sets can handle. The NTSC palette includes 256 colors that are legal and should look good on video, although on an RGB monitor they tend to look pretty blah. Colors outside the NTSC palette tend to change color when you tape the animation to video; also, highly intense or saturated colors that are not legal seem to spread beyond the image and "bloom," as TV types say. I can almost hear my old schoolmarm screaming, "Don't go outside the lines now, children!" She must have been a card-carrying member of that NTSC. For a full description of the other palettes included with Director, check out Chapter 10.

6. **Press the Purge Priority pop-up menu.**

I know, this one's a little frightening. You've heard of purges in other parts of the world. That's bad enough, but not in the good, old U.S. of A. No, this is a different kind of purge. Remember the Purge Memory button in Director's About box? (If not, flip back to Chapter 2 to refresh your memory.) That's the kind of purge I'm talking about, Director's way of managing memory. When memory runs low, Director starts trashing, or purging, stuff from memory, including Cast Members. The Purge Priority pop-up menu lets you decide what gets tossed and when by selecting a Cast Member from the Cast window, opening the Cast Member Info box, and setting a purge priority based on the following criteria:

- *Priority 0:* Gives a very important Cast Member that is going to be used frequently in the movie Priority 0, meaning, "Never purge Mr. Big Shot from memory. Too important."
- *Priority 1:* A little lower on the totem pole than Priority 0; giving a Cast Member Priority 1 means, "Save this puppy for last."
- *Priority 2:* The normal setting, meaning, "Expendable but nice. Keep it if you can." Sounds like a real casting couch situation to me.
- *Priority 3:* The lowest priority; mow 'em down along with gaffers, technicians, accountants, and assistant directors.

Different types of Cast Members open different types of Cast Member Info windows. For example, you can add a set of custom colors, called a palette, to the Cast window as a Cast Member. Selecting the Palette type Cast Member and clicking Cast Member Info opens a Palette Cast Member Info dialog box.

Director's hard cell

A thumbnail of the first Cast Member you import rests in cell 1 of the Cast window. Actually, the Cast window is a set of 32,000 cells. If you have a screen large enough to display them all, congratulations. (By the way, I know where you can get a great deal on industrial-size containers of sun blocker. Please, give me a call.)

Each occupied cell in the Cast window gives you the following info:

- The type of Cast Member
- The position of the cell in the window by name
- An optional name for the cell

You can learn a lot about a Cast Member by noting its thumbnail's icon(s) listed directly ahead in Table 4-1:

Table 4-1 Cast Member Type Icons

Icon	*What It Represents*
	Unlinked bitmap Cast Member. May have been imported from an unlinked PICT, PICS, Director movie, MacPaint, or Scrapbook file, or created with Paint window tools.
	Linked bitmap Cast Member. May have been imported from a PICT, PICS, Director, MacPaint, or Scrapbook file.
	PICT Cast Member. Copied to the Cast window from the Clipboard with the Past as PICT command under the Cast menu.
	Sound Cast Member. Imported sound sample, or recorded in Director with the Record Sound command under the Cast menu.
	Palette Cast Member. Custom Palette imported with an external graphic file, or chosen from the Palette window in Director.
	Script Cast Member. Scripts become Cast Members as you add scripts to your movie, or may be added when you import another Director movie.
	Text Cast Member. Text typed from the Text window, or with the Text tool from the Tools window.
	Button Cast Member. Created with one of three Button tools in the Tools window.
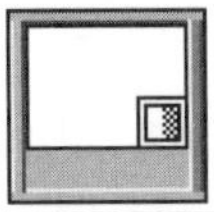	QuickDraw Cast Member. A shape created with Drawing tools in the Tools window; similar to object-oriented drawings created with programs such as ClarisDraw.
	Digital Video Cast Member. An imported QuickTime movie, plays in its own Digital Video window on the Stage.
	Linked Director movie Cast Member. Not directly editable within current movie; need to use File menu's Open command.

(continued)

Table 4-1 *(Continued)*

Icon	*What It Represents*
	Film Loop Cast Member. Created within the current movie by copying a range of frames in the Score and pasting them into an empty Cast window cell.
	Combined with one of the above, indicates a Cast Member containing a Script. Any Cast Member may contain a set of Lingo commands called a Script.

You can customize which icons appear in the Cast with the Cast Window Options command under the Cast menu.

Notice that standard Edit menu commands are available, but some command names change to reflect that the Cast window is active (such as Copy Cast Members, Paste Cast Members, and Clear Cast Members in Figure 4-7). Your Mac's menu bar is very dynamic, meaning that the menus displayed and their commands constantly change, depending on which window or tool is currently chosen. Don't let these chameleonlike menus trip you up. Confidence. Ohmmm-m-m-m-m-m-m-m.

Edit
Undo Cast ⌘Z
Cut Cast Members ⌘X
Copy Cast Members ⌘C
Paste ⌘V
Clear Cast Members
Select All ⌘A
Play ⌘P
Stop ⌘.
Rewind ⌘R
Step Backward
Step Forward
Disable Sounds ⌘~
✓Loop ⌘L
Selected Frames Only ⌘\
Disable Lingo
Lock Frame Durations

Figure 4-7: The Edit menu, customized to work with the Cast window.

What's an active window?

In the Macintosh world, only one window is available at any one time (with one exception coming up). Whichever window you've just selected is the currently active window; all other open windows are inactive. Looking at Title bars is the key to knowing which window is active. An *active window* displays its name in black text in the Title bar at the top of the window, and gray, horizontal stripes adorn the width of the Title bar. All other open windows become inactive, their Title bars lack gray stripes, and window names are grayed out, or disabled. (There's that "d" word, again.)

Ah, the exception; I'm glad you reminded me. A special Macintosh window called a floating window appears active at all times and appears to, well, float in front of the regular active window. Director doesn't use this kind of window but many other programs, including Adobe Photoshop, use floating windows for tool, layer, and color palettes.

Screening the Cast Menu

So, knowing a lot about the Cast window isn't good enough for you? Now you want to get close and personal with the Cast menu too, huh? Why, for two cents . . . (said to the voice of Edward G. Robinson, mmmyehhh).

OK, be sure the Cast window's selected before you take a peek. Choose Cast from the Cast window menu bar; the Cast menu appears as in Figure 4-8.

Cast

Cast Member Info... ⌘I
Open Script ⌘'
Edit Cast Member
Launch External Editor ⌘,

Record Sound...
Paste as PICT
Convert to Bitmap
Transform Bitmap...
Align Bitmaps

Cast to Time
Duplicate Cast Member ⌘D
Find Cast Members... ⌘;
Sort Cast Members...
Cast Window Options...

Figure 4-8: Director's Cast menu.

Ready to dive into this hotbed of commands? Right.

- *Cast Member Info:* See the section, "Using the Cast Member Info button," earlier in this chapter for how this command works and how the Cast Member Info dialog box lets you change the Cast Member type.
- *Open Script:* Another way to enter a Cast Member's script where Lingo commands are stored. You'll understand this better when you get to Lingo. Oh, you can't wait? OK, Mr. Ants-in-Your-Pants, take a look at Chapter 17 and Part V, "The Part of Tens," where tons of, well, thirty give or take, tips and tricks await your reading pleasure.
- *Edit Cast Member:* Depending on the type of Cast Member, takes you either to a window where you can modify the Cast Member or to the Cast Member Info dialog box. For example, selecting a bitmap Cast Member in the Cast and choosing Edit Cast Member takes you to the Paint window.
- *Launch External Editor:* Allows you to launch an external application to edit a *linked* file. After you modify the file and quit the external editor, you return to Director with an updated Cast Member.
- *Record Sound:* Takes you to a VCR-type recording window, where you can record sounds in Director. You need a Mac model equipped with a Sound In port, a sound card with the Sound In port, or an external sound sampler such as MacRecorder connected to a serial (printer or modem) port.
- *Paste as PICT:* Allows you to paste a PICT from the Clipboard into a cell in the Cast window without turning it into a bitmapped graphic. The benefits: PICTs print out better for handouts and storyboards, are usually smaller in size, and may be resized more successfully in Director than bitmapped graphics. Also allows you to make extra good espresso with a nice frothy top.
- *Convert to Bitmap:* Allows you to convert a PICT Cast Member, created with the Paste as PICT command, into a bitmapped graphic. Once converted, the Cast Member may be modified in Director's Paint window. Bitmapped Cast Members provide greater animation speed, too. Convert to Bitmap also converts QuickDraw text typed with the Text tool in the Tools window. Why would you want to do this? Once the text becomes a bitmap, you don't have to worry about having the right font in your System folder. It's just paint!
- *Transform Bitmap:* As the name implies, bitmaps only — no others need apply. Allows you to change a bitmap's size, number of colors (color depth), and palette of colors. The change is permanent, in contrast to modifying a bitmap through its Cast Member Info dialog box.
- *Align Bitmaps:* Lines up bitmap "registration marks," visible in the Paint window. Next and Previous buttons in the Paint window allow you to view sequences of Cast Members like a flip book to test animation sequences.

- *Cast to Time:* An essential command to add Cast Members to the Score and Stage. After selecting Cast Members in the Cast window, choose Cast to Time to place each Cast Member sequentially in frames of the Score.
- *Duplicate Cast Member:* Allows you to place a "clone" of the selected Cast Member in the next available cell of the Cast window. After duplication, the clone is an independent Cast Member; modifications to the original Cast Member have no effect on the copy and vice versa.
- *Find Cast Members:* Allows you to find and select Cast Members in the Cast window by Type, Name, and Palette with the Find dialog box.
- *Sort Cast Members:* Allows you to rearrange Cast Member order in the Cast window by Name, Type, Size, Order in the Score, or Order in the Cast. Director automatically updates information, so animations in the Score are unaffected. The command also acts to displace empty cells from the set of occupied cells in the Cast window.
- *Cast Window Options:* Takes you to the Cast Window Options dialog box, where you can set the Maximum Visible Cells, Row Width by Cell, Size of Cast Member Thumbnails, Cast ID Style, and Cast Type Icons.

Selecting multiple Cast Members

Director's a little strange when it comes to making multiple selections in the Cast window. The Shift key works in most other Mac applications, but not Director. That's not good enough for Mr. Fancy Pants Director.

When you need a noncontiguous selection of cells, use the Command key and click the desired cells, useful for selecting Cast Members throughout the Cast window to drag to the Stage or to change their palettes. To make a contiguous selection of cells in the Cast window, that is, without jumps, stay with the old Shift-and-click trick. Click the first cell to highlight it. Move to the last cell to be included in the selection, press Shift, and click the last cell. You'll wind up with a contiguous string of selected cells.

Chapter 5

As Time Goes By: Opening Director's Score Window

In This Chapter

- Exploring the Score window
- Using icons in the Score window
- Adding Cast Members to the Score window
- Finding the hidden cells
- Coloring in the Score window — stay inside the lines!
- Manipulating cells

Most programs don't need a Score window. Word processors don't have one. Have you ever heard of a Score window in a desktop publishing program? I don't recall seeing a Score window for PageMaker or QuarkXPress. Why am I talking like Andy Rooney?

Information in other programs doesn't intrinsically change with time. Sure, you return to a PageMaker newsletter or a Word memo to modify it, maybe use it as a template for a new file. But once you make your changes, you can stare at the file night and day, and it doesn't change. If it does, you've got the makings for the next Spielberg hit.

From its start as VideoWorks in 1985, Director was designed to handle information that changes over time, information that cries out for a Score-type window. It's in the Score window where you design your Director movie, deciding which Cast Members appear and vanish on the Stage at your every whim. With client approval, of course. Of all Director's windows, the Score window allows you to play director to the hilt.

So hitch up your riding boots, get a good grip on that riding crop. Berets on . . . now. With your best guttural grumbling, shades of Erich von Stroheim resonating in the air, demand that the Score make its appearance this instant. Of course, it helps to go up to the Window menu and choose Score.

The Score Window: And You Thought NeuroLinguistics 101 Was Complicated

Choosing Score from the Window menu calls up the Score window. I've got to admit, it's a mighty intimidating window. Everything has its place for a purpose, though, and soon you'll be reading it like the back of your hand. You can read the back of your hand, can't you? That's a must quality for multimedia types. Good.

The Score window is where you really create your movie. In our culture, lots of stuff moves from left to right: type, days of the calendar, pages of a book, even images. Ever notice how figures in a film moving left to right seem effortless? Film the same scene moving right to left, and it's uphill all the way. Add a little dramatic music, some popcorn, and you've got great, dramatic footage. So think of the Score as a graph of time moving left to right in your animation, earlier stuff to the left, later stuff to the right.

Icon thingies

I guess you noticed, plenty of new icon thingies to explain. Start from the top left of the Score window, shown in Figure 5-1, and note the following:

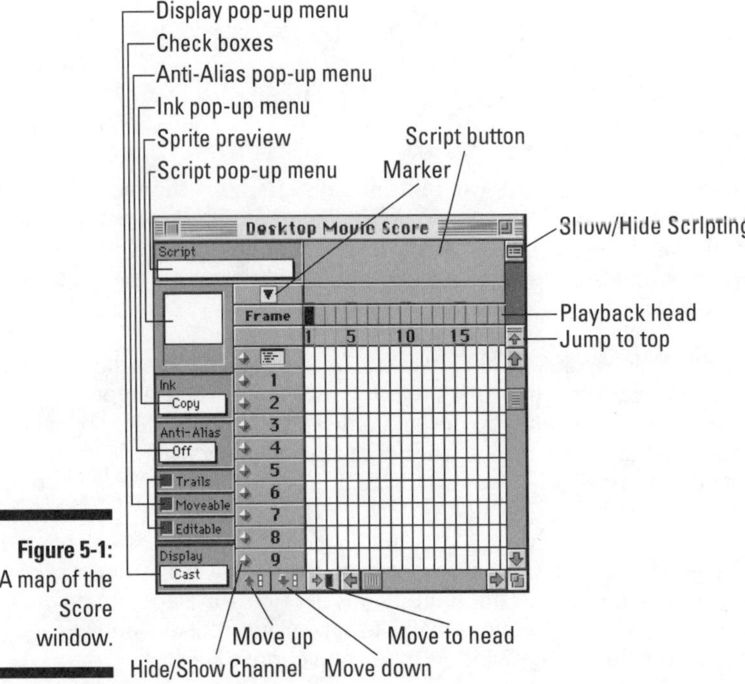

Figure 5-1: A map of the Score window.

- *Script pop-up menu:* Below the word *Script,* you see a long, white, shadowed box. Remember that a shadowed box in MacLand means a pop-up menu. When you start adding scripts to your movie, you'll find them listed by number and name under this Script pop-up menu.
- *Script button:* To the right of the Script pop-up menu is a larger gray area that looks more like a button. In fact, it is a button. When you have scripts in your movie, it reflects the number and name of the currently selected script in the Script pop-up menu. A click of the Script button opens the Script window where you may modify the script to your heart's content — or as much as you can stomach, depending on how you and your internal organs feel about scripting.
- *Show/Hide Scripting button:* To the right of the gray Script button (at the top of the vertical scroll bar) is a tiny button to hide and show the two scripting areas described in the preceding paragraph.
- *Sprite preview:* Below the Script pop-up menu button is a small preview of the currently selected sprite in the Score window along with its distinctive icon type in the lower-right corner of the preview. If the sprite itself contains a script, you'll also find the script icon in the lower-left corner of the preview. If the sprite is a bitmap, double-clicking the preview takes you to the Paint window where you can modify the bitmap.
- *Marker button:* To the right of the upper-right corner of the preview is the Marker button. With it, you can label specific frames of your movie. You can find out how this works in Chapter 15.
- *Playback head:* Below the Marker button is the *Frame,* which names the row called the scratch bar where you find the playback head of your movie, like the playback head of a VCR. You can press the playback head with the mouse and drag left or right across the scratch bar to other frames of your movie.
- *Frame number:* Just below the playback head is a row of numbers. That's it. That's all it is. I know, you should get more than numbers for a pricey package like Director. But they're useful, trust me. They break the Score down into sets of five frames; makes counting them real easy. Good, I'm glad you feel better.
- *Ink pop-up menu:* I'd like you to swing to the left, just under the sprite thumbnail. OK, here's a riddle. What has a box around it and a shadow giving it a phenomenal 3-D effect? Right, a pop-up menu; have another lump of sugar. The Ink pop-up menu lists an impressive set of *ink effects* worthy of George Lucas. The idea is to select one or more bitmap sprites and apply one of the ink effects to them with startling results.
- *Anti-Alias pop-up menu:* Just below the Ink pop-up menu, the Anti-Alias pop-up menu allows you to apply *anti-aliasing* in varying strengths to selected bitmap sprites in the Score. Anti-aliasing is a technique that smoothes out the "jaggies" by blending edges where contrasting areas meet in a bitmap.

- *Trails, Moveable, and Editable check boxes:* Below the Anti-Alias pop-up menu, the Score window presents you with three check boxes that you can turn on for selected sprites: Trails, Moveable, and Editable. Trails leaves a streak of the sprite as it moves around the Stage during the animation; Moveable allows the user to move a selected sprite while the movie plays — the user could drag a folder into a file cabinet, for example, using the mouse pointer; and Editable refers to text sprites, allowing a user to enter text in a text area while a movie is running.
- *Display pop-up menu:* Below the three check boxes is the Display pop-up menu, used to customize the view in the Score window, similar to changing the view of a window at the Desktop with the View menu.

  For example, when you choose Extended from the pop-up menu, you get larger cells with more info, as in Figure 5-2.

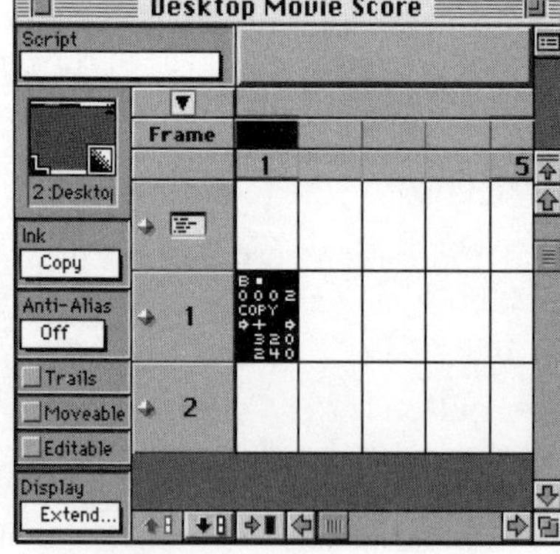

Figure 5-2: Score window cells in Extended view.

  In Figure 5-2, the first line displays *B* for bitmap and a bullet to indicate the sprite's lack of movement (if the sprite moved to the right in the next frame, you'd see a small right-pointing arrow rather than a bullet); the second line displays 0002 for the Cast number of the sprite; the third line displays COPY for the ink type; the fourth line displays a script code; and the next two lines represent the center of the sprite in pixels measured from the upper-left corner of the Stage window (the zero point).

- *Move up, Move down, and Move to head buttons:* To the right of the Display pop-up menu is a row of three utility buttons. From left to right, the button on the left moves selected sprites up the Score window with each click, the second moves selected sprites down the Score, and the third button takes you wherever the playback head currently rests.

- *Channel numbers:* To the right of the Ink and Anti-Alias pop-up menus is a column of numbers labeling nine visible rows of small white rectangles that your sprites rest in. For each frame of your animation, 48 total rows or channels are available. Think of channels as plastic overlays used in traditional animation. Going along with this analogy, channel 1 is similar to static background art, such as the canyon where Wile E. Coyote is chasing Road Runner; channel 2 is the next oldest acetate layer with Road Runner running away from you toward the background; channel 3 is the next layer with Wile E. Coyote tearing after Road Runner; channel 4 is a great yellow cloud of dust that Road Runner and Wile E. Coyote kick up as they race down the canyon. And look, you've got 44 channels left to play with.
- *Hide/Show Channel buttons:* Just to the left of each channel number is a button that hides or shows the channel. Strangely enough, you can't save this setting with the rest of the movie.

Using Trails for easy and unusual special effects

OK, you Roy Rogers fans, happy Trails is a special ink you apply to a selected sprite in the Score so that it leaves a copy of itself wherever it moves on the Stage. In effect, the sprite becomes a brush that paints itself behind its movement to build unusual shapes and patterns. In addition, when you turn off Trails in a subsequent frame, the same sprite begins to erase its own trail wherever it passes over the trail on the Stage.

You nostalgia buffs can build your own psychedelic "flower power" happening on Director's Stage. (Don't forget beads, flowers in hair, and tie-dyed bell bottoms.) Or use Trails with the In-Between command to animate a line-type chart. As someone once said in answer to the query, "How do I get to Carnegie Hall," practice, practice, practice.

Transitions, transitions! (to the tune from Fiddler on the Roof)

Built-in transitions help you quickly build professional-looking multimedia with Director. You can heighten the drama of a bullet chart by setting a new line of text to dissolve into place on the Stage. Or you can create quick animation effects by "wiping" from one frame to another. I've used this trick to create an animation sequence with only two sprites and one wipe transition.

Imagine a sprite in Frame 1 that looks like a deck of cards neatly squared on the table. The second sprite in Frame 2 depicts the deck fanned out across the Stage. You double-click Frame 2 in the Transition channel and choose Wipe Right from the pop-up menu of transitions. When you rewind your movie with the Control Panel window and click the Play button, the Wipe transition creates a slick illusion that the deck of cards has magically fanned itself.

In case you didn't notice, the Transition pop-up menu gives you over fifty transitions to choose from. In other words, if you think I'm going to cover each one of them in this book, I've got a great piece of property I'd love to show you in a quaint little village called Chernobyl. Frankly, I wouldn't touch most of these transitions with a ten-foot pole. Someone find me a twenty-foot pole, quick.

Anyway, once you've chosen a transition, Director allows you to modify most of them by one of the following:

- *Duration:* Available for most transitions, you can set a duration in 1/4-second units.
- *Chunk Size:* Factory set at the best rate for a particular transition, you're invited to experiment with the number of pixels or chunks affected in the image from one unit of time to the next. Generally, the larger the chunk, the coarser the effect of the transition.
- *Stage Area/Changing Area:* Some transitions allow you to apply the effect only to the part of the Stage that changes. For example, a new sprite may dissolve into view from the background, which won't display the Dissolve transition effect itself.

Never set a transition in the first frame of a movie. You won't see anything happen because setting a transition in a frame of the Transition channel kicks in visually going from the previous frame to the current frame (the frame resting under the Playback Head). When you set a transition in the first frame, there's no previous frame to begin the transition.

Find out more about the Transition channel later in this chapter in the section, "Hidden, top-secret channels."

That's MISTER cell to you, Bud

The small, white rectangles in the Score window are called *cells.* Cells hold sprites that come from the Cast window and serve as building blocks for the visual timeline you build in the Score window. You can change the view of these cells in much the same way you change window views at the Desktop. For example, if motion info is most important to you at a particular time in your movie's development you can switch to Motion view from the Display pop-up menu.

To move to the right in the Score window, press Command and then the right-arrow key or press 3 on the keypad. To move left, press Command and then the left-arrow key or press 1 on the keypad. Next, you put your left foot in . . . .

Hidden, top-secret channels

Just above the bold number labeling channel 1 is a small icon representing one of a set of special channels waiting to be explored. Pith helmets on now, everyone. To begin your safari through the steaming jungle hell of hidden channels, notice the small scroll bar in the top right corner of the Score window. At the bottom of the small scroll bar is a special Jump to Top button.

When you click the Jump to Top button, the top five hidden channels zip into view, as in Figure 5-3. Aren't you glad you had your pith helmet on?

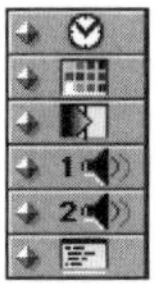

Figure 5-3: Hidden channels in the Score window.

So, that makes a grand total of six special channels, outlined in Table 5-1.

Table 5-1 Special Score Channels

Icon	*Channel*	*Add a Sprite in This Channel to*
	Tempo	Set the pace and add limited interactivity to your movie from the selected frame.
	Palette	Change the set of colors used in your movie from the selected frame.
	Transition	Set dissolves, wipes, and more effects; starts on the previous frame.
 1	Sound Channel 1	Play imported sounds including SoundEdit, AIFF, AIFC files, and snd resources.
 2	Sound Channel 2	Play left and right stereo sound from stereo-capable Macintoshes such as Quadra and Power Mac AV models.
	Script	Store scripts in the Score that activate when the playback head reaches the appropriate frame.

- SoundEdit sound files are the proprietary file type from Macromedia's SoundEdit Pro, an application for editing digitized sounds. AIFF (Audio Interchange File Format) files represent Apple's nomination for an industry standard sound file type. AIFC files are similar to AIFF but compressed. And snd files are bits of code that become part of the movie file itself when imported.

- There *are* two spaces between "snd" and "files" in the previous sentence because this type of file, called a resource, always has a four-character resource type to identify it. The fourth character for a snd resource is an invisible space character.
- If you intend to import and play back sound from both Sound channels, make sure that you have Sound Manager 3.0 or later installed in your System folder.

- It's not a bad idea to get into the habit of entering a Tempo setting in the first frame of the Tempo channel for each movie. Otherwise, Director will play your movie at 15 fps (frames per second), the default tempo setting that won't necessarily match your needs. Also, be sure to brush after every meal.

Adding a Cast Member to the Score

Have you noticed one thing the Score shares with other windows? Aside from the gizmos, numbers, and icon thingies, it's pretty bare when you first open it. You see, you're responsible for putting content into the Score, which is a pretty frightening thought considering your old SAT scores. But you've come a long way, and something that would sure brighten up that old Score window, aside from a couple of throw rugs and a little paint, is to add a Cast Member. Not to mention that you build a movie by adding Cast Members from the Cast window to the Score.

1. **Make sure that the Score window is visible.**
2. **Choose Window⇨Cast to display the Cast window.**
3. **Move the mouse pointer over the Cast Member that you want to add to the Score window.**

   Notice that the cursor changes from the mouse pointer to the grabber hand, illustrated in Figure 5-4.
4. **Press the mouse and begin dragging slowly to the right.**

   Two things happen at this point. The grabber hand cursor turns into the menacing Fist cursor, and the Cast Member follows in ghostly outline form, both visible in Figure 5-5.

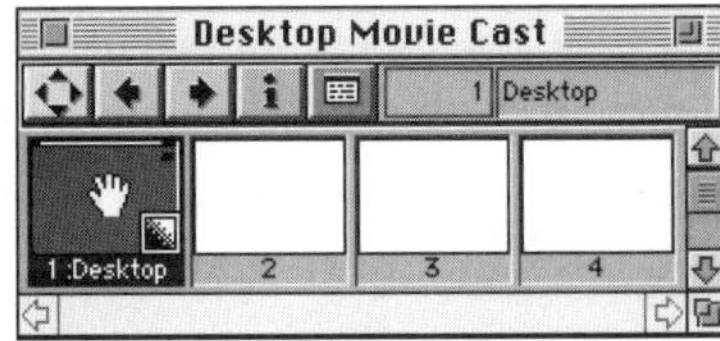

Figure 5-4: The grabber hand cursor in the Cast window.

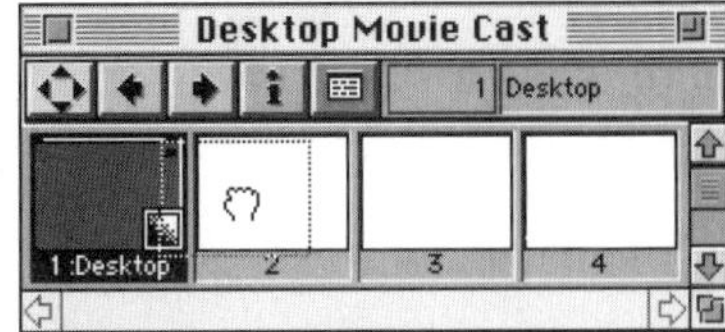

Figure 5-5: The grabber hand cursor turning into the Fist cursor.

5. **When the Cast Member and the Fist cursor loom over the second cell in the Cast window, release the mouse.**

   Now you've moved your Cast Member from the first cell to the second. I had you make a small detour to show how you can move Cast Members from cell to cell within the Cast window. You're going to make one more detour to see how hard Director goes out of its way to be helpful to you.

6. **Press the mouse over your Cast Member in the second cell and begin dragging slowly upward.**

   Look at the Fist cursor. As you drag over areas where you shouldn't release the mouse, the cursor changes into the infamous Fist with a "No-No" symbol inside, as in Figure 5-6. Kind of like Robert Mitchum with Love and Hate tattooed on his knuckles. Now that's macho.

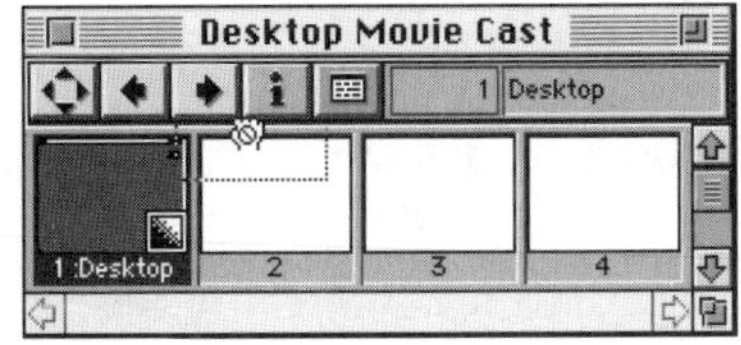

Figure 5-6: The Fist cursor displaying the "No-No" symbol.

7. **With the mouse still pressed down, drag up past the Cast window and over the Stage.**

The cursor returns to the regular fist, meaning you could release the mouse here. Chances are that your Cast Member would wind up off center, and you'd have to fudge it into place. There's a better way, trust me.

8. **Drag the mouse into the Score from the bottom of the Score window.**

   Two events worthy of notice occur at this point:

   - The rectangle currently resting under the fist turns black, highlighted with a bold white border to indicate its readiness to receive your offering.
   - The black rectangle to the right of the word *Frame* follows your mouse as you drag left or right.

   Following along with the VCR analogy, the black rectangle represents the playback head of your movie in the making, as seen in Figure 5-7.

Figure 5-7: The playback head in the Score window.

9. **When the Fist cursor hovers over the rectangle to the right of the bold number 1, as in Figure 5-7, release the mouse.**

Now a number of events take place at the same time. See if you catch them all; no fair peeking at Figure 5-8, which reflects most of these changes:

- Your pants fall down. If not, the program's defective; return it immediately and demand a fresh copy. Pull your pants up first.
- Your Cast Member instantaneously appears, centered on the Stage.
- The small, highlighted rectangle becomes reversed and designates a number that represents which Cast Member it is. If your screen looks different, shame on you. Just kidding. It only means you released the mouse a little too soon, and your Cast Member wound up in a different rectangle. If so, press the mouse over the rectangle where your Cast Member is and drag it over the first rectangle, as shown in Figure 5-8.

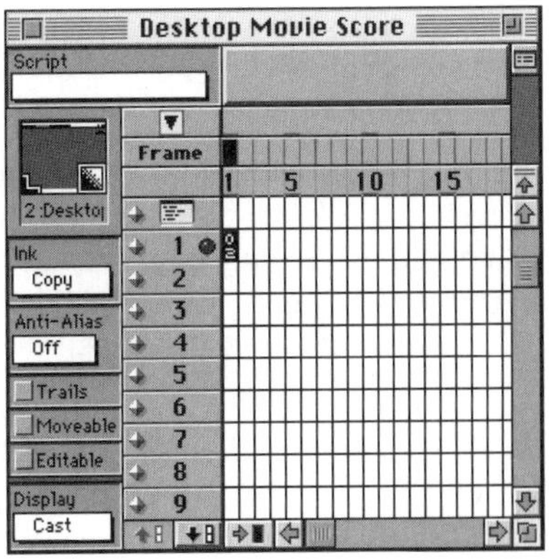

Figure 5-8: The Score window after adding a Cast Member.

- A small preview of the Cast Member appears in the upper left corner of the Score window.
- The cursor becomes the mouse pointer again. If you're following along in Director, notice that the Cast window is still the active window. Adding a Cast Member to the Score doesn't automatically make the Score the active window.
- The Step Recording Indicator appears just to the right of the bold number 1. Creating a movie by dragging Cast Members into the Score window puts Director into frame-by-frame or Step Recording mode.

Now this is *very* important. It's not a bad idea to tattoo the following on your forehead so you don't forget. You call the contents of the Cast window Cast Members. After you drag a Cast Member into the Score window, you refer to it in the Score as a *sprite.* Hey, I didn't make this up, blame Macromedia. It's the honest truth, I swear. So, a bitmap in the Cast window is a Cast Member. Same bitmap in the Score, sprite. Good. Cut. Print.

All This Ink and Not a Drop on Me — Oops

I know, I whizzed by that Ink pop-up menu pretty quickly in the "Icon thingies" section earlier in this chapter. Now you can relax, get a cup of coffee, loosen your belt, take off your shoes — wait, better put your shoes back on — and investigate the mysterious world of ink effects in Director.

The most useful and frequently used inks under the Ink pop-up menu include

- *Copy:* The out-of-the-box or default ink for sprites, it uses the least amount of memory and is the fastest running ink of all. The bitmap is contained in a rectangular *bounding box* of white pixels indicating the image's width and height.

- *Matte:* Makes transparent the white pixels surrounding a sprite in its bounding box so that the sprite displays a cut-out effect against the background.
- *Bkgnd Transparent:* Similar to Matte but turns transparent all background-colored pixels surrounding and within the sprite, allowing you to achieve the infamous "donut" effect. You could use Bkgnd Transparent to make a sprite such as a large *A* dance around the Stage. The so-called *counter* in the center of the *A* becomes transparent, allowing the background to show through.
- *Mask:* Similar to Matte but goes a step further. When set up correctly, Mask allows selective, background-colored areas in a complex sprite image to remain opaque and still deliver the "donut" effect. To complete the Mask ink effect, you need to select the Cast Member in the Cast window, clone it in the very next cell, and turn it into a black and white, bitmapped silhouette. Applying the Mask ink effect to the sprite in the Score is the finishing touch.

Other inks allow you to create some very unusual effects, especially when two or more sprites overlap.

The wild, wacky world of foreground color, background color, and pattern

When you're exploring ink effects, you need to keep in mind that Director always recognizes a set of three, related conditions: current foreground color, current background color, and current pattern. Because inks make use of these two colors and the current pattern in creating their effects, being aware of these conditions can help you anticipate an effect. Even if you're running a black and white monitor, you've got a current foreground color, black, and a current background color, white. Running color, you can switch from black to a color chip with the foreground color selector and switch from white to another color—including black—from the background color selector in the Paint or Tools window.

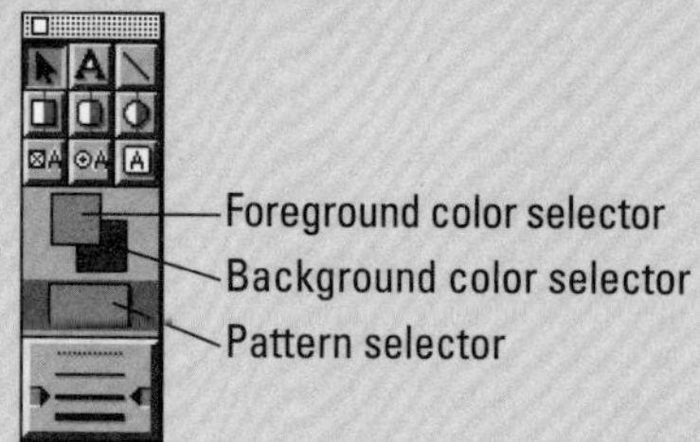

When you're painting with solid black paint, the current pattern is simply solid black. If you're considering a waffle pattern in the Pattern pop-up menu, the pattern itself is black, its negative space white. Running color, the current foreground color replaces black, the current background color white.

The price you pay for using ink effects other than Copy — you knew this was coming — is speed. Ink effects greatly slow down the playback speed of your animations on the Stage, some more than others.

These additional ink effects include

- *Transparent:* Intended mainly for black and white screens, makes any white or background-colored pixels in the selected sprite transparent.
- *Reverse:* Intended mainly for black and white screens, black or foreground-colored pixels in a selected sprite become white, and white or background-colored pixels become transparent revealing the background. With color monitors, color-on-color effects are hard to predict so save time for plenty of experimentation and breaking of fine china against the wall in fits of aesthetic frustration.
- *Ghost:* Intended mainly for black and white screens, black pixels in the selected sprite turn pixels of underlying sprites white and transparent.
- *Not Copy, Not Transparent, Not Reverse, Not Ghost:* Not as in "The check is in the mail. . .NOT," first reverses pixels of the selected sprite, then adds the corresponding ink effect to them.
- *Blend:* Averages the selected sprite's color with the color of underlying sprites creating a transparency effect.
- *Darkest:* Compares pixels of the selected sprite to the current foreground color and colors pixels only in the selected sprite that are darker than the foreground color.
- *Lightest:* Compares pixels of the selected sprite to the current foreground color and colors pixels only in the selected sprite that are lighter than the foreground color.
- *Add:* Adds the color values of each pixel in the selected sprite to the color values of each underlying pixel. The Add ink effect looks like a blend at first glance, but doesn't hold true on close inspection. Also, as its name implies, Add often makes a new, lighter color after the addition, but not necessarily. Some color combinations in Add loop past the highest color value in a palette, white, to the lowest color value, black, or to a subsequent color in the palette, resulting in surprising color changes. Check out the Technical Stuff sidebar coming up soon about colors and their associated values to see how all this works, as if anyone cares.
- *Add Pin:* Similar to Add, but doesn't allow the final color to loop past the highest color value. The result is that many color additions with Add Pin wind up white, the highest color values that a pixel can register.
- *Subtract:* Subtracts the color values of each pixel in the selected sprite from the color values of each underlying pixel, resulting in a new color. If the result is a negative value, the color restarts from black to subsequent colors in the palette.

- *Subtract Pin:* Similar to Subtract, but doesn't allow a color value to loop back and continue up the scale of color values. Applying Subtract Pin to a sprite often results in many black pixels, the lowest color values that a pixel can register.

Technical drivel about color values

To really understand how ink effects do their magic you need to understand how a color image appears on your screen. Each pixel you see on your screen is the result of red, green, and blue light mixing together, which is why monitors are often referred to as RGB displays (or as #@%%^&*!! displays when they're not working).

By the way, these red, green, and blue lights come from three, tiny, electronic "guns" inside your monitor, one for each color, pointed at the phosphorescent surface of your screen. Your color TV at home works basically the same way.

It happens that each color has its own recipe of red, green, and blue light. Where you see a black pixel, no red, green, or blue beam of light strikes that particular area of the monitor. So another way of saying black in the Macintosh world is Red=0 (for 0 percent), Green=0, Blue=0. Where you see a white pixel, maximum (or 100 percent) red, green, and blue light meet and mix at that precise point on your screen. You can designate white as Red = 100, Green = 100, Blue = 100.

When you're mixing light together instead of Crayolas, red and green equals yellow, believe it or not. Here's a simple test to prove I'm right. Rent three standard klieg lights and three filters, red, green, and blue, each about two yards wide. Overlap their mega-volt beacons on the wall of any nearby skyscraper and what do you get in the center? That's right, pure white light. Now turn off the blue klieg light (watch your fingers, those klieg lights get hot). Voilà, a beautiful diaphanous yellow. And it only cost you a few thousand dollars in equipment and hauling to demonstrate the additive approach to mixing color. Don't worry, it's probably tax-deductible.

So, with so-called additive color, any color can be designated with a set of red, green, and blue values. When you select a sprite from the Score and apply the Add ink effect, Director adds the red, green, and blue values of each pixel in the selected sprite to the red, green, and blue values of each underlying pixel. Remember, these values are percentages of color, so you might see a case where adding values gives you a sum over 100 percent. When this occurs with the Add ink effect, Director makes the excess percentage the new value. On the other hand, when you choose Add Pin, you're telling Director to ignore color values over 100 percent, resulting in a number of new colors with 100 percent red, green, and/or blue.

Getting Close and Personal with the Score Menu

Chances are you've guessed that the Score menu is related to what goes on in the Score window. Glad to see you're not asleep out there in ReaderLand. Why don't you see what's under the ol' Score menu?

- *Sprite Info:* Takes you to the Sprite Info dialog box where you can change a selected sprite's scale (width and height), restore a sprite's original size (after resizing), and alter the sprite's location on the Stage.
- *Delete Sprites:* Allows you to delete selected sprites directly from the Stage. Remember, press Shift while clicking to select sprites on the Stage.
- *Set Sprite Blend:* Brings up the Set Sprite Blend dialog box for one or more selected sprites where you can set the percentage of transparency from 0 to 100 percent with a sliding control.
- *Set Tempo, Palette, Transition, Sound:* Each of the four commands takes you to the respective dialog box where you can modify your movie at the point of a selected frame in the Score. Just like double-clicking a cell in the Tempo, Palette, Transition, or Sound channel.
- *Insert Frame:* Creates a duplicate frame in the Score to the right of the frame with a selected cell. Each time you select Insert Frame, all frames to the right of the new frame move one frame to the right. If a range of frames is selected, Insert Frame inserts a frame to the right of the last selected frame.
- *Delete Frame:* Removes all 48 cells of a frame containing a selected cell. All frames to the right of the deleted frame move one frame to the left.
- *In-Between Linear:* Refers to an animation technique called *in-betweening,* or *tweening,* for short, to create animation from beginning and ending frames of a sequence. You can paste a copy of a sprite along with its current location on the Stage to a place in the Score two or more frames apart from the original sprite, change the copy's location on the Stage, and select the range of frames from the original sprite to the copy. When you choose In-Between Linear, Director creates the "In-Between" sprites for you in even steps calculated by how many frames apart the original sprite and copy are in the Score.
- *In-Between Special:* Similar to In-Between Linear but offers you several options in an In-Between Special dialog box to create more realistic, animated sprites.
- *Space to Time:* Places Cast Members selected in the Cast window into consecutive frames in the Score, one frame per Cast Member.
- *Paste Relative:* A special Paste command that pastes copied frames of a sprite automatically after the last selected sprite so that you can easily extend a sequence of repetitive movement.

- *Reverse Sequence:* Reverses the order of a selected range of frames so that the first frame of the selection becomes the last, the last the first, and so on. You get the idea.
- *Switch Cast Members:* Allows you to replace a sprite selected in the Score with a Cast Member selected in the Cast window.
- *Auto Animate:* Offers you a pop-up menu of semi-automated special effects including Banner (text scrolling horizontally across the Stage), Bar Chart (a chart using an animated sprite to represent a unit of value increasing or decreasing over time), Bullet Chart (a chart that "builds" from point to point, featuring both animated bullets and text), Credits (text scrolling vertically as in many "Hollywood" films), and Text Effects (including Zoom Text, Letter Slide, Typewriter, and Sparkle).
- *Score Window Options:* Allows you to customize the Score with colored cells and magnified cells, setting the playback head to follow selections, and something called Drop and Drop where you can move a selection of cells in the Score by pressing the mouse inside the selection and dragging it to a new location.

Now that you've got a better idea how the Score window and menu commands work together, check out how you can easily add eye-catching effects with built-in Director features. Drop by someday and I'll show you my personal collection of eyes I've caught over the years. Paté, anyone?

As time goes by: using Space to Time

One of the monster challenges you face when you use Director is how to get Cast Members from the Cast window to the Score. Space to Time under the Score menu allows you to select a number of Cast Members from the Cast window and instantly place them as sprites in consecutive frames of the Score. When you choose this command, the Space to Time dialog box appears. There you can change the number of frames apart that each sprite winds up as it becomes part of the Score. The default value is 1; you can change it to whatever value you enter.

Sometimes you'll want to visually check how a set of selected Cast Members relate to each other by dragging them to the Stage as sprites. What happens when you drag Cast Members to the Stage? Excellent, have a lump of sugar. They're placed in separate channels under the *same* frame in the Score. Once you check each sprite's position and possibly modify some of their locations, you can select the sprites from the Score by dragging out a selection marquee, or by pressing Shift and clicking them, then choose Space to Time from the Score menu to rearrange the sprites' cells from consecutive channels to consecutive frames. This places them in the Space-Time Continuum that Einstein proposed, and the end of the world occurs in a blinding flash of searing heat. Or maybe it just places the sprites in adjacent frames. Are you brave enough to take the chance?

What to do between takes? In-Between Special, of course.

Objects in the real world don't usually start and stop in equal units of space from moment to moment. For example, imagine a bouncing ball. It speeds up or accelerates as it approaches the floor, bounces off the ground with stored up energy, and begins to slow down or decelerate as it reaches its highest point in the air because of the effects of gravity.

Using In-Between Special, you can call up the In-Between Special dialog box and enter a so-called Ease-In value to accelerate a selected sprite as it's "tweened." You can also enter a so-called Ease-Out value to decelerate the sprite.

In addition, In-Between Special allows you to set up non-linear movement for tweened sprites. Remember how you needed beginning and ending sprites for the In-Between Linear command under the Score menu? In-Between Special requires at least one additional, intermediate sprite to determine the "path" followed when Director creates the full set of tweened sprites with In-Between Special.

If little of this makes sense to you, don't worry. The following chapter details working with sprites in the Score, and everything will come together. Trust me.

Chapter 6

Too Graphic for You? Director's Paint Window

In This Chapter

- Accessing the Paint window
- Reviewing some familiar icons
- Hammering away at Director's Paint tools

You know, Director's pretty generous. For the price of the top animation program in MacLand, Macromedia throws in a pretty slick paint program just because they like you so much. Oh, you think there might be an ulterior motive? Well, it's a good program anyway. With the built-in paint program hiding under the Paint window, you can handle any kind of bitmap from 1-bit, black and white graphics to what techies call 24-bit images, meaning graphics with over 16 million colors. How did I get that figure? You don't want to know. (If you'll just burst not knowing, read the Technical Stuff sidebar later in this chapter.)

Director also gives you a number of ways to display and use the Paint window, including:

- *Choosing Paint from the Window menu:* When you want to start from scratch, you can go the basic route, call up the Paint window, and begin scratching away on a blank, electronic easel. Not an easy thing to do, even with a degree from the Sorbonne and the big set of crayons you got for Christmas.
- *Double-clicking a Bitmap Cast Member:* With one or more Cast Members happily waiting for the role of their lives in the Cast window, you can double-click on a Bitmap Cast Member's thumbnail and find the actual-size bitmap in the Paint window ready and willing to be edited. This route is a lot easier than starting from scratch because the Cast Member could have been imported from a good collection of clip art, an image you scanned

yourself and saved as a bitmap, a screen shot you took with the old Command+Shift+3 trick (or better yet, with a commercial utility such as Capture or CameraMan), a chart generated from raw data in Excel, or a roll of film you had your friendly photo dealer turn into a PhotoCD for you.

- *Double-clicking a bitmap sprite in the Score window:* As long as the sprite is a bitmap, you get the Paint window with the bitmap ready for editing.
- *Double-clicking the small thumbnail of the currently selected sprite in the Score window:* Same result, you'll wind up with the bitmap staring back at you from the Paint window, anxiously awaiting modification.

Oh, No! Thousands of Icon Thingies!

OK, hold on. You went to the menu bar and chose Paint from the Window menu. Now you see icon thingies everywhere, as in Figure 6-1.

First, the number of icons is much less than a hundred, let alone "thousands." A lot of the icons are standard Mac stuff: a Close box in the upper-left corner of the Title bar, a Zoom box in the upper-right corner, a Resize box in the lower-right corner, and a set of horizontal and vertical scroll bars. So far, so good.

Then there's the mysterious stuff. You have a row of icons in the upper-left corner of the Paint window. Below them, you see a double column of enticing icons, and below the enticing icons, a number of small panels. You can handle this. You made it through the Score, you and I can get through the Paint window, together. Trust me.

Colors, colors everywhere

Getting over 16 million colors from 24-bit graphics comes from the way computers understand information. In the final analysis, all computers know is *binary,* which is why Macs make such rotten houseguests for the weekend. Boring! Anyway, binary is a system of counting that uses only two numbers, 0 and 1. To your Mac, 0 is *off* and 1 is *on.*

However, various combinations of 0s and 1s, on and off *states,* have unique coded meanings to your Mac. To a computer, 24-bit means a number in binary that looks to you like a string of 24 1s in a row. Rocket scientists like to call this value "2 to the 24th power." 24-bit, 24 binary 1s in a row, 2 to the 24th power; they all stand for the same value — 16,384,000.

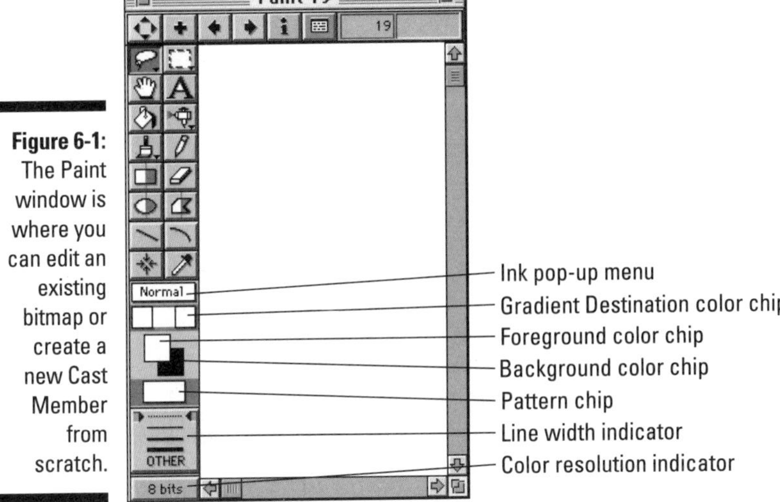

Figure 6-1: The Paint window is where you can edit an existing bitmap or create a new Cast Member from scratch.

Now, wait, some of these icons look familiar, eh?

Come to think of it, doesn't that row of icons in the upper-left corner of the Paint window look suspiciously familiar? Hello, all but the second button are in the Cast window, too.

- The first icon lets you drag the contents of the Paint window to the Stage or Score.
- Now for the new + icon. Clicking this button gives you a blank electronic easel to paint on with the many tools in the Paint window; this will create a new Cast Member that occupies the next available cell in the Cast window.
- The Previous and Next icons allow you to click through Cast Members in the Cast window.
- The i icon takes you to the Cast Member Info dialog box.
- The Script button takes you to the Cast Member's Script window where you can enter or modify Lingo commands.

To the right of these buttons is an area displaying the currently selected Cast Member's number in the Cast window and the Cast Member's name.

Additional Paint window areas

Now — to wake some of you drowsing off in ReaderLand — I'd like you to look at the areas of the Paint window from the bottom left on up, represented in Figure 6-1.

- *Ink pop-up menu:* Allows you to choose an ink effect for a selection in the Paint window. Many of the ink types are similar to the inks available in the Score window, but others, such as Smudge and Smear, are specifically used to expand the potential of Director's paint tools. Double-clicking the Ink pop-up menu several times gives you a terrific headache as the pop-up menu wildly appears and disappears with each click.
- *Gradient Destination color chip:* Hey, don't blame me; I didn't make these names up. Allows you to select the beginning and ending colors for a gradient, or blend of colors, by pressing the left and right sides of the chip and selecting a color from the available colors. Double-clicking the chip takes you to the Color Palette dialog box where you can choose a different palette for the bitmap.
- *Foreground color chip:* Allows you to select the current foreground color by pressing the Foreground color chip and choosing a color from the current set of available colors. The number of colors depends on the current color depth setting of your monitor (in the Monitors control panel under the Apple menu). Double-clicking the chip takes you to the Color Palettes dialog box where you can select a different palette for the bitmap.
- *Background color chip:* Allows you to select the current background color by pressing the Background color chip and choosing a color from the current set of available colors. The number of colors depends on the current color depth setting of your monitor (in the Monitors control panel under the Apple menu). Double-clicking the chip takes you to the Color Palettes dialog box where you can select a different palette for the bitmap.
- *Pattern chip:* Allows you to select the current pattern by pressing the Pattern chip and choosing a pattern. Double-clicking the Pattern chip takes you to the Pattern dialog box where you can create custom patterns.
- *Line width indicator:* Allows you to choose the current line width for several of Director's paint tools. Double-clicking the Line width indicator takes you to the Paint Window Options dialog box where, among other options, you can select a line width up to 64 points with a sliding control.
- *Color resolution indicator:* Displays the color depth of the current bitmap in the Paint window. *Color depth* is techy talk for how many colors a bitmap can display at one time. For example, a 1-bit graphic can show only black and white, while an 8-bit graphic can display up to 256 different colors at once. Double-clicking the Color resolution indicator takes you to the Transform Bitmap dialog box where you can, among other options, set the bitmap to a higher or lower color depth.

Director's Paint Tools

The other mysterious areas of the Paint window represent tools and paint option areas that you use to modify bitmaps or create new Cast Members from scratch. Row by row, Director's paint tools include the following:

Lasso tool

You use the Lasso tool to create irregularly shaped selections in the Paint window. Think of using the Lasso as "roping in" an area you want to include in a selection.

You can modify the way the Lasso tool works by pressing the tool in the Paint tool palette and choosing one of three commands from the Lasso pop-up menu, described in Table 6-1.

Table 6-1 Lasso Pop-Up Menu

Command	*How the Lasso Tool Works*
Shrink	Changes the selection to exclude contiguous pixels, matching the color first pressed with the Lasso.
No Shrink	Sets the selection to include all pixels "roped in" with the Lasso.
See Thru	Within the selection, sets pixels matching the color first pressed to Transparent ink.

Table 6-2 describes the different results you get when you use the Lasso tool with and without modifier keys.

Table 6-2 Using the Lasso Tool

Action	*Result*
Press Option and click	Establishes a starting point to make a polygonal selection with repeated clicks of the Lasso.
Click	Creates the first and remaining segments of a polygonal selection after establishing a starting point by pressing Option and clicking the Lasso.
Double-click	Closes a polygonal selection.

(continued)

Table 6-2 *(continued)*

Action	*Result*
Press Option and drag a selection	Creates an identical copy, or clone, of the selection. Each time you release, then repress the mouse button, you may press Option and drag a new clone to another area of the easel.
Press Shift and Option and drag a selection	Creates a clone and constrains movement of the clone horizontally or vertically, depending on the direction of the initial move.

Selection Rectangle tool

The Selection Rectangle tool is another basic selection tool for making, of all things, rectangular selections.

You can modify the way the Selection Rectangle tool works by pressing the tool in the Paint tool palette and choosing one of four options from a pop-up menu, as described in Table 6-3.

Table 6-3 Selection Rectangle Pop-Up Menu

Command	*Behavior*
Shrink	Snaps to the height and width of a graphic, eliminating background-colored pixels from the selection.
No Shrink	Includes all pixels in the selection.
Lasso	Notes the color first pressed and eliminates matching pixels from the selection. Also, switches to the Lasso tool.
See Thru Lasso	Notes the color first pressed and turns all matching pixels in the selection and all background-colored pixels transparent, then switches to the Lasso tool.

The Selection Rectangle tool is also the key to quickly making copies of and resizing bitmaps, either proportionally or to distort a bitmap horizontally or vertically. Table 6-4 outlines the result of applying modifier keys to the Selection Rectangle tool.

Table 6-4 Using the Selection Rectangle Tool

Action	*Result*
Press Option and drag a selection	Creates an identical copy, or *clone.* Each time you stop and repress the mouse, you may press Option and drag a new clone to another area of the easel.
Press Shift and Option and drag a selection	Creates a clone and constrains movement of the clone horizontally or vertically, depending on the direction of the initial move.
Press Command and drag a corner of a selection	Resizes the selection horizontally and/or vertically. Dragging away from the selection increases the selection's size. Dragging into the center of the selection reduces the selection's size.
Press Command and Shift and drag a corner of a selection	Proportionally resizes the selection horizontally and vertically. Dragging away from the selection increases the selection's size. Dragging into the center of the selection reduces the selection's size.

One of Mr. Bitmap's most serious disadvantages is how poorly it scales up or down. A bitmap resized in Director's Paint window rarely results in an acceptable image for professional work. Not withstanding Director's fine built-in Paint program, the best approach to resizing a bitmap is to use a sophisticated paint program like Photoshop. A program on Photoshop's level calls on highly refined routines for scaling graphics that even allow successful, limited enlargement of a bitmap. *Limited* is the key word.

Some kindly advice for scaling graphics in Director

- Reducing a bitmap works better than enlarging in Director or any paint program, especially with a relatively simple graphic.
- If a bitmap is moving, loss of quality is harder to detect and less critical to the eye.
- If you know that changing scale is going to be an important part of a Cast Member's role, add it to the Cast as a PICT from the Clipboard with the Paste as PICT command in the Cast menu; then rescale the PICT as a sprite on the Stage by pressing Shift and dragging a corner handle (for proportional scaling).
- If you've pulled and stretched a sprite, bitmap, or PICT, on the Stage and wished it back to its original size in desperation, stop wishing. Choose Sprite Info from the Score menu and click the Restore to Size of Cast Member radio button.

Hand tool

Pressing the Hand tool in the easel of the Paint window allows you to shift the view on-screen so that hidden sections of full-size bitmaps, such as a screen shot, or oversized bitmaps come into view.

A common fear of novice Director types is that moving a bitmap in the Paint window messes up the position of artwork on the Stage. Director is smart enough to know you don't want changing the location of a bitmap in the Paint window to alter a artwork's location on the Stage. Give Director some credit, will you? Sheesh!

If the position of a bitmap in the Paint window is important to you, press the Option key and drag the Hand tool around the easel so that you move around the screen without changing the placement of the bitmap relative to the top-left corner of the easel.

Other than the Text tool, temporarily change the currently selected tool in the Paint window to the Hand tool by pressing the spacebar.

Text tool

The Text tool in the Paint window is for creating text that becomes a bitmap as soon as you do just about anything other than type or set text attributes like Font, Size, and Style.

Try this out:

1. **Choose Paint from the Window menu.**
2. **Click the + button near the upper-left corner of the window.**

   To quickly return to the upper-left corner of a bitmap in the Paint window, click the Next button in the top-left corner of the window, then click the Previous button to return to the bitmap. You'll find you're back at the upper-left corner of the bitmap with the scroll bars rearranged like magic.
3. **Click the Text tool.**

   Once you move back to the easel, your mouse pointer should look like the classic I-beam cursor of word processing programs such as Microsoft Word and Claris MacWrite.
4. **At the I-beam, type some text; copy from Figure 6-2 if you want.**
5. **Type a period and then type three spaces.**

   OK, those of you out there who typed "a period" and "three spaces," go stand in the corner for at least three hours. And no supper.
6. **Press the Delete key once.**

Your text should appear as something similar to Figure 6-2. My guess is the typeface is Geneva, Director's default typeface. And the size is probably 12 point, Director's default size. Aren't defaults pathetically boring? (They do save time, though.)

Figure 6-2: Editable text created with the Text tool in the Paint window.

Today is the first day
of the rest of your life.

The only reason I added three spaces and then deleted one space was to get a better view of the insertion point following the period that looks like an upside-down cross. The short horizontal line at the bottom of the insertion point marks what typographer types call the baseline, where lowercase characters visually rest horizontally on the page.

You should also see a bold gray border around the text you typed. As long as you retain the gray border, also shown in Figure 6-2, and insertion point, you can modify the text in several ways. For example, you can

- Delete characters to the left of the insertion point one character at a time with the Delete key.
- Move editable text without losing the border or insertion point by pressing the mouse anywhere within the gray border and dragging.
- Choose Font, Size, and Style commands from the Text menu. These changes are immediately visible in editable text.
- Choose the Text Shadow command from the Text menu. Text Shadow changes are not visible until you change the text to a bitmap.
- Double-click the Color resolution indicator to change the scale, color depth, and/or palette of the text with the Transform Bitmap dialog box. *After this operation, you lose the ability to edit the text.*
- Press the Pattern chip to change the current pattern. You don't see pattern changes until you change the text to a bitmap.
- Press the Background color chip to change the current background color; it colorizes the white space within the bold gray border that contains the text. You don't see background color changes until you change the text to a bitmap.

- Press the Foreground color chip to change the current foreground color, which will colorize the text. Changes to foreground color are immediately visible in editable text.
- Press the Gradient Destination color chip to set up first and last colors for a custom gradient. This action alone does not modify the editable text. To apply a gradient to the editable text, you need to take one more step, selecting Gradient from the Ink pop-up menu. Also, changes are not visible until you turn the text into a bitmap.
- Press the Ink pop-up menu to change the current ink type. Changes are not visible until you turn the text into a bitmap.

As soon as you lose the bold gray border and insertion point, text typed with the Text tool in the Paint window becomes a bitmap, no different than any other bitmap imported or painted into being with one of Director's paint tools.

The biggest disadvantage of losing the insertion point is that you can no longer edit the text. If you want to make edits, bitmapped text must be literally erased and retyped, care being taken to match the previous artwork and blend the text appropriately into its surroundings.

Every cloud has a silver lining. That's an old saying I just made up since it seems appropriate at this time. You see, a great big wonderful advantage of bitmapped text is not having to worry about having the right typeface installed in the system, a never-ending concern when using "real" text. What if the right typeface isn't installed in the computer? What if the user doesn't have the same typeface? What if you have halitosis? And on and on. Once bitmapped text sits on a page, you're one giant step closer to old man, Carefree Day.

Just make sure that you avoid on-screen "jaggies" by choosing a TrueType font or installing Adobe Type Manager, a commercial product, into your system before opening Director. For serious type aficionados who want extra-smooth looking type, you can also turn on Anti-Alias from the Score window, although this option tends to slow down animations.

Bitmapped text also animates faster than "real" or so-called QuickDraw text.

Paint Bucket tool

Use the Paint Bucket tool to fill an area with the current foreground color and pattern.

The Paint Bucket tool also fills an area with the current gradient set in the Gradient Destination color chip, if you choose Gradient from the Ink pop-up menu. The Paint Bucket tool works best with solid areas of color, or as techy types say, contiguous blocks of pixels of matching color. You see, the Paint

Bucket is sensitive to the color of the pixel you initially click on; it seeks out contiguous pixels of a matching color and says, "Today is your lucky day. I have come to color, pattern, and gradient you."

Double-clicking the Paint Bucket tool takes you to the Gradients dialog box shown in Figure 6-3. By the way, a gradient is a blend of colors. The beginning color is defined by the current foreground color, the ending color by the current color chosen as the Destination color chip.

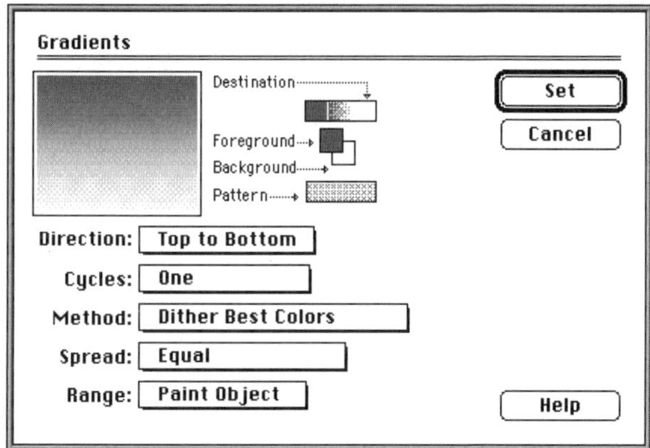

Figure 6-3: The Gradients dialog box.

As you can see, Director offers you many options in this dialog box:

- Direction of the gradient.
- Number of cycles in the gradient.
- Method of producing the gradient.
- Spread of the gradient, meaning evenly spread or favoring the first or last color.
- Range, meaning where Director places the beginning and ending colors of the gradient (for example, across the dimensions of the Cast Member versus the window size).

Air Brush tool

Use the Air Brush tool to create soft, feathered shapes of color and splatter effects with the current foreground color and pattern.

If you're used to Photoshop's Airbrush tool, you'll be disappointed with Director's Air Brush tool. There's no contest, although Photoshop's Airbrush tool doesn't create the interesting splatter effects you can achieve with Director's built-in tool. So you just may find yourself sneaking away one day from Photoshop to get an effect that you can only achieve in Director.

Double-click the Air Brush tool to display the Air Brushes dialog box, where you can customize the spray, size of dots, and speed of spraying paint. To modify the Air Brush effect even more, change the current ink style from the available inks in the Ink pop-up menu.

Press the Air Brush tool to reveal a pop-up menu of five customizable Air Brush settings.

Paintbrush tool

The Paintbrush is, perhaps, Director's most intuitive paint tool. It looks and acts like a brush.

When coupled with inks such as Smudge or Smear from the Ink pop-up menu, you'd swear you're painting with real oil or acrylic paint. Double-click the Paintbrush to display the Brush Shapes dialog box shown in Figure 6-4.

In the Brush Shapes dialog box, you can select from 30 installed brush shapes or create custom shapes of your own by pressing Custom in the pop-up menu.

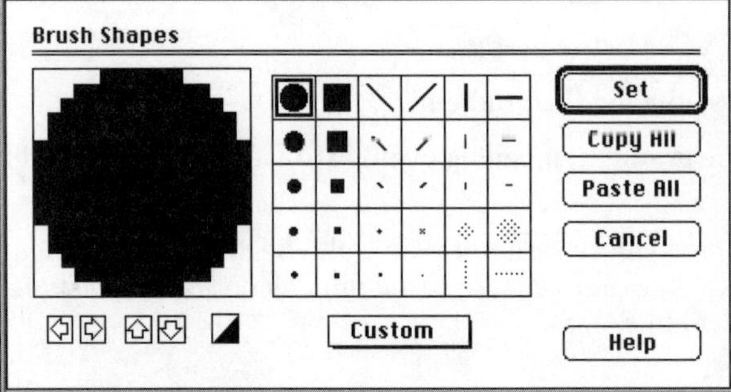

Figure 6-4: The Brush Shapes dialog box

Pencil tool

Use the Pencil tool for freeform painting with the current foreground color in the Paint window. Use the Pencil tool with the Option key pressed to paint with the current background color.

The Pencil doesn't display the current pattern or the current ink setting; its ink type is always set to Normal, and it always paints with one-pixel-wide paint. Must be the Republican in the bunch.

Press the Shift key to constrain the Pencil's movement to straight horizontal or vertical lines.

Use the Pencil for critical, pixel-by-pixel retouching of a bitmap, too.

Press the Command key to temporarily change any tool in the Paint window to Director's hidden Zoom tool for critical editing of Bitmap Cast Members. Click once to zoom in; click again to zoom back to normal view. By the way, the Zoom tool reflects the last degree of magnification set with the Zoom In command under the Paint menu.

Rectangle tool

Use the Rectangle tool to. . . You're getting warmer. . . . Come on, you can get it. Did my ears deceive me? Did you say paint rectangles? Have a lump of sugar! I don't know how you do it.

The hollow side of the Rectangle tool

Ah, but wait, your little friend has a dual personality. Click the left, hollow side to paint a rectangle with a transparent fill, bordered with the current foreground color in the current line width. To add a little zip to your life, press the Option key when painting to add the current pattern to the border. And to make life so exciting you can hardly stand it, add an ink effect from the Ink pop-up menu. Now that's living on the edge. Whoo.

The fill side of the Rectangle tool

Click the right side of the Rectangle tool to paint rectangles filled with the current foreground color in the current pattern and bordered in the current line width. The border won't display the current pattern.

Hold down the Option key to paint a filled rectangle with a border displaying the current pattern, which effectively draws a rectangle with no border.

Press the Shift key and drag a rectangle to paint a perfect square. There's no law against tossing in the Option key, except in Orange County maybe, to paint a perfect square with a border displaying the current pattern.

Double-click the fill side of the Rectangle tool to display the Gradients dialog box.

Eraser tool

Use the Eraser tool to remove pixels from a bitmap in broad strokes.

Director doesn't allow you to change the shape of the Eraser. For critical, pixel-by-pixel erasing, switch to the Pencil tool, set the background color to the color behind the graphic, and press Option and click with the Pencil tool to "erase" unwanted pixels. When I think of all the unwanted pixels in the world, I could just bawl.

To instantly erase the current easel in the Paint window, just double-click the Eraser.

Some programs are thoughtful enough to warn you when you're about to do something drastic, such as erasing the entire contents of a file or window. They'll bring up an alert box asking, "Are you sure you want to erase the entire window?" giving you an out by clicking a Cancel button. Not Director. So think twice before using the double-click Eraser trick to erase everything in the window.

If you do erase the entire easel by double-clicking the Eraser tool, stop. Do not pass Go. Immediately choose Undo Bitmap in the Edit menu if you want to restore the graphic. You have this one chance to save your skin.

Ellipse tool

Use the Ellipse tool to paint an ellipse or oval. Like the Rectangle tool, the Ellipse tool has a split personality.

The hollow side of the Ellipse tool

Click the left, hollow side to paint an ellipse with a transparent fill, bordered with the current foreground color in the current line width. Press the Option key when painting to add the current pattern to the border. To add an additional effect, choose an ink effect from the Ink pop-up menu.

The fill side of the Ellipse tool

Click the right side of the Ellipse tool to paint ovals filled with the current foreground color in the current pattern and bordered in the current line width. The border won't display the current pattern.

Hold down the Option key to paint a filled oval with a border displaying the current pattern, which effectively paints an oval with no border.

Press the Shift key and drag an ellipse to paint a perfect circle. To paint a perfect circle with a border displaying the current pattern, add the Option key to the preceding recipe.

Double-click the fill side of the Ellipse tool to display the Gradients dialog box.

Polygon tool

Use the Polygon tool to paint a polygonal shape in the Paint window. Click and drag to establish the first side of the polygon; continue to click and drag to add a side. Double-click the Polygon tool to close the polygon.

Like the Rectangle and Ellipse tools, the Polygon tool has a split personality.

The hollow side of the Polygon tool

Click the left, hollow side to paint a polygon with a transparent fill, bordered with the current foreground color in the current line width. Press the Option key when painting to add the current pattern to the border. To add an additional effect, choose an ink effect from the Ink pop-up menu.

The fill side of the Polygon tool

Click the right side of the Polygon tool to paint polygons filled with the current foreground color in the current pattern and bordered in the current line width. The border won't display the current pattern.

Hold down the Option key to paint a filled polygon with a border displaying the current pattern, which effectively paints a polygon with no border.

Double-click the fill side of the Polygon tool to display the Gradients dialog box.

Line tool

Use the Line tool to paint straight lines at any angle in the current foreground color on the Paint window's current easel.

Press Shift and drag the Line tool to draw horizontal, vertical, or 45-degree angled lines. Press Option and drag the Line tool to draw horizontal, vertical, or 45-degree angled lines in the current background color.

Arc tool

Use the Arc tool to paint curved segments.

Press the mouse to establish the beginning of the arc, drag in any direction to create the arc on the easel, and release the mouse to complete the arc.

Press Shift and drag to create perfect quarter circles with the Arc tool. Press Option and drag the Line tool to draw arcs in the current background color.

Registration tool

In traditional animation, artistes draw their initial sketches on highly translucent paper called *onion skin.* They learn to hold several pages in one hand and, with inconceivable dexterity, flip back and forth through the pages to test the sequence. This technique is called, oddly enough, "onion-skinning." Artistes with eight or more fingers per hand are highly prized, chained to their desks, fed special diets, and groomed daily.

Viewing a sequence of bitmaps in the Paint window by pressing the Next button is Director's equivalent of onion-skinning. Each bitmap in the Paint window starts out in life with a registration point centered in the graphic. You can see the registration point of a bitmap by choosing the Registration tool and noting where the special dotted lines that appear intersect on the easel. Click the Registration tool to fine-tune a bitmap's registration point.

To test an animation sequence in the Paint window, follow these steps:

1. **If the Cast window is not displayed, choose Window⇨Cast.**
2. **Press Shift and select a range of contiguous Cast Members in the Cast window belonging to a particular animation sequence.**

   If necessary, manually rearrange Cast Members by dragging them, in the correct sequence, into contiguous cells.
3. **Choose Cast⇨Align Bitmaps.**

   This command causes the registration point of selected bitmaps to line up at a common point in the Paint window.
4. **Double-click the first Cast Member of the animation sequence.**

   Director takes you to the Paint window where you see the Cast Member's bitmap.
5. **Simulate "onion-skinning" by pressing the Next button and letting subsequent bitmaps pass by.**
6. **If necessary, adjust one or more bitmaps' registration point with the Registration tool.**

After adjusting registration points, you need to repeat Steps 2 through 4 to realign the registration points before viewing the sequence, again using the Next button in the Paint window.

The Align Bitmaps command works best with relatively small bitmaps of similar shape. If the Align Bitmaps command doesn't seem to work, you may have chosen bitmaps too diverse in size or registration point location; try limiting your selection.

To re-center a bitmap's registration point, its default setting, double-click the Registration tool in the Paint window.

Eyedropper tool

Click the Eyedropper tool on a pixel to sample its color and pattern and set the current foreground color and pattern to the sample.

Press Shift and click the Eyedropper to set the current background color and pattern to the sample. Press Option and click the Eyedropper to set the end or destination color in the Gradient Destination color chip to the sample.

Chapter 7

Drawing, er, Painting on Director's Paint Window

In This Chapter

- Setting colors in the Paint window
- Exploring mysteries of the Line width indicator
- Handling graphics too big for their own good
- Making masks even when it's not Halloween

OK, you've perambulated through the mysteries of the Paint window, although I'm not sure perambulating is legal to do in public, at least until the kids are sound asleep. Anyway, there are some people whose ice cream always falls from the cone to the street one minute after they buy it, who wind up every time with one less sock at the laundromat, who always choose Brand X in those taste tests. For those of you out there in ReaderLand whose Paint window came up with black as the current foreground color and white the current background color, let me assure you that Director is a 24-bit program; it can handle over 16 million colors at one time, provided your monitor and Mac can handle 24-bit color.

No, You're Not Limited to Just Black and White

It's a cinch to change colors, too. The Foreground color chip on the Paint window is actually a pop-up menu. When you press the chip with the mouse, a collection of colors, or a *palette,* appears; you may highlight any one of the colors to become the new foreground color. It's that simple.

Even if you have a Mac and monitor set up to display so-called 24-bit color, or over 16 million colors, you can only have one current foreground color at a time. This is the color that your paint tools will paint with, unless you alter their actions with modifier keys.

Director's Paint window also provides you with a Background color chip, visually underneath the Foreground color chip, and it's a pop-up menu too, with the same set of colors from which you may select a new background color at any time with the press of the mouse.

One other important color option exists. Do you know which one? Wonderful, here's an extra large lump of sugar. That's right, the destination or ending color in the Gradient Destination color chip. Both the beginning and ending colors in the chip are actually pop-up menus hiding a full palette of available colors, although the beginning color is always the current foreground color. So you could say that the beginning color of the Gradient Destination color chip is merely another way of choosing the foreground color, whereas — and forthwith — the destination color can be a completely independent choice from the current foreground and background colors.

How Do I Change the Size of My Lines?

I see you're painting with the Line tool, and you're getting frustrated because you can't figure out how to change the size of the line. You've cussed at it, which is usually highly effective with high technology, but this time, zippo. You've pouted, but with the same result.

You must have forgotten the Line width indicator in the Paint window, lovingly hand-painted in Figure 7-1.

Figure 7-1: The Line width indicator in the Paint window.

The Line width indicator offers you the following:

- *Dotted line:* Click to paint an invisible line. Only affects the so-called shape tools, the Rectangle, Ellipse, and Polygonal tools, so that with the invisible line selected, shape tools produce an object without a border (if you're too lazy to press the Option key).

- *1-pixel, 2-pixel, 3-pixel lines:* Click to choose one of three ready-made line widths for down-to-the-wire, heart-thumping, last 15-seconds-on-the-clock art making.
- *Other:* Kinda silly 'cause just clicking Other doesn't do a thing. You need to *double-click* Other to display the Paint Window Options dialog box, where you can choose a line width from 1 to 64 pixels using a sliding control. But then, you can double-click anywhere on the Line width indicator to display the same box. I don't get it, Director, and I'm supposed to be the know-it-all here.

When a Graphic's Too Big for Its Own Good

What's a person to do when a graphic's too big to see everything at once in the Paint window? The following sections give you a clue.

First, you need to view your Cast Member in the Paint window. You have a number of ways of accomplishing your mission, should you choose to accept:

- Find the Cast Member in the Cast window and double-click its thumbnail.
- Find the Cast Member in the Score and double-click the sprite.
- Select the Cast Member in the Score and double-click the small preview in the upper-left corner of the Score window.
- Select the Cast Member in the Score and double-click its bitmap on the Stage.
- Throw chicken bones on floor, chanting, "Aboo — abow — aboo" (archaic language predating pig Latin).

Using scroll bars

When a full-size graphic is too large to see at one time in the Paint window, a wonderful Mac invention should come to mind: scroll bars. A vertical scroll bar is on the right side of the Paint window with an up arrow at the top, a down arrow at the bottom, and a weird little box in between that techies call the elevator. Also, you'll find a horizontal scroll bar at the bottom of the Paint window with its own arrows and elevator.

To see a different portion of the Paint window, you can

- Click on the up or down arrow of the vertical scroll bar.
- Click on the right or left arrow of the horizontal scroll bar.
- Press and drag the elevator on the vertical or horizontal scroll bar.

Now you know all you ever wanted to know about scroll bars.

Using the Hand tool

Another trick that should come to mind when you've got a bitmap too large to see at one time is Director's Hand tool.

1. **Select the Hand tool from the tools in the Paint window.**
2. **Press the Hand tool over a portion of your bitmap and drag in the direction you want to view.**

   Notice that the bitmap slides along with your motion.
3. **Now try dragging vertically up and to the left.**

   Note that once the upper-left corner of the bitmap hits the upper-left corner of the easel, Director doesn't allow you to drag any farther. That's when you want to add the Option key.
4. **Press the Option key and continue dragging up and to the left.**

   You'll find that now you can drag past the upper-left corner of the easel, but notice that the scroll bars move on their own as if you were manually using the elevator or one of the scroll bar arrows. That's how pressing Option and dragging with the Hand tool works.

Monitoring monitor size

This whole topic of working around extra large bitmaps leads to why we multimedia developer types like monitors larger than the standard 13-inch variety. With a 17-inch monitor or larger, you can place all those tricky windows to the side of the screen and still see the entire bitmap on the Stage, which you'll usually set to the ever-popular 13-inch size. When you opt for a larger monitor, find out if your Mac model allows you to install extra *VRAM,* the video RAM that provides a larger screen without losing colors, which you'll probably need.

Another solution is to install a second monitor, not necessarily color, where you can drag all those annoying extra windows and palettes. The prime monitor and any others that you add merge in cyberspace into one "virtual" screen so that you can literally drag a palette from one screen to the next. Adding another monitor usually means adding another video card to the innards of your Mac, although Power Macs are set up for running two monitors without additional add-ons. Check your particular model.

Wow! A New Menu

Anyone notice? When you choose Paint from the Window menu, a new menu appears along with the Paint window: the Paint menu, meticulously reconstructed in Figure 7-2. Actually, a second new menu appears, the Effects menu, but it's dimmed, or disabled, because you haven't made a selection with the Selection Rectangle or Lasso tool, yet.

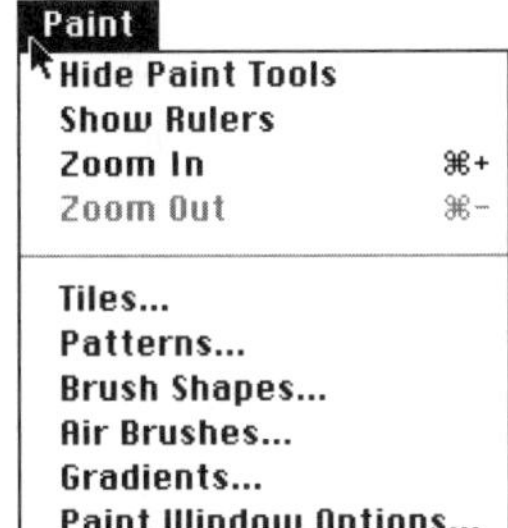

Figure 7-2: The Paint menu.

Well, I know that you're just dying to see what this menu's all about, so dive in. The paint's fine. From top to bottom, you find the following commands:

- *Hide Paint Tools:* Allows you to hide the set of tools in the upper-left corner of the Paint window, another way of eking out a little extra space with 13-inch or smaller monitors. This is one of those toggle commands; it switches between Hide Paint Tools and Show Paint Tools.
- *Show Rulers:* Allows you to display vertical and horizontal rulers in the Paint window, as shown in Figure 7-3.

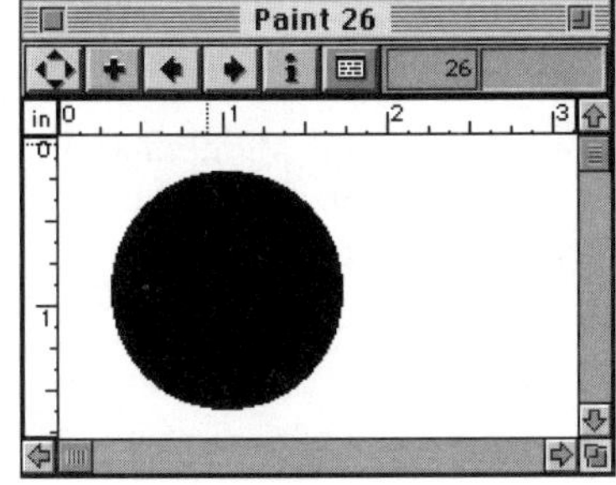

Figure 7-3: Vertical and horizontal rulers displayed in the Paint window.

Show Rulers is also a toggle command, switching from Show Rulers to Hide Rulers. Notice the dotted line within each ruler marking the current position of the mouse.

- *Zoom In:* With each selection of the command, allows you to double the image size, up to 800 percent, at which point Director disables the command.
- *Zoom Out:* With each selection of the command, allows you to decrease an enlarged image by half, to the image's actual size, at which point Director disables the command.

Notice that Director doesn't increase the size of the ruler when you view a bitmap at any size other than actual size. For accurate measurements, you'll need to do a little arithmetic based on the current view of the bitmap.

- *Tiles:* Takes you to the Tiles dialog box, shown in Figure 7-4, where you can select one of Director's eight built-in tiles or build a custom tile from one of the Cast Members in the Cast window. Tiles allow you to fill a selection with a pattern of tiles rather than with the foreground color or with a pattern.

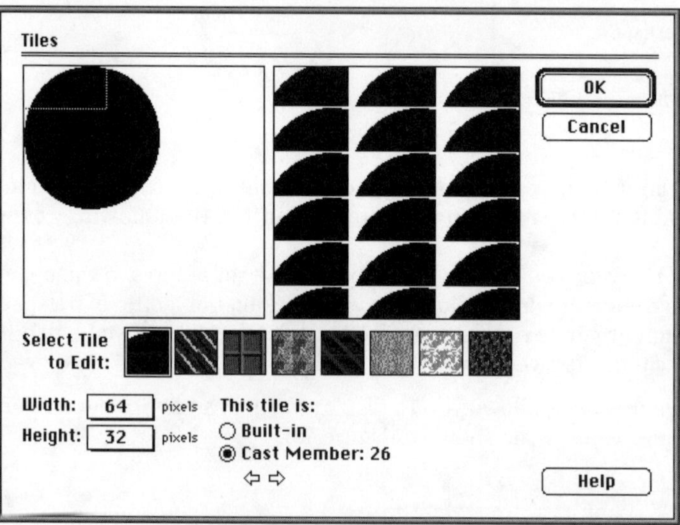

Figure 7-4: The Tiles dialog box, where you can design your own tiles for the Paint window from Cast Members in the Cast window.

The small left and right arrows under the Cast Member radio button allow you to cycle through each Cast Member from which a custom tile is created. The Width and Height pop-up menus allow you to set the dimensions of the tile from 16 to 128 pixels, reflected in the left panel of the Tiles window as a ghost-outlined box and in the right panel as a sample of the tile pattern itself.

- *Patterns:* Takes you to the Patterns dialog box, shown in Figure 7-5, where you can choose Gray, Standard, or QuickDraw pattern sets from the Patterns pop-up menu, copy the set of patterns, and paste the set into the Custom set of patterns to modify to your heart's content.

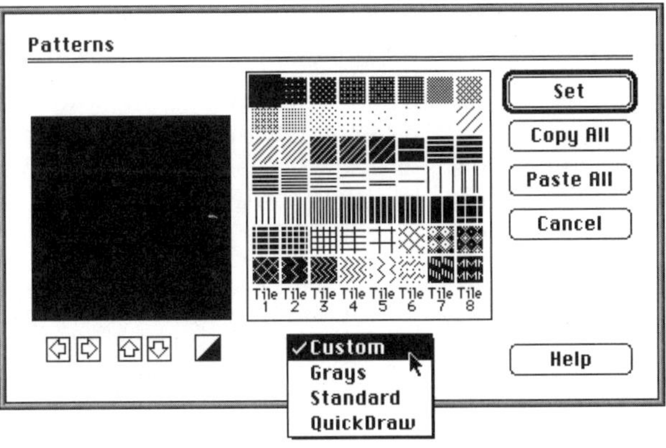

Figure 7-5: The Patterns dialog box, where you can design your own custom patterns for the Paint window.

Click inside the large panel on the left of the dialog box to turn pixels black or white, click the arrows at the bottom of the dialog box to shift the pattern left, right, up, or down, and click the black/white box to the right of the arrows to reverse the pattern.

- *Brush Shapes:* Opens the Brush Shapes dialog box, shown in Figure 7-6, where you can select one of 30 standard brush shapes or modify any of the 30 custom brushes pixel by pixel in the large panel on the left of the window.

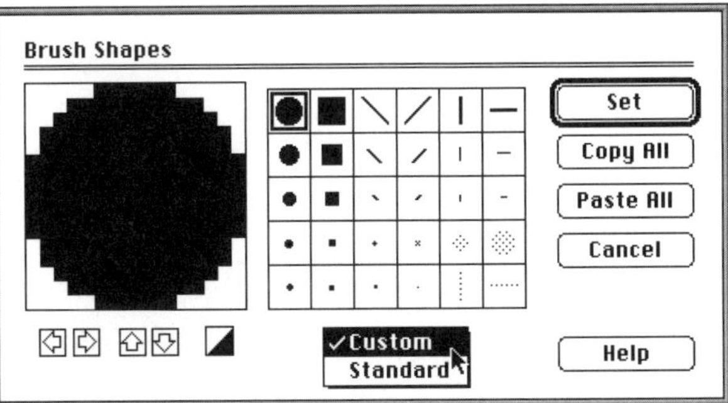

Figure 7-6: The Brush Shapes dialog box, where you can create custom Brush Shapes for the paint window.

Use the arrows at the bottom of the window to shift a brush shape left, right, up, or down. Click the black/white box to the right of the arrows to reverse the brush shape. The Copy All button allows you to copy brush shapes to the Clipboard so that you can restore them later with the Paste All button.

- *Air Brushes:* Takes you to the Air Brushes dialog box, pictured in Figure 7-7, where you can customize the Air Brush tool in the Paint window.

  Choose one of three Air Brush modes by clicking the Normal, Speckle, or Brush Shape radio button. You can modify the Size, Dot Size, and Flow Speed with sliding controls. A preview of the Air Brush shape and dot size appears in the large panel on the left of the window.

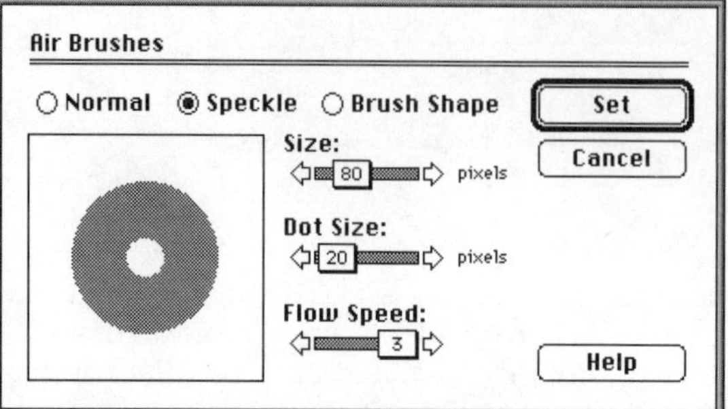

Figure 7-7: The Air Brushes dialog box, where you can customize the Air Brush tool.

- *Gradients:* Takes you to the Gradients dialog box, illustrated in Figure 7-8, where you can design your own gradient of colors for Director's paint tools.

  In the Gradients dialog box, you can set the current foreground color, which serves as the beginning color of a gradient, from the Foreground color selector, and the ending or destination color of the gradient from the Destination color selector. You can also set the current background color and pattern from this dialog box.

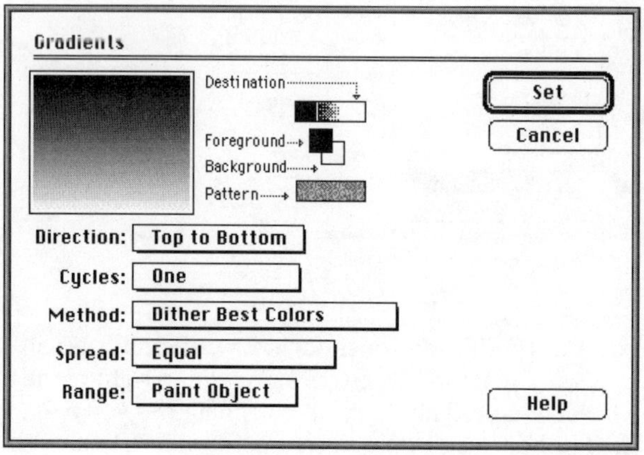

Figure 7-8: The Gradients dialog box, where you can create custom gradients for the Paint window.

The Gradients dialog box provides five pop-up menus to choose the direction of the gradient, number of cycles in the gradient (for example, one as opposed to four smooth cycles of color, giving a banded look to the gradient), method of creating the gradient for smoothest transition or special effect, distribution of gradient spread (for example, equal as opposed to more destination color for a gradient favoring the current destination color) and range of the gradient (for example, a gradient applied to the paint object as opposed to the entire window).

- *Paint Window Options:* Allows you to customize the Paint window with the Paint Window Options dialog box shown in Figure 7-9.

  The Paint Window Options dialog box is organized into three panels. With the Display panel radio buttons, you can choose to display 1 easel or 50 at a time in the Paint window.

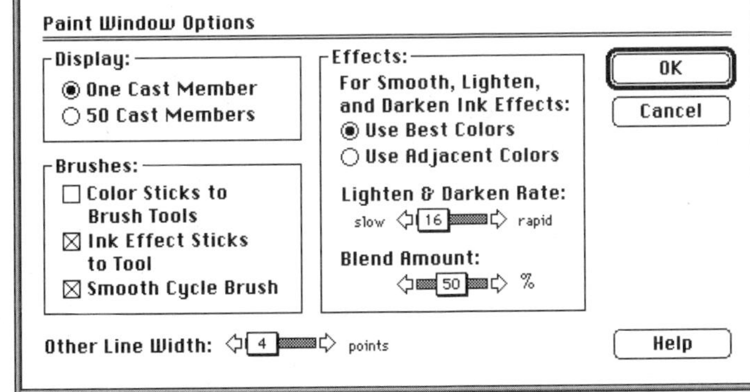

Figure 7-9: The Paint Window Options dialog box, where you can customize Paint window options.

In the Brushes panel are three check boxes you can check. The Color Sticks to Brush Tools box allows each brush to "remember" the last color selected for its use. The Ink Effect Sticks to Tool box allows each tool to remember the last ink effect applied with its use. The Smooth Cycle Brush box allows you to paint gradients that display a foreground to destination color gradient and then reverse to a destination to foreground color gradient for increased smoothness of color change; if this box is unchecked, a gradient simply loops from foreground to destination color, creating a banded effect in extra wide gradients.

In the Effects panel, you can click either the Use Best Colors or Use Adjacent Colors radio button for a smoother color transition or for a special effect. You can also adjust the rate of the Lighten and Darken ink effects and adjust the amount of the Blend ink effect with special slider controls.

A separate slider control allows you to adjust the current line width from 0 to 64 pixels.

You can "sample" a pattern or brush shape by simply clicking the mouse anywhere outside the Patterns or Brush Shapes dialog box. Your sample will appear in the large panel on the left of the respective window where you can further modify the bitmap by clicking individual pixels.

Director saves custom tiles in the file where the custom tiles are created. However, Director saves custom patterns to the Director 4.0 Preferences file in the Preferences folder of your System folder. If you want to archive custom patterns you've created, be sure to drag the Director 4.0 Preferences file to the Desktop before reinstalling the System or Director; then replace the archived Director 4.0 Preferences file in the System folder after installation.

Shhhh — secret features of Paint window rulers

Notice the small box as illustrated below where the vertical and horizontal rulers intersect in the upper-left corner of the Paint window; it includes the letters "in," for inches. You can change the unit of measure by simply clicking the small box and cycling from unit to unit. The other units of measure available are the following:

- cm = centimeters
- Pixel = 1/72 of an inch (your display's unit of measure)
- Pica = 1/6 of an inch (a typographic unit of measure)

The small box also marks the *zero point,* or *origin,* of the rulers, where measurement begins. You can set the zero point to any other location by positioning the mouse pointer in either ruler and pressing and dragging to some point on the current easel. Resetting the zero point allows you to take measurements from the center of a bitmap or its upper-left corner or any other arbitrary point on the easel.

To return the zero point to its default setting by the small box, position the pointer in either ruler and press and drag into the small box.

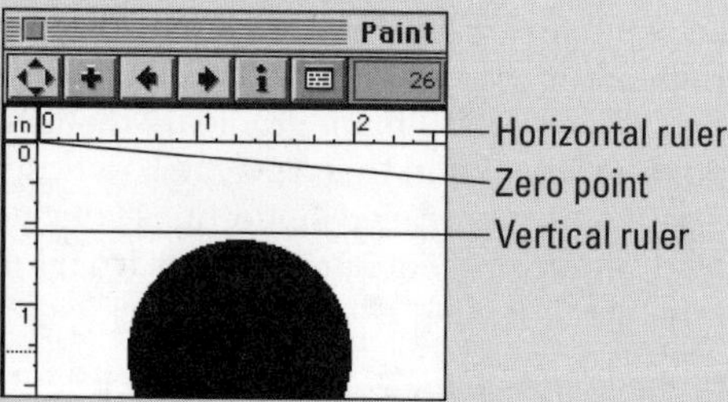

SuperTechniRamaVision: All about System and Custom Palettes

There's something about a known quantity that's so comforting, so cozy, so. . . known. I think it's safe to say that people don't really like surprises, except for listeners of Howard Stern maybe. A surprise birthday party is about as strong a surprise as most of us can take.

Same thing goes when using a Mac. The System palette is a known quantity. It has exactly 256 different colors. White is the first color, black is the last. Always. In between is a range of colors, each color in its own unvarying slot — what techies call a *color lookup table* (CLUT). No surprises.

Using the System palette

You can see this set or palette of colors by choosing Color Palettes from the Window menu. The Color Palettes dialog box appears, looking suspiciously like Figure 7-10.

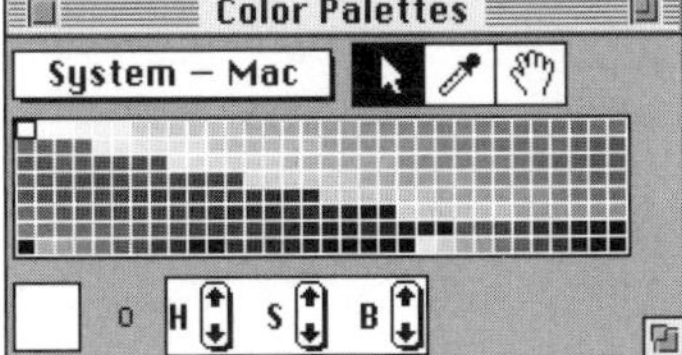

Figure 7-10: The Color Palettes dialog box.

Take a look at the Palette pop-up menu (Figure 7-11) and you'll find a bouquet of palettes, nine in all, including the steadfast System — Mac palette. A palette named VGA is grayed out if you're not running a VGA-type monitor from the PC world. Kaaak, someone give me a breath mint, fast.

Figure 7-11: The Palette pop-up menu in the Color Palettes dialog box.

When you choose System — Mac from the selection of palettes, you know what to expect. As a multimedia producer, you constantly need to anticipate what the user, the intended audience for your epic, is going to see. Chances are the user's going to be running off the same, ubiquitous System palette.

Facing problems with the System palette

Which is not to say that problems don't arise from sticking with trusty, old System palette. The same 256 colors that make us feel so smug also limit us in a critical way — to 256 colors. Some of the problems that the System palette presents us with include the following:

- Poor rendering, or display, of certain color gradients because of the limited number of colors to work with, depending on specific foreground and destination colors chosen.
- *Posterization,* or blockiness, of some areas of scanned photographs and computer-based images, basically because of the same limited color choice problem.
- *Artifacts,* or defects, in an image, which are little thingies in a bitmap that don't belong there, created in your Mac's attempt to display a range of colors it really doesn't have the resources to create.

Living with 16 million headaches

So, as multimedia types, we face a classic dilemma. Use fast, 8-bit color and stay with the System palette to ensure that the user sees on-screen what we intend to show, but put up with problems like posterization and artifacts that degrade the aesthetics and effectiveness of our multimedia product.

Or go with a higher color depth, typically 24-bit color, giving us over 16 million colors to play with, that looks nearly photographic on a matching monitor. And risk suffering a whole new set of performance problems. You see, 24-bit color asks your Mac to handle three times the amount of data and computation as 8-bit color. The result? Your multimedia slows to a grinding halt on all but the fastest machines.

The question becomes, do you really want to assume that your user is going to run your beautiful multimedia on the latest, greatest computing dynamo Apple has to offer? Or will the machine turn out to be an old clunker, such as a Mac Plus? With 1 megabyte of memory?

Living with compromise

There's this thing I've heard of called, what was it, oh yes, compromise. Which is why Director offers a Method pop-up menu, shown in Figure 7-12, in the Gradients dialog box with 10 options for rendering a gradient in 8-bit color.

Figure 7-12: The Method pop-up menu from the Gradients dialog box, where you can choose one often rendering methods for displaying a gradient.

✓Pattern Best Colors
Pattern Best Colors See Thru
Pattern Adjacent Colors
Pattern Adjacent Colors See Thru
Dither Best Colors
Dither Adjacent Colors
Dither Two Colors
Dither One Color
Standard Dither
Multi Dither

Given a specific set of foreground and destination colors, one rendering method may work better than another. Pattern Best Colors, for example, may work better than, say, Dither Adjacent Colors. It's a visual decision rather than an intellectual one (thank goodness); if one rendering method makes a gradient look better, it's the better rendering method.

Another way of compromising — staying with 8-bit color when you want 24-bit, photographic quality color — is to modify a 24-bit image in a high-level paint program such as Photoshop, Painter, or DeBabelizer. These programs offer special routines that reduce 24-bit color's 16 million colors down to the System palette's 256 colors with a special trick called *dithering.* Optimum dithering fools the eye into thinking that it sees more colors than really exist. The result is an 8-bit image that often can pass as 24-bit color.

Compromising, and then compromising

An even better solution when using high-end paint programs such as Photoshop, Painter, or DeBabelizer is to choose an option called an *adaptive palette* when reducing a 24-bit image down to 256 colors. The result is a graphic no longer based on the System palette, but a palette of 256 custom colors analyzed by the paint program for optimum effect and combined with a special dithering routine. The effect is an 8-bit image nearly indistinguishable from its 24-bit original.

When you choose File⇨Import, select a bitmap with an adaptive palette, and click Import, Director displays an alert, shown in Figure 7-13, asking what Director should do with such a bitmap.

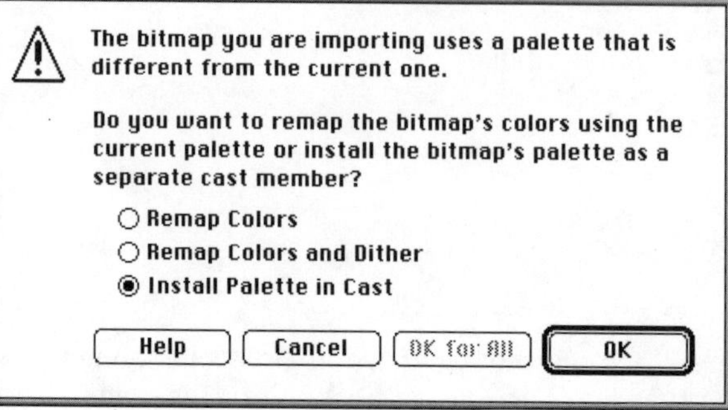
The bitmap you are importing uses a palette that is different from the current one.
Do you want to remap the bitmap's colors using the current palette or install the bitmap's palette as a separate cast member?
Remap Colors
Remap Colors and Dither
Install Palette in Cast
Help
Cancel
OK for All
OK

Figure 7-13: The Custom Palette alert that appears when you import a graphic with a custom palette.

Director gives you one of three radio buttons to click:

- *Remap Colors:* Meaning redo colors to accommodate the standard System palette. Remapping colors usually results in less than satisfactory artwork.
- *Remap Colors and Dither:* Meaning redo colors and apply a special dithering routine to accommodate the standard System palette. The dithering routine improves the translation but is still inferior to the third option coming up next or to importing the original 24-bit image.
- *Install Palette in Cast:* Imports the special adaptive palette, created by Photoshop or a similar program, and the graphic as cast members in the Cast window. In the Score, you can add the custom palette in the Palette channel to correctly display the special bitmap in Director's Stage.

Checking out those other built-in palettes

Why so many other built-in palettes? In Figure 7-11, in addition to the System palette, you see eight other built-in palettes.

I'll take you through them and give you an idea why they're there and what you can do with them:

- *System — Win:* A palette of colors that transfers successfully to the Windows platform. Since Director movies are often designed to run in both Mac and PC platforms, Director provides a palette that is compatible for Windows to help prep your movie for cross-platform compatibility.
- *Rainbow:* A special palette of bright colors, heavy on primary colors, as seen in a rainbow, for special effects and extra smooth color gradients. Simply add the palette to the Score in the Palette channel.
- *Grayscale:* A special palette of 256 values for extra smooth gray scale bitmaps and gradients. Add this Palette to the Score in the Palette channel when needed.
- *Pastels:* Another special palette of colors "softer" than the standard System palette, lighter and less saturated, with 0 percent cholesterol.
- *Vivid:* A special palette similar to Rainbow but not so focused on primary colors. A more sophisticated yet bright set of colors for special effects. Take a look at this palette after drinking ten or twelve cups of coffee for a real cheap thrill.
- *NTSC:* A special palette for prepping your movie for transfer to video. Novice multimedia types are often shocked at how different a Director movie looks on TV. One of the most dramatic changes in video transfer occurs with color. *NTSC* (National Television Systems Committee) TV, which is the kind of TV we currently watch, can only handle a very limited range of colors and *saturation levels* (that is, how red a particular red really is). For example, colors on NTSC TV above 70 percent full saturation or thereabouts appear to spread beyond the image and bloom, meaning the color seems to fluoresce or glow. Other colors simply translate into ugly browns, grays, and greens or make totally unexpected color shifts in the spectrum. So Director supplies you with a set of NTSC-legal colors to help reduce NTSC shock after you've transferred your beautiful multimedia to videotape.
- *Metallic:* Another special effects palette of subtly metallic colors, designed mainly for robots who become interested in developing multimedia in their spare time. You haven't heard of robot-spawned multimedia? Well, that's 'cause robots have so little spare time. Workaholics, every one of them, bless them.

- *VGA:* A special palette for working with VGA monitors from the PC world that many of Apple's newer Mac models can easily accommodate. VGA monitors display a color shift from standard Mac models; the VGA palette attempts to properly translate the color shift. By the way, VGA is dimmed in the Palette pop-up menu if you're not running off a VGA monitor, so don't feel cheated or something.

The best way to work on Director movies intended for video transfer is to work directly with an NTSC monitor or at least to frequently refer to an NTSC monitor during development. AV Mac models can switch between your computer monitor and an NTSC TV through the Monitors control panel. Some third-party video cards supply a separate port for outputting NTSC signals so that you can work with two monitors. Check the capabilities of your own monitor. Some settling of contents may occur. Over. Out.

Who Was That Masked Man? And How Do You Make a Mask, Man?

One of the most important ink types available from the Score window's pop-up menu is the Mask ink effect. The Matte ink effect removes the white, rectangular bounding box marking the width and height of a bitmap, resulting in a silhouette effect and allowing the background to show beyond the outline of the graphic. But white pixels within the graphic remain opaque, which is not always the effect you want. That's when you want to turn to the Mask ink effect.

For example, the Matte ink effect on a text cast member such as the letter *A* (that's a capital *A*) won't give you the effect you need. In the center of a capital *A* is that little bit of what typographer types call the *counter,* or negative, space. It looks like a tiny pyramid and by all rights, the background should show through the counter.

When you use the Matte ink effect on the letter, what happens? Sure enough, the bounding box surrounding the *A* sprite turns transparent, and you get a silhouette effect; but the *A*'s counter remains white and defeats the effect you intended to create, that this is an independent little object floating around on the Stage.

Creating a mask

Follow these steps to create a mask that you can add to a sprite as an ink effect:

1. **Make sure that a sprite is selected on the Stage and that the Paint window is your active window.**
2. **Choose Cast⇨Duplicate Cast Member.**

   Don't let this one trick you up. After choosing this command, you're now viewing the duplicate cast member's easel; notice that it has a new cast member number. In fact, if it's not one number higher than the original cast member, you'll have to do a little extra fudging for masking to work properly.
3. **Choose a color from the Foreground Color selector.**
4. **Select the Paint Bucket tool and click inside the area of the cast member that requires the mask to fill it with black paint.**

   In my earlier example (the letter *A*), you would need to fill the pyramid area in the middle of the letter.
5. **Double-click on the Color Resolution indicator containing the phrase, "8 bits," in the bottom-left corner of the window.**

   The Transform Bitmap dialog box appears.
6. **Choose 1 bit from the Color Depth pop-up menu.**

   An alert appears warning that you cannot undo the operation.
7. **Click on OK.**

   Director returns you to the duplicate cast member in the Paint window, now a 1-bit graphic, which is exactly what you need to create a mask.

The only step left before you apply Mask ink to the sprite is to ensure that the duplicate, 1-bit cast member rests in the very next cell to the right of the original A in the Cast window, a requirement to complete the masking procedure:

1. **Choose Window⇨Cast and locate your cast member.**

   When you duplicated the cast member, Director placed the copy in the next available cell in the Cast window. If you find that the duplicate is not next to the original, go to the next step; otherwise jump to the next section.
2. **Move the mouse pointer over the duplicate cast member.**

   The Hand cursor appears.

3. **Press and drag the duplicate cast member to the cell just to the right of the original cast member and release the mouse.**

   Director rearranges the cast members in the Cast window and automatically takes care of accounting for such changes in the Score.

Applying Mask ink to a sprite

To apply the Mask ink effect to a sprite, follow these steps:

1. **Click the Score window and make sure that the original sprite is still selected.**

   The sprite also appears selected on the Stage.

2. **Choose Mask from the Ink Effect pop-up menu in the Score window to complete the masking procedure.**

Once Mask ink is enabled, the area of your sprite that needed the mask will turn transparent and reveal the colored Stage in back. If you drag the sprite within the Stage, you'll see the effect remains until you decide to change the ink effect.

While pressing the Command key, click on a selected sprite on the Stage to reveal the secret Ink Effect pop-up menu from which you can choose a different ink for the sprite. With the purchase of this book, you have agreed to guard this secret with your life. Always read the small print

Chapter 8

And Now for Something Completely Different: The Text Window

In This Chapter

- Using the Text tool
- Looking at the Text menu
- Examining different text types

Although we think of multimedia as a visual experience, content in the form of words plays a big part of most multimedia productions. Working with Director is no exception. There's a strong textual element among all the jumping, gliding, hip-hopping, generally hyperactive sprites dancing around the Stage window. Director makes use of text on the Stage with labels, with blocks of text meant to be read, and in sets of buttons giving the person viewing the movie choices as the movie plays back. Why Director provides a Text window for you in the first place, I guess.

Whoa, Pardner, Thought I Saw a Text Tool in That Paint Window

Now, for those of you out there in ReaderLand who are thinking to yourselves, "Selves, I know where the Text tool is because I just read about it in the last chapter," you're thinking about the Text tool in the Paint window. You even tried it yourself, clicking on a spot on the easel and typing text on the screen. In a state of confused agitation, you're wondering, "Isn't that where text comes from?" My suggestion? Cut way down on the coffee.

The Text window

Anyway, I'd like you to choose Text from the Window menu. You may notice that the Text window has the same row of buttons displayed in the upper-left corner as the Paint window mentioned in Chapter 6. To review, the buttons include the following:

- *Place button:* Allows you to drag the contents of the Text window to the Stage or the Score where it becomes an active sprite in your movie.
- *New button:* Allows you to create a Cast Member from the Text window, which Director places in the next available cell in the Cast window.
- *Previous and Next buttons:* Allow you to click through the Text Cast Members in the Cast window. Bitmaps and other non-text Cast Members do not appear in the Text window.
- *Info button:* Takes you to the Text Cast Member Info dialog box where you can customize the Text Cast Member.
- *Script button:* Takes you to the Script window for the Text Cast Member where you can create or edit a Lingo script.

To the right of the buttons are the Cast Member number and Cast Member name panels to aid in identifying the current Text Cast Member.

The Text Cast Member Info dialog box

Take a closer look at the Text Cast Member Info dialog box shown in Figure 8-1.

The Cast Member text box

At the top of the dialog box is a Cast Member text box, where you can enter a meaningful name for the Text Cast Member. Instead of referring to a Text Cast Member by its position in the Cast or the Score (which can change over time and cause unexpected results), you can use this field to provide a stable, meaningful name for the Text Cast Member.

The Style pop-up menu

From the Style pop-up menu, meticulously reproduced by Alsatian artisans (see Figure 8-2), you can choose one of four options for text display on the Stage, including the following:

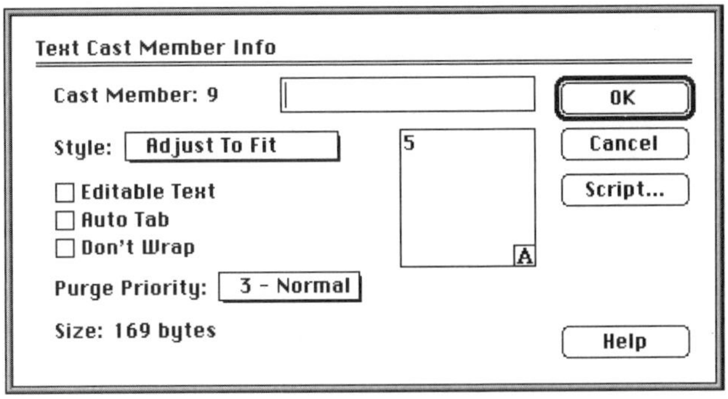

Figure 8-1: The Text Cast Member Info dialog box, where you can customize a Text Cast Member.

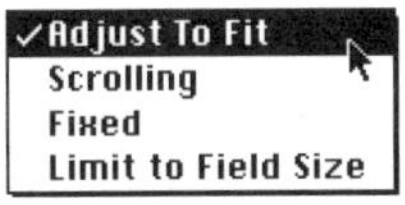

Figure 8-2: The Style pop-up menu.

- *Adjust To Fit:* Creates a field that automatically adjusts its vertical depth to contain the current amount of text.
- *Scrolling:* Creates a field with a vertical scroll bar on the right side, allowing you to enter a large amount of text without resizing the text field. The user simply scrolls with the up- and down-arrows to see different parts of the field's contents while the movie plays.
- *Fixed:* Creates a text field with a fixed depth regardless of the amount of text typed in the field, although it may be manually reshaped to reveal more of the text.
- *Limit to Field Size:* Creates a field that limits the amount of text that can be entered to its fixed width when text is entered from the Stage. This feature is very useful for one-line entry fields commonly seen in database applications.

Three Text Cast Member check boxes

Below the Style pop-up menu are three check boxes, including

- *Editable Text:* Checking this check box allows users, that is, persons viewing the movie, to type text into the field while the Director movie is playing. If you leave this option unchecked, users can't enter text after the movie begins playing.

- *Auto Tab:* Checking this check box allows users to navigate from editable text field to editable text field by pressing Tab when the movie is playing, which is especially useful for a database-type screen with many single-line entry boxes. If you leave this option unchecked, pressing Tab in an editable text field while the movie is running adds an invisible space character to the text.
- *Don't Wrap:* Checking this means the text field doesn't automatically wrap a line longer than its width to the next line. Such a line simply disappears off the right side of the text field; in this case, only a hard return wraps text to a new line. If you leave unchecked, text automatically wraps to the next line as it does in most Mac word processing programs.

These options apply to text fields you add to a movie during development, as well as to text fields you present to the viewer as the movie plays.

The Purge Priority pop-up menu

Use the Purge Priority pop-up menu to tell Director which Cast Members may be *purged* or removed from memory when not visible on the Stage. You also name the conditions for purging. Check out an extended discussion of the Purge Priority pop-up menu in "Cast Member Info button" in Chapter 4.

Miscellaneous stuff

You'll find a few other goodies in the Text Cast Member Info dialog box.

- *Size Indicator:* At the bottom-left corner, Director displays the size in bytes of the Text Cast Member in question.
- *Text Cast Member Preview:* Just off-center of the window is a preview, representing the contents of the Text Cast Member, with a Text Cast Member icon in the lower-right corner of the preview.
- *Script button:* Under the OK and Cancel buttons, Director provides a Script button to take you to the Text Cast Member's Script window.
- *Help button:* The ubiquitous Help button displayed in all dialog boxes to quickly take you to Director's built-in Help system.

A Good Look at the Text Menu

Cast window, Cast menu. Paint window, Paint menu. So we've gotta have a Text menu, right? Actually, the Text menu's been there all along, in case you haven't noticed. The problem is, nearly all the commands are disabled most of the time. When you choose the Text tool from the Paint window, a few commands become enabled, but most remain disabled.

Reshaping a text field on the Stage

When you place a scrolling text field on the stage it appears as in the illustration below.

To be or not to be. That is the question. Whether 'tis nobler in the mind to suffer the slings and arrows of outrageous fortune. Or to take arms against a sea of troubles and by opposing, end them.

Notice the bold gray border that signifies that the field is selected. Also notice the three, bold gray handles, one at the bottom of the field, another on the field's right side, and a third in the lower-right corner of the field. You may press any one of the handles to reshape the dimensions of the field.

Other field types display fewer handles. For example, a field given the Adjust to Fit style displays only one handle on the right side to manually adjust the field's width; the field's depth changes automatically to contain the full contents of the text field.

To move a text field, press anywhere in the gray border of a selected text field, other than a handle, and drag to a new location.

Only after you choose Text from the Window menu does the Text menu really come alive. All but three commands referring to scripts become enabled and ready to rock and roll. Press the Text menu to see the list of commands shown in Figure 8-3. The only difference on your screen is that Comment, Uncomment, and Recompile Script may be grayed out because these commands are reserved for when the Script window is active.

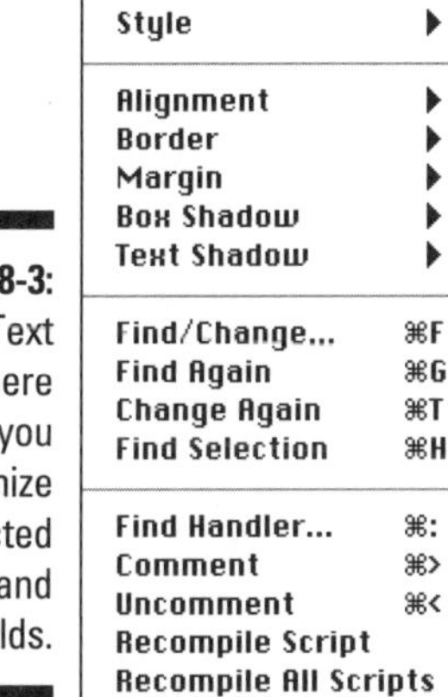

Figure 8-3: The Text menu where you customize selected text and fields.

Formatting text

Note that the Text menu is divided by a gray line into groups of related commands. From top to bottom, the following commands are under the first group of the Text menu:

- *Font:* Displays a submenu of all fonts currently installed in the system. With System 7.5, this menu includes all the fonts in the Fonts folder.
- *Size:* Displays a submenu of standard font sizes measured in *points* (a vertical, typographic measure that has 72 points to the inch); includes Other Size if none of the listed sizes do it for you (see Figure 8-4).

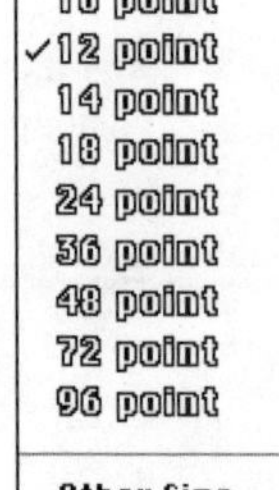

Figure 8-4: The Size command's submenu from the Text menu.

Choosing Other Size takes you to the Other Font Size dialog box where you can enter a non-standard point size for selected text in a field.

- *Style:* Displays a submenu of standard Mac font styles. Styles include Plain, Bold Italic, Underline, Outline, Shadow, Condense, and Extend. Choose one of the options to style a selected text field.

In case you are wondering, the standard set of sizes displayed in outline style in Figure 8-4 indicates that the current font is a TrueType font, probably one of the fonts that comes with System 7.5's installation. If the list only has sizes 10 to 24 in outline style, you can assume that the font is a PostScript font with built-in screen fonts for these limited sizes.

Displaying text

The second group of commands under the Text menu deals mainly with how the field appears on the Stage:

- *Alignment:* Displays a submenu of alignment options including Left, Center, and Right, referring to whether text in the selected field is flush with the left or right side of the field or centered between left and right sides. The selected option applies the same type of alignment to all paragraphs in a selected field.

- *Border:* Displays a submenu that lets you choose whether to add a border to a field and its thickness. Choose None to eliminate a border around a selected field; choose from 1–5 to add a border of the desired thickness in pixels to a selected field. The Border option works only with QuickDraw text on the Stage, meaning that it only works with text typed in a text field or with the Text tool from the Tools palette.
- *Margin:* Displays a submenu that lets you choose the width in pixels of the margin or to have no margin at all surrounding text in a selected field. Choose None to eliminate a margin a selected field; choose from 1–5 to add a margin of the desired width. As with Border, the Margin option works only with QuickDraw fields on the Stage.
- *Box Shadow:* Displays a submenu that lets you choose the width of a box shadow or to have no box shadow at all. Choose None to eliminate a shadow falling to the right of a selected field; choose from 1–5 to add a shadow of the desired width in pixels falling to the right of a selected field. This option works only with QuickDraw fields on the Stage.
- *Text Shadow:* Displays a submenu that lets you choose the width of a text shadow or to have no text shadow at all. Choose None to eliminate a shadow falling to the right of selected text in a field; choose from 1–5 to add a shadow of the respective width in pixels falling to the right of selected text in a field. For readability's sake, Text Shadow works best with large text sizes and heavier weights of fonts. The Text Shadow option may be applied to both bitmapped and QuickDraw text.

Searching for text

The next set of commands under the Text menu deals with finding and changing text in a field:

- *Find/Change:* Displays the Find/Change dialog box shown in Figure 8-5 below.

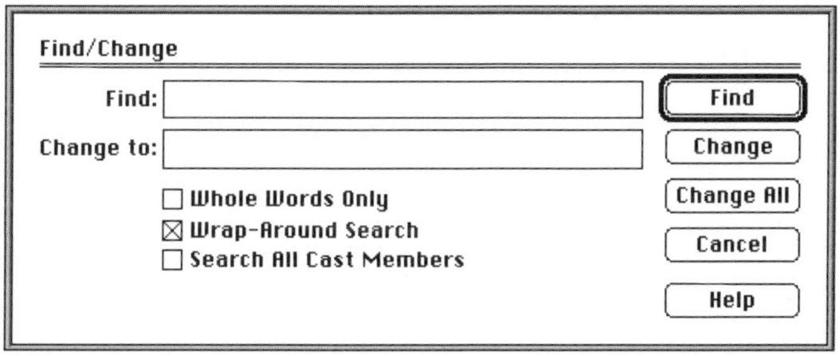

Figure 8-5: The Find/Change dialog box where you can search for specific words in Text Cast Members of a Director movie.

- *Find Again:* Allows you to search again for the last Find entry entered in the Find/Change dialog box.
- *Change Again:* Allows you to replace found text with the last substitute text entry made in the Find/Change dialog box.
- *Find Selection:* Allows you to make a selection in the current text field using the Find entry. If the Search All Cast Members check box has been checked in the Find/Change dialog box, Director continues to search the other same-type Cast Members in the Cast window after the first search in the current text field.

The Find/Change dialog box features a Find entry field to type the word or phrase to find and a Change to entry field to enter substitute text in case of a "hit." Director begins searching from the current location of the insertion point in the selected text to the bottom of the field. Click on Find to begin searching, and click on Change to change the entry. Click on Change All if you want Director to change all text in the field regardless of the insertion point's initial location.

Underneath the entry fields in the Find/Change dialog box are three check boxes. Checking Whole Words Only makes Director search for a match of complete words rather than partial words. For example, if you enter *part* as the search criteria with Whole Words Only checked, Director ignores words like *partner* or *partisan* with *part* in them and only accepts the complete word *part* as a legitimate find.

Checking Wrap-Around Search makes Director search from the insertion point to the end of the selected field, then search from the first character in the field to the original location of the insertion point, coming full-circle in its search.

Checking Search All Cast Members makes Director note the kind of text beginning the search (meaning QuickDraw text or script text) and then search for the Find entry in all Cast Members of the same kind. For example, if the current text field is a script and you choose Search All Cast Members, Director searches the current field for the Find entry and then searches through every Script Text Cast Member in the Cast window for the Find entry.

Working with script text

The last five commands under the Text menu are all script related. They include the following:

- *Find Handler:* Displays the Find Handler dialog box, pictured in Figure 8-6.

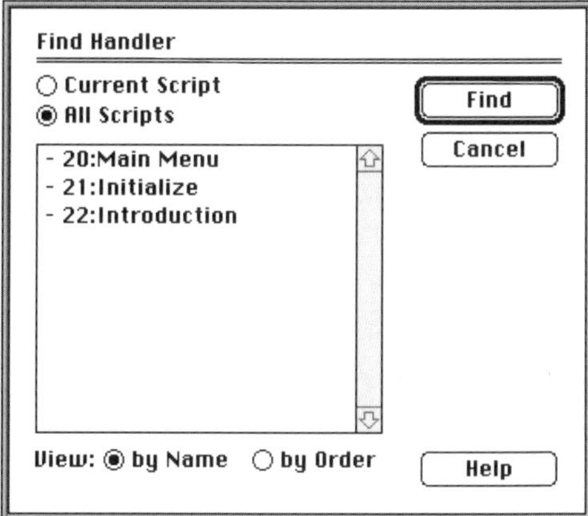

Figure 8-6: The Find Handler dialog box appears when you choose Find Handler from the Text menu.

Underneath the window title you can see two radio buttons, Current Script and All Scripts. When you click All Scripts, a list of handlers in the current movie appears under the radio buttons. Under the list you can change the view from By Name to By Order (of creation). It's not a bad idea to give meaningful names to your scripts so that they're easy to recognize in this dialog box.

Simply double-click on the script in the list that's of interest to you to go to that script's text window for edits.

- *Comment:* Grayed out until you choose a Script window, this option allows you to add two hyphens at the beginning of the line currently displaying the insertion point. Director understands the hyphens to mean that text following the two hyphens is a note to yourself or other Lingo-ites and is not scripting code. Without comment hyphens, Director would probably object to the line by displaying an error message and might even refuse to have lunch with you ever again.
- *Uncomment:* Grayed out until you choose a Script window, this button undoes comment hyphens at the beginning of the line currently displaying the insertion point. Director then recognizes the line as Lingo code and will object if the line is not properly written. So keep it clean; this is a family application.
- *Recompile Script:* Grayed out until you choose a Script window, this option turns the contents of the currently active Script window into *machine code* (basic instructions your Mac understands). Compiled Lingo code runs faster than uncompiled Lingo and, in the final product, adds protection from prying eyes, except for speed readers of machine language.
- *Recompile All Scripts:* Turns the contents of all Script windows into machine code.

Using the Comment command in the Text menu always places two hyphens at the beginning of the line displaying the insertion point; Uncomment only recognizes two hyphens at the beginning of the line. You may manually enter hyphens after a command to "uncomment" out the rest of the line. Director does not recognize text following the hyphens as code. To uncomment hyphens other than at the beginning of a line, you'll have to manually select and delete them the old-fashioned way that granny did.

Everything You Can Do with Text in the Text Window

So we've got all this text. What good is it? I mean, is it going to change your life? Is it going to change the life of one other person in the world? Well, come to think of it, maybe. Actually, a lot of people with multimedia burning in their soul envision just such a thing happening with their work. And I seem to recall an old saying, "The pen is mightier than the sword," from some marketing schnook at Bic, no doubt.

Anyway, by definition multimedia is a mix of text along with all the other goodies our computers can augment content with — sound, music, narration, color, animation, QuickTime movies, and on and on. Then there's this concept of hypertext — the ability you possess with Director and Lingo to create a web of links across your multimedia production that allows users to delve into ever deeper layers of related information. All this is a little ambitious at this point but you're well on your way with the help of this book and a little hard work. Wait, come back!

To review, Director offers you two basic flavors of text: bitmap text and QuickDraw text. If Director were an ice cream parlor, it'd have been out of business long ago. But two text types is all we really need.

Bitmap text

You create bitmap text in the Paint window with the Text tool. As long as you see a blinking insertion point in the text and a thick gray border around the text you can edit the text by pressing Delete as needed and then retyping, change the font, style, and size, and even add a shadow effect to the text.

But the moment you do nearly anything else in Director, the text you typed with the Text tool becomes transformed into a bitmap, meaning a painting just like one you might create in Director's Paint window. In Chapter 6, you find that paintings are nothing but a collection of pixels that (usually) look like something recognizable from a standard viewing distance. Once transformed into a bitmap, you can zoom in and edit bitmap text one pixel at a time, if you like, to fine-tune the shapes. Sometimes this isn't a bad idea, especially with smaller type sizes. You might enhance the text's readability by adding or removing a pixel here and there.

Why should you use bitmap text? Well, one of the greatest benefits of using bitmap text in Director is not having to worry about what fonts are installed in your System, or to try to guess the fonts installed in a user's Mac. Fonts installed in the System are no longer generating the bitmap text you see on-screen. Again, it's just a graphic, with pixels turned on or off.

You can *kern* (adjust the space between characters) bitmap text, a feature not directly built into Director, by selecting individual letters or groups of letters with a selection tool and adjusting their spacing in a line of type. Many character pairs, such as *W* and *O* or *V* and *A,* benefit from kerning or tightening the space between characters because their particular shapes create unsightly gaps of space with standard spacing.

Another benefit of bitmap text is that, used as a sprite on the Stage, it animates faster than QuickDraw text. Speed is a constant consideration when developing Director movies, and it's not usually wise to assume your users are fixed up with the latest, greatest bit-chomping computer to view your work.

Bitmap text comes with disadvantages, too. Once turned into a bitmap, you can't return to the text later, select a word or phrase, or edit the selection. There's really no text to select or modify. The only way to "edit" bitmap text is to erase it with the Eraser and retype from scratch. You can't search for bitmap text with Director's Find commands. Lingo commands can't recognize bitmap text and manipulate its contents. Also, when it comes to printing, bitmap text falls flat on its face (no pun intended, or was it?). If you've ever printed out a screen font without the printer font available, you know what to expect — ugly! You'll see the infamous jaggies in the output. And for quality storyboards and reports to present to clients, the results will be disappointing, to put it gently.

QuickDraw text

Director also allows you to use QuickDraw text. Using QuickDraw text is similar to entering text in a word processing program, especially because you can edit the text at any other time. QuickDraw refers to routines coming from your Mac's system board allowing objects to display on-screen, including QuickDraw text. One great advantage of QuickDraw text is it remains text; you can always return to it and edit changes or correct typos just as you can reopen a memo you wrote a week ago in Word and make changes.

Because QuickDraw text is real text, you can search it for specific content with Director's Find commands. In movies featuring advanced Lingo scripting, a movie can "read" text input from the user, for example, and modify it or check the contents of a field for errors or inappropriate or missing entries.

Another area where QuickDraw shines is printing. Output of QuickDraw text is comparable to output you expect from a word processing program and a LaserWriter or better. So consider your needs as you develop a movie in Director. If you know a block of text is going to be output to a printer, you better go with QuickDraw text.

Unfortunately, Director doesn't offer kerning to improve character spacing in problem character pairs like *W* and *O*, and trying to do it manually isn't as good an idea as it sounds. Results can be very unpredictable, and working with little bits and pieces of QuickDraw text is maddening. How do you think I wound up like this?

However, one technique makes life easier when importing a movie from Director for Windows to the Mac version. The Movie Info command under the File menu takes you to the Movie Info dialog box beautifully reproduced by

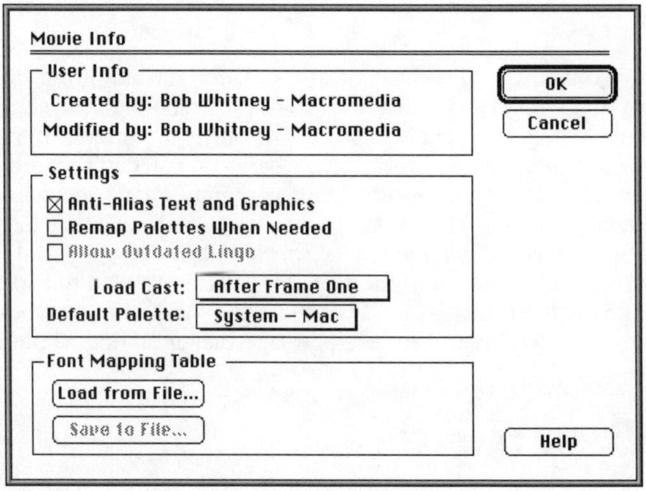

Figure 8-7: Use the Font Mapping Table panel of the Movie Info dialog box to improve translation of a Windows font into a Mac font.

Carpathian eunuchs in Figure 8-7.

At the bottom left of the Movie Info dialog box, notice the Font Mapping Table panel. When you're using a font coming from a Director for Windows movie, click the Load from File button to incorporate the font's mapping table that Windows generates for its fonts.

As for disadvantages, QuickDraw text animates slowly. If you can't guarantee your movie's going to be running off a fast machine, you better stay away from QuickDraw text sprites on the Stage, if possible. If you must animate QuickDraw text, make sure its ink type is Copy. Other Ink Effect types can slow even the fastest sprites down to a crawl.

For a quick overview of what you can and can't do with Director text, keep the following Table 8-1 handy.

Table 8-1 Advantages and Disadvantages of Director Text

Type of Text	*Advantages*	*Disadvantages*
Bitmap	Shapes are editable pixel by pixel	Not editable for content
	Extensive kerning by dragging	Limited global spacing
	Speedy animation	Poor printing output
		Not searchable with Director Find commands
		Not recognized as text by Lingo scripts for manipulation
QuickDraw	Editable at any time	Shapes not editable pixel by pixel
	Limited kerning possible	Limited global spacing
	Excellent printing output	Slow animation
	Searchable with Director Find commands	
	Recognized as text by Lingo scripts for manipulation	
	Font mapping table for cross-platform movies	

Part III
Manipulating Director with More Windows

"No, they're not really a gang, just the new multimedia division."

In this part...

There's an old saying I just made up: When you're designing multimedia, you can never have too many windows and their tools. Someone at Macromedia must agree with me since they slipped even more windows with assorted tools to explore into Director while we weren't looking. Maybe these windows don't have the glamour of the Score or Cast windows, but boy, would you miss them if they walked out on strike.

In this next part, I walk you through QuickDraw, QuickTime, 24-bit palettes, H-B-S, scripts and their associated windows, and a gaggle of other intriguing characters just itching to become part of your movie.

Chapter 9

Yet Another Set of Tools: The Tools Window

In This Chapter

- Fiddling around with QuickDraw's tools
- Using the shape tools to create and change shapes
- Exploring the importance of the Tools window
- Discovering the meaning of life

One of the great pleasures of learning Director is plowing through the kazillion windows the program has to offer — that is if you also happen to look forward to paper cuts during the day. As if you don't have enough windows to become close personal friends with, allow me to present the Tools window and its entourage, the QuickDraw tools. Now, it's my personal belief that Macromedia added the QuickDraw tools to Director on April Fool's Day as a techy's idea of a practical joke. Somewhere there's a sadistic developer chuckling over the thought of sneaking in QuickDraw tools to make your day a little more rotten. But don't let the techy win this one. Just keep in mind that you can use those other tools in the Paint window to modify existing bitmaps and to create bitmaps from scratch, and don't let this new set of QuickDraw tools in the Tools window confuse you. Besides, the tools are actually useful.

A Brief Explanation of QuickDraw

So far, I've talked about QuickDraw this and QuickDraw that. You just might be wondering, what the heck is QuickDraw? Well, without getting too technical, QuickDraw refers to a set of very basic computer routines that your Mac calls on to draw images to your screen. Some programs use these same routines to create graphics. ClarisDraw, the latest and greatest version of one of the Mac's oldest programs, calls on QuickDraw routines when you use its tools to create images, such as circles, rectangles, polygons, and even freeform shapes.

When you use a program like ClarisDraw, you're drawing, not painting. And as much as I hate to admit it, when you use one of Director's tools from the Tools window, you're really drawing, too, not painting. I feel so ashamed I didn't bring this up earlier . . . well, not that ashamed.

Painting in Director

Anyway, what's the difference between painting and drawing? In a painting *environment,* to use the big kids' lingo (no pun intended), you add *digital paint* to the page pixel by pixel as you push the Brush or Pencil tool around. Another way of saying this is, you turn on individual pixels on the page that look, from a normal viewing distance, like a recognizable image. This collection of pixels may look like a circle, an apple, or even text if you used the Paint window's Text tool. But it's all an illusion, it's nothing but individual pixels glowing on your computer screen. I know, another illusion shattered forever.

Drawing in Director

Imagine that you're drawing in ClarisDraw or, better yet, using one of Director's QuickDraw tools from the Tools window. Whether you realize it or not, you're creating a description of an object using the same routines your Mac uses to draw to the screen. Your Mac accepts the result as an *object,* or whole entity, not just a collection of pixels that look like something due to a trick of the eye. When you draw an oval with the Circle tool from the Tools window, you get a real oval; you can click anywhere inside the oval with the mouse pointer and drag the circle around the Stage. Try this on long, rainy weekends; the time will just fly by.

Got a StyleWriter II? It's a QuickDraw printer using the same routines to print out your report, memo, or letter. Maybe you've noticed it's not so good at printing out complex graphics because QuickDraw has some problems with intricate images. But QuickDraw shines for drawing rectangle, ovals, rounded rectangles, real squares, perfect circles in Director, and even type.

Watch My Lips — T-h-e-s-e A-r-e Q-u-i-c-k-D-r-a-w T-o-o-l-s

What makes the tools unique in the Tools window is they draw QuickDraw objects, very different from the bitmap-making tools in the Paint window. If the word, *QuickDraw,* made you utter, "Huh?" I've got a suggestion for you. On second thought, maybe I'd better keep it to myself. Anyway, in the next section, I give you a painless idea of what QuickDraw is all about.

Drawing QuickDraw shapes on the Stage

Functionally, one of the biggest differences between QuickDraw tools in the Tools window and those in the Paint window is that you can draw directly on the Stage with QuickDraw tools. Several events occur, actually, when you draw on the Stage with a QuickDraw tool. To better understand what happens, set up your screen as follows:

1. **With the help of the Window menu, display the Tools, Cast, and Score windows.**
2. **Drag the Resize box in the lower-right corner of the Cast window to make the window about two inches square and click the appropriate scroll bars so an empty Cast Member cell is visible in the window.**
3. **Drag the Score's Resize box in the lower-right corner in toward the center of the window to make the Score window as small as possible.**
4. **Click inside the first empty cell in the Score window.**
5. **Click one of the shaded tools in the second row of the Tools window.**
6. **From the upper-right region of the Stage, drag the tool diagonally down and to the right about $1^1/_2$ inches.**

   The Stage is the one window you never have to select. It's always there, like happy, smiley-face sunbeams in California. And, oh yes, like death and taxes, too.

Notice what happens the nanosecond you release the mouse; several events occur instantaneously. In fact, if you have an atomic clock handy, it's great fun timing the following as a family project for that daily fix of quality time together:

- A rectangular QuickDraw sprite appears on the Stage, bordered with a bold, gray selection outline.
- Director automatically adds the QuickDraw sprite you just painted to the Cast window as a new Cast Member.
- Director automatically adds the sprite to a free cell in the current frame of the Score window.

And you thought Director was just another pretty face.

Modifying a QuickDraw Cast Member

As for the type of sprite, the sprite you just painted directly on the Stage is dramatically different from any you may have created in the Paint window, Well, don't act so smug about it. For example, when you double-click on a Bitmap Cast Member on the Stage, Director takes you to the Paint window, where you can edit the graphic, pixel-by-pixel if you like.

The Shape Cast Member Info dialog box

Don't expect the same thing to happen when you double-click a QuickDraw sprite. What happens when you do? Double-clicking a QuickDraw sprite takes you not to the Paint window but to the Shape Cast Member Info dialog box as in Figure 9-1.

Figure 9-1: The Shape Cast Member Info dialog box for a QuickDraw object painted with a Shape tool.

You can easily recognize a QuickDraw Cast Member in the Cast by the icon in the lower-right corner of its cell, looking for all the world like the icon of the tool you just used — a small square, half white and half gray.

You can't edit QuickDraw shapes pixel-by-pixel, but the Shape Cast Member Info dialog box allows you to modify the graphic in a number of significant ways, including

- Giving the shape a unique and meaningful identify by entering a name in the Name entry field at the top of the window.
- Changing its shape by choosing one of the QuickDraw shapes in the Shape pop-up menu under the Cast Member number.
- Changing it to an unfilled shape by unchecking the Filled ballot box.

The Shape pop-up menu

Take a look at the Shape pop-up menu, shown in Figure 9-2, featuring four Shape options based on the dimensions of the currently selected QuickDraw shape. You can use the Shape pop-up menu to transform the shape of a previously drawn QuickDraw shape.

Figure 9-2: The Shape pop-up menu.

Shape options in the Shape pop-up menu include the following:

- *Rectangle*: A rectangular QuickDraw shape with 90-degree corners.
- *Round Rect*: A QuickDraw shape with rounded corners.
- *Oval*: An oval QuickDraw shape.
- *Line*: A straight line whose angle reflects the dimensions of the original shape you drew with a tool from the Tools window.

QuickDraw shape resizing handles

Another way of modifying a QuickDraw shape is to resize it by dragging one of its selection handles, as shown in Figure 9-3.

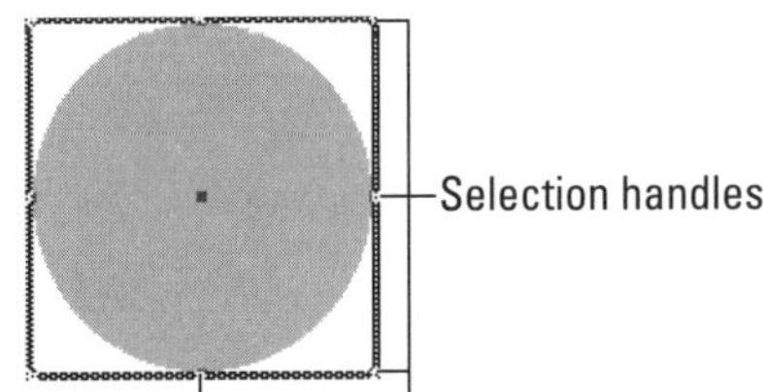

Figure 9-3: The selection handles of a QuickDraw sprite.

Ah, some of you wide-awake types remember that selected bitmap sprites display selection handles, too, and that they can be resized by dragging a handle. However, an advantage of a QuickDraw sprite is that you can resize without "jaggies," those infamous stairstepped jagged edges you get with enlarged bitmaps. When you want to increase the size of a QuickDraw sprite, hold down the Shift key until you begin dragging, if you want to maintain proportions, press a handle of the sprite, and drag away from the center of the sprite. As you drag the handle, you should see something like the result pictured in Figure 9-4.

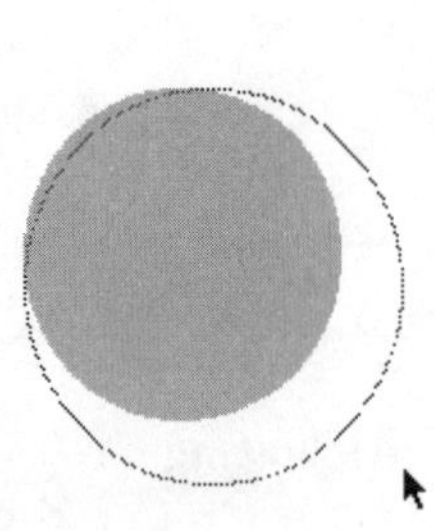

Figure 9-4: Proportionally scaling a QuickDraw sprite by pressing Shift and dragging one of its handles.

The selection marquee and handles disappear and a ghost outline of the sprite grows in size as you continue dragging the mouse. After you release the mouse, the result is an enlarged QuickDraw sprite as shown in Figure 9-5, without the "jaggies" associated with rescaled bitmaps.

Figure 9-5: An enlarged QuickDraw sprite — and no "jaggies."

Now compare the QuickDraw sprite in Figure 9-5 with the bitmap sprite in Figure 9-6, which has been scaled up to similar dimensions. Note the classic and, may I add, ugly "jaggies" that result whenever you try enlarging bitmaps in Director.

Another important difference between QuickDraw and bitmap sprites is that QuickDraw sprites are *objects,* self-contained shapes that aren't just an assemblage of pixels on-screen. Bitmaps only look like self-contained shapes, they're really nothing more than a block of pixels that trick the eye into looking like something from a typical viewing distance. It gets a little confusing in Director because a bitmap sprite on the Stage takes on some QuickDraw-like characteristics. You can click anywhere on a bitmap sprite on the Stage and select the whole sprite, and when it's selected, the bitmap sprite displays handles just like its QuickDraw cohorts. Don't you see? Director has designed things this way so that we multimedia types can work with bitmap sprites more easily on the Stage. But double-click that bitmap sprite, get it in the Paint window, and its bitmap characteristics come through. Zoom in and whammo. Pixels! Nasty individual pixels that give the show away.

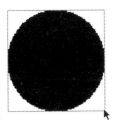

Figure 9-6: The infamous "jaggies" of a rescaled bitmap.

Checking out the Tools window tools

Several of the tools in the Tools window, smartly reproduced in Figure 9-7, look similar to tools you find in the Paint window. As you'll find out, other tools are, however, unique to the Tools window.

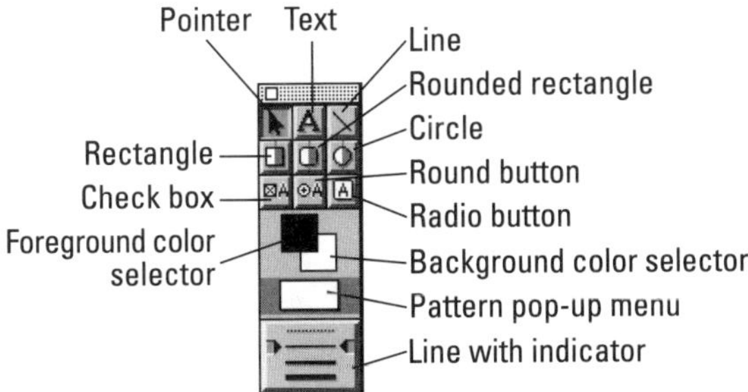

Figure 9-7: The Tools window, used for creating QuickDraw shapes, text, and buttons.

Misfit tools

The first area of the Tools window that you meet may be the set of nine tools at the top, organized by type into three rows. You could say that the top row is a collection of misfit tools. From left to right, they include the following:

- *Pointer tool:* The classic mouse cursor, moves — interestingly enough — both QuickDraw and bitmapped sprites around the Stage.
- *Text tool:* Not to be confused with the Paint window's Text tool of the same name, offers you another way of making a Text Cast Member with the advantage of typing directly on the Stage. The field adopts the current background color in the Tools palette; the text itself reflects the current foreground color. (The resulting object — or text in a field — is the same kind of object that results from typing text in the Text window and then dragging the text on the Stage.)

- *Line tool:* Paints straight lines at any angle directly on the Stage; remember to press Shift and drag to paint a horizontal or vertical line or a line at a 45-degree angle. The QuickDraw line adopts the current foreground color and line width displayed in the Tools window. While the line is selected, you can change the graphic's color with the Foreground color selector and the line width with the Line width indicator. Notice that QuickDraw line width options in the Tools window are very limited compared to sizes available for bitmaps in the Paint window. You win some, you lose some. *C'est la vie.*

QuickDraw shape tools

The second row of QuickDraw tools are the Shape tools with split personalities — hollow on the left, shaded on the right. Come to think of it, I have a couple of friends who fit that same description. Anyway, from left to right, the Shape tools include the following:

- *Rectangle tool:* Allows you to paint a hollow rectangle bordered in the current foreground color using the left side of the tool, and a rectangle filled with the current foreground color using the right side of the tool. Remember to press Shift and drag to paint a perfect square.
- *Rounded rectangle tool:* Allows you to paint a hollow, rounded rectangle bordered in the current foreground color using the left side of the tool, and a rounded rectangle filled with the current foreground color using the right side of the tool. Remember to press Shift and drag to paint a rounded square shape.
- *Circle tool:* Allows you to paint a hollow oval shape bordered in the current foreground color using the left side of the tool, and an oval filled with the current foreground color using the right side of the tool. Remember to press Shift and drag to paint a perfect circle shape. And to eat plenty of leafy green vegetables each and every day.

When you double-click on a QuickDraw sprite created with one of the Shape tools, Director takes you to the Shape Cast Member Info dialog box. From here, you can change the shape of the sprite with the Shape pop-up button. For more information on the Shape pop-up button, see "The Shape Cast Member Info dialog box" section earlier in this chapter.

Button-making tools

The third row of QuickDraw tools comprise Director's QuickDraw button-making tools. From left to right, they include the following:

- *Check box button tool*: Creates a check box-style button, as shown in Figure 9-8.

  During playback, the user may check one or more check boxes, initiating a respective script for each checked button. You could use check boxes, for example, to enable users to change the formatting of a screen title.

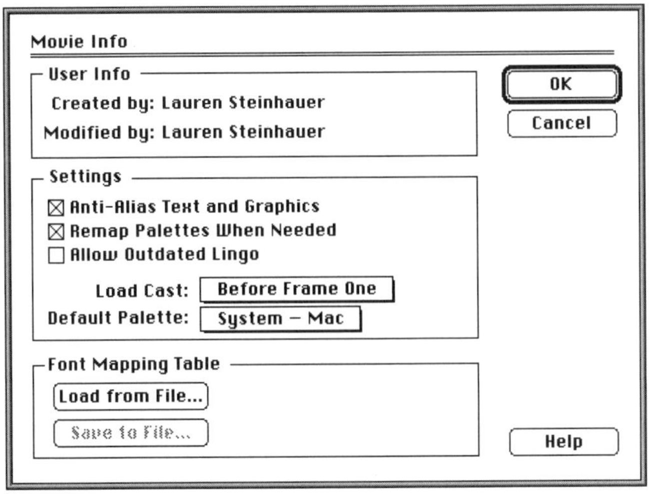

Figure 9-8: Check box-style buttons in the Settings panel of the Movie Info dialog box, used to offer options that are not mutually exclusive.

- *Radio button tool*: Creates a radio button. Figure 9-9 shows radio buttons used in the Export dialog box to give you some choices when exporting a Director movie as a QuickTime mooV.

  During playback, the user may check one of the radio buttons from a set, initiating an associated script. You — who else? — are responsible for writing the script that both initiates the desired action and unchecks any other radio buttons in the group. For more info on writing scripts in buttons, jump to the "Scripts" section in Chapter 17.

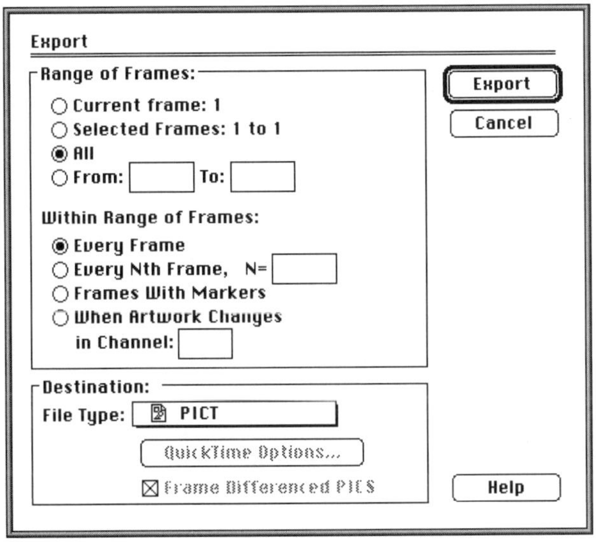

Figure 9-9: Radio buttons in the Within Range of Frames area of the Export dialog box, used to offer one choice from a set of mutually exclusive options.

- *Round button tool*: Your plain vanilla round button tool; creates a rounded button, as shown in Figure 9-10, that you can name.

  During playback, the user activates an associated script after clicking a round button. Guess who gets stuck writing the script?

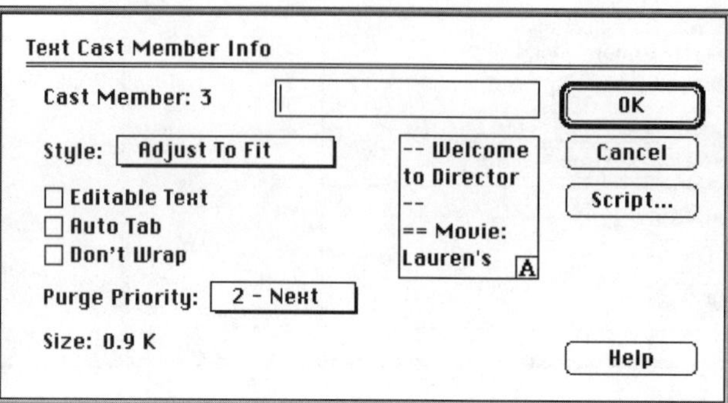

Figure 9-10: OK, Cancel, Script, and Help are similar to buttons you can make with the Round button tool.

You can easily change the button style of a button sprite. Double-click the button to go to its Button Cast Member Info dialog box where you can select a different style from the Style pop-up menu.

When double-clicking a button sprite to go to its Button Cast Member Info dialog box, be sure to double-click within the selected button's bold, gray selection border. Otherwise, you'll only place an insertion point in the field area of the button or select part or all of the button name. Very frustrating.

If you can't wait to play with making buttons and adding secret messages in them, what we multimedia types call *Lingo scripting,* peruse Chapter 17. For more on when to use check boxes and radio buttons, flip back to the sidebar, "Round versus square: the politics of selection buttons," in Chapter 3.

More Tools window stuff

Beneath the nine QuickDraw tools at the top of the Tools window are the following areas:

- *Foreground color selector:* Allows you to select the current foreground color from the current palette of colors when you click the selector area.
- *Background color selector:* Allows you to select the current background color from the current palette of colors when you press the selector area.

- *Pattern pop-up menu:* Allows you to select the current pattern from a set of patterns when you click the pop-up menu area.
- *Line width indicator:* Allows you to set the line to invisible or to one of three different widths by clicking the desired option.

The Meaning of Life

Oh, yeah, the meaning of life. Who knows?

Why You Should Care about This Window

The product and features of the Tools window are very useful, really. I've listed a number of reasons why. Not necessarily ten reasons, so no drum roll please:

- You can paint — excuse me — draw directly on the Stage.
- You can type directly on the Stage.
- You can search and replace text typed with the Text tool.
- You can easily edit text typed with the Text tool.
- You can instantly change the shape of a QuickDraw sprite, manually or by using Lingo commands to create magical transformations.
- You can instantly change the color of a QuickDraw sprite, manually or by using Lingo commands to create magical color changes.
- QuickDraw text prints out at high resolution without "jaggies," making it the text of choice for printing out storyboards for client approval and for reports generated by your multimedia product.
- Lingo scripts can recognize, modify, or manipulate text typed with the Text tool.
- You can reduce or enlarge a QuickDraw sprite right on the Stage without getting the infamous "jaggies."
- QuickDraw sprites and text take up less memory than bitmapped equivalents.

Well, what do you know? Ten reasons! OK, I'll take that drum roll after all. YES!

Chapter 10

Getting to Those Scrumptious Palettes: The Color Palettes Window

In This Chapter

- Creating a custom palette
- Working with the Color Palettes window
- Using the Apple Color Picker
- Discovering the mysteries of 65535

Throughout this book I talk about sets of colors called palettes that you use when developing movies with Director. Surprise, they have their very own window. And some clever devil at Macromedia named it, of all things, the Color Palettes window.

Decisions, Decisions, Decisions

To see your very own Color Palettes window, choose Window⇨Color Palettes, and, like magic, the Color Palettes window appears on-screen, looking uncannily like the hand-tooled engraving shown in Figure 10-1. Remember, this figure is only an artist's representation, not the real thing.

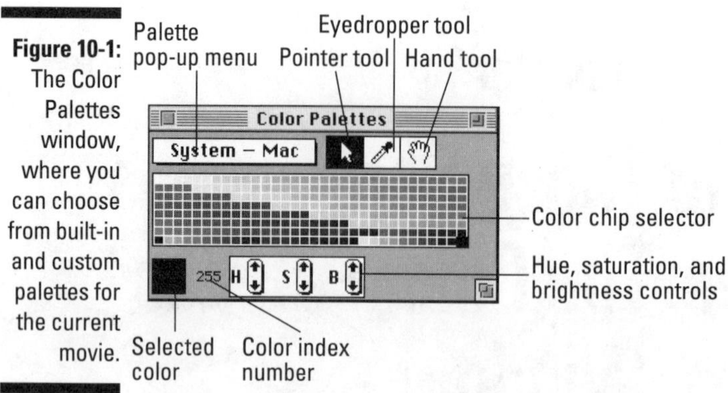

Figure 10-1: The Color Palettes window, where you can choose from built-in and custom palettes for the current movie.

Okay, so the Color Palettes window isn't quite as imposing as, say, the Score, but it's very important in its own little way. By the way, the Color Palettes window reflects the current palette. If you have a number of custom bitmap sprites in the Score and run from one to the other with the mouse, the palette in the Color Palettes window updates to the current palette. On the other hand, you can change the current palette by selecting a different palette from the Palette pop-up menu in the Color Palettes window.

Before finding out how the Color Palettes window contributes to your Director movies, you should make sense of all the goodies in the window.

The Palette pop-up menu

When you click the box near the upper-left corner of the Color Palettes window, a menu pops up, as in Figure 10-2, revealing nine built-in palettes and any custom palettes of your own that accompany an imported Cast Member.

Figure 10-2: The Palette pop-up menu, in which you find nine built-in palettes and any custom palettes.

Director's built-in palettes

Here are the nine built-in palettes listed in the Palette pop-up menu (see Figure 10-2):

- *System — Mac:* The System palette, the *default* palette, or the palette of choice of your Mac right out of the box while it's still warm. This palette is a collection of 256 standardized colors that the look of your Desktop and most program interfaces are based on. Most of the PICTs you import into Director display these same 256 colors.
- *System — Win:* A collection of 256 colors intended to translate well when porting bitmaps between your Mac and Windows — you know, that copycat program from . . . Well, anyhow . . .
- *Rainbow:* A bright collection of 256 colors meant to flower forth images of doves, angels, big fluffy clouds, and a sky full of McDonald's-like arches shimmering before our galvanized eyes. Good for kids' games.
- *Grayscale:* Sometimes nothing's better than a beautiful set of colorless values, from pure white through incremental shades of gray to deepest velvet black. That's when you choose good, old Grayscale palette for near photographic-quality, black-and-white images in your movie.
- *Pastels:* A collection of 256 colors inspired, no doubt, by watching too many "Barney" episodes. A plethora of soft, snugly, coochie-coo colors for designing disposable undies packaging.
- *Vivid:* Whoever designed this set definitely needs to cut way down on the coffee. Two hundred fifty-six *very* bright colors. The word *vivid* pales in comparison to the actual palette of colors.
- *NTSC:* A special collection of colors meant to translate well when *printing to video,* as multimedia types are apt to say.
- *Metallic:* An interesting collection of colors that definitely brings to mind thoughts of rusting tin cans, Robbie the Robot, and auto derbies. Not for everyone, but that's what makes life a confusing mess. Just kidding.
- *VGA:* Grayed out in Figure 10-2; this set of VGA (Video Graphics Array) colors is available only when you're viewing Mac stuff off a PC-type computer monitor. Another attempt to translate someone else's idea of a color scheme into the System palette we've grown to love — in this case, with a whopping 16 colors. Love those PCs.

Free to be NTSC

Novice multimedia types are often alarmed at how dramatically colors change after videotaping their work and playing it back on a real TV. *NTSC* is a set of standards for TV broadcasting adopted, while the crust of the earth was still cooling, by a stodgy group of frustrated, old media moguls called the National Television System Committee. Fact is, we had a number of ways to transmit and receive color television in 1953, but some people thought that we needed to agree on some basic specifications, lest chaos prevail.

Until contemporary debate over standards for high definition and wide-screen television, NTSC standards have dictated the quality of color images broadcast to the huddled masses yearning for cable to be free. These standards include a limited range of colors, bringing us back to the NTSC palette, a collection of 256 NTSC-legal, or safe, colors. None of these colors are so bright as to *bloom,* or fluoresce, and smear beyond the image's outline on the TV screen or be so far removed from NTSC's *gamut,* or color range, as to transform into an unexpected color or some drab green or brown tone.

Custom palettes

At the very bottom of the Palette pop-up menu in Figure 10-2, just below a gray rule demarcating built-in palettes from custom palettes, you'll find the line, `33:Palette 33`. It's a reference to a custom palette that tagged along with a bitmap I imported into Director while you weren't looking.

When a bitmap's built on a set of colors other than the System palette, the bitmap carries custom color info in a secret place within its own file. To import a bitmap that has a custom palette, choose File⇨Import, select the bitmap from the Directory dialog box, and click Import. Director displays a warning — showoff that Director is — boasting it knows you're trying to sneak in a bitmap with special colors. In this alert box, recreated in Figure 10-3, Director asks you to decide on one of three options by clicking the appropriate radio button.

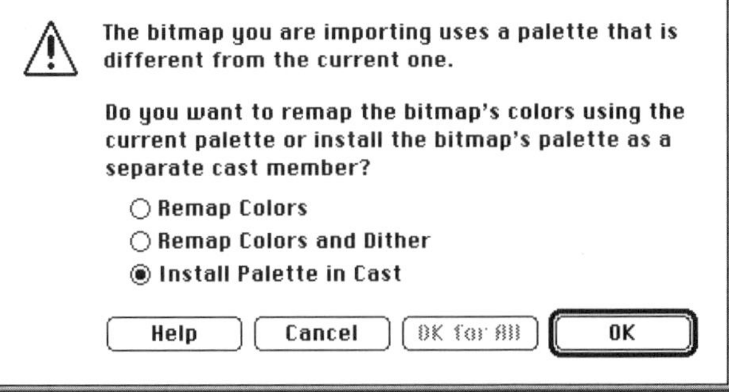
The bitmap you are importing uses a palette that is different from the current one.
Do you want to remap the bitmap's colors using the current palette or install the bitmap's palette as a separate cast member?
Remap Colors
Remap Colors and Dither
Install Palette in Cast
Help
Cancel
OK for All
OK

Figure 10-3: The Remap Bitmap alert box that appears when you import a bitmap with its own custom palette.

The alert box offers you three choices:

- *Remap Colors:* If you check this option, Director changes the colors of the bitmap as best it can using the current palette of colors so that no change of palette occurs while your movie is running. Director doesn't do a knockout job of changing colors much of the time; you can benefit by standardizing on one palette, usually the System palette. Switching palettes during playback takes time and may slow down a movie running on an older, slower Mac.
- *Remap Colors and Dither:* If you click this option, Director uses a dithering routine to create the illusion of seeing more colors than actually exist on-screen. *Dithering* is similar to how a magazine prints a color picture of a photographic image using just four inks — cyan, magenta, yellow, and black. You can see the separate, little blobs of color on the page with a magnifying glass; at normal viewing distance, the minuscule blobs of cyan, magenta, yellow, and black blend together in various percentages to produce an illusion of the millions of colors we're accustomed to seeing in real life. For multimedia types, the blobs of color are the pixels on their screens, typically 72 pixels per inch. (One day, you may hear an associate refer to *pixels per inch* or *ppi* as the resolution of the screen. At that point, exclaim in a loud, boisterous voice, "Oh yes, know all about that! Resolution of the screen, ppi, stands for pixels per inch." Be prepared to eat lunch alone for several months.)
- *Install Palette in Cast:* If you click this option, the custom palette tags along to become a Cast Member alongside the new Bitmap Cast Member. Then you may add the Palette Cast Member to the Palette channel in the Score window when the special bitmap appears on the Stage. Director continues using the new palette until you change palettes.

Color Palettes window tools

To the right of the Palette pop-up menu (Figure 10-1) are three tools:

- *Pointer tool:* Your basic mouse pointing tool for pointing, clicking, and dragging within the color chip selector below the tools. For example, you can drag the Pointer tool through a number of colors in the System palette, selecting colors in preparation for shifting them as a block to another area of the palette with the Hand tool. Or you can select a block of ten colors and choose, for example, the Blend Colors command from the Palette menu in Director's menu bar; Director creates a blend using the first selected color as the beginning color and the last selection as the destination color.
- *Eyedropper tool:* Common to many high-powered paint programs, including Photoshop, the Eyedropper allows you to *sample* a color anywhere on the Stage, that is, record a color's percentage of red, green, and blue light that makes up all colors on your RGB monitor. For example, suppose that you're working with the System palette and you have the image of a bright sun on the Stage; you click the brightest area with the Eyedropper, and the sixth color from the top-left of the color chip selector area is highlighted. The same color also becomes the selected color in the lower-left corner of the Color Palettes window. The number to the right of the selected color changes to 5 to display the color's *index number.* For more information on indexed color, see the next section.
- *Hand tool:* Use the Hand tool to move one or more selected colors in the color chip selector of the Color Palettes window by clicking inside the selection and dragging to another area of the palette. Director considers this action a creative endeavor on your part and brings up a window in which you can name your new palette.

Just in case you're concerned, after you switch from the Pointer to one of the other two tools in the Color Palettes window, your mouse cursor automatically turns back into the Pointer when you enter the window's Title Bar to drag the window to a new location or to click the Close or Zoom box. If you use the mouse outside the Color Palettes window and then return to the window, Director switches you back to the Pointer tool. You have to start all over again . . . jheech!

Color and index numbers

Below the Palette pop-up menu and tools is the set of 256 colors making up a particular palette. (Yes, we're still in Figure 10-1.) By the way, when Director first brings up the window, it's tiny. Real tiny. To really open up what you're working with, click the Zoom box in the upper-right corner of the window to fill the screen with the Color Palettes window. Simply click the Zoom box again to return the window to its original size.

Going from palette to palette, have you noticed something striking? No, running out of beer doesn't count. White is always the first color in the upper-left corner of the palette, and black the last. In other words, white is always index number 0, and black is always index number 255. Always and forever. You can bet your life on it, just don't bet mine. You never know when someone at Apple is going to slip up and put black in the center or something.

Anyway, this black and white thing applies to all of Director's built-in palettes and custom palettes. That's right, your Mac won't allow you to move or modify white or black, regardless of how weird the other colors in your custom palette happen to look. Some other programs that let you rearrange colors in a palette even offer a command called Macintize that puts white at index 0 and black at index 255.

In the System palette, things get even more draconian. Each color is always the same color in its respective position and always has the same index number to identify it. Of course, this boring predictability is the whole point of the System palette. The only problem is the real world, or even the world of the imagination, doesn't always fit so neatly into this handful of colors, provided you can hold 128 colors in each hand.

Miscellaneous Color Palettes window stuff

Across the bottom of the Color Palettes window, from left to right in Figure 10-1, you find the following:

- In the lower-left corner, a large color sample reflecting the color that is currently selected in the Color Palettes window.
- To the right of the selected color, the index number of the currently selected color.
- Lastly, *H-S-B* (Hue, Saturation, Brightness) controls for modifying the selected color from this view of the Color Palettes window. If the current palette is the System palette, the nanosecond you begin clicking on one of these controls Director takes you to the Please name this Palette dialog box, where clicking OK automatically creates a custom palette.

Something new, something old

If you ever decide you need a color that is missing from the System palette selection, you can make up your own custom palette. Here are the steps you need to make a new color with the Apple Color Picker – one of the more ingenious names for a dialog box; but what the heck, life's too short to worry about ingeniously named dialog boxes, right?

1. **Choose Window⇨Color Palettes.**
2. **Click the Zoom box in the upper-right corner to fill the screen with the Color Palettes window.**
3. **Choose System – Mac from the Palette pop-up menu.**
4. **Double-click a color you can live without in the Color Selector to display the Apple Color Picker, shown in Figure 10-4.**

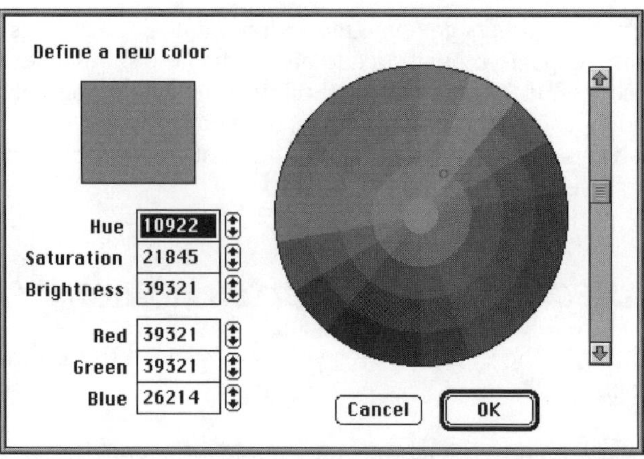

Figure 10-4: Double-clicking on a color in the Color Palettes window opens the Apple Color Picker.

Notice the color you double-clicked on shows up in the large color sample under `Define a new color`. Directly below the color are its components in two kinds of color space: Hue, Saturation, and Brightness (*H-S-B*) and Red, Green, and Blue (RGB). Your monitor, by the way, uses RGB color to create the images on your screen.

Very few people picture colors as numbers, like the ones you find in Figure 10-4, but numbers add a certain accuracy to the whole business of defining a color. For example, I might think of a special color, a kind of British racing green that's very difficult to describe any more accurately. But having noted a very similar color in the Apple Color Picker, I can pass on the color's components in one of the color models, H-S-B or RGB, to you to reproduce fairly accurately on your monitor.

5. **Enter new RGB or H-S-B values.**

   If you wanted that great Austin Healy green, try the following: 8963 for Red, 14928 for Green, and 20129 for Blue.

   Notice how the upper-half of the color sample reflects changes to the red, blue, and green values so that you can compare the original color to any modifications you make. As usual, your Mac gives you an out with the Cancel button, but you're not going to squirm out of this one. Go on. Go on now, read the next step.

6. **Click OK.**

   As soon as you click OK, Director knows that you tried to make changes to the System palette and displays a dialog box that looks like Figure 10-5, where you can christen your own palette with a meaningful name.

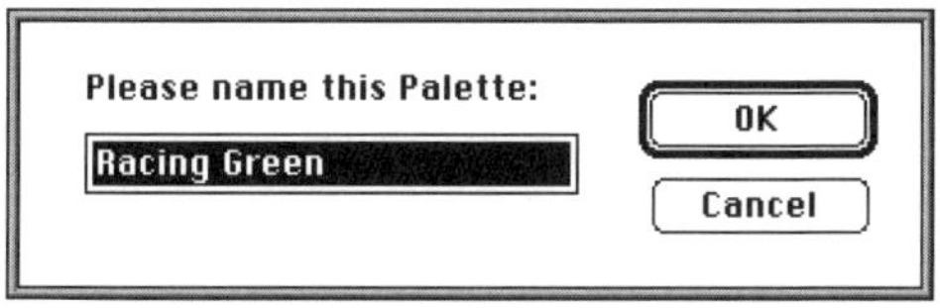

Figure 10-5: The Please name this Palette dialog box.

Please name this Palette:
Racing Green
OK
Cancel

7. **Enter a name for the new palette in the dialog box and click OK.**

   With a click of the mouse, you add a custom palette to the list under the Color Palettes window and a Palette Cast Member to the Cast window.

Anyway, I hope you noticed the Color Wheel in the Apple Color Picker dialog box. Otherwise, I'm not the only one who needs a new pair of glasses. Also, I hope you noticed the tiny, circular indicator jumping around inside the Color Wheel as you made changes to the original color.

Like any Mac scroll bar, you can click the up and down arrows or drag the elevator on the scroll bar. The scroll bar technique makes broad changes to all colors in the Color Wheel. The higher the elevator, the brighter the colors. If you drag the elevator to the bottom, all colors shift to black because you've effectively set brightness to zero.

You can also change a color by dragging the color indicator in the Color Wheel and/or moving the elevator in the scroll bar.

The Palette pull-down menu

Okay, the first time Director sneaks the Palette pull-down menu into the menu bar when you open the Color Palettes window, it's funny. Got me doubled up on the floor, personally. The second time, if you're in the right mood, it may get a laugh out of you. By the third time it gets really old. Call it someone's idea of cyber-humor.

As irritated as you may become, the Palette pull-down menu contains some interesting commands (see Figure 10-6).

Figure 10-6: The Palette pull-down menu magically appears in the menu bar when you display the Color Palettes window.

Commands under the Palette pull-down menu include the following:

- *Duplicate Palette:* If you're dead set on creating a custom palette by hand, first read "Something new, something old," found earlier in this chapter. No, reading doesn't make people go blind, trust me. An easy and safe way to start off is to choose a built-in or custom palette from the Color Palettes window and then choose Duplicate Palette. Director gives you a dialog box to name your new palette; after you click OK, you've got yourself a new palette to play with to your heart's content, plus a new Palette Cast Member in the Cast window.
- *Reserve Colors:* Allows you to protect colors in bitmaps on the Stage not being used for special effects like *color cycling* (an easy method of creating animation by cycling through a range of colors that I discuss in Chapter 22). For example, if you intend to animate a bitmap of a roaring fireplace with color cycling, you don't want colors chosen for the fire effect to cycle in other bitmaps. Choosing Reserve Colors can help to avoid this messy situation.

- *Invert Selection:* After making a selection in the Color Palettes window, choosing Invert Selection selects the unselected colors and de-selects the selected colors. On long, rainy weekends, I find that I can pass the time very quickly by selecting and inverting colors, and in no time, it's Monday. Try it.
- *Set Color:* For the double-clickably challenged, click *once* on a color in the Color Palettes window and choose Palette⇨Set Color to go to the Apple Color Picker, where you may modify the color in H-S-B or RGB color mode.
- *Blend Colors:* Creates a blend from the beginning and ending colors of a contiguous block of selected colors in the Color Palettes window. If you look back at the System palette, you'll find that it lacks a contiguous block of smoothly graduated colors to give you a good color cycling effect; the solution to creating effective color cycling animation is to create a custom palette with a wider range of graduated colors. You can select the block of colors by either dragging through colors with the Pointer or Hand tool or by clicking a beginning color and then pressing Shift and clicking the ending color with the Pointer or Hand tool. Keep in mind that you lose the colors in between beginning and ending colors of the selection — a small price to pay for color-cycling masterpieces.
- *Rotate Colors:* Shifts a contiguous block of selected colors one color over with each issue of the command. Rotate Colors reproduces what happens to a block of selected colors in color-cycling animation, only more slowly. If you're having trouble picturing what happens, think of a selection of colors as a "rosary" of color, each color a bead in the chain. Each time you choose Rotate Colors, you move the rosary by one bead. OK, that covers all the Catholics out there; now, there are these things called worry beads. . . .
- *Reverse Color Order:* Exactly what the command says, reverses the order of a contiguous block of selected colors. Try Reverse Color Order on the gradation of grays in the System palette at the tail end of the colors, except for black. Remember, your Mac won't allow you to move or modify either black, at index number 255, or white, at index number 0, in any palette, let alone the System palette. Also, remember that the moment you try to reverse color order with the System palette, Director basically forces you to create a new palette, going so far as to open a dialog box strongly hinting to give the palette a meaningful name. The big bully.
- *Sort Colors:* Another command based on first selecting a contiguous block of colors in the Color Palettes window, and then choosing Sort Colors to display the Sort Colors dialog box, shown in Figure 10-7.

Sort Colors

Sort Selected Colors by:

◉ Hue

○ Saturation

○ Brightness

Sort

Cancel

Help

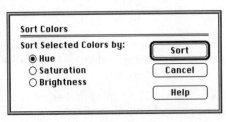

Figure 10-7: Choosing Palette⇨Sort Colors opens the Sort Colors dialog box, in which you decide how to sort selected colors.

You decide how to sort the selection of colors by clicking one of three radio buttons: *Hue* (by red, for example, rather than blue or green), *Saturation* (by intensity or purity of color), or *Brightness* (by lightness or darkness of color).

- *Select Used Colors:* Tallies up the colors in the bitmap displayed in the Paint window and automatically selects them in the Color Palettes window. This option is grayed out in Figure 10-6 and probably on your screen because it is dependent on three conditions: the command must have a bitmap in the Paint window (whether or not the Paint window itself is visible), the Color Palettes window has to be visible, and the Color Palettes window needs to be the active window.

I'll bet my mother's hot water bottle you see an iridescent flash when switching palettes, not one of Director's most fetching traits. To avoid the flash, try adding a transition to the Transition channel in the same frame where you placed the custom palette. The Transition palette is just underneath the Palette channel. The Set Transition dialog box appears, as shown in Figure 10-8.

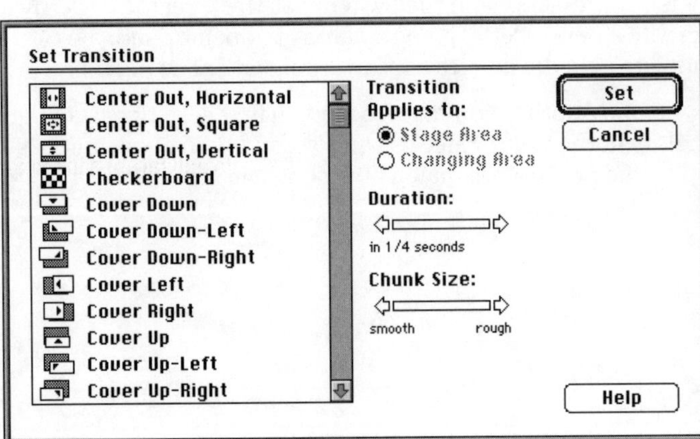

Figure 10-8: The Set Transition dialog box, where you may choose from a wide range of transition effects.

Switching palettes in your movie

I can think of at least three reasons why you'd want to switch palettes in a movie; there are probably 5,895 other reasons, give or take a reason. Big reason number one is due to the limitations of the default System palette. Its 256 colors just don't do justice to many bitmaps, especially photographs scanned into your Mac at millions of colors (what techy types call *24-bit color*) and then reduced to the System palette's paltry 256 color choices. Often, the result resembles a technique called *posterization,* in which light and shade are reduced to solid blocks of color. Sometimes, you may actually want this effect. It can be very dramatic, graphic, and artful. But not if you're aiming for realism and photographic quality.

That's when you go into Photoshop, open up the 24-bit scan, and choose Indexed Color from the Mode menu. A dialog box appears giving you a number of choices for reducing the millions of colors to a limp 256. But one special choice called the Adaptive method creates a custom palette that optimizes results. Amazingly, the new bitmap with a 256-color adaptive palette looks almost as good as the original with its 16 million-plus colors. Director tries to do the same thing after you begin importing a bitmap built on any palette but the System palette. You'll notice a dialog box with a radio button named Remap Colors and Dither.

Wonderful as Director is (kiss, kiss), Photoshop is the expert at remapping bitmaps. So if you choose the Photoshop route, be sure to click the Install Palette and Cast radio button in the dialog box that appears after selecting the file in the Import dialog box and clicking Import. The imported bitmap and its palette become separate cast members in the Cast window.

Why would you reduce all those beautiful 16 million colors to 256 in the first place? Well, that's reason number two for making a custom palette. Twenty four-bit bitmaps are gigantic; they slurp up room on your hard drive and stretch your poor Mac's computing power to or beyond its limit, especially with animation sequences. Unless you can count on developing and running your movie on the latest, greatest computing dynamo Apple has to offer with umpteen gigabytes of storage and a terabyte or two of memory chips, the most common solution is to drop the number of colors, which means that you either go with the System palette's interpretation of your image or let Director do it with the Remap Colors and Dither radio button. Or you could try Photoshop's adaptive palette method.

By the way, the third reason I can think of for creating a custom palette is color cycling. If you're downright antsy to find out more, jump to "Try Color Cycling" in Chapter 22. Just keep in mind, since the color cycling palette will be a limited palette, you'll probably have to swap back to your regular palette during playback of your movie by adding it to the Palette channel in the Score at the appropriate frame.

After you place your bitmap on the Stage, the bitmap will probably look weird, almost psychedelic. OK, all together, "Like wow, man, yeah, psychedelic." Now that we've got that out of our system. . . .

To properly view the bitmap, you need to add its accompanying Palette Cast Member to the Palette channel in the Score window. Place the Palette Cast Member in the same frame that your bitmap makes its appearance in the Score. Until you change palettes, Director continues to use the custom palette, which may or may not be what you want. If not, add your regular palette, probably the System palette, to the Palette channel at the appropriate frame.

Only a few transitions really overcome the flashing that occurs when switching palettes. I've used the Dissolve, Pixels Fast transition set to Changing Area with great success. Why does it work, you ask? It boils down to trial and error. I'm trying to save you the pain, the agony I've endured experimenting, experimenting, night and day, day and night. And to what end? To end up the shell of the man you see before you. Aargh.

Another technique that helps when you plan to switch Palettes is to choose File⇨Preferences and check Black and White User Interface (see Figure 10-9).

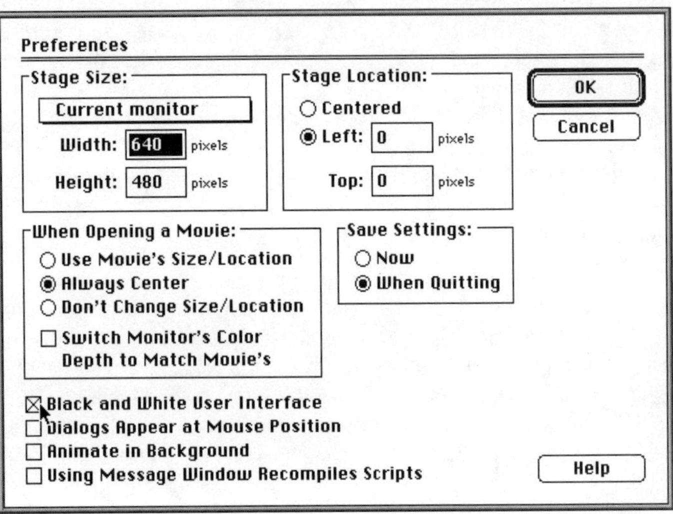

Figure 10-9: Checking the Black and White User Interface check box in the Preferences dialog box helps reduce flashing when switching palettes in a Director movie.

Checking this check box helps because Director's interface becomes black and white and doesn't need to update the interface's colors every time you switch palettes. It uses less memory, and many developers find the black-and-white interface less distracting, too.

There's dithering, and then there's *dithering*. Great as Director may be, Photoshop and other high-end paint programs offer dithering routines that produce superior results. A fascinating, peculiar, irritating, and necessary program called DeBabelizer, from Equilibrium, does a particularly excellent job of dithering bitmaps.

DeBabelizer also solves one of the most irksome enigmas that come up when using two or more palettes in a Director movie. How can images common to Director sequences with different palettes appear the same on the Stage? DeBabelizer can analyze a wide range of color requirements in different images and create a Super Palette that is usually a terrific compromise palette for all the images. This is the palette you'll want to import as a Cast Member along with the special bitmaps themselves. As you're saving the bitmaps in DeBabelizer, be sure to save the files in PICT2 with CLUT file format from the pop-up menu in DeBabelizer's Save As dialog box.

I'd Like You to Run Through This H–S–B Thing, Again

Earlier in this chapter, I took you on a tour of the Apple Color Picker, one of the most ignominious names I can think of for a dialog box. You discovered that colors on-screen are described in the Apple Color Picker with numbers in two different color *models,* or systems: H-S-B and RGB.

Hue, saturation, and brightness

H-S-B stands for hue, saturation, and brightness — not an old vaudevillian team that worked with seals — and is one of the major color models that multimedia types use to develop products. Take another look at the Apple Color Picker in Figure 10-10 and how the H-S-B model relates to colors in its Color Wheel.

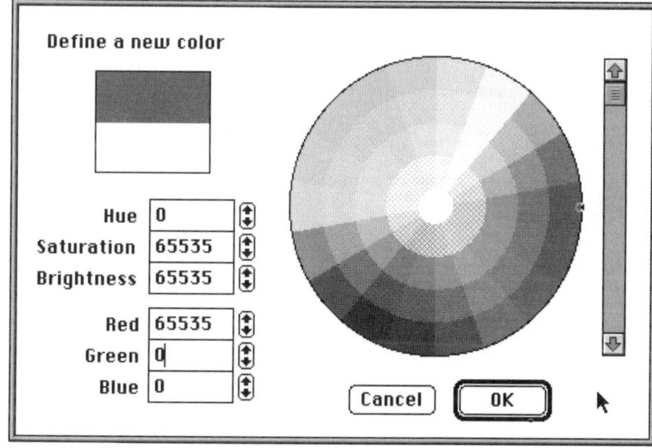

Figure 10-10: The Apple Color Picker as it looks with your monitor set to 8-bit color giving you 256 colors to use at any one time.

In the H-S-B color system, *Hue* refers to pure color. Picture a distinctive color in your mind; that's a hue. As a color changes hue in the Apple Color Picker, it moves around the circumference of the Color Wheel.

Saturation refers to intensity of hue. How red is a particular red? A washed out or pastel red is less saturated than pure red, candy red, or apple red. In the Apple Color Picker, as a hue becomes less saturated, it moves closer to the white center of the Color Wheel.

Think of *Brightness* as the amount of light shining on a hue. When you turn off lights in a room at night, all hues go black, even yellow. When you set Brightness to 0 in the Apple Color Picker dialog box, you're turning off all the lights. The Apple Color Picker visualizes this scenario with the "elevator" in the scroll bar sliding to the bottom.

Additive and subtractive primary colors

Remember school? I'll bet you learned primary colors are red, yellow, and blue. Close, but no turkey. Actually, you need to work with two different sets of primary color schemes when playing with color. Additive primaries — red, blue, and green — are for working with pure (or incident) light, such as the light that your monitor uses. That's why monitors generally use red, green, and blue (RGB) light. Mix all three colors at the highest saturation and brightness levels and what do you get? White light. If you're a fan of the theatre, those lighting technicians use the same scheme to light the stage; when the director wants a golden glow on her leading man and lady, the lighting crew had darn well splash red and green spots on them to make yellow light. That's the wacky world of additive color for you.

On the other hand, when you're dealing with light reflected off objects, you turn to subtractive primary colors: cyan, yellow, and magenta — printers' colors or process colors. In the desktop publishing world, printers customarily sneak in black as a fourth color to add punch to the printed image.

That mysterious 65535

In Figure 10-10, the selected hue happens to be pure red, as red as you can get on an RGB computer screen. Below the H-S-B values, RGB mode represents the same hue with red at maximum, the mysterious value 65535, while green and blue are set to 0. With saturation and brightness in the H-S-B color model turned up all the way, the additive and subtractive primaries are evenly divided in 60-degree intervals around the Color Wheel with pure red at number 0, pure green at 21845, and purest blue at 43690; subtractive primaries work out to pure cyan at 32768, pure yellow at 10922, and pure magenta at 54614. All based on 65535 divided by 6. And boy, wouldn't you love to know why! That makes two of us, because I haven't a clue.

I lied. Actually, I have a good idea why that mysterious 65535 keeps coming up. The Apple Color Picker is designed to handle up to 16-bit color. One way of defining 16-bit color is 2 multiplied by itself 16 times. Which is "2 to the 16th power." Which is 65,536. Isn't all this math stuff bringing back fond memories of old school days, wilted peanut butter sandwiches, and the school bully grinding your new glasses into the pavement at recess? Anyway, since computers start counting from 0, subtract 1 and the remainder becomes . . . 65,535! That's 65,536 hues to click through, each color with its own identifying number in the H-S-B system.

Complementary colors

You can also use the Apple Color Picker to find *complementary* colors. Four out of five rocket scientists agree, a complementary color is the color that creates white light when added to the original color. The technique of finding a color's complement is simplicity itself. After choosing a color either by clicking on the Color Wheel or entering values in H-S-B or RGB mode, find the complementary color directly opposite on the Color Wheel. You can safely build a color scheme around these two colors.

Or try a group of three complementary colors, which is what primary colors are. To make things more interesting, start with a more subtle color and then find its complements by finding the other two colors a third of the way around the Color Wheel in each direction. For example, say you decide on a yellowish color by eye-clicking hither and thither on the Color Wheel. Better yet, click hither and yon. You note in H-S-B color mode the color you pick is Hue 14626, a little more interesting than pure yellow. To find a set of complementary colors, imagine dividing the Color Wheel into thirds like a pie starting at your yellowish color. The other two "slices" wind up at around hues 36338 and 58316. To make things more interesting, brighten one hue by moving your choice in toward the white center of the Color Wheel and darken another color by scrolling down with a couple of clicks to the down arrow. The colors are no longer "perfect," but that's OK; it's visually more exciting.

Have you noticed that computers start counting with 0? For example, 8-bit color gives you 256 colors but the first color is index number 0 and the last color index number 255. Also, the Apple Color Picker offers 65536 hues in H-S-B color mode, but the first hue is 0, the last 65535. You'll see this kind of thing very frequently when working with your Mac. Don't let it throw you, especially if you wind up programming for NASA.

Chapter 11

QuickTime and Your Very Own Digital Video Window

In This Chapter

- Reviewing QuickTime
- Setting up your movie for QuickTime
- Getting close and personal with codecs
- Exporting your movie to QuickTime
- Touring the Digital Video window
- Playing QuickTime in Director
- Using Director as a QuickTime editor

Depending on whom you speak to, QuickTime is either the biggest thing since sliced bread or a sham technology, doling out postage stamp-sized, cataract-inducing animations to a swelling crush of catatonic, multimedia wannabes swayed by a movement more subversive than those Tupperware parties you've heard of. Where lies the truth?

Could You Review That QuickTime Thing Again?

Adding video to the rest of the mix that multimedia is made of has been the dream of developer types for some time. We tried all sorts of Rube Goldberg, Scotch tape, and rubber band kinds of solutions. Some actually worked, but none turned out to be as on target as Apple's QuickTime.

By the way, if you really don't want to review the history of QuickTime and are ready to get right to work, skip ahead to the section, "QuickTime to the Rescue."

Pre-QuickTime technology

Before QuickTime, multimedia types longed to bring video effortlessly into productions. We had techniques, however contrived, for including video, but "effortless" doesn't leap to mind when reviewing them. For example, we could include an external television monitor (you know, real TV) in our multimedia setup, hook up a laser disc to the TV, and control the laser disc with our Mac. In fact, Director still comes with a set of XObjects, used for controlling external devices, including laser discs from various manufacturers.

Why laser discs? Laser discs are similar to hard drives, floppy drives, and CD-ROMs in an essential way: instant access. You can move to any point on a laser disc seemingly without delay; in Lingo, using these XObject commands, you can write a script taking you instantly to a particular frame on a laser disc. On the other hand, what do you do with videotape when you want to skip a half hour of the material? You need to fast-forward or rewind, and usually shuttle back and forth until you find the right frame. Actually, we multimedia types have worked that way, too, planning delays into the production to cover rewinding and fast-forwarding by Igor, our helpful but pathetic assistant. The mess works, but boy, is it kludgy.

Another pre-QuickTime method for bringing video into the Mac is called bringing video into the Mac. Is there an echo in here? Actually, expansion cards from several different third-party manufacturers or vendors allow you to include a picture-in-picture style "video window" directly on your Mac's monitor with video from real-time broadcast, live video camera sources, or prerecorded video from a laser disc or VCR. Just before the announcement of QuickTime, I noticed the release of a number of software/hardware solutions providing "video-in-a-window" to video-hungry multimedia types like me.

By the way, these pre-QuickTime techniques are still viable solutions for certain demands of a multimedia production; in fact, AV Macs allow you to display video-in-a-window whenever you like with their built-in video capabilities and Video Monitor, a small program included with these models. The major contribution of QuickTime technology has been to enable more people than ever before to view and use video-style information on their own Macs, however humble they may be. The Macs, not the people.

Introduction of QuickTime

In 1993, Apple introduced QuickTime to the world. Depending on your perspective, QuickTime was: a major event on the same plane as the invention of writing, movable type, or the dawn of desktop publishing; "nice"; or insignificant. Old-time videographers laughed at the stamp-sized images everyone was suddenly showing on their monitors and, even then, the poor quality of the video.

But they missed the point. QuickTime technology was destined to improve, and more important, QuickTime gave birth to *desktop video,* enabling anyone with a Mac the opportunity of accessing and manipulating video-style information with the ease of using text and still graphics.

Ordinary data

You really need to compare video as an information or data-type with "ordinary" data to appreciate Apple's achievement with QuickTime. Ordinary data, basically text and *still* graphics, demands a certain level of performance from your Mac's software and hardware, built within limits to handle these anticipated demands at a reasonable performance level. Of course, a more powerful Mac handles ordinary information at higher performance levels.

The important characteristic of ordinary data is it doesn't change with time; until QuickTime, your whole computer system designed with this basic assumption in place. Your hard drive, for example, is designed to read or write short bursts of information at an acceptable performance level. Maintenance routines have even been added to your hard drive that periodically halt information exchange between the drive and your Mac at millisecond intervals, too small an interval to be significant when you're reading or writing memos, spreadsheets, or even painting an enormous bitmap masterpiece in Director's Paint window. Your system software has been developed around this basic assumption, too, with file types and performance levels engineered in to handle the expected data types at acceptable levels of performance.

Demands of video

Remember contemplating your navel in the '60s and '70s? OK, contemplate video. Video looks like a radically new data type standing next to its traditional lineage. It's like an invasion of pod people out of those old science fiction movies from the '50s. Most important of all, video *changes over time.* Video presents a new image approximately every thirtieth of a thecond, excuse me, second. If you're asking your Mac to "read" video or record video, you're suddenly making enormous, unexpected demands on your Mac's software and hardware. And until QuickTime, your Mac didn't even have a file type to handle this kind of information.

Now consider the size of a video-style file. A good rule of thumb is to count on about 27 megabytes per second of video. 27 MEGABYTES! Sorry, I lost it for a second, I'm all right now. Trust me. Without getting too technical, consider the demands that a second of video, about 30 frames, makes on your hardware, keeping in mind your Mac's many, so-called *bottlenecks.* Bottlenecks are areas that slow down performance regardless of how fast a machine you have. The so-called NuBus, one of the channels that information flows through when running your Mac, can handle, at best, about 10 megabytes of information per second. Your video wants 27 megabytes of info to flow per second. The SCSI bus allows your Mac to communicate with your hard drive at about 1.5 megabytes of information per second. Even so-called SCSI-2 hard drive technology ups the rate of data flow to a mere 8 megabytes per second when video demands over 3 times that amount of information flowing consistently from second to second. To top things off, this enormous requirement of video — 27 megabytes of info flowing *consistently* from second to second — is what cripples standard hard drives, built to handle lackadaisical text and graphic data that doesn't mind an occasional (pronounced, "every few milliseconds") missed beat as your drive cleans up after itself with built-in maintenance routines.

I used the phrase, "about 30 frames per second," earlier in discussing video characteristics. I wasn't stuttering; I meant to imply that video's frame rate is *not* 30 frames per second. The actual frame rate is 29.97 frames per second, established by the National Television Systems Committee back in 1953 when it tried to solve the problem of adding color to broadcasts without requiring a nation full of black-and-white TV set viewers to ante up for expensive new color sets. The solution was this odd value, 29.97, a compromise solution arrived at with some mighty convoluted mathematics. What was this convoluted mathematics? You don't want to know. Trust me.

To make things more interesting, video-style information often includes sound effects, narration, and/or music. Not only are you asking your Mac to take care of this additional burden but also to somehow synchronize these sounds to the images. What does your Mac do if video with narration is running on a slow computer? Does the whole movie slow down so that the speaker sounds like Goofy on Prozac? Or does the narration get completely out of sync so that your movie looks like a really bad Ninja film? What's a Mac to do?

QuickTime to the Rescue

Maybe now you can see why Apple developed QuickTime. What exactly is QuickTime? Well, I'll start you off with a round about answer by telling you how to load QuickTime on your computer. First of all, QuickTime comes with your system since System 7.1, so if you've got Apple's latest system, then you've got QuickTime somewhere on your hard drive. Otherwise, QuickTime now comes bundled with a number of software packages, too. And Apple sells a QuickTime kit, including a set of utilities along with the QuickTime system extension itself, smartly displayed in Figure 11-1.

Figure 11-1: QuickTime, Apple's extension for digital video.

However you get your hands on QuickTime, you install QuickTime by dragging its icon over your System folder and allowing System 7.5 to place QuickTime in the Extensions folder where it belongs. Or an Installer — System 7's or an application's — places QuickTime in the Extensions folder for you. With bated breath, you restart your Mac, and ka-boom! Nada. Nothing happens, not a darn thing. Your Mac doesn't rev up like a Lamborghini or double in size. The little Happy Mac icon that greets you when you start up your Mac doesn't even get a broader grin on its face. Zip.

You find yourself asking, "Self, what's the big deal about QuickTime, anyway?" Well, the QuickTime extension e-x-t-e-n-d-s your system. In and of itself, QuickTime doesn't do anything apparent. QuickTime works its magic after you launch a QuickTime-dependent program such as Adobe Premiere or CoSA After Effects. Then the program shifts into overdrive with QuickTime's special capabilities.

Codecs

QuickTime 2.0, the latest version as I write this book, contains a number of built-in compression schemes. Multimedia types like to call them *codecs* for *co*mpression/*dec*ompression or *co*der/*dec*oder, depending on whom you talk to at Apple. In Director, you meet QuickTime's codecs when you save your production as a QuickTime mooV to your hard drive. You may remember that you can import QuickTime movies into Director, but you may also choose to turn your Director production into a QuickTime mooV using the Export command under the File menu.

After choosing Export from the File menu, Director takes you to the Export dialog box, shown in Figure 11-2. Notice that Director gives you some powerful options under this dialog box, including which frames to export: a single frame, all frames, or every fifth frame, if you so choose.

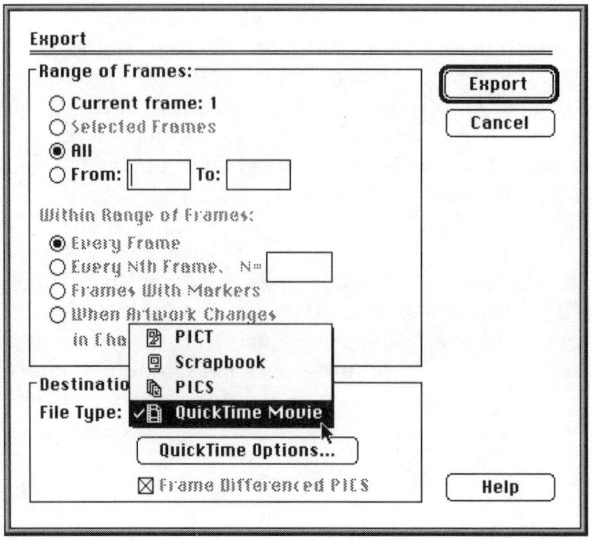

Figure 11-2: The Export dialog box, where you may choose to turn your Director movie into QuickTime, PICTs, a Scrapbook file, or a PICS file.

Focus now on the File Type pop-up menu and the QuickTime Options button near the bottom of the Export dialog box. If you choose QuickTime Movie from the File Type pop-up menu straight away, you're telling Director that you accept the default, out-of-the-box setting for a QuickTime mooV, and you miss the opportunity to custom select a codec. So the first step after coming to the Export dialog box really is to click the QuickTime Options button. Director takes you to the QuickTime Export Options dialog box, shown in Figure 11-3, to introduce you to your set of QuickTime codecs.

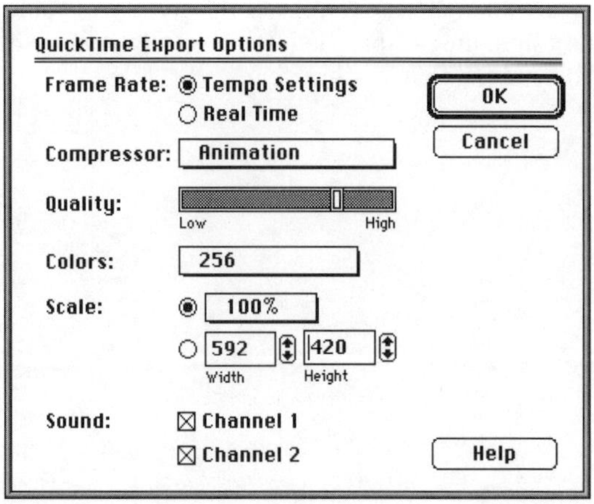

Figure 11-3: The QuickTime Export Options dialog box, where Director offers you a choice of codecs for turning your movie into QuickTime.

Pressing the Compressor pop-up menu displays a list of codecs, shown in Figure 11-4 below.

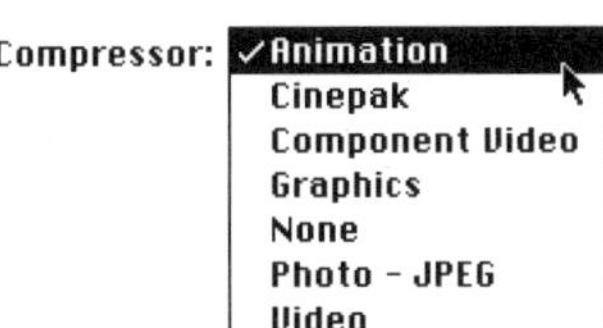

Figure 11-4: The list of QuickTime 2.0 codecs under the Compressor pop-up menu.

The set shown in Figure 11-4 is QuickTime 2.0's current list of codecs, each designed to compress a specific type of file. QuickTime 2.0's codecs include the following:

- *Animation:* This codec's main purpose is compressing computer animation, such as a sequence created in a 3-D program that takes you on a tour of a make-believe city existing only on computer. This type of file has unique characteristics that the Animation codec is designed to compress most efficiently.
- *Cinepak:* The codec of choice for many developers, especially useful for preparing QuickTime movies destined to run off a CD-ROM. The Cinepak codec takes a very long time to compress information into a QuickTime mooV; figure about two minutes per frame on average. But once compressed, Cinepak mooVs decompress quickly on playback and look very good. Developers often choose to compress their work overnight with the Cinepak codec, often in combination with utilities allowing *batch compression* (that is, compressing a log of selected QuickTime files).

  In addition to controls for setting the degree of compression for the Cinepak codec, some QuickTime applications and utilities — not including Director, unfortunately — allow you to set the *data rate* (how much information is sent to the Mac) in kilobytes per second. For example, using a useful utility called MovieShop, you'd want to set a QuickTime mooV's data rate to around 90 kilobytes per second for QuickTime destined to play on older CD-ROM drives and around 150 kilobytes for double-speed CD-ROM drives. If you're interested, you can find MovieShop on various commercial and independent bulletin boards.
- *Component Video:* For you to better understand the Component Video codec, I need to give another mini lecture on how real TV works. What we get broadcast to our homes and received on our real TVs is NTSC *composite video,* meaning the image-making signals are essentially mixed together, as opposed to separate red, green, and blue signals. Our real TV

attempts a translation back to red, green, and blue data for the picture tube to work properly, but there's that old saying about stuff losing something in translation. NTSC TV's a perfect example.

Video composed of separate red, green, and blue signals is called component video and results in significantly higher image quality than composite video. When you're about to make a QuickTime mooV from a component video source, the Component Video codec is the one to go with to save all the extra info that component video offers.

- *Graphics:* The codec of choice for 8-bit graphics, that is, bitmaps that display 256 colors, and a special situation for at least two reasons and possibly 3,472 more. First, QuickTime is optimized to display thousands of colors. And second, 256-color bitmaps are limited in color range. The Graphics codec is developed to achieve good compression and optimum results with 8-bit graphics, resulting in few *artifacts* (flawed pixels in the image) that typically occur during the compression process.
- *None:* I'll give you one guess. You got it, this selection turns off all codecs and results in a QuickTime mooV with no compression. None offers the highest quality QuickTime results but is only a practical choice for Mac users who own behemoth hard drives with names like Bruiser and Powe-r-r-r-r-r-D-r-r-r-rive and Macs accessorized with a Cray computer or two.
- *Photo — JPEG:* Developed for compressing full-screen, 24-bit (16 million) color *still* images. Now you may be asking yourself, "Self, why offer still-image compression in a movie-making program?" Well, it's important to remember that part of the beauty of QuickTime is its ability to incorporate virtually all file types into the Movie file type, including still images. For example, you can use a series of still images, such as a tour of famous paintings from the Louvre in Paris, as a QuickTime sequence, compressed with the Photo — JPEG codec and spliced together in Director with other QuickTime sequences, each compressed at its optimum value with its best codec.
- *Video:* The Video codec offers fast compression and decompression for files with moving images and sound. Moving images present special problems for compression schemes because all the pixels that make up the image tend to change from frame to frame. All this change disables what any self-respecting compression scheme tries to do, cut down on info by recording only what changes from frame to frame.

Notice the Quality slider under the Compressor pop-up menu in Figure 11-3 earlier in this chapter, used to set the degree of compression. (If only we had a Quality slider for Congress.) In general, you'll aim for the highest possible quality by selecting the least amount of compression, but you'll have to balance quality against frame rate and image size. If a large video window and/or high frame rate are paramount, you'll need to consider compromising on quality by upping the compression rate.

Some developers use QuickTime for purposes other than making digital movies. Since QuickTime can incorporate still-image file types such as PICT files and sounds, you might consider using QuickTime as a way to archive various file types into one QuickTime standard, using no compression or the Animation codec, which is sometimes used to organize and store high-quality PICTs. An additional benefit of this kind of QuickTime archive is easily taping animations to video, one PICT per frame, the so-called single-frame technique that some hardware components offer.

Preparing QuickTime for Export

Take another look at the QuickTime Export Options dialog box in Figure 11-3. You checked out the Compressor pop-up menu and learned about QuickTime 2.0's various codecs and how to adjust the amount of compression with the Quality slider, keeping in mind the inverse relationship between image quality and amount of compression. Now you can become close, personal friends with the dialog box's other features.

Tempo settings versus real time

Director gives you a choice between Tempo Settings and Real Time when saving part or all of your Director movie as QuickTime. Choose Tempo Settings to create a QuickTime movie based on sprites in the Tempo channel of the Score window. Be warned that using regular transitions in the Transition channel and/or Palette transitions help determine a QuickTime mooV's file size and playability. Choose Real Time to duplicate a playback of a movie on Director's Stage running off a specific Mac model to a QuickTime mooV exported to your hard drive.

QuickTime's advantage over Director in playing a movie accurately at various speeds is its built-in routines for dealing with information that changes over time and making necessary adjustments, basically dropping frames. A Director sequence of 30 frames given a tempo setting of 15 frames per second will time out at precisely two seconds in QuickTime, while sync between frames and sound cues is precisely maintained. The same sequence played in Director as sprites on the Stage may or may not play for two seconds, depending on machine type, color depth, and a number of other factors, while sync between sound and action cannot be relied on without anticipating the model fated to play the Director movie.

Director is frame-based while QuickTime is time-based. Big difference. Director will play all frames no matter what, even if it limps to an agonizing crawl on an old, festering Mac. QuickTime keeps a sharp eye on the timer, dropping frames rather than running long or getting picture and sound out of sync.

What color is your pop-up menu?

Set the desired color depth of the final QuickTime mooV. Keep in mind that color depth options are dependent on the chosen codec. For example, after choosing the Animation codec from the Compressor pop-up menu, you'll find a complete choice of color depths under the Colors pop-up menu, as shown in Figure 11-5; choose Graphics for your codec and only 256 colors will be available.

QuickTime Export Options
Frame Rate: Tempo Settings
Real Time
OK
Cancel
Compressor: Black & White
4
Quality: 16
256
High
Colors: ✓Thousands
Millions
Scale: 100%
592 420
Width Height
Sound: Channel 1
Channel 2
Help

Figure 11-5: The Animation codec allows a complete choice of color depths from the Colors pop-up menu.

You can create your QuickTime mooV in black and white, although I don't recommend it. The result is dithered black-and-white frames, possibly justified when considering as wide an audience as possible. There's just one problem. It's ugly.

You can choose 256 colors, which multimedia types call 8-bit color. However, if you remember my rantings in the previous section on codecs, the Graphics codec is specifically engineered to optimize 8-bit QuickTime mooVs.

Anyway, you can move up to thousands of colors or even millions. Keep in mind that QuickTime is optimized for thousands of colors, what developer types call 16-bit color. As tempting as millions of colors sounds, 24-bit QuickTime mooVs make enormous demands on anyone's computer. And doctors agree, based on a five-year survey, only three people in the whole world can tell 16-bit color from 24-bit color, and one of them lives in Siberia.

Scale options

Director gives you one of two scale options. Choose the final scale for your QuickTime mooV from the shadowed Scale pop-up menu, shown in Figure 11-6, or enter Width and Height values manually. (You can also click the little up and down arrows.) That done, Custom automatically appears in the Scale pop-up menu along with a check mark reflecting your hand-chosen Width and Height values.

Custom
200%
150%
✓100%
75%
50%
25%
Other...

Figure 11-6: The Scale pop-up menu in the QuickTime Export Options dialog box.

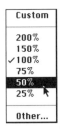

You may also choose Other from the Scale pop-up menu and enter a specific percentage in the Scale dialog box, reproduced in Figure 11-7.

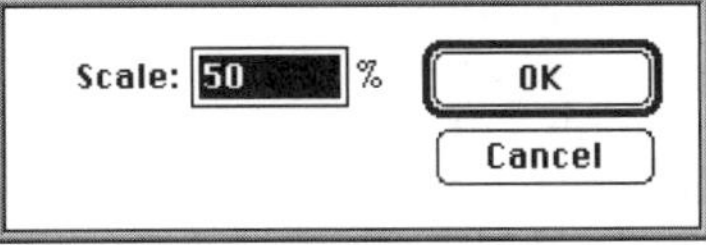

Figure 11-7: The Scale dialog box.

In real life, only a handful of dimensions work well with QuickTime mooVs, all based on the classic 4-to-3 screen ratio inherited from the film industry since the silent screen days, passed on to NTSC TV, and now QuickTime. The proportions of the ubiquitous 13-inch monitor, 640 × 480 pixels, reflects this 4-to-3 ratio; you can derive other dimensions by simply halving these values again and again until you arrive at the stamp-sized QuickTime window that started it all in 1993, a whopping 160 × 120 pixels.

Sound decisions

You may choose to include sound channels along with your animations by clicking the appropriate check boxes. In Figure 11-3, I decided to include both channels of sound with the QuickTime movie. If your Mac doesn't support stereo sound, only one sound check box will be enabled.

How do you export a color Director movie as a gray scale QuickTime mooV? Simple, you don't. In Director, your options are limited to importing the color QuickTime mooV, placing the QuickTime mooV into the Score, and then setting the Palette to Grayscale in the Palette channel of the Score window. Thinking positive, it's relatively easy and all done in Director; the downside is that all other sprites in the same frames turn gray along with the QuickTime mooV until you change palettes. The best way is to turn to a utility program such as MovieShop or a heavy-duty application such as Premiere, open the color QuickTime movie, and then save it as gray scale QuickTime.

Setting up for Real-Time QuickTime mooVs

Use the following steps to prepare your QuickTime mooV for Real-Time playback:

1. **Turn off all Lingo commands by checking Disable Lingo under Director's Edit menu.**
2. **Establish a beginning tempo by double-clicking the Transition channel in frame 1, clicking the Tempo radio button in the Set Tempo dialog box, and sliding the Tempo control to 15 fps, a standard rate for on-screen animation barring high-end equipment, pronounced EXPENSIVE. Click OK.**
3. **Set desired tempos in other frames of the Tempo channel, as in Step 2.**
4. **Set desired transitions in the Transition channel by double-clicking the Transition channel in each frame you decide to place a transition, scroll to the preferred transition in the Set Transition dialog box, and be sure to customize the transition with its specific set of check boxes and other controls, and then click OK.**

5. **Uncheck Loop in the Edit menu.**
6. **Rewind the movie with Command+R.**
7. **Make popcorn.**
8. **Salt and butter popcorn.**
9. **Play the movie with Command+P.**
10. **At the conclusion of the movie, choose File⇨Export.**
11. **Be sure to click QuickTime Options in the Export dialog box and check the Real Time radio button in the QuickTime Export Options dialog box.**
12. **Select an appropriate codec from the Compressor pop-up menu. To review codecs and their uses, jump back to the "Codecs" section earlier in this chapter.**
13. **Make any other desired modifications to Director's default settings in the QuickTime Export Options dialog box.**
14. **Finish exporting your movie.**
15. **Play back your QuickTime movie to test results.**
16. **Clean fingers of salt and butter from popcorn.**

What Good Is an Empty QuickTime Window?

It's time to dive into using QuickTime in Director with the infamous Digital Video window. Just remember that for now, digital video means QuickTime; what it'll mean in the future is anybody's guess.

When you choose Digital Video from the Window menu, surprise! It's blank. That outrageous price that Macromedia wants for Director, and you get a blank window. As blank as Figure 11-8.

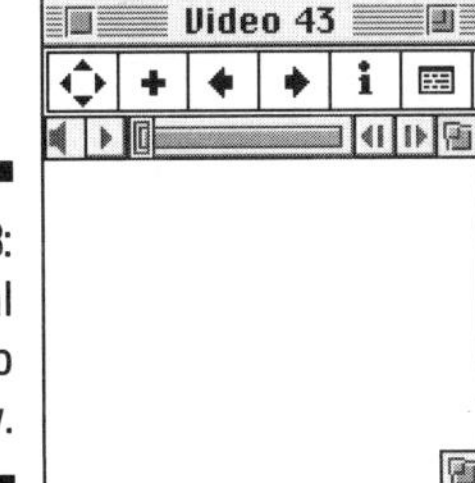

Figure 11-8: The Digital Video window.

Not even a Digital Video menu in the menu bar. Try copying a bitmap and pasting it into the empty Digital Video window; you can't. It's a great practical joke that may keep you entertained for a couple of hours. Then it dawns on you. You realize you *can* use a blank Digital Video window in Director to glue together snippets of imported QuickTime mooVs with the Copy and Paste commands.

By the way, you may open as many Digital Video windows in Director as your memory or RAM allows; more RAM, more windows.

Once you import a QuickTime mooV, you can use all the standard Copy, Paste, and Clear commands under the Edit menu to move, rearrange, and delete QuickTime frames *between* Digital Video windows. Until you get Adobe Premiere or Avid VideoShop, you can copy and paste between Digital Video windows for playback in Director. You may also choose to export your new digital video as a QuickTime mooV.

When you export a Digital Video Cast Member cut and pasted together in Director as a QuickTime file, the result is what we multimedia types call a "flattened" file, meaning all the bits and pieces it took to put the Digital Video Cast Member together in Director are now part of the final QuickTime file, independent of the original QuickTime sources.

Touring the Digital Video window

Take a closer look at that blank Digital Video window. Some of the features look familiar; some are unique to this window. Notice that the top row of buttons duplicates what you find in the Paint window. To review Paint window buttons in depth, take one giant step back to the section, "Now, wait, some of these icons look familiar, eh?" in Chapter 6.

To briefly review these Digital Video window buttons, from left to right, they include the following:

- *Place button*
- *Add button*
- *Previous button*
- *Next button*
- *Info button*
- *Script button*

I lied. One of the buttons is actually fairly unique. Its name is unique, and clicking the button takes you to a window unique to Digital Video Cast Members. Isn't that unique? Of course, I'm speaking of the Digital Video Cast Member Info button as opposed to the run-of-the-mill Cast Member Info button.

Make the distinction clearly in your mind between a Digital Video Cast Member in the Cast window, its sprite placed on the Stage, and its Digital Video window that appears when you double-click the Digital Video Cast Member's thumbnail — three very different views of an imported QuickTime mooV, as shown side-by-side in Figure 11-9. By the way, Figure 11-9 shows an impossible situation in one respect; each window is shown in its active form, when in real life only one of the windows may be active at any one time. Don't let this throw you.

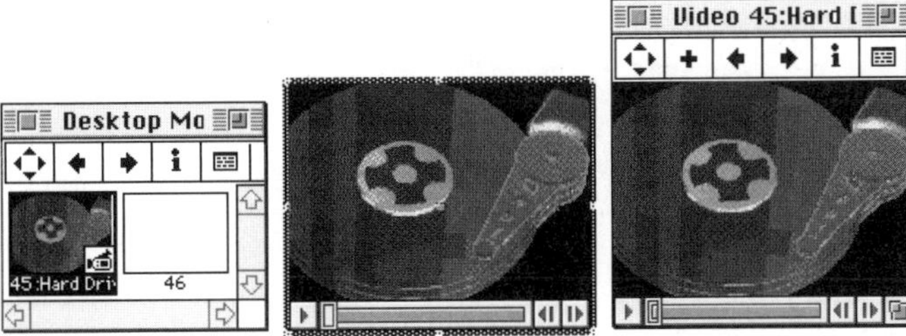

Figure 11-9: The three faces of an imported QuickTime mooV: its Digital Video Cast Member, its sprite on the Stage, and its Digital Video window.

The first view, from left to right in Figure 11-9, shows an imported QuickTime mooV as a Cast Member in the Cast window. Note the row of Cast window buttons at the top, the Cast Member's telltale thumbnail size, its cell number under the thumbnail followed by as much of the name as can show in Geneva 9 point type, and the Digital Video icon in the lower-right corner.

The second view in Figure 11-9 is the Digital Video Cast Member's sprite after placing it on the Stage. Notice the selection rectangle and handles that appear when you select the sprite. Displaying the controller at the bottom of a Digital Video sprite is optional; you may choose to hide it by selecting the Cast Member, clicking the Cast Member Info button, and unchecking the Controller check box.

The third view in Figure 11-9 shows the Digital Video Cast Member's Digital Video window. Display it by double-clicking a Digital Video Cast Member in the Cast window or its sprite on the Stage. Notice the telltale Add button at the top of the window with its distinctive cross icon and the Digital Video's permanent controller. Director doesn't allow you to hide a Digital Video window's controller any more than its Close box, Zoom box, or Resize box.

Setting up your digital video

Click the Digital Video Cast Member Info button and Director takes you to the Digital Video Cast Member Info dialog box, depicted with excruciating accuracy in Figure 11-10.

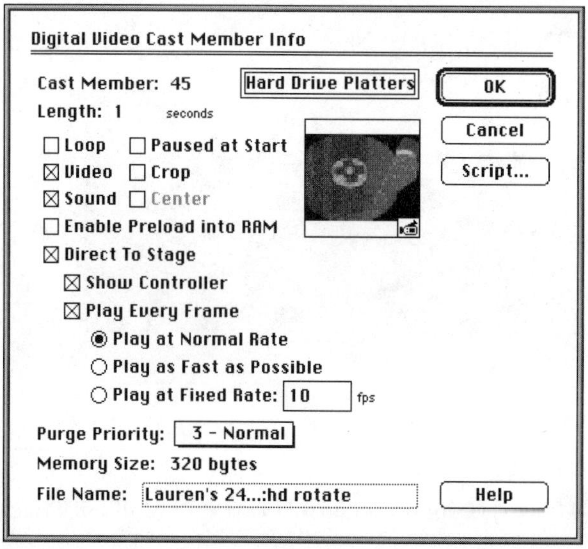

Figure 11-10: The Digital Video Cast Member Info dialog box, offering a number of options for the recreational angler — caught you.

The Digital Video Cast Member Info dialog box gives you important information on a Digital Video Cast Member, including its position in the Cast window. In Figure 11-10, the QuickTime mooV is Digital Video Cast Member 45. To the right, Director gives you the Digital Video Cast Member's name, which may be different from the source file's name on the hard drive; remember, you can name a Cast Member in its Info dialog box. Underneath, you learn the mooV runs for one second. At the bottom, you can read the source file's size in memory, 320 bytes in this case, and the source file's *path* (its address on the hard drive). In addition to all this info, Director offers you the following options at no additional expense:

- *Loop check box:* Check to make the mooV jump from the last frame of the playback, or loop, to frame one and replay, continuing the loop until you click the Stop button.

To stop a QuickTime mooV, press the spacebar. Press the spacebar again to resume playback. By the way, this keyboard shortcut works with most QuickTime-related programs.

- *Paused at Start check box:* Check to keep the QuickTime sprite from automatically playing when it appears on the Stage; you can then click the Play button on the controller at any time. With the check box unchecked, Director plays the QuickTime sprite when it appears on the Stage.
- *Video check box:* Check to show the QuickTime sprite on playback. An unchecked Video check box hides the QuickTime sprite, except for the controller when you check its check box in this same dialog box. With only the controller showing, you can still click the Play button to play any sound imported with the source QuickTime mooV.
- *Crop check box:* Check to turn the QuickTime sprite's *bounding box* (its outline that highlights when you select the sprite) into a frame showing more or less of the sprite as you drag the bounding box by a selection handle into various dimensions. If the sprite's controller is set to be visible, you can crop out the controller along with part of the image. If this box is unchecked, dragging a QuickTime sprite's selection handle simply resizes the sprite; press Shift and drag a selection handle to resize proportionally. Regain a sprite's original size by choosing Stage➪Sprite Info and clicking the Restore to Size of Cast Member radio button.
- *Sound check box:* Check to enable any soundtracks embedded in the QuickTime sprite.
- *Center check box:* When the Crop check box is unchecked, Director disables the Center option, as in Figure 11-10. Once you check Crop, the Center check box becomes enabled. Then you can check this option to center the QuickTime sprite in the dimensions of its bounding box.
- *Enable Preload into RAM:* Checking this box automatically issues a Lingo command, `preLoadCast`, that initiates the copying process into memory before Director plays the QuickTime sprite.

  Director has two ways to call up QuickTime information from the source file to play back on the Stage. The slower way is to read one frame of the source file from disk, display the frame on the Stage, read the next frame, display it, and so on. The faster method is to copy the entire source file into memory or, in a limited memory situation, copy as much of the file as possible to memory and then play the mooV from memory. The faster method is where the Enable Preload into RAM check box comes in to play.

  Be sure to uncheck the Enable Preload into RAM check box when you anticipate or need to assume a low memory situation.

When you import a QuickTime mooV, Director always sets up the source QuickTime mooV as a *linked* file; the Digital Video Cast Member that appears in the Cast window refers to the external QuickTime mooV on your hard drive when you play back the QuickTime sprite in the Stage window.

- *Direct To Stage:* Checking this box forces Director to play the QuickTime sprite at the highest layer, regardless of its real channel position in the Score.

Each frame of a Director movie contains 48 channels to work with, like transparent layers one on top of the other. Channel 1 is the furthest back, like a background layer; channel 48 is the closest layer to you. Playing QuickTime in the closest or highest channel maximizes playback speed because Director doesn't have to deal with the possibility of calculating the effect of other sprites overlapping the QuickTime sprite.

Two rules are associated with this option. One, no other sprites can be in higher channels in the Score when calling on this option, and two, the only acceptable ink type is the default ink, Copy. In other words, when you need to apply a custom ink type to a QuickTime sprite, or you want other sprites overlapping or crossing a QuickTime sprite in your animation, don't use Direct To Stage. You may cause the magnetic fields of the North and South Pole to swap places, causing havoc throughout the world and some really bad traffic jams.

- *Show Controller:* Only enabled after you check the Direct To Stage check box, the Show Controller check box displays a QuickTime mooV's controller, the subject of the next section.

- *Play Every Frame check box:* The Play Every Frame check box becomes enabled when you check the Direct To Stage check box. Check the Play Every Frame radio button to force QuickTime to play every frame in he mooV.

QuickTime is a so-called time-based file format, meaning its mission by default is to play a mooV at the proper duration and maintain sync between picture and soundtrack. The basic technique for accomplishing its mission is to drop frames when required. The Play Every Frame option allows you change its mission.

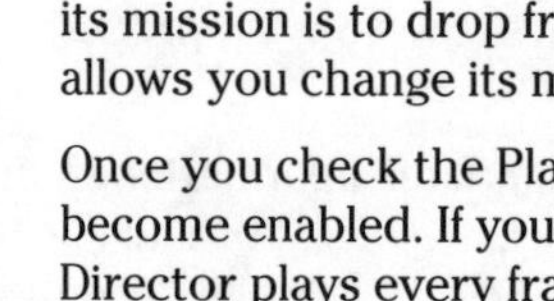

Once you check the Play Every Frame check box, three radio buttons become enabled. If you check the Play at Normal Rate radio button, Director plays every frame of the mooV, attempting to stay at its set frame rate. Check the Play as Fast as Possible radio button so that Director plays every frame at the fastest frame rate available with your Mac's *CPU* (the central processing unit chip, the brains of your Mac), amount of memory, and all other factors contributing to its maximum performance level. Check the Play at Fixed Rate radio button and enter a value in the *fps* (frames per second) entry box to have Director play every frame and do its best to play the frames per second rate you entered.

The Play at Fixed Rate radio button option only works properly when the entire QuickTime mooV plays at the same frame rate. Some mooVs vary frame rate from sequence to sequence, or you may decide to create such a mooV.

- *Purge Priority pop-up menu:* Choose one of the Purge Priority options, as shown in Figure 11-11, for the Digital Video Cast Member.

Figure 11-11: The Purge Priority pop-up menu.

Purge Priority: ✓3 - Normal
2 - Next
1 - Last
0 - Never

For detailed info on Purge Priority options, jump back to the section, "Cast Member Info button," in Chapter 4.

Controlling your digital video

Back to the Digital Video window. The really unique area of this window is the second row of controls. These controls are actually a standard QuickTime feature called, of all things, the controller. QuickTime movies usually appear with the controller, although you can hide it in most programs, including Director. Notice how similar the controller buttons are to VCR or remote control buttons. From left to right, the controller features the following:

- *Sound Control:* Press to adjust the sound, from off to full volume, with a sliding control. Sound may be adjusted during QuickTime mooV playback. If no slider appears when you press the Sound Control button, the original QuickTime mooV has no soundtrack, or it wasn't imported along with the graphics for any of 5,392 reasons.
- *Play and Stop:* Click to begin mooV playback. On playback, the button changes its icon to a square and functions as the Stop button.
- *Scroll Bar:* Press and drag to the right to fast forward or to the left to fast rewind as with the shuttle control on some VCRs.
- *Step reverse control:* Moves the QuickTime mooV back one frame for each click of the mouse.
- *Step forward control:* Moves the QuickTime mooV forward one frame for each click of the mouse.
- *Resize box:* Like the Resize box on most Macintosh windows. Press and drag to manually resize the Digital Video window's dimensions.

If you don't want to assume the person viewing the mooV knows how to use a QuickTime controller, either include a Help area somewhere on-screen or hide the controller by unchecking the Show Controller check box and include a custom Play Movie button somewhere on-screen that plays the QuickTime mooV.

Unfortunately, there's no simple Play command for QuickTime mooVs in Director. Following is a method for playing a QuickTime mooV from a button that avoids a lot of Lingo scripting. It looks like a lot of work, but the whole process goes pretty quickly when you're really setting it up.

Playing QuickTime Lite

First, you need to set up a new Digital Video Cast Member in the Cast window that has only the first frame of the mooV you'd like to play.

Setting up your window

1. **Choose Window⇨Cast and double-click the QuickTime mooV you'd like to play to bring up its Digital Video Cast Member window.**
2. **Click the Info button and check that the Paused at Start check box is *not* checked.**
3. **Click OK.**
4. **Choose Edit⇨Copy Video.**

   Basically, you've copied the first frame of the mooV, known as the *poster* since it acts as a preview image for the file, to the Clipboard.
5. **Click the Add button in the Digital Video Cast Member window to display a blank Digital Video Cast Member window and choose Edit⇨Paste Video.**
6. **In the Save As dialog box that appears, name the new mooV something original, like "Poster," using the Directory window, select the location where you'd like to save the file, and click Save.**

Preparing the Score

Now you need to set things up in the Score window.

1. **Using the Score window's playback head, move to the frame where you'd like to insert a QuickTime mooV.**

   Remember the frame number and the channel. You'll use the same channel throughout the rest of these steps.

2. **Drag your mooV from the Cast window to the Score, noting the channel number.**

   Of course, placing your mooV in the Score also centers the mooV on the Stage.

3. **While the mooV is highlighted in the Score, choose Edit⇨Copy Cells.**
4. **Highlight the frame that is two frames to the right of the frame you chose in Step 1 and choose Edit⇨Paste Cells.**
5. **In the Cast window, highlight the original full-framed QuickTime mooV.**
6. **Choose Score⇨Switch Cast Members.**
7. **Highlight the original mooV in the Score, noting its frame number, and choose Edit⇨Copy Cells.**

   The next part's a little dicey. You need to guess approximately how many frames your animation runs. For example, if your movie's running at 15 *fps* (frames per second), and you guess that the QuickTime mooV runs for 3 seconds, that's 45 frames.

8. **Guess the number of frames your QuickTime mooV takes and add that number to the frame number you noted in Step 7.**
9. **Whatever number you arrive at in Step 8, highlight that frame and choose Edit⇨Paste Cells.**

   You're preparing to use the In-Between Linear command in the Score menu.

10. **Press Shift and click the first copy of the full-framed mooV to select the range of frames you guessed the mooV would take to play completely.**
11. **Choose Score⇨In-Between Linear.**

Adding a little Lingo

Remember, I said that these steps avoid *a lot* of Lingo; it's hard to avoid it altogether.

1. **Return to the frame where your mooV is, noting the frame number, and double-click the Script channel in the same frame.**
2. **Type** go to this frame **and click the Script window's Close box.**

   When you play the Director movie, this line of Lingo locks you in this frame until another command tells Director to do something else.
3. **Choose Window⇨Tools and select the basic Button tool.**

   For more on the Tools window, page back to Chapter 9.
4. **Drag out a button at the bottom of the Stage and enter a name for the button where you see the blinking insertion point: for example,** Play Movie.
5. **Double-click the thick gray border of the selected button to open its window and click the Script button at the top of the window.**
6. **In the button's Script window, type** go to frame.
7. **Add a space and then the number of the frame where the real full-framed QuickTime mooV begins; click the Close box.**

Testing it out

Now you're ready to test your work.

1. **Choose Edit⇨Play.**

   What should happen? Your Director movie should play to the frame where your QuickTime mooV (in this example, "Poster") appears. Director waits until you press the button you created (in this example, "Play Movie"). When you finally do decide to press the button, the Lingo command hidden in the button jumps you to the full QuickTime mooV and plays to its conclusion, *providing* you guessed correctly about the number of frames it would take. If you didn't guess correctly, go to Step 2.
2. **Add some additional frames to the set of duplicate frames allowing your mooV to play to completion and retest.**

Using Director as a QuickTime Editor

If you don't have an honest-to-gosh QuickTime editing program such as Adobe Premiere, Avid VideoShop, or several other fine software packages on the market, you can use Director itself as a QuickTime editing application. Of course, Director isn't meant to be solely a QuickTime editor, so don't expect to replicate all the wondrous special effects you've heard about with dedicated QuickTime editing programs; but for basic editing, cutting, and pasting, Director works just fine. In fact, in a way it offers some features those fancy editing programs lack.

To use Director as a QuickTime editor, you need to start with some QuickTime. In other words, opening the Paint window, creating a masterpiece on a blank easel, copying it to the Clipboard, and trying to paste your graphic into a blank Digital Video window just doesn't work. Try it if you don't believe me. Gjeeeech.

Start from scratch

Remember that old saying about where there's a will . . . Just as soon as the words leave my lips (that is, my keyboard), I find myself backtracking on them a bit. Director actually does provide a way to create a QuickTime mooV from scratch — in a roundabout way, but it works! For example, you decide to develop an animation sequence in Director, maybe the old-fashioned way, one drawing at a time, making small, incremental changes to your actors (or sprites, as we Director-types call them) from frame to frame. You build your sequence over the days, the weeks, the months. You forget to make your car payment; they tow your car away. You build your sequence. Your spouse leaves you; your children run away. You build your sequence, fine-tuning each frame to perfection until you have ten frames Disney would be proud of. Sure, you've sacrificed a little, but hey, that's the path of the artiste.

Anyway, you've got your ten frames. Then again, perhaps you're not so dedicated and you decide to use Director's Auto-Animate features discussed later in Chapter 16. You build an animated bullet chart Disney would be proud of. The topics fly in; the bullets fly in. Full color, stereo sound, with just a couple of clicks of the mouse. You seriously consider CinemaScope, but finally pass on that one. Either way, one drawing at a time or taking advantage of Director's built-in animation capabilities, you build your ten frames. Then you realize what makes the darned thing so powerful is the sync between graphics and sound. Now, you *did* swipe that musical intro from *Star Trek: The Next Generation,* so you'll be spending some big time in a maximum security federal penitentiary, but you're an artiste, willing to sacrifice a little for your art. A few years in the slammer's nothing compared to building ten great frames Disney would be proud of.

What I'm trying to say is, Director is a frame-based application. With a lot of tweaking and perspiration, you can make graphics and sound sync pretty well together. Wondrous as Director is however — kiss, kiss — Director's just not designed to do the job as well as QuickTime. QuickTime is time-based, bone-deep. Apple developed QuickTime to play at a user-set rate, to stay in sync with any accompanying soundtracks, and to drop frames if necessary in order to accomplish its mission, should it so choose to accept. Impossible, you say? No, QuickTime works very well indeed for synchronizing graphics with soundtracks. So why not export your ten frames as a QuickTime mooV, resolve any sync problems and, if you want to stay with Director as the software "engine," simply import your QuickTime mooV back into a Director movie? Now you have the best of both worlds for your editing pleasure, QuickTime's time-based technology and Director's interactive capabilities.

Prebuilt QuickTime

Another way to use Director's built-in QuickTime editing features is to start with some prebuilt QuickTime. A list of sources might include the following:

- *Your own digital videos:* That's what AV Macs are all about, complete with Video In and Video Out ports, Stereo Sound In and Out ports, a *DSP* (Digital Signal Processor) chip on the system board, along with other special architecture to digitize *analog video* (your videotapes) into digital info that your Mac understands and that Director can display in a Digital Video window. Power Mac versions of AV models offer all the above, plus three to four times the performance. More powerful models are coming up, and finally, Mac AV clones are tiptoeing onto the market.
- *Freeware and shareware QuickTime mooVs:* You say you don't have a camcorder, a VCR, or talent? All the major commercial bulletin boards, such as America Online, CompuServe, and Prodigy, have tons of QuickTime mooVs for you to *download* (copy via a modem to your Mac). And don't forget the Internet. Many mooVs are freeware with unlimited usage rights granted you by the originator, with or without sword touched to the shoulder; other files may be shareware-style files where you're obliged to send in a relatively low fee for ownership and/or usage, or perhaps a licensing fee per one-time usage of the mooV based on the honor system. In these legally combative times, it's important to read all fine print and completely understand the contract you're agreeing to before adopting someone else's work to your own.

Freeware doesn't necessarily translate into "no strings attached." Always read the fine print. How do you think I wound up getting married twice?

- *QuickTime mooVs on floppy and CD-ROM media:* Countless sources of third-party commercial QuickTime mooVs and still images on floppies are on the market. Better yet, purchase a CD full of QuickTime. A CD-ROM disc can store up to 650 megabytes of info, and its shelf life is yours, give or take a year or two. Assuming that the image and sound quality is high, prices for CD-ROM collections are usually very reasonable. Again, check and double-check usage rights before you purchase anything. My recommendation is to look for unlimited usage to get your full money's worth, unless you just can't live without that CD full of one-time usage kitties lapping up milk, ripping sofas, sinking needle-sharp, little fangs into toes, et cetera, et cetera.

A QuickTime edit

OK, say your client, Mr. Big, wants you to re-edit some scenes from a couple of QuickTime mooVs and make Director the QuickTime "engine" that plays the digital video. Mr. Big wants to use Director because he has plans for you to add some animation and interactivity to the project in about a month from now. Here's a basic plan I recommend following:

Setting up

1. **At the Desktop, make a project folder by choosing File⇨New Folder.**
2. **Name the folder.**

   Typing *ƒ* at the end of a folder name has become something of a Macintosh convention. If you like the look, just type Option+F to add the swash letter *f* to the name of your folders. It's also useful, identifying a folder in a directory list without any icons to go by.

3. **Drag your QuickTime mooVs into the folder.**

   Figure 11-12 shows a couple of QuickTime mooVs, Hard Drive CU.mooV and HD Platters.mooV, ready for editing.

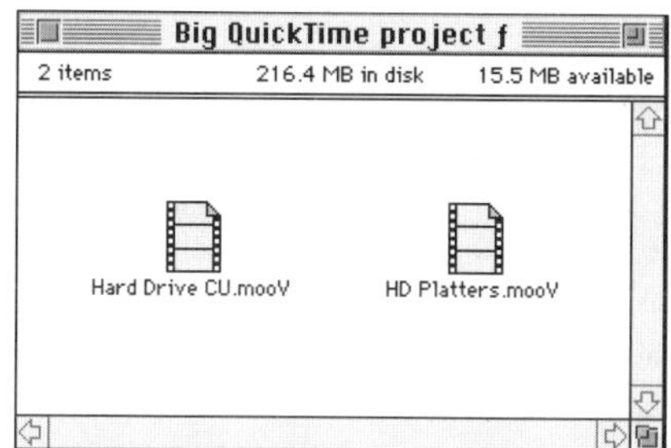

Figure 11-12: Two QuickTime mooVs in their own project folder on the Desktop.

By the way, CU stands for close-up, as in "I'm ready for my close-up, Mr. DeMille."

Importing the QuickTime mooVs

1. **Highlight Director's icon at the Desktop.**
2. **Choose File⇨Open or simply double-click Director's icon.**
3. **When you arrive at Director's blank Stage window, choose File⇨Import.**
4. **In the Import dialog box, click Desktop.**
5. **From the Type pop-up menu, choose QuickTime Movie.**

   Your view should look something like Figure 11-13.

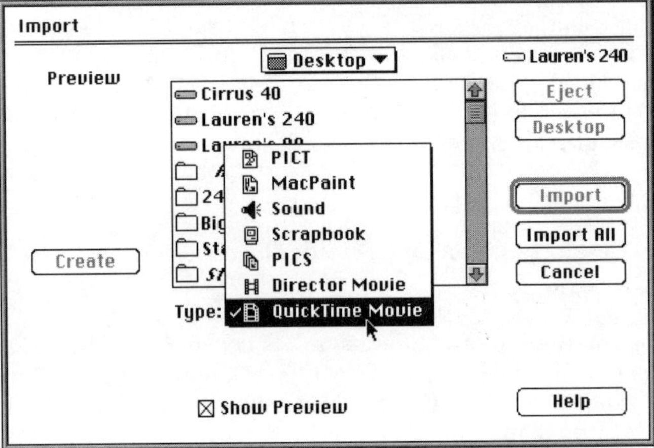

Figure 11-13: Selecting QuickTime Movie from the Type pop-up menu in Director's Import dialog box.

Selecting the right file type from the Type pop-up menu in the Import dialog box is very important. Not choosing QuickTime results in hiding the very files you're looking for in the directory.

Notice the absence of a Link To File check box under the directory in the Import dialog box after you choose QuickTime from the Type pop-up menu. This is because Director imports each QuickTime file as a *linked file,* meaning its content doesn't become incorporated into the Director file. Only a link pointing to the source file is established; when playing a Digital Video sprite, Director reads QuickTime data from the original file in the project folder on the Desktop.

6. **Double-click the project folder in the directory.**

7. **If you want to import more than one QuickTime mooV into Director, be lazy and click Import All.**

   Clicking the Import All button in the Import dialog box automatically imports all files shown in the open folder in the directory window. Director returns you to the Stage, where you find the Cast window with your Digital Video Cast Members in place, as in Figure 11-14.

Figure 11-14: Digital Video Cast Members in the Cast window after being imported.

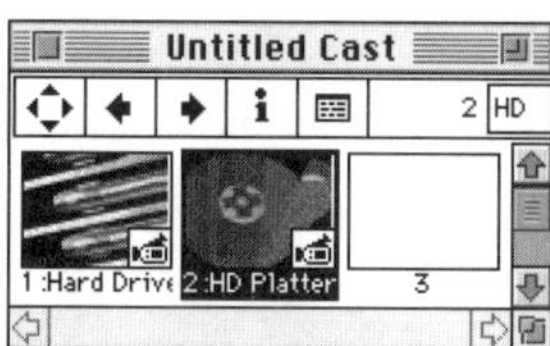

Notice the tiny Digital Video icon in the lower-right corner of each thumbnail.

Displaying the Cast Members' Digital Video windows

1. **Double-click the first Cast Member to display its Digital Video window.**

2. **Press Option and double-click the second Cast Member to add its Digital Video window to the screen.**

   Why the Option key? If you simply double-click the second Cast Member, it replaces the first Cast Member in the current Digital Video window, and you wind up with only one Digital Video window, which probably isn't what you want at this point.

3. **Drag the visible Digital Video window by its Title Bar so that you expose the first Cast Member's window.**

   By now, if you have the traditional 13-inch screen, you're already running out of real estate (room). In PageMaker, if you've ever used it, you can use a special technique for resizing bitmaps called *magic stretching* that pops the bitmaps into small set of optimized dimensions. You can use a similar technique in Director to resize Digital Video windows when running out of room.

4. **While pressing Shift, press the Resize box of the first Digital Video window.**

5. **While pressing Shift and the Resize box, press Option and drag into the center of the window.**

   The window will snap to a smaller set of proportional dimensions. Why not simply press Shift and Option together? You wind up with Director's Help cursor, and after pressing the mouse, you'll suddenly find yourself in the Help system.

6. **Continue dragging into the center of the window until it snaps to one size smaller, and then release the mouse.**
7. **Repeat steps 4 through 6 to resize the second Digital Video window.**

Now that the two Digital Video windows are one-fourth their original size, you should have plenty of extra room on-screen.

Making a new Digital Video window

1. **Press Option and click the second window's New button (with the + icon) to display a new Digital Video window.**

   Pressing Option and clicking the New button in the Digital Video window creates a new blank Digital Video window so that you wind up with three Digital Video windows on-screen.

2. **Magic stretch (see the preceding section) the blank Digital Video window and assemble all three windows as in Figure 11-15.**

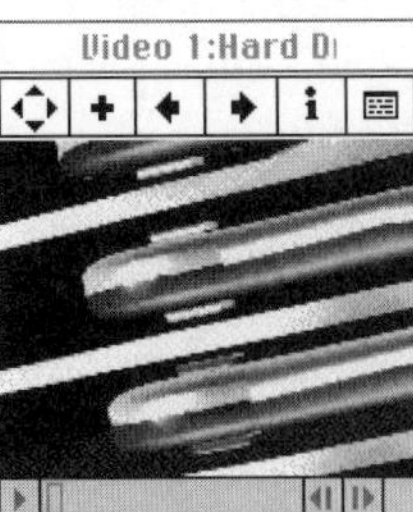

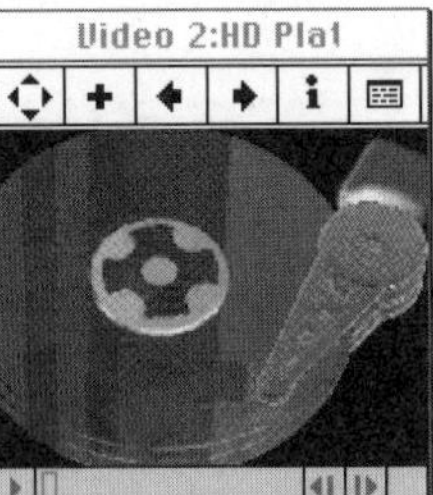

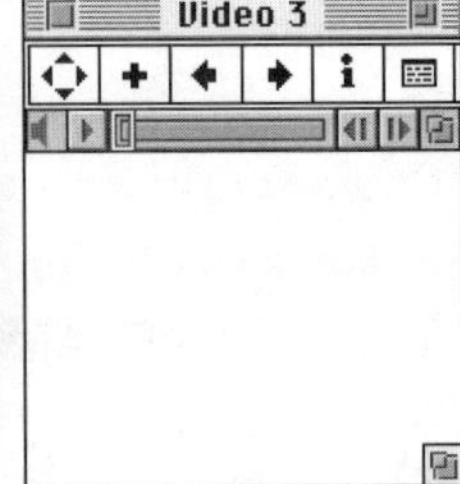

Figure 11-15: Three Digital Video windows lined up in preparation for digital editing in Director.

Editing together a new Digital Video Cast Member

1. **To select a range of frames, press Shift and drag your mooV's scroll bar in the controller, as in Figure 11-16.**

   Notice that the selected range appears black in the Controller.

2. **Choose Edit⇨Copy Video to copy the selected frames to the Clipboard.**
3. **Click in the empty Digital Video window to make it the active window.**
4. **Choose Edit⇨Paste Video.**

   As soon as you choose Paste Video, Director automatically presents you with the Save As dialog box, depicted in Figure 11-17, so you can save the new QuickTime mooV to your hard drive.

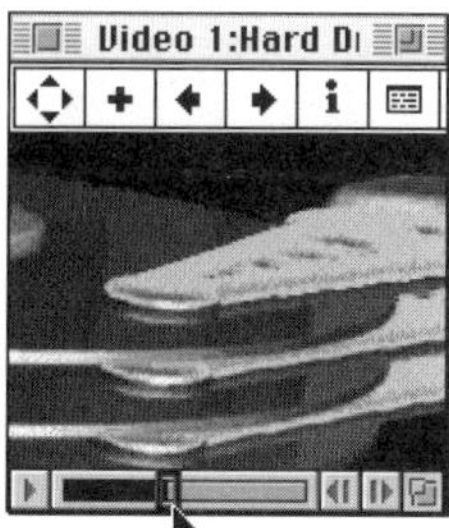

Figure 11-16: Selecting a range of frames in a Digital Video window by pressing Shift and dragging the controller's scroll bar.

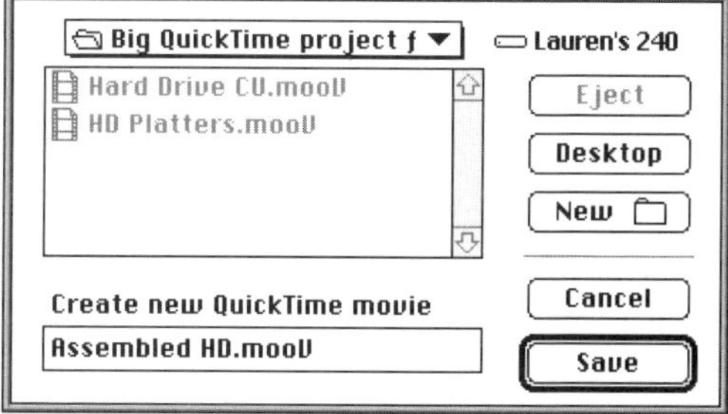

Figure 11-17: Director presents you with the Save As dialog box after you paste video into a new Digital Video window.

5. **Enter a name for the new file and click OK.**

QuickTime mooVs always import as linked files, so they can be shared among a number of Director movies without adding to the size of your complete presentation. Also, edits you make to QuickTime mooVs with other programs such as Premiere will be automatically updated in Director because the QuickTime files are linked to their Director documents.

From here on, it's just a matter of more cutting and pasting, and you can edit together your new QuickTime mooV in Director, using the mooV exclusively in the Director file or using the new QuickTime mooV in the project folder in some other application or even another Director movie.

Chapter 12

And the Winner of Script of the Year: The Script Window

In This Chapter

- Learning Lingo
- Creating a script
- Adding a script to a movie

No doubt about it. There's excitement in the air. The crowd's restless, the fans are pushing, shoving, scratching, and straining to get autographs. Eyes flashing, flashbulbs bulbing. I've never seen anything like it. For tonight's the night all bits and bytes have been waiting for. Dressed in their little tuxedos and sequined evening gowns, the royalty of Macdom has convened once more in their annual ritual of mutual backpatting.

Now is the moment. The envelope is torn. We're always tearing the envelope. Pouty lips mouth incomprehensible words among the rising din of apprehension. And, what's that? Yes, the winner is of script of the year is . . . the Script window!

Well, it's all over now until another 1,892,160,000 ticks pass by. There's nothing left but streamers tossed carelessly to the floor, a rainbow of confetti strewn in the aisles, here and there an empty champagne glass. Wait, there's not an empty champagne glass, pardon me.

By the way, Macs keep time in ticks per second (60 ticks per second).

So, the Script window won, again. And why not. It's one of the more important windows Director has to offer. In fact, the Script window and the scripts it contains are the keys to Director's interactive possibilities. Scripts are important themselves because they're snippets of text containing Lingo commands. Lingo is Director's built-in programming language that you can use to do really neat things.

Did You Happen To Notice That New Lingo Menu?

When you open the Paint window, Director gives you a Paint menu in the menu bar. When you open the color Palettes window, Director gives you a Palette window in the menu bar. So when you open the Script window, what do you get? The Lingo menu?

I guess with some twisted logic it all makes sense. Come to think of it, having a Lingo menu appear makes a lot of sense, since Lingo is what you enter in a Script window. By the way, Lingo is Director's built-in programming language. Hey, come back.

Whatever you do, don't miss the last section in this chapter. I walk you through writing a couple of scripts, and believe it or not, you live to tell about it. One night a long time from now, you'll gather your grandchildren around by a crackling fireplace and tell them how you once wrote two scripts in Director and survived; see what you'll miss. But it doesn't have to stop there. Plenty of scripting awaits you. If you find your hands quivering, read my little pep talk further down in this chapter called "Scripts: The Secret Sauce of Interactive Multimedia." Then jump back here to explore the Lingo menu, captured with whimsical precision in Figure 12-1.

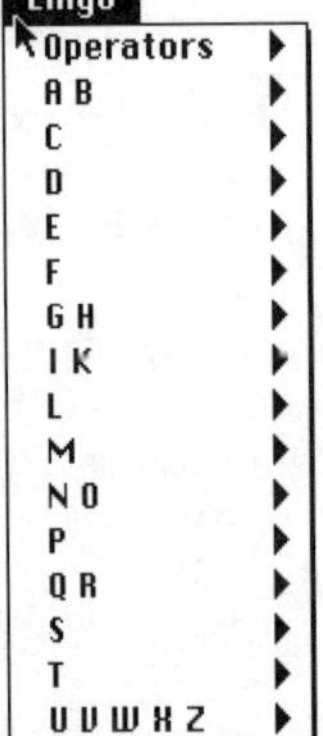

Figure 12-1: Lingo's Operators and commands revealed under the Lingo menu.

Lingo operators don't exist alone. You add them to a Lingo script to contribute to the meaning of the script, basically guiding Director to do what you want the program to do. Slide the mouse over to the Operator submenu and take a peek at Lingo's operators. Notice the operator my pointer has highlighted in Figure 12-2.

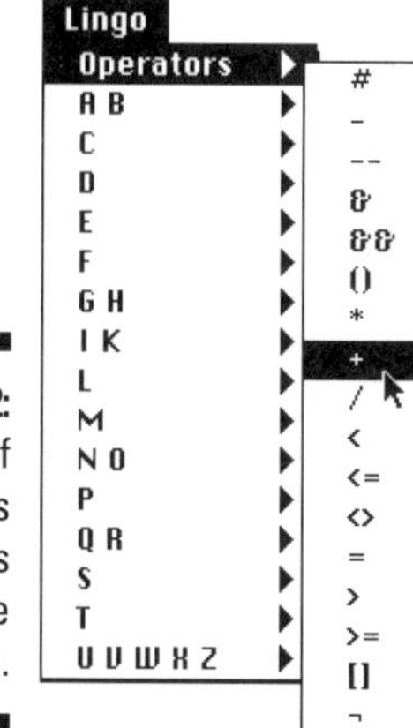

Figure 12-2: The list of Lingo's operators under the Lingo menu.

The operator is the old + sign — as in 1 + 1 = 2. And how about the = sign? Another operator. See, you've been using operators all your life; Director just collectively calls them operators, puts them together in a submenu, and scares the heck out of a few of you, as if jumping out of a closet and shouting, "Boo." Don't let Director get away with that.

Director organizes the rest of Lingo alphabetically under more submenus. To make your selection, simply slide the mouse down the pull-down menu to the letter of interest and drag horizontally to the submenu that appears. Most of these other menu options are Lingo commands, statements that tell Director to take some specific action such as *beep, delete,* and *go.* Words that look suspiciously like verbs tend to be Lingo commands.

A few of the items are what Lingo types call *properties.* A property helps to describe a Lingo object, such as a button. For example, say you select a button tool from the Tools window and draw a button on the Stage. (If you feel like reviewing button tools, jump back to Chapter 9.) While a Director movie is playing, a button may be highlighted or not highlighted. By the way, in Lingo, we spell highlight as "hilite." A button's "hilitedness" is one property of the button; Lingo types refer to this property as *the hilite of button* followed by the button name in quotes. That's all a property is. Knowing a lot about an object's set of properties helps define the object, just as describing your hair color, eye color, skin color, and shape of face helps to define you.

I hope you see that Lingo isn't so scary after all. It may be something new to you and some concepts may strike you as more difficult than others. But you can see that the whole set of Lingo stuff fits under the Lingo menu. Most of the items are commands, most of the rest are properties. Child's play. Can someone find me a child, quick? I talk lots more about Lingo stuff in Chapters 17 and 23.

Where Good Scripts Go

If the Script window isn't visible, check to see whether your eyes are closed. Otherwise, choose Window⇨Script from Director's menu bar. Director presents the Script window to you, looking amazingly like Figure 12-3.

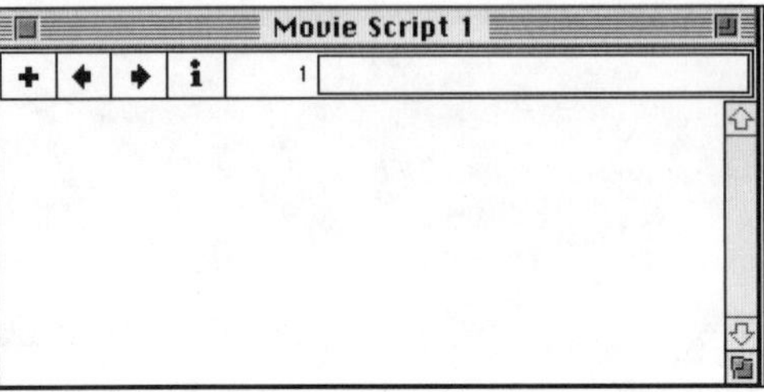

Figure 12-3: The Script window, where good scripts go when they try.

The Script window has all the accoutrements of a basic Mac window: the Close box in the upper-left corner, the Zoom box in the upper right, a Resize box in the lower-right corner, and an area on the right set aside for a scroll bar.

In addition, just above the scroll bar area is a Name panel in a black frame that displays the name of the current script. In Figure 12-1, it's blank. Just to the left is a number 1, meaning the script waiting to be entered is destined to be Script Cast Member 1.

On the left, beneath the Title Bar, you find a row of buttons. From left to right, they include the

- *New Script button:* After you enter a script in a blank Script window, you can click the New Script button to display a new Script window. You can have as many Script windows open as you like, limited only by the amount of memory you have installed in your Mac.
- *Previous Script button:* Each script has its own ID number that reflects its position in the Cast window. Clicking the Previous Script button takes you to, lo and behold, the previous script. Nothing could be simpler, and nothing could be finer than to be in Carolina in the mo-oh-orning.
- *Next Script button:* Clicking the Next Script button takes you to the following script.
- *Script Cast Member Info button:* Clicking the Script Cast Member Info button takes you to the Script Cast Member Info dialog box, shown in Figure 12-4.

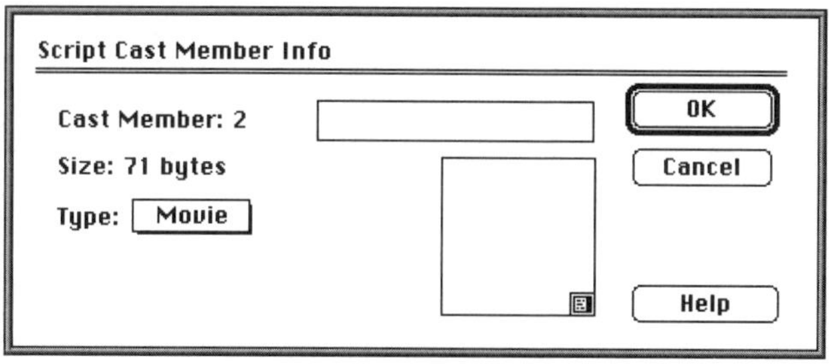

Script Cast Member Info

Cast Member: 2

Size: 71 bytes

Type: Movie

OK

Cancel

Help

Figure 12-4: Click the Info button in a Script window to go to the Script Cast Member Info dialog box.

In the Script Cast Member Info dialog box, you find the Script Cast Member number, the Script Cast Member's size in bytes, and preview box of the script's contents, with the distinctive Script Cast Member icon in the lower-right corner. In the top entry box, you can enter a name for the Script Cast Member.

In the lower-left corner, notice the Type pop-up menu. Clicking the pop-up menu reveals options for two kinds of scripts, shown in Figure 12-5.

Figure 12-5: The Type pop-up menu in the Script Cast Member Info dialog box.

The Type pop-up menu in the Script Cast Member Info dialog box is the key to making what Director types call a movie script, meaning a Script window that contains a set of commands intended to be available anytime during playback of a Director movie. Movie scripts are often initialization-type scripts, too, that set up the movie on startup. Movie scripts may check the type of computer running the movie, set the color depth of the monitor as well as other critical values such as the sound level and the beginning palette from a number of different Palette Cast Members, and generally prepare the movie for optimum playback.

The other option under the Type pop-up menu, Score, refers to scripts found in the Script channel of the Score window that activate only when the playback head enters or exits a particular frame during playback. For example, a Score script in Frame 15 may kick in a timing routine that jumps the playback head forward 10 frames to a special animation sequence if you don't press the mouse or a key on the keyboard within 30 seconds of reaching Frame 15.

For another example, a Score script placed in frame 10 may read `go to frame 1`, causing the playback head to jump back repeatedly to the first frame of the Director movie so that the movie *loops,* or repeats, until some special condition is met. For a thorough discussion of Score window features, hop back to Chapter 5. For a thorough discussion of conditions, read *The Physicians' Handy Desk Reference.* Boy, are there a lot of conditions. Some are really disgusting.

Scripts: The Secret Sauce of Interactive Multimedia

If your main interest in purchasing Director and reading this book is taking advantage of Director's interactive features, sooner or later you need to take the plunge and face the terror of terrors. Right, I'm talking about . . . *programming!*

Gu, ghaa, du, uh, ormpf

Programming. For the technically challenged, the very thought turns flesh and blood hands to jello, voices to high-pitched squeaks, and normally intelligible adults to zombie-like nightcrawlers uttering phrases like, "Gu, ghaa, du, uh, ormpf." I know, I've been there. I know the cold beads of sweat breaking across the forehead, the trembling hand turning to the chapter on code, programming, scripts, variables, and so on.

There's an old saying I just made up. Sometimes you can be your own worst enemy. This thing about scripting is a perfect example. Think about it. Out there in real life, thousands and thousands of people no smarter than you are making a good living at scripting. They buy a nice home, drive a great car, find the perfect spouse; people think they're smart. And all because they do scripting. The only difference between them and you is they're them and you're you. Also, they've broken past that invisible barrier that exists only in the mind.

If you think learning Lingo's hard, try English

If all I've said so far hasn't touched you, consider this. Humans are born to use language. Somehow it's in our genes. Learning English — which I'm still working on, personally — means learning thousands of words and gosh knows how many rules about how to meaningfully put these words together in an infinite number of ways. Do you see my point? Learning English was a monumental accomplishment. Learning a language like Lingo, the key to scripting, involves learning a list of commands, that fits under one menu in Director's menu bar, and a handful of other concepts. Child's play. And remember, adding scripts to your movies is the key to all those interactive goodies. So, find me a three year-old child, and we'll begin scripting.

No, Mother, I want to do it myself

Just because you want to use Director's interactive features doesn't necessarily mean that you have to write all the scripts yourself. You can do a number of things to make your scripting life easier.

Ready-made scripts

A number of scripts are *out there* for you to use, requiring only the most rudimentary knowledge of how a script should look and where to place one in your Director movie. Where do find these scripts? Well, in this book for one. Although my intention in this book is only to give you a friendly nudge in the scripting direction, I do include some sample scripts you're welcome to use. In Appendix B, I recommend free and commercial resources available to you. Of course, Macromedia includes a full set of demos and tutorial files on all of Director's features, including Lingo, with the purchase of Director. Be sure to study them, not only for scripting but also for graphic and interface design. And don't forget the technical support Macromedia includes with your purchase of Director. A veritable bonanza of technical staff is eagerly awaiting your call with bated breath.

Simple scripts

After you overcome any negative mind-set interfering with the learning process, work on grasping scripting fundamentals and try writing some easy scripts. Believe it not, the most frequently used scripts are often extraordinarily simple. Take the go command, one of the most frequently used Lingo commands. Tack on the word "to" and a frame number, and you've created a powerful line of Lingo that jumps the user from one frame to another of your choosing. I discuss this option in more detail in Chapter 17.

User groups

Macintosh and Director user groups meet on a regular basis throughout the states with enormously generous members more than willing to help you through tough scripting problems. It's a place to receive and share information, make contacts and some friends, and keep in touch with what's going on in the rest of the multimedia world.

One of the most famous user groups is BMUG, Berkeley Macintosh User Group, listed in Appendix B. BMUG holds frenetic, high-energy meetings and has tons of freeware and shareware software on floppies and CD-ROM, with a software directory that looks more like the telephone book for greater New York. If you're unlucky enough to not live anywhere near Northern California, call User Group Locator at 800-538-9696 for a user group in your area. They'll even help you start your own user group with a free User Group starter kit.

Bulletin boards

Both commercial and private bulletin boards abound in the ether, both with sample scripts, utility software, roundtable discussions, and technical help for scripting wannabes. The Internet, America's newest love affair, offers tons of resources for Director scripting and technical aid, not to mention the likes of America Online, CompuServe, and Prodigy. You just might wind up cybertalking with Mr. Macromedia Director himself: Marc Cantor. By the way, these resources are listed in the Appendix B, too.

Scripters

Without being facetious, I suggest that you hire a scripter. My goal in this book is two-forked, which makes eating eggs over easy very difficult. One, I'd love to nudge some of you into trying scripting yourself. It's fun. Until you try it yourself, you may find it hard to realize or even believe how much fun and creative scripting can be. All this book or any other book can do is walk you through the essentials. From then on, scripting becomes a process as creative as the visual arts. We have only so many colors to work with, but for thousands of years, artists have been combining them in seemingly endless variety to produce unique and creative results. The same thing applies to scripting.

Two, I want to show that you don't need to do scripting to create winning multimedia with Director. In fact, in the real world, more often than not, multimedia development is a team effort, much like filmmaking. Ever sit through those eternal credits at the end of a movie? All those people contributed to the film; no one person could possibly have done everything. The same approach applies to multimedia. It helps to know your strengths and a little about scripting so that you know whether what you want to accomplish is reasonable. I talk more about the team nature of multimedia in Chapter 20.

Come On, Try One On for Size

Ready for some fun? Are you set to have the time of your life? Okay, let's script. Say you've been developing a business presentation for a mysterious client, Mr. Big. Actually, you're not sure what business Mr. Big is actually in, but it involves lots of calls from public phones, wearing dark suits and sunglasses, and meeting someone carrying a bass cello carrying case at the airport every few weeks. Everyone loves your presentation, but Mr. Big contracts you again to add some scripting so that he doesn't have to work so hard presenting the darn thing. The presentation will look a lot slicker, and Mr. Big won't have to stand up from his gold-plated, wing-back chair so often. Anyway, he makes you an offer you can't refuse.

The movie is called *Introduction.* Mr. Big wants it to go automatically to a new movie, *What We Can Do for You.* Sounds pretty exciting already, let me tell you. Anyone have a megadose of No-Doz handy?

Actually, this scenario's pretty common in producing Director presentations. The question is, how do you go to another movie smoothly? Can this be done with Lingo in the first place?

After Mr. Big begins his movie *Introduction,* he wants to jump from Frame 35, the last frame, to the second Director movie, have it play automatically, and then return to the first movie.

Okay, here's how you'd handle an assignment like this. Remember, this mini-tutorial is just an example, a simple template for you to use as an aid for working with Director and Lingo scripts.

1. **At the Desktop make a folder for the project by choosing File⇨New Folder.**

   Making a project folder where you place all files is usually a pretty good idea. Otherwise, keeping track of everything, especially linked files, can be pretty hairy.

2. **Give your folder a meaningful name.**

   For example, I named my project folder, *Mr. Big Presentation ƒ.*

   You can make the special character at the end of the folder name by pressing Option+F. To many Mac types, ƒ has come to indicate a folder.

3. **Drag the essential contents of Director's application folder into the new folder, including the Director application, Director 4.0 Help, Director 4.0 Help Settings, and Director 4.0 Resources.**

4. **Drag all movies and linked files into your project folder from wherever you have them stored.**

Some of the files might be from different folders in your internal hard drive. Others may come from external drives and possibly CD-ROM clip art collections.

5. **Open the folder so that you can arrange the icons as in Figure 12-6 to hide the "gears and pulleys" from public view.**

   The layout of icons is very deliberate. At the top, I place the Director movies representing the entire presentation. The gears and pulleys running the presentation — Director and its auxiliary files — are underneath the movies. You can resize the window so that only the starting movie is displayed in the window. The layout is purely aesthetic, in case the audience watching the movie sees the Desktop and the open project folder.

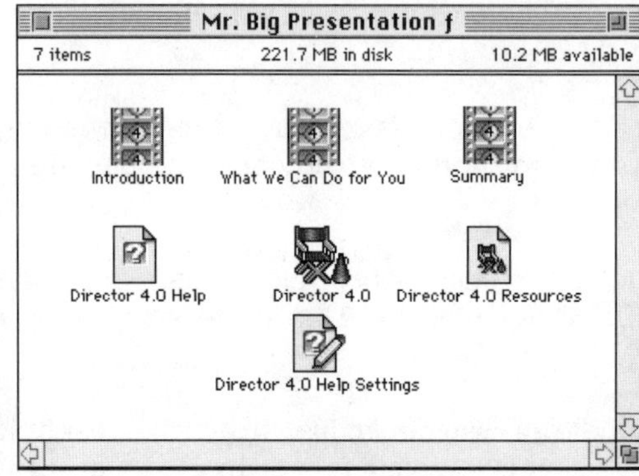

Figure 12-6: The layout of the folder, *Mr. Big Presentation ƒ.*

The content of the folder is important, too. When you tell Director to find a file, the first place Director looks is just inside its own folder, the *root level* of the folder, so placing necessary movies in the Director folder is especially important for a presentation when you want everything to go as smoothly as possible.

6. **Press the Resize box of the project's window and resize the window so that only the beginning Director movie file is displayed, as in Figure 12-7.**

7. **Double-click the movie visible in the window to open Director and the movie.**

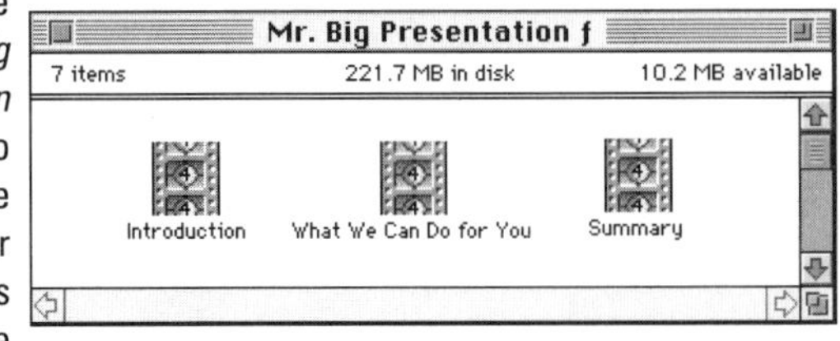

Figure 12-7: Resizing the *Mr. Big Presentation ƒ* window so that only the Director movie files are displayed.

Adding a script to a movie

The following steps show you how to add some scripting that tells Director to go to the next movie and play it, using an exitFrame script that kicks in when the playback head begins to leave the frame that holds the script. Use the play command to tell Director to play the movie named in your script, and then return to the place where the play command was issued.

1. **If the Score window isn't visible, choose Window⇨Score.**
2. **Locate the frame in the movie where you want to place your script.**

   In Figure 12-8, I'm getting ready to select frame 35 in the movie, *Introduction.*

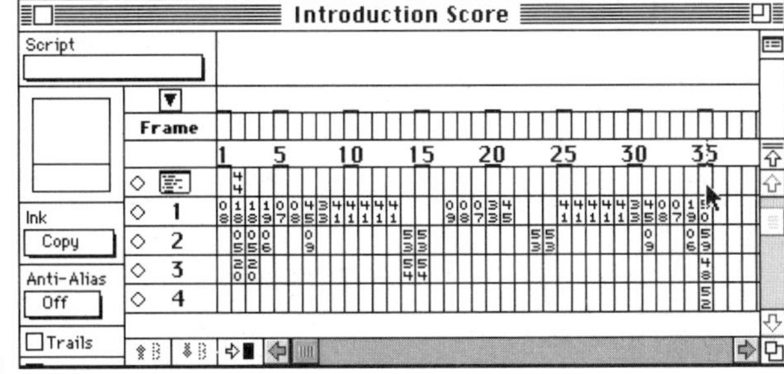

Figure 12-8: Locating frame 35 in the Score window of the Director movie, *Introduction.*

3. **Double-click the Script channel in the frame where you've decided to add the script.**

   Director displays the blank Score Script window as shown in Figure 12-9.

If Director provides you with a couple of lines of text, that's a good sign; it means Director likes you. Actually, it happens automatically. The first line of a Score script is set to `on exitFrame`, as in Figure 12-9, one of the most common types of scripts you'll use in Director.

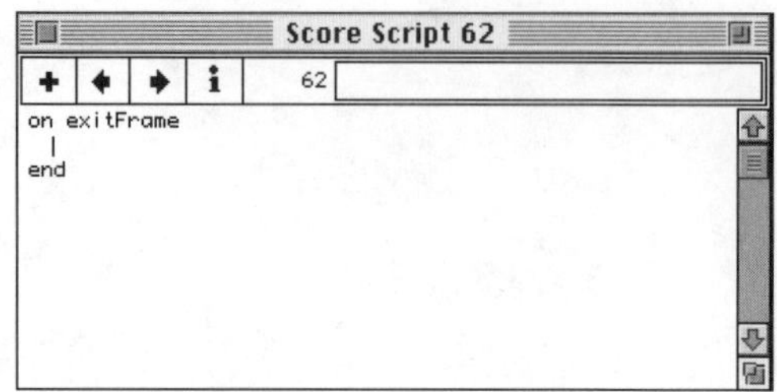

Figure 12-9: Double-clicking a cell in the Script channel of the Score window displays the Score Script window.

What does *exitFrame* mean? Well, Director knows when you're about to go to the next frame of a movie. The line `on exitFrame` tells Director to carry out any commands in the Score Script for that frame as the playback head leaves, or *exits,* the frame. The other line Director gives you automatically in the Score Script window, `end`, is simply required to end a script. There's a rule there somewhere, I think #5,793. Whenever you write a script in Director, the last line must end with the word `end`.

Notice one other thing. Director sets you up with a blank second line, too. The vertical line shown in Figure 12-9 between the two lines of script isn't a character. It represents the blinking insertion point Director provides so that you can start typing immediately.

4. **Enter** play movie, **followed by a space, and then the name of your movie surrounded by quotation marks.**

   The play movie command looks for a movie by name on the hard drive and opens the movie. The play movie command needs the name of a movie surrounded by quotes to operate successfully.

   Trying to use the play movie command without the name of a movie prompts an alert from Director. After you write a script with something missing, misspelled, or some syntax problem, Director presents you with a script error alert as in Figure 12-10. It's Director's attempt to be helpful and *debug,* or troubleshoot, a problem script for you. Without getting technical about what an *operand* is, notice the alert tells you that Director expects it in the script. (In this example, the operand that's missing is the name of the movie you want to play.) The alert includes the name of the problem command, play movie, and the question mark confirming something's wrong. When you click Script to return to the Score Script window to correct the problem script, Director kindly provides the blinking insertion point at the end of the bad line.

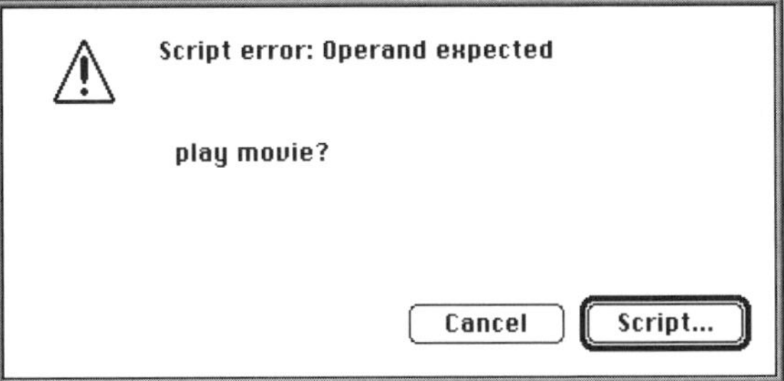

Script error: Operand expected
play movie?
Cancel
Script...

Figure 12-10: Director presents a script error alert when you try to save a problem script.

In my example, the line would now read

```
play movie "What We Can Do For You"
```

Quote marks in scripts are the plain vanilla variety, the same character you type to specify inches. Don't even think of adding fancy quotes in a script. You'll reverse the polarity of the Earth's magma, and everything will be sucked into the blackness of outer space where no one can hear you scream.

5. **Click the Close box in the upper-left corner of the Score Script window to save the script.**
6. **Choose File⇨Save to update the Director movie.**

   The way the play movie command works is to go the movie named in the script, play the movie, and— providing no command is found at the last frame of the new movie— *return* to the movie and the frame following where the command was issued.

   Congratulations, Professor Higgins. You've just written your first Director script. Anyhow, there's one critical step you haven't taken: testing your work. Always test your scripts thoroughly. Try to mess things up. Everyone else will.

Testing your scripts

1. **Choose File⇨Open.**
2. **Select the movie in the Directory containing the play movie command and click Open.**
3. **Press Command+P to play the Director movie.**
4. **Check that Director goes to the second movie, plays it and returns to the first movie following the frame where play movie was issued.**

Now, where's that bottle of champagne?

Chapter 13

Messages from Beyond: The Message Window

In This Chapter

- Playing with beeps
- Watching your movie from the Message window

If there's one thing you can say of Director, it doesn't lack windows. The Stage window is always around. It's the one window that you can't hide. Sure, you can change its dimensions in the Preferences dialog box, but you can't close it because it doesn't even have a Close box. Aside from the Stage window, you'll probably do most of your work in the Score window, the timeline of your movie. You may also do a lot of work in the Cast window, depending on how many files you import and whether you like to rearrange the Cast Members every half hour so that things look nice. After you take the plunge and start scripting in Lingo — Director's built-in language — you'll find yourself in the Script window for one Director object or another.

After you start working with Lingo and the Script window, you may find the Message window your best ally. Macromedia designed the Message window to be your very own digital pal.

Playing with Scripts from the Message Window

When you're just learning to script with Lingo, the Message window is a great way to play with bits and pieces of Lingo as long as you use the Message window from the perspective of playing a game and having a great time while learning the idiosyncrasies of a somewhat bizarre language. After all, you are learning to talk to your Mac and its little chips of silicon on the system board.

Why do I make this suggestion? Frankly, because learning Lingo can be frustrating. Just as learning English may have been frustrating, or just as that French or Italian class in your freshman year at college in which you weren't allowed to speak a word of English may have been frustrating. The properties, commands, and other Lingo stuff you learn about here are just tools. If you're an artist, after you learn how to pick up a pencil and hold it in your hand, it's up to you to draw something beautiful, powerful, or terrifying with it. Beyond a certain basic mastery of Director's tools, including Lingo, you need to use the tools creatively. Even after scripting for a while you may find that you need to experiment. That's where the Message window comes in. It's a great window for being creative because it gives you instant feedback.

I'm sure you've heard your system beep many times. You can go into your Sound control panel and switch the simple beep to a quack or one of several other dippy alternative sounds. But there's nothing like the pure, resonant, almost poignant crispness of the simple, system beep.

You can use the Message window to alter that beep. To do so, you need to open the Message window by choosing Window⇨Message from Director's menu bar. Note the warm `Welcome to Director` message that Mac types have come to expect (see Figure 13-1).

Figure 13-1: The Message window, where you can experiment with lines of Lingo scripting.

Your message window should include a blinking insertion point — your Mac's classic signal to you that it's waiting for you to start entering text in the window. To play with one of Lingo's commands, the beep command, you need to follow only two basic rules. First, you type the command, and then you press Return. It's as easy as that.

After you take a few minutes to memorize the basic rules, you can use the beep command in the Message window to create a beep by typing **beep** and pressing Return.

Director plays the system beep. Instant feedback. That's what makes the Message window so great. You don't need to create a button or even call up the Script window.

The beep command is a kind of command that accepts optional information modifying its result. Lingo types call this optional info a *parameter.* The beep command accepts a value followed by a space and the word *times* after its name and plays the system beep accordingly. For example, type **beep 2 times** and press Return.

Great, Director plays the system beep two times. But as you go along with your Lingo career, you learn that some words are just window dressing to make Lingo sound more English-like. Director doesn't even need the word *times.* For example, type **beep 2** and press Return.

Director still beeps twice, so the word *times* is really unnecessary, just smoke and mirrors. Now, sometimes you may forget the proper *syntax* or arrangement of words when writing Lingo scripts. If you type **beep for 2 times** and press Return, Director objects to using the word *for* and presents you with a script error alert, as in Figure 13-2.

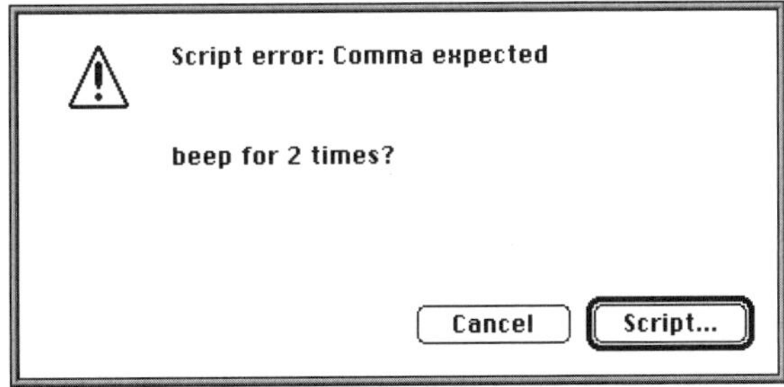

Figure 13-2: Director presents you with a script error alert when you try to get away with bad Lingo.

Notice what the script error alert says and what it doesn't say. According to the alert, Director expects a comma in the line of Lingo. Then the alert repeats the line you typed, `beep for 2 times`, and adds a question mark. That's the problem with many script error alerts. Part of the message may be nonsensical, another part too ambiguous to be of much use. The script error alert doesn't say anything about it being wrong to use the word *for* in the beep command. So you need to take part of the message with a grain of salt (an old saying I just made up), accept the fact that something's wrong with the line of Lingo, and find out whether the alert gives you any solid clues pointing to the problem and its solution.

Much of the time, the problem with a line of Lingo script is a simple typo. Carefully look over the script for any misspelled words. After that, the problem is typically a syntax problem, meaning the line of Lingo isn't written in the right order or a necessary parameter is missing.

Watching Your Movie in Action from the Message Window

You eagle-eyed readers out there in ReaderLand may have caught me. I haven't mentioned a very distinctive feature of the Message window. That's it, the Trace check box on the bottom-left corner of the window.

When you turn on the Trace feature, Director logs messages and scripts in the Message window as they occur in your movie on playback. Without getting too technical, *messages* are descriptions of what Director-types call *events*. For example, every time you click the mouse, you generate a `mouseDown` event and a `mouseUp` event that refer to the action of the mouse button. Director describes these events with `mouseDown` messages and `mouseUp` messages. You only have to worry about ten different types of messages in Director. For more details on message types, see the "Events" section in Chapter 17.

With the Trace check box in the Message window turned on, the Message window logs scripts as they're executed. You can think of a script as a customized mousetrap waiting for one particular type of "mouse" or message to trap. The message travels through the Cast Members of your movie and their associated scripts and through a maze called the *message hierarchy*. A script beginning with the line `on mouseDown` is a custom trap just waiting for a `mouseDown` message to pass by. At that time, the `mouseDown` script catches or traps the `mouseDown` message, preventing it from traveling through the rest of the message hierarchy and the script is executed.

All this craziness is what the Message window records — as it happens — when you turn on the Trace check box, as in Figure 13-3.

Why turn on the Trace check box in the first place? Well, it's a great way to kill a rainy weekend. Just turn on your Trace check box, settle down with a hot cup of java, and before you know it, it's Monday. Didn't someone once say, "Time flies when you're having fun"?

The more conventional reason to turn on the Trace check box is to help uncover a problem area in your movie — a process that Lingo types call *debugging* — a crucial part of the development process when you're trying to iron out all the kinks.

Message
== Frame: 1 Script: 14 Handler: startMovie
--> set the mouseUpScript to "set the foreColor of cast 13 = random(255)"
--> end
== Script: 15 Handler: exitFrame
--> go to the frame
--> end
--> go to the frame
--> end
== MouseDown Script
--> go to the frame
--> end
--> go to the frame
--> end
== Clickon Script for sprite: 1
== Script: 13 Handler: mouseUp
--> beep 2
--> end
== MouseUp Script
== Script: 0 Handler:
--> set the foreColor of cast 13 = random(255)
== Script: 15 Handler: exitFrame
--> go to the frame
--> end
--> go to the frame
--> end
Trace

Figure 13-3: With the Trace check box turned on, the Message window records messages and scripts as they occur on playback.

The Trace feature is pretty clear when it detects a problem. It slams on the brakes, and your whole movie comes to a screeching halt. Take another look at Figure 13-3. The Message window has recorded the following:

- The Welcome message.
- The playback head beginning on frame 1, an action marked in the Message window with ==.
- A handler named `startMovie` encountered on frame 1.

- A script in its own Script window is made up of one or more *handlers,* a number of lines of Lingo beginning with *on* followed by a space and the name of the handler (`on mouseDown`, for example), followed by one or more Lingo commands and ending with the line, end.
- The lines of Lingo commands of startMovie, in this case — `set the mouseDown Script to "mousingAround3"` marked in the Message window with --> as it's read and executed by Director.

  Don't be too concerned about what this handler means right now. Focus on what the Message window does and why you should care.
- The last line of the handler, `end`, marked again with --> as it's read by Director.
- Encountering a second handler named `exitFrame` in frame 5, marked with ==.
- The one line of the handler, `go to frame 10`, marked with -->.

- Arriving at frame 10, another action marked with ==.
- The last line of the `exitFrame` handler, `end`, executing and marked with -->.
- Encountering a third handler named `exitFrame`, in frame 10 and marked with ==.
- Executing the one line of the `exitFrame` handler in frame 10, `go to the frames`, marked with -->.

Which is where the Message window and movie abruptly stop, telling you Director has found a problem in the last line. In addition, just to hit you over the head with it, Director brings up a script error alert, such as the one shown in Figure 13-4. Director tells you it's found a script error; a property hasn't been found in the first line of the handler `go to the frames`.

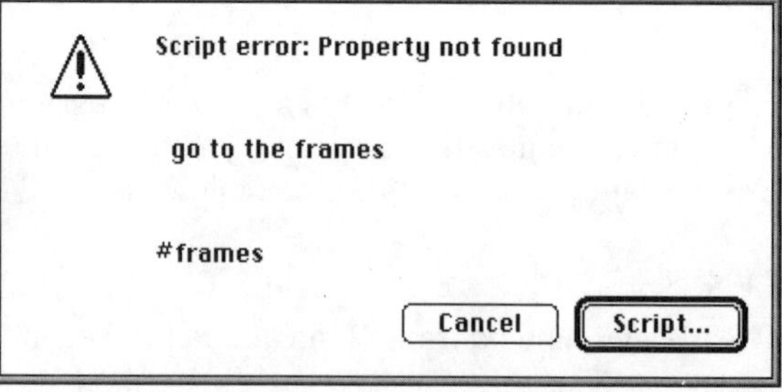

Figure 13-4: A Script Error alert from Director informing you of a problem line of Lingo scripting.

This box means that you look for typos and syntax problems. Notice `go to the frames`, a form of Lingo's go command that allows the movie to continue playback but keeps you in the same frame, except it should read `go to the frame`, without an *s*. That's the typo the Message window and script error alert have been trying to point out, as if your Mac were playing charades with you. First word, sounds like . . . .

Chapter 14

Trick or Tweak: The Tweak Window

In This Chapter

- Having fun with the Tweak window
- Reviewing the X-Y coordinate thing

What can you say about a window that is about the size of a thumb with two cryptic words in it (ΔX and ΔY) and a button with a silly name (Tweak)? It's got to be the funniest window in all Directordom. Oh, yes, I almost forgot. It's got a square on the left with a one pixel dot in the center of the square. That ups the Tweak box from funny to hilarious in my book.

Anyway, it's actually useful.

When Mousing Around Just Isn't Enough

The Tweak window is under the Window menu, I promise. Choose it and up comes the . . . heh, ha-ha, hee-hee-hee, oh hah-ha. Excuse me, I just can't help myself. Self-control, Lauren Steinhauer.

Okay, once you've got the (hee) Tweak window up and running, it doesn't look very (ha-ha) impressive. But there are times when moving an object with the mouse is a royal pain. In the early days of Macdom, someone once likened using the mouse to drawing with a cake of soap. Ergo, the Tweak window as shown in Figure 14-1.

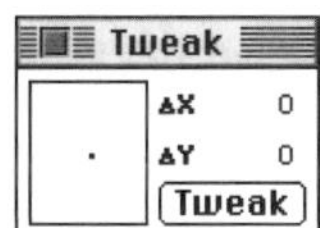

Figure 14-1: The Tweak window, the funniest window in Director.

Notice the zeros to the right of ΔX and ΔY. You say you're having a hard time finding them? Ho-ho-ho. Hee-hee. Please, my sides. Oh, yes, the values, right. These are the X and Y coordinates of the *Cartesian plane.* For an explanation of a *Cartesian plane,* check out the next section; it may also save your reputation at your next cocktail party (pronounced beer bust).

With a sprite on the Stage that you'd like to move in small steps, try the following.

1. **Click the sprite on the Stage.**

   After clicking, if the sprite's a bitmap, the gray selection rectangle appears, marking its *bounding box* with eight resizing handles. If it's a text sprite, a thick, gray selection rectangle appears, featuring one or two thick resizing handles.

2. **If the Tweak window is not visible, choose Window⇨Tweak.**

   At this point, make believe the sprite starts out sharing the same coordinate values displayed next to ΔX and ΔY (pronounced *delta X* and *delta Y,* by the way) in the Tweak window.

3. **Press halfway between the dot in the center of the square and the upper-right corner of the Tweak window.**

   A thick, black line emerges from the center of the square as in Figure 14-2 below.

Figure 14-2: The Tweak window displaying how far and in which direction a selected sprite is to be displaced.

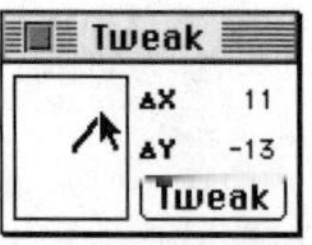

4. **Keeping the mouse button down, drag the mouse in various directions.**

   Note how the thick black line follows the mouse and how Director continuously updates the values by ΔX and ΔY. By the way, you're not limited to staying inside the small dimensions of the Tweak (ha-ha-ha) window.

5. **If you haven't tried, drag the mouse beyond the Tweak window.**

   The black line doesn't visibly extend beyond the Tweak window but clearly follows the movement of the mouse, and the X and Y values continue to update, as in Figure 14-3.

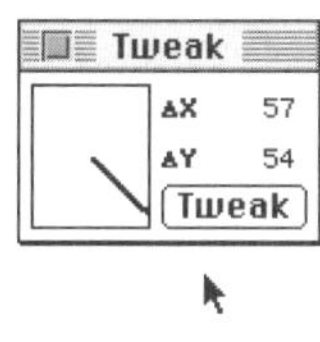

Figure 14-3: The Tweak window can record X and Y values beyond its small dimensions.

6. **Click the mouse when the Tweak window indicates values close to how much you'd like to move the sprite.**
7. **Click Tweak.**

   Note how the selected sprite moves according to the values displayed in the Tweak window. Each time you click the Tweak button, the sprite moves again by the values currently shown.

Please keep in mind the values displayed in the Tweak window are *relative* values, meaning that they don't show a selected sprite's actual location on the Stage but merely how far up, down, or across from its current location the sprite will move with a click of the Tweak button.

OK, Let's Review That X-Y Coordinate Thing

Back in the moldy, old 17th century, a Frenchman by the name of Renatus Cartesius worked on a number of grand projects, including changing his name. Better known as René Descartes, he's given credit for establishing the foundation of analytic geometry and for the famous saying, "Never put Descartes before the horse." Or was it, "I think, therefore I am"?

Anyway, we are interested in Descartes for his creation of a coordinate system used for pinpointing any location on a surface. Horizontal locations are set along the X axis and vertical locations along the Y axis. You can designate any point on a surface by giving its location along the X and Y axes. Starting from an origin at 0,0 (0 for X and 0 for Y), locations move in a positive direction down and to the right and negative directions up and to the left. If this stuff confuses you, you can check out Figure 14-4 to get a better idea.

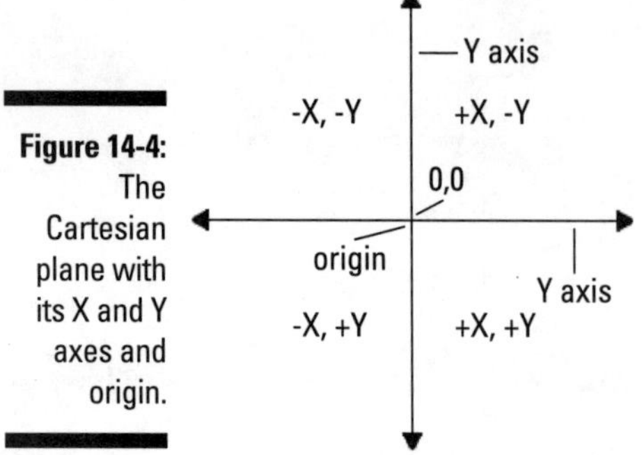

Figure 14-4: The Cartesian plane with its X and Y axes and origin.

In fact, click the Tweak window and drag it up and to the left of center of the square and note the negative values displayed by ΔX and ΔY. In Director and most other Macintosh programs, the origin is in the upper-left corner of the screen, so all X and Y coordinates remain positive. Of course, the units of measure can be anything from inches, millimeters, and typographers' points to *pixels,* the unit of measure of the (ha-ha-ho) Tweak window. I can't take (hee-hee-ha-ha) it anymore. We'd better go on to the next chapter. Oh, my sides.

Chapter 15

Your Pal, the Markers Window

In This Chapter

- Creating markers
- Using the Duplicate Window command

Never let it be said that Director lets you down. Macromedia gives you all these windows out of the kindness of its heart, and then it gives again. Introducing your pal and mine: the Markers window.

So, What Is the Markers Window?

It's a note to yourself, a permanent ID for your frames, a printable outline, and a great dessert topping, too.

Choose Window⇨Markers, and Director displays the unique Markers window, hand illuminated with Old World craftsmanship in Figure 15-1.

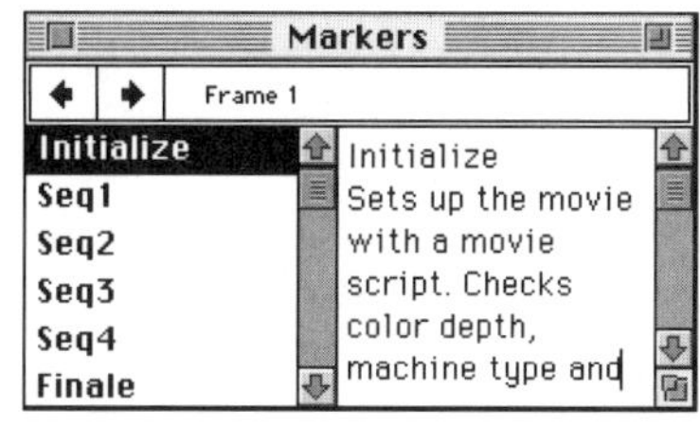

Figure 15-1: The Markers window, in which you can make notes to yourself on rainy weekends.

Think of markers as bookmarks, only better. As you create your Director movie in the Score window, you can give important frames distinctive labels by pressing the Markers button, shown in Figure 15-2, and dragging markers above frame numbers in the Frame channel. If you need to review markers in the Score window, jump back to Chapter 5.

The Markers window lists all markers in the Score in sequence in its left scrolling field, as in Figure 15-1. Click any marker in the list to display its name in the first line of the scrolling field on the right. You can then add a note in the blank area underneath.

Why are markers important, you ask? Good question. Well, for one thing, markers help organize your movie in the Score window and flag important frames in your movie, as shown in Figure 15-2.

The Markers window prints out QuickDraw text so that you can enter notes in the right scrolling field for yourself, your design team, or your client.

The first line in the scrolling field becomes the marker label. If you want to add notes to the field, be sure to reserve the first line for the label name and press Return. Notes can start from the second line. If you continue typing text on the first line after you enter a label name, whatever text follows the label name becomes incorporated into the name itself, causing problems with Director's capability to identify markers in the Score.

The Markers window prints good-looking output on a LaserWriter or QuickDraw printer such as the Apple StyleWriter. To print, activate the Markers window. Choose File⇨Print and consider the options in the Print Options dialog box shown in Figure 15-3. Be sure to click the Marker Comments radio button and decide whether you want the currently highlighted marker only or a range of marker comments printed. When you are ready, click Print.

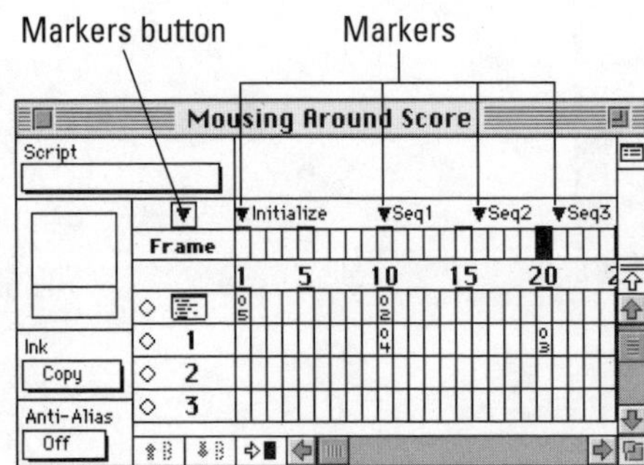

Figure 15-2: The Score window with markers for Frame 1, where an initialization script kicks in, and for other important frames.

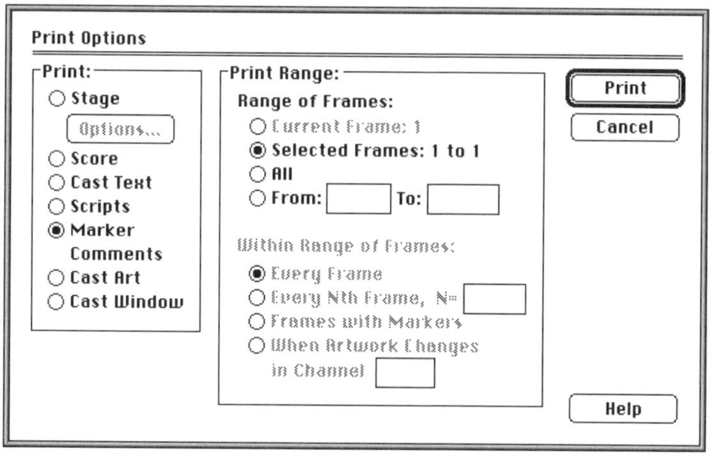

Figure 15-3: The Print Options dialog box, where you can print output from QuickDraw text in the Markers window.

When you start writing numerous Lingo scripts in a movie, you can use the go command with a frame's marker name to add meaning to the line of Lingo. For example, instead of saying, `go to frame 10`, in Lingo — which doesn't say much — you can say instead, `go to marker ("Finale")`. Director moves the playback head to the frame marked `Finale`. You know there are some dynamite special effects starting on that frame just waiting to sweep your audience off their feet.

In addition, markers stay with their frames even when frame numbers change after you edit a movie. If you have a movie that's 30 frames long, and you add three frames to the beginning, frame 30 is now frame 33. A script that refers to frame 30 now affects or references the frame that was frame 27 before the edits. In other words, Markers move with their frames, and all references to frame 27 refer to frame 30 after you add those three frames.

A Word about the Duplicate Window Command

Duplicate Window, the last command under the Window menu, is great when using Director to edit QuickTime mooVs, either to use in a Director movie as a Digital Video Cast Member or to export as a stand-alone QuickTime file. For more info on Digital Video and QuickTime, jump back to Chapter 11.

In Chapter 11, I discuss cutting and pasting a new QuickTime mooV together. During this editing process, calling on the Duplicate Window command can be very useful, especially for a long sequence. After choosing Window➪Duplicate Window for an active Digital Video window, you can use the new window to move to a different part of the QuickTime mooV as shown in Figure 15-4.

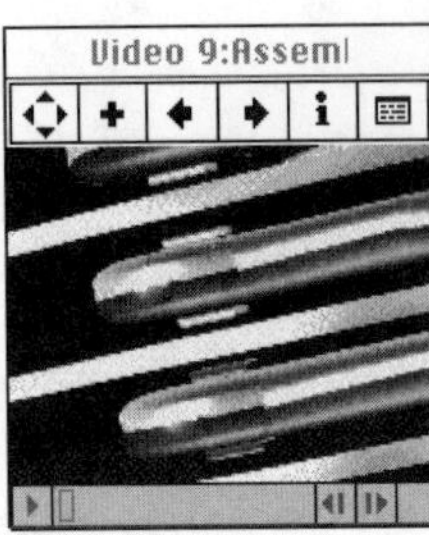

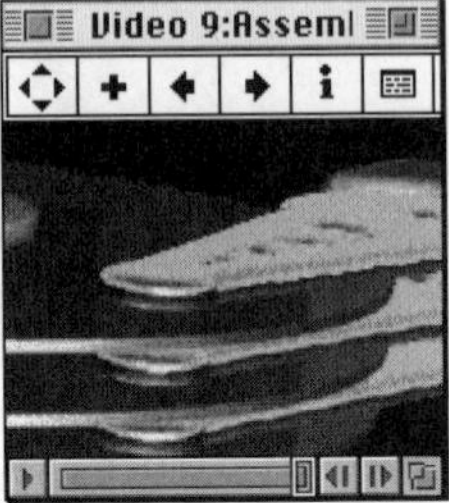

Figure 15-4: Two different views of the same Digital Video Cast Member, thanks to the Duplicate Window command.

Suppose that one window shows the beginning sequence, as usual. In the second window, you may fast forward to the middle sequence and cut between the beginning sequence, the middle sequence, and a blank Digital Video window. It's hard to duplicate the ease of this kind of editing in high-powered QuickTime editing programs, even Adobe Premiere.

Be sure that you understand that the original and duplicate windows refer to the same Cast Member, so edits in either window change the Cast Member. You should remember this fact especially when editing Digital Video windows in Director because the original, source file is always linked to the Cast Member. Edits in Director actually change the original external file on disk.

Part IV

More Interaction, Please!

The 5th Wave **By Rich Tennant**

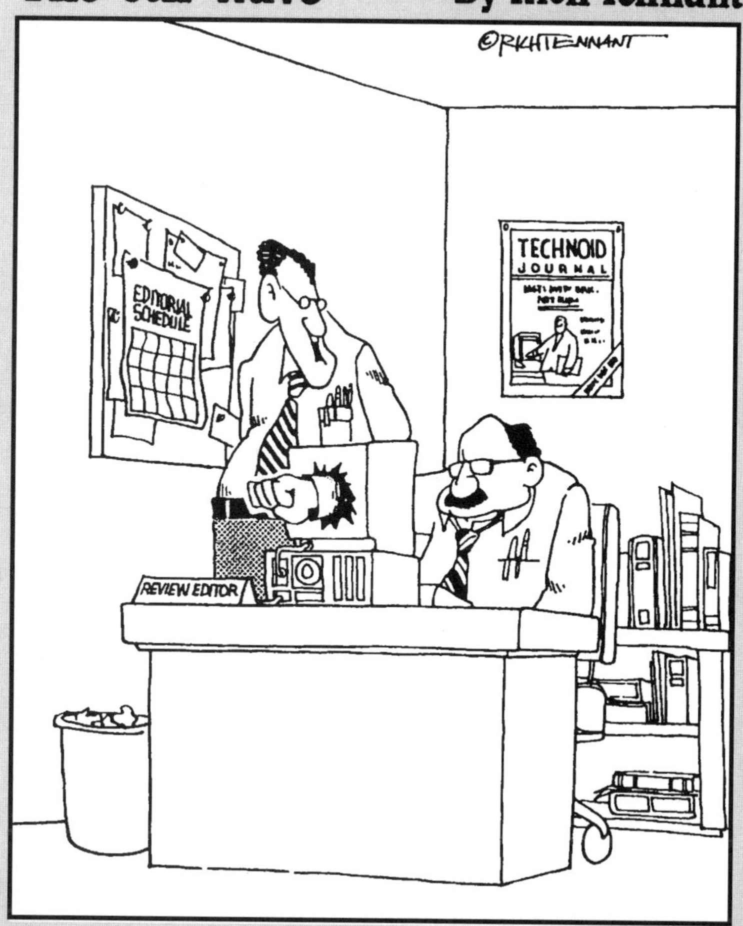

"Let me guess. Another example of interactivity gone awry."

In this part...

When the Altair 8800, the world's first personal computer, hit the stands on the cover of *Popular Electronics* back in 1975, people couldn't wait to busy their hands assembling it. Funny thing was, no one could say why, or what they were going to do with all that silicon.

If you've got the same kind of trouble articulating why you were just born to do interactive Director stuff, Part IV has a haystack full of fodder for you, from Auto Animating charts with the push of a button to why Lingo should be high on your To Do list.

Chapter 16

Six Easy Pieces with Auto Animate

In This Chapter

- Introducing Auto Animate
- Setting up Auto Animate
- Creating animation effects

One of the easiest, most pleasant ways to get into animation is with Director's Auto Animate feature. Better and easier to use than ever in Director 4, it's about as close as you can get to instant animation. Some settling of contents may occur.

Discovering Auto Animate Effects

A whole slew — or is that a gaggle? — of wondrous text effects is hiding at the bottom of the Score menu, and it's called Auto Animate effects. By choosing Score⇨Auto Animate, something like Figure 16-1 should appear.

```
Banner...
Bar Chart...
Bullet Chart...
Credits...
Text Effects...
Zoom Text...
```

Figure 16-1: The Auto Animate submenu.

By choosing one of these effects, deciding on a bouquet of options in the effect's dialog box to customize the animation, and clicking a Create button, you tell Director to create the sprites, place them in the Score, and set you up for flying, zooming, and gesticulating text and chart graphics.

Once all this frenetic action is set up for you, the fun doesn't stop there. The objects are now in the Score and on the Stage, ready and waiting for you to modify them. You can add gradients to bullets for a 3-D effect, fudge bars in an Auto Animate chart closer together, or replace the out-of-the-box object with a new glitzy one using the Switch Cast Members command in the Score menu. Let Director do the leg work, then add the final spit and polish yourself.

Setting Up for Auto Animate

Getting to Auto Animate is pretty easy. But first, be sure you have a good selection of fonts loaded in your System. After all, we're dealing with text effects; it doesn't hurt to have great fonts ready to experiment with. Try a variety of styles; for example, sans serif fonts such as Helvetica and Avant Garde, serif fonts such as Palatino and Goudy, and a mix of display type, that is, unusual, ornamental, and heavy-faced type for graphic impact that you wouldn't use for columns of body text. At the same time, it's easy to get carried away. The general rule is to be careful when you use more than two different types of fonts in one screen.

If ever there was a time you wanted to have a product called ATM (Adobe Type Manager) installed in your system, this is it. ATM works with PostScript fonts to build screen text on the fly at any point size you choose. You can recognize PostScript fonts by the couplet of files per font you install in your system, the screen font that looks like a little suitcase, and the printer font that usually looks like a laser printer. The suitcase font provides a limited number of font sizes for displaying the font on-screen, usually from 8 to 24 point. Without ATM, your goose is cooked if you need anything larger than 24 point text. That's where ATM comes in to save the day. The result? No more infamous "jaggies," those ugly stair-stepped diagonal lines so common to bitmaps displayed on-screen. If you're not using ATM yet, get it and will it to your progeny. Trust me.

You can also use TrueType fonts to get rid of the jaggies that occur with fonts displayed at large screen sizes. These days, Apple includes a standard set of TrueType fonts with System 7.5. You can purchase any number of additional TrueType fonts, too. What's so great about TrueType fonts? They have ATM-like routines built into them; a similar technology builds the screen font on the fly at the required size so that you and your family avoid the social stigma of jaggies. By the way, if you decide to add fonts to your System, you'll need to quit Director first. If you're not sure where your fonts are in your System, check Table 16-1 to find out where to find your fonts and how to add them to your System.

Table 16-1 Where Do Fonts Go in My System?

System Version	Where Fonts Go	Add a Font by
6.08	Screen fonts in System file	Using Apple Font/DA Mover
	Printer fonts in the System folder	Dragging over the System folder
	TrueType fonts in the System folder*	Dragging over the System folder
7.0	Screen fonts in the System file	Dragging over the System folder
	Printer fonts in the System folder	Dragging over the System folder
	TrueType fonts in the System file	Dragging over the System folder
7.1–7.5	All fonts in the Fonts folder	Dragging over the System folder

* System 6.07 and 6.08 require a TrueType INIT to use TrueType fonts.

Whatever type of font you drag over the System folder with any flavor of System 7.0, System 7.0 will recognize the type of font you're installing and where the file(s) should go in the System folder. You'll see an alert, asking whether you'd like your Mac to do the work. Click OK and grab a cup of java.

After you add some great looking fonts to your system file, open Director and choose Score➪Auto Animate. Drag the mouse to the right to view the submenu of effect choices. Or is it choice effects? Anyway, take a gander at Figure 16-1 for a peek at the goodies hidden in Auto Animate's submenu.

Auto Animate effects are push-button animation sequences Director builds for you in a matter of seconds. All you have to do is replace placeholder text with your own text and set options with various controls including buttons, sliders, and pop-up menus. That's part of the fun of using Auto Animate features, don't be afraid to experiment.

The following sections show you how to set up each of the effects listed in Figure 16-1.

Creating an Auto Animate Animation

I've hinted that Auto Animate animation is push-button heaven, like some decadent dream out of the '50s when people envisioned the coming age of automation and a push-button world of leisure. You've probably seen the images in old movies and commercials. Push a button and your bed gets made by invisible mechanical hands; as a climax, the bed somehow swings into the wall leaving no seams. Push another button and a tray of steaming food slides into view from a stainless steel slot, utensils set properly, a flower and vase popping into place by themselves. Yes, it's the Food-O-Matic, folks.

Auto Animate's basic scenario

Auto Animate is kind of like this mad, push-button utopian dream. Basically, you go through a grueling couple of bouts of button-pushing. Here's the basic scenario in a little more detail.

1. **Choose the effect you want from the Auto Animate submenu.**

   The dialog box for that particular effect appears. All these effects are based on animated text, sliding, gliding, crawling, and generally acting hyperactive. The dialog box provides a highlighted line of sample text so that you don't even have to select anything. Talk about decadent!

2. **Type your text.**

   By now, you should know that typing automatically replaces selected text anywhere in the Mac universe. Same thing here. Couldn't be easier unless you train Igor, your trusty assistant, to do the typing for you.

3. **Press Create.**

Did that go by too fast for you? Really, that's it. Director takes over, creates all the frames for you, sets up the Score, adds Cast Members to the Cast window and sprites to the Stage, and all but gives you a manicure and pedicure, no extra charge.

Of course, the real fun is in gorging on all those delicious options for each effect through pop-up menus, buttons, and slider controls. A handful of the options are specific to each Auto Animate effect and described later in this chapter. But many of the options show up in all or most of the dialog boxes. For now, I'll take you on a whirlwind tour of these options, available in the dialog box for most of the Auto Animate effects. Figure 16-2 displays the Banner dialog box, which contains most of the options.

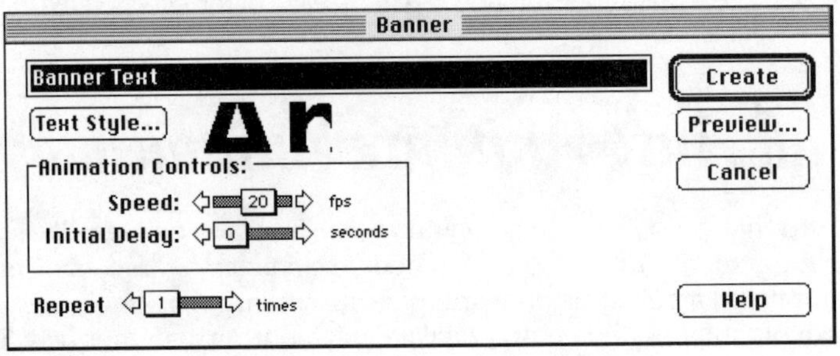

Figure 16-2: Animation options are available in the Banner dialog box.

Text Style button

Since Auto Animate effects rely on text, it should be no surprise to find a Text Style button that takes you to the Text Style dialog box, where you can customize your text.

1. **Click the Text Style button.**

   The Text Style dialog box appears as in Figure 16-3.

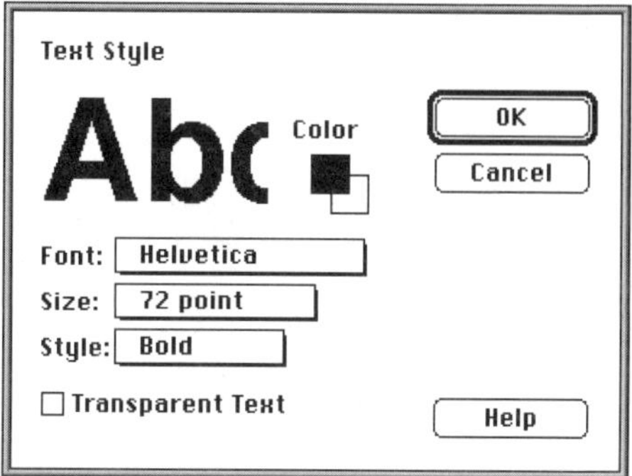

Figure 16-3: The Text Style dialog box, where you can customize text for Auto Animate animations.

   The Text Style dialog box is very *interactive.* In the upper-left corner is a preview that updates with every decision you make in this dialog box.

2. **Press the Text color selector to display the current palette and drag the pointer over the color you want for the text before releasing the mouse.**

   The Text color selector is the black square near the top of the dialog box in Figure 16-3. It's black until you choose a color from the current palette, when it reflects the chosen color.

3. **Press the Background color selector to display the current palette and drag the pointer over the color you want behind the text before releasing the mouse.**

   The Background color selector is the white square in Figure 16-3. Like the Text color selector, it reflects the color you choose from the current palette.

4. **Click the Font, Size, and Style boxes and choose what you want for your text from their pop-up menus.**

5. **Decide whether you want to check the Transparent Text check box.**

   Be warned. The Transparent Text check box is highly misleading! For shame, Director. With the Transparent Text check box *unchecked,* the text appears surrounded by a frame in the color you choose from the Background color selector in Step 3.

Choosing Transparent Text is the equivalent of choosing white for the background color of the text, and then going to the Score window to select the text sprites in the Score and apply Background Transparent ink to the sprites. The result? The space *surrounding* text shapes becomes transparent, allowing whatever is on the Stage to show through. What's really misleading is the preview image in the Text Style dialog box when you choose Transparent Text, displaying the background color you choose in Step 3 as a pastel shade, suggesting it blends with the background color or image on the Stage. DO NOT let Director fool you. Tish, tish. What has this world come to?

6. **Click OK.**

Preview button

The Preview button shows you a preview of an Auto Animate effect, with selected options in place, *without* doing the work of setting up the animation in the Score. It also displays the Preview dialog box, shown in Figure 16-4 below.

Banner Preview			
Play	Center	Cancel	OK

Figure 16-4: The Preview dialog box.

The first time around, the preview plays automatically, centered vertically on the Stage. Click on a location in the Score to change the vertical placement of the animation and replay the preview in its new location. You can also click Play in the Preview dialog box to replay the preview and Center to re-center the Auto Animate sequence vertically in the Score. Once you're satisfied with the result, click OK to return to the dialog box for the Auto Animate effect you've chosen.

Help button

The ubiquitous Help button, actually an amazing invention second only to angel hair pasta, appears in every effect's dialog box. Click the Help button, and does Director take you to an old-fashioned main menu where you actually have to select a topic? No, no. This clever devil whisks you straight to the section in the Help system that deals with the very concerns on your mind. Careful, there be witchcraft there.

Animation controls

Since we're talking about animation, you'd expect some kinds of animation controls. And sure enough, Director comes through for us with a number of options.

- *Speed slider control:* Chances are, for any one of the Auto Animate effects you choose, you'll find a Speed slider control to set the tempo in fps (frames per second). Simply press on the little button-like object displaying the current setting and drag left or right to adjust the setting. Try a middle setting for starters.
- *Initial Delay slider control:* Use the Initial Delay slider control to delay the beginning of the animation sequence in units of seconds. Again, the processor running your Mac will affect the actual delay.
- *Ending Delay slider control:* Use the Ending Delay slider control to pause at the conclusion of the animation sequence in units of seconds.

Just remember that in real life, tempo is highly conditional on the processor running the show. Slower machines run the same setting more slowly, faster machines run the same setting more quickly, possibly too fast. For a solution to this vexing problem, make a date with the section, "Can I Set Up My Movie to Play at the Right Speed on Any Mac?" in Chapter 21.

Repeat slider control

Set the number of times the Auto Animate sequence repeats with the Repeat slider control. If you really want to see your bar charts rise to the occasion three times, this is the baby that makes it happen.

Now for a whirlwind tour of each of the Auto Animate effects.

Creating the Banner effect

With the Banner effect, text scrolls across the screen horizontally, bringing Times Square and crackly old MovieTone newsreels of World War II and the like to mind.

When you choose Banner from the Auto Animate submenu, Director displays the Banner dialog box, as in Figure 16-2, found earlier in this chapter, with sample text highlighted for you.

1. **Type the text you'd like to animate.**

   Chances are the selected dummy text in the Banner dialog box isn't quite what you had in mind. Typing *your* text automatically replaces the highlighted sample text. Now, all you have to do is decide on the smorgasbord of options in the rest of the dialog box.

2. **If you want to change text attributes for the title, click Text Style, choose your options, and click OK.**

   Take a look at the "Text Style button" section earlier in this chapter for detailed info on all the options.

3. **Set Speed, Initial Delay, and Repeat values with the control sliders, described in the "Animation controls" section earlier in this chapter.**
4. **Click Create and play your movie with Command+P.**

After admiring your movie, check the Cast window to find a new Bitmap Cast Member, that is, the text you entered in the Banner dialog box entry field. It should look something like Figure 16-5.

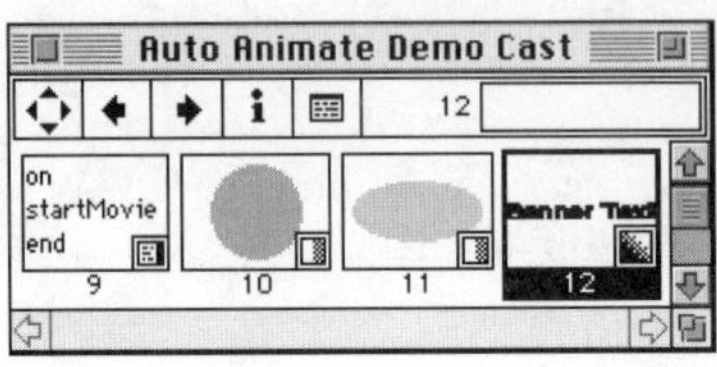

Figure 16-5: Creating a Banner effect makes a new Bitmap Cast Member in the Cast window.

Also, check the Score window to find that Director automatically placed the Text Cast Member in the first available cell of the Score and created the required frames for you to produce the Banner animation, reproduced in Figure 16-6.

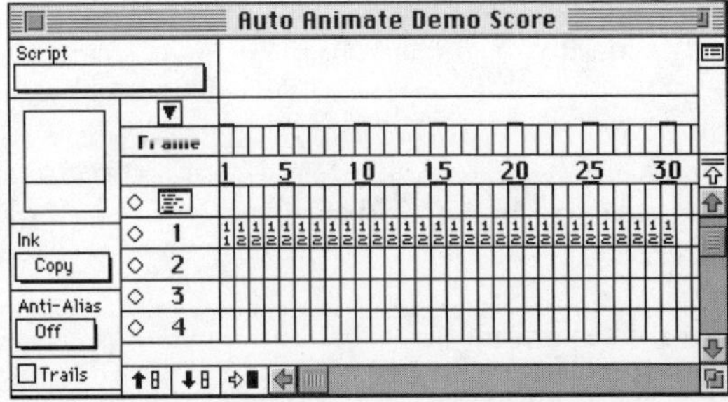

Figure 16-6: Director magically whips up the required frames for the Banner effect in the Score window.

Although Director's done much of the work for you, if you want to enhance the animation with background graphics, buttons, or other objects on-screen, you'll probably want to call on the In-Between commands in the Score menu. You'll find info on using the In-Between Linear and In-Between Special commands in Chapter 5.

Test your work often by playing back a movie. Test Director's work, too, when you use the Auto Animate feature.

Creating the Bar Chart effect

Auto Animate's Bar Chart whips up an animated bar chart with up to six bars that rise to their respective values with five choices for bar style: solid, concrete, coins, bullion, and hands. Choosing Bar Chart from Auto Animate's submenu opens the Bar Chart dialog box shown in Figure 16-7.

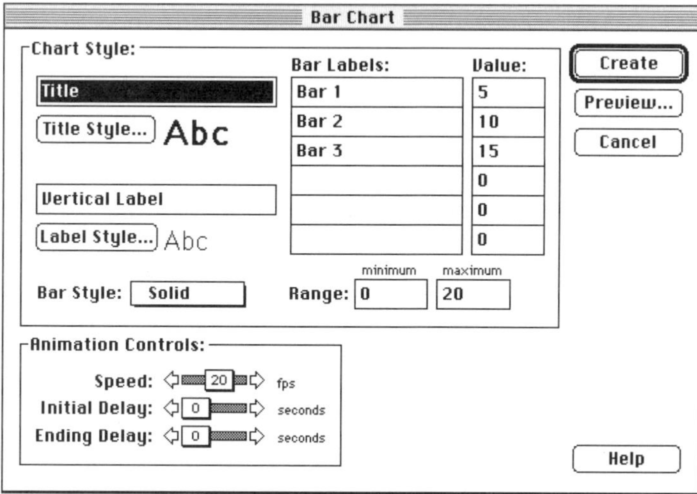

Figure 16-7: The Bar Chart dialog box, where you can choose one of six bar styles, along with several other options to customize the final animated sequence.

Director starts you off with a placeholder title highlighted and ready to retype, as well as placeholder bar names and values for three of six bars for the chart.

1. **Type the text for the title you'd like to animate in the Bar Chart.**
2. **Tab to the Vertical Label entry field and type your custom label name.**
3. **Tab to the first Label entry field and enter a custom label name.**
4. **Tab and type for the remaining label and value fields.**
5. **If you want to change text attributes for the title, click Text Style, choose your options, and click OK.**

   Take a look at the "Text Style button" section earlier in this chapter for detailed info on all the options.

6. **If you want to change text attributes for the labels, click Label Style, choose options identical to Text Style options, and click OK.**
7. **Choose one of five bar styles from the Bar Style pop-up menu (see Figure 16-8).**

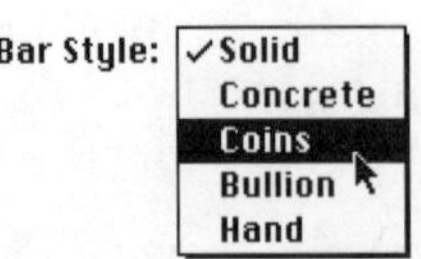

Figure 16-8: Five styles to choose from for your animated bar chart.

8. **Enter minimum and maximum range values in the Range entry fields.**
9. **Set Speed, Initial Delay, and Ending Delay values with the control sliders, described in the "Animation controls" section earlier in this chapter.**
10. **Click Create and play your movie with Command+P.**

Choose Window⇨Cast and note that Director created a number of new Cast Members to make the Bar Chart, as shown in Figure 16-9.

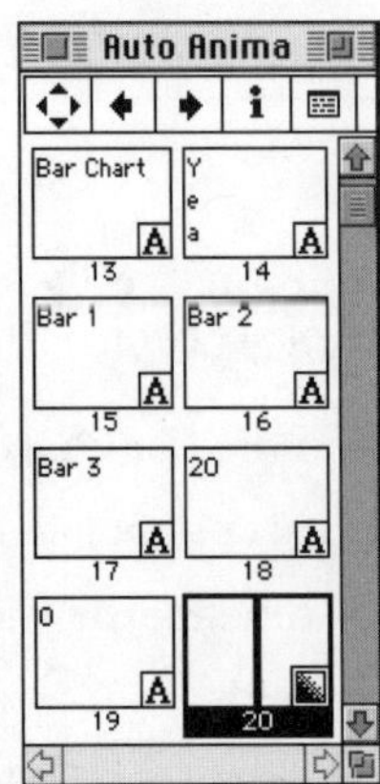

Figure 16-9: The Cast window with new Cast Members after Director builds a Bar Chart animation sequence.

The Cast window now includes Text Cast Members for the title, label, one Cast Member for each bar label, maximum value and minimum value, and a Bitmap Cast Member for the longest bar you specified in the Bar Chart dialog box.

Choose Window⇨Score and notice that Director produces all the required frames for the animation sequence, as shown in Figure 16-10.

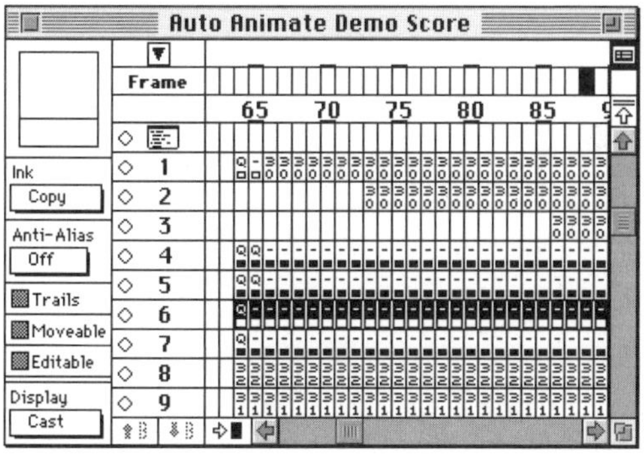

Figure 16-10: The Score window after Director builds an animated Bar Chart.

Creating the Bullet Chart effect

Auto Animate provides an animated bullet chart with flying titles, bullet points, and oh yes, bullets. Watch your head. After you choose Bullet Chart from Auto Animate's submenu, the Bullet Chart dialog box appears, shown below in Figure 16-11.

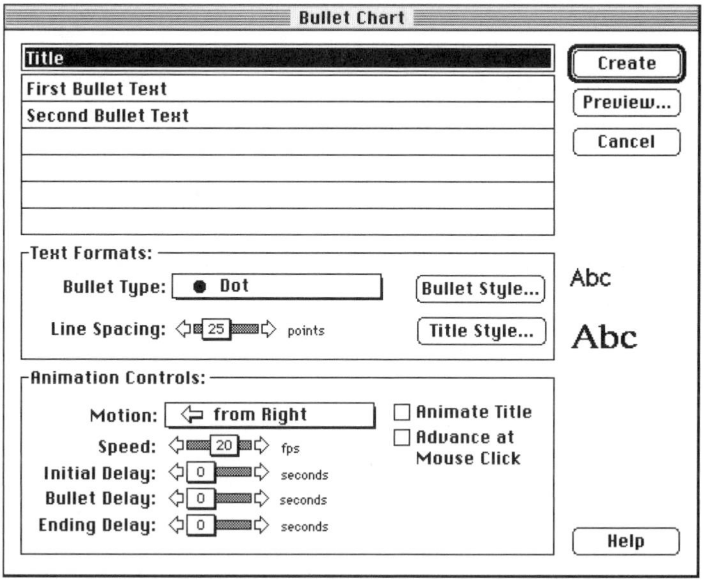

Figure 16-11: The Bullet Chart dialog box, where you can enter up to six lines of bullet text and choose an animated bullet type.

1. **Type the text for the title of your Bullet chart.**
2. **Tab to each bullet text entry field you'd like to display and enter custom text.**
3. **Choose a bullet type from the Bullet Type pop-up menu, shown in Figure 16-12.**

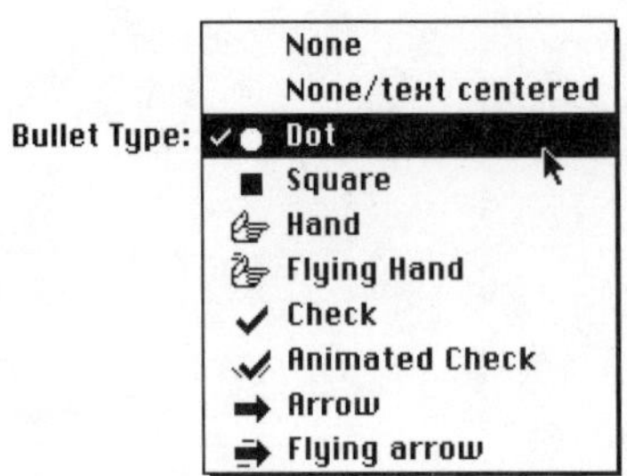

Figure 16-12: The Bullet Type pop-up menu displays ten options for customizing an Auto Animate Bullet Chart.

4. **If you want to change text attributes for bulleted text, click Bullet Style, choose options identical to Text Style options, and click OK.**

   Take a look at the "Text Style button" section earlier in this chapter for detailed info on all the options.

5. **Set Line Spacing with the slider control by pressing the button-like object that displays the current setting for line spacing and dragging left or right to change the setting.**

   Line spacing is what old-timers would call *leading,* the vertical distance in pixels from line to line. The larger the line spacing value, the greater the distance between lines. Try an initial setting of 120 percent of the text size for line spacing and adjust if needed.

6. **If you want to change text attributes for the title, click Text Style, choose your options, and click OK.**
7. **In the Animation Controls panel, choose an option for how bullet text animates on-screen from the Motion pop-up menu shown in Figure 16-13.**

   For example, choose From Right and the bullet topics glide into view the right side of the screen.

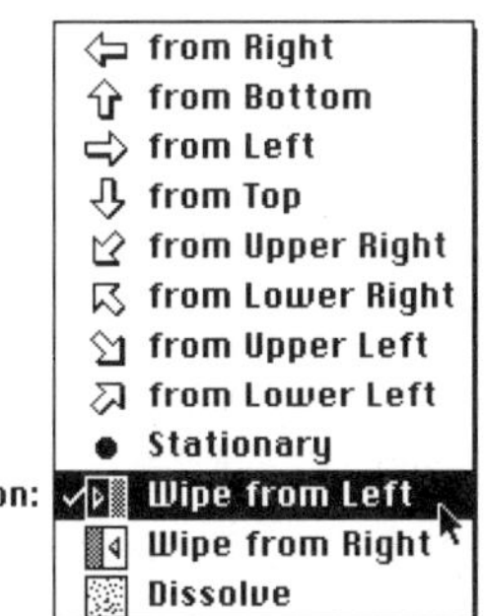

Figure 16-13: The Motion pop-up menu in the Bullet Chart dialog box with 12 different motion types for the bullet topics.

8. **Set Speed, Initial Delay, Bullet Delay, Ending Delay, and Repeat values in the Animation Control panel with the control sliders, as described in the "Animation controls" section earlier in this chapter.**

   Go with the default settings first and preview the effect with the Preview button. You can always change the settings. Giving you specific values isn't going to be that helpful because the real life rates will vary from Mac model to Mac model.

9. **Decide whether you want to check the Animate Title check box.**

   If you turn on this check box, the title animates along with the bullet points. Otherwise, the title simply appears on the Stage, followed by the animated bullet points.

10. **Check the Advance at Mouse Click check box if you prefer to control when each bullet topic appears in the animation.**

   If Advance at Mouse Click is checked, each bullet point pauses to animate into view until you click the mouse.

   Beware when previewing this effect. If you click the mouse within the Stage, Director thinks you're clicking to reset the vertical location of the sequence, and the preview freezes up. The only safe place to click is the title bar of the Bullet Chart Preview dialog box.

11. **Click Create and play your movie with Command+P.**

If it happens to be a long, rainy weekend, choose Window⇨Cast to find out how many Bitmap Cast Members Director made when you created your bullet chart. Then choose Window⇨Score to find out how Director set up the animation and how many channels it took in the Score window.

Creating the Credits effect

For film-style credits that scroll vertically on the screen, choose Credits from Auto Animate's pop-up menu. The Credits dialog box appears, vividly reproduced in Figure 16-14.

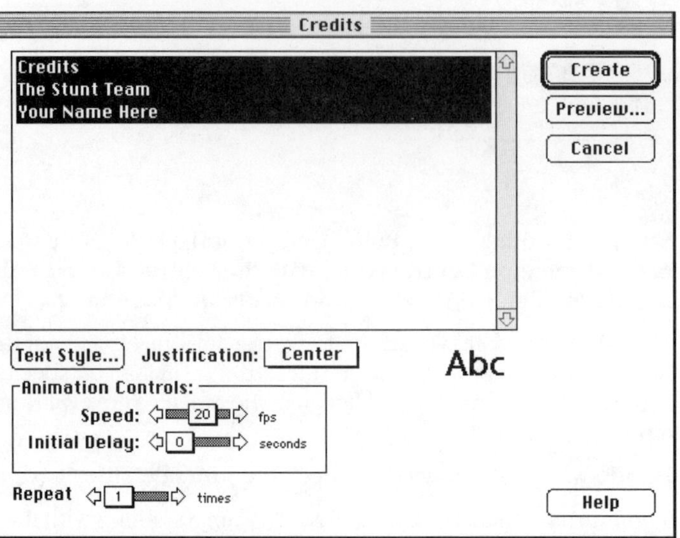

Figure 16-14: The Credits dialog box, where you can set up Hollywood-style scrolling credits in your Director movie.

1. **Enter the text you'd like to animate.**

   By the way, the field scrolls to accommodate a long list of credits, à la George Lucas epics.

2. **If you want to change text attributes for the title, click Text Style, choose your options, and click OK.**

   To review Text Style options, jump back to the "Text Style button" section earlier in this chapter.

3. **Press the Justification pop-up menu and choose from Left, Center, or Right.**

4. **Set Speed, Initial Delay and Repeat values with the control sliders, detailed in "Animation controls," earlier in this chapter.**

5. **Click Create and press Command+P to play your movie.**

Creating Text Effects

If you'd like to spice up a particular presentation with some Hollywood-style tricks, choose Text Effects from Auto Animate's submenu. The Text Effects dialog box presents itself, an almost photographic likeness coming up in Figure 16-15.

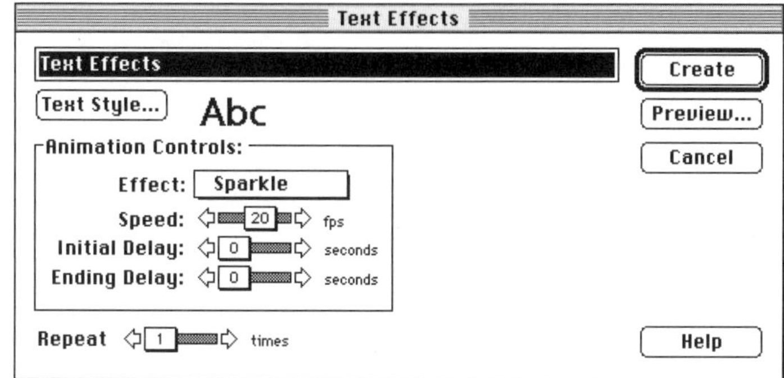

Figure 16-15: The Text Effects dialog box offers you several eye-popping animation sequences for an important presentation in Director.

You can choose one of three special effects to apply to your text, including Sparkle, Letter Slide, and Typewriter. Typewriter? What's that? Oh yes . . .

Sparkle is like flossing your text. Sharp glints of light roll across the characters of your title like Burt Lancaster's teeth, or for a more contemporary analogy, Jim Carrey's 70mm-wide toothy grin.

Letter Slide puts rollerblades on your title's little feet. Each character skates into place from the edge of the screen, screeching to a halt with gymnastic precision.

If you're a fan of "Murder, She Wrote," you'll love the Typewriter effect! Each character of your text appears on the page as if typed by a ghostly hand with a ghostly typewriter. By the way, Jessica, please don't come anywhere near me.

For any one of these effects, the setup is the same. Plug in your favorite effect of the day, and — shazam! — you've got Hollywood on your screen.

1. **Enter the text you'd like to animate.**
2. **If you want to change text attributes for the title, click Text Style, choose your options, and click OK.**

To review Text Style options, jump back to the "Text Style button" section earlier in this chapter.

3. **Press the Effect pop-up menu pictured in Figure 16-16 and drag the pointer to the effect you'd like to use for the Auto Animate sequence.**

Figure 16-16: The Effect pop-up menu.

4. **Set Speed, Initial Delay, Ending Delay, and Repeat values with the control sliders, detailed in "Animation controls," earlier in this chapter.**
5. **Click Create and enjoy your movie.**

Remember, movies are your favorite entertainment.

Creating Zoom Text

If you're after an eye-crossing, old-fashioned 3-D movie with a red and green glasses type of effect, choose Zoom Text from Auto Animate's submenu. Choose one of three options for creating the effect of a zoom lens that places you closer and closer to its subject with a Zoom in, Zoom out, or Zoom in, then out effect. Comes complete with an airline bag.

The Zoom Text dialog box appears, looking for all the world like Figure 16-17.

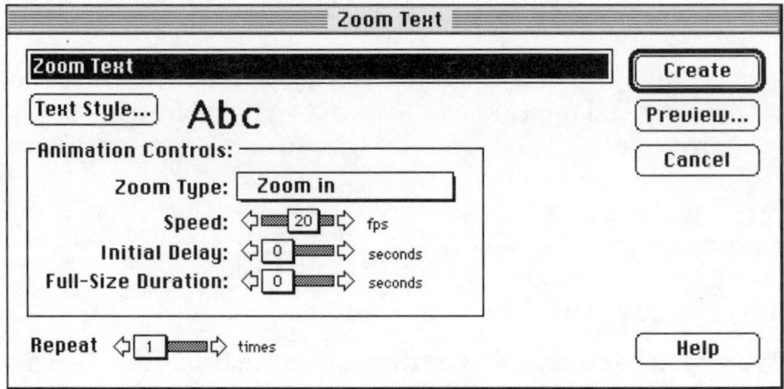

Figure 16-17: The Zoom Text dialog box, where you can set up text to zoom in, out, or back and forth.

1. **Enter the text you'd like to animate.**
2. **If you want to change text attributes for the title, click Text Style, choose your options, and click OK.**

   To review Text Style options, jump back to the "Text Style button" section earlier in this chapter.
3. **In the Animation Controls panel, press the Zoom Type pop-up menu, shown in Figure 16-18, and drag the pointer to the effect you want.**

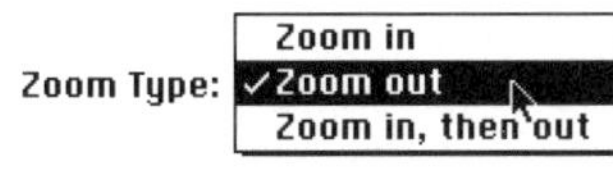

Figure 16-18: The Zoom Type pop-up menu in the Zoom Text dialog box.

4. **Set Speed, Initial Delay, and Repeat values with the control sliders, detailed in "Animation controls," earlier in this chapter.**
5. **Set Full-Size Duration with the control slider by pressing the button-like object displaying the current setting and dragging it left or right to change the setting.**

   A setting of 0, of course, means no pause before the next sequence begins to play back. Try an initial setting of two seconds if you do want a slight pause and adjust as needed. Here again, the speed of your processor will affect the real life duration of the pause.

Check out the new Cast Members in the Cast window by choosing Window➪Cast. You can also see the sprites that Director automatically added to the Score window by choosing Window➪Score.

Chapter 17

A Closer Look at Lingo

In This Chapter

- Dealing with Lingo
- Creating handlers
- Working with scripts

Lingo's something you have to talk yourself into, like putting on a tie, washing the car, or getting married. You may have heard scary stories about Lingo. They're all true. But it's not as bad as it used to be. Lingo's a lot more like everyday speech in version 4. Of course, if you're still working on everyday speech . . .

Anyway, if you need a morale booster, jump back to Chapter 12. I show you that learning Lingo is something a 4-year-old child can handle. So if you have a 4-year-old child handy, you're all set. You can even try the sample script in that chapter and live to tell about it.

OK, Take a Deep Breath — Lingo's Not That Hard

As programming languages go, Lingo's a breeze. Lingo's referred to as a high-level computer language, meaning it sounds and feels like everyday conversation. The opposite of Lingo is a low-level programming language such as machine language, in which you wade through 0s and 1s, or assembly language, which uses hexadecimal code (a numbering system with 16 digits). How'd you like to cozy up to stuff that looks like 5765 6C63 6F6D 6520 746F 2040 6163 696E 746F 7368 for eight or ten hours at a stretch? That's hexadecimal, by the way, for "Welcome to Macintosh."

Although Lingo feels conversational, the experience of learning Lingo is very close to tackling a foreign language with its special rules, distinctive *syntax,* and unique set of words to learn, small in number though they may be in Lingo. Oh, yes, *syntax* is the way words are arranged to form meaningful clauses or sentences. Lewis Carroll had a great time playing with syntax in *Alice in Wonderland* when, for example, the Mad Hatter exclaims, "You just as well as might say, 'You eat what you see' as, 'You see what you eat.'" Or was that the Disney version?

And don't forget Director's on-line help. I don't even attempt to cover everything about Lingo, not even all the basics. Use this chapter as a kind of social event without the booze to turn Lingo from stranger to warm acquaintance. When you encounter something you don't understand while playing with Lingo, remember to go to the Apple menu and choose Help. Better yet, press Command+?, and Director's special Help cursor appears. If you're working in the Script window, the Lingo menu is visible in Director's menu bar. Choose a problem Lingo item under the menu with the special cursor, and Director takes you right to that topic in Help. For a refresher course on Director's built-in Help system, jump back to Chapter 1.

Touring Basic Lingo Concepts

Now, I'm going to take you on a whirlwind tour of some basic programming concepts that apply to Lingo and most other computer languages. If something doesn't make sense, take a break, wash the cat, and return to this book, reminding yourself that plenty of people no smarter than you use Lingo everyday, as a mantra chant and not a programming language. Still, there's hope yet.

Lingo

Lingo is Director's built-in programming language. Director hasn't always had a language. Its auspicious beginning as VideoWorks in 1985, one year after Apple introduced the Macintosh, gave us Mac types a delightful black-and-white animation program to play with, but without Lingo and interactivity. Later, special editions of the program called VideoWorks Interactive introduced Lingo to the world. I'd typify the first several versions of Lingo as "difficult," and I think I'm being kind. VideoWorks Interactive was also flaky, causing numerous freezes and all-around mayhem on the Mac.

Today's program is a far cry from its VideoWorks days. Director 4 is a slick, solid program, and Lingo is conversational and approachable. Lingo is still a computer language, though, and the time has come to face a few unusual characteristics all programming languages share, including Lingo.

If something doesn't make sense, don't worry. It doesn't mean your IQ has slipped. It's new, that's all; with time it all comes together. Trust me.

Operators

With the Script or Message window is active, check out the Lingo menu. The first item you see is Operators with its submenu as shown in Figure 17-1.

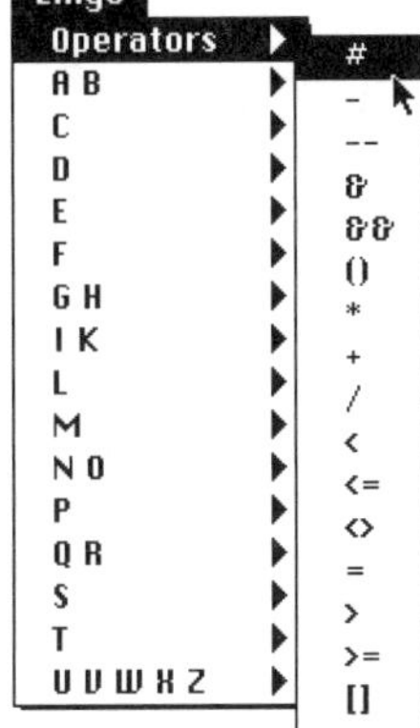

Figure 17-1: Lingo's operators under the Lingo menu.

On second look, many of the symbols shown in the Operators submenu should be familiar. They're arithmetic operators like +, –, =, and *. In fact, in your halcyon school days, the teacher probably referred to them as *arithmetic operators.* Lingo's other operators are simply an extension of the same idea. You'll find a set of *comparison operators* in the submenu, too. For example, < means "less than," and >= means "greater than or equal to." You can use these operators in a line of Lingo to compare one value with another. Table 17-1 contains basic explanations of the operators in the order listed in the Operators submenu.

Table 17-1 The Operators Submenu

Operator	*Function*	*Example*
#	Used to create a symbol instead of a variable for increased speed	put #Lauren into firstName
–	Subtracts one value from another	9 – 3
--	Disables a line of Lingo in a handler to include notes in a script	-- The following line gets the Mac model running Director

(continued)

Table 17-1 *(continued)*

Operator	*Function*	*Example*
&	Used to "glue" text, values, and variables together in a line of Lingo	set the text of cast "Welcome Message" = "Hello, " & firstName & "."
&&	Same as above but automatically adds a space character between two elements	set the text of cast "Welcome Message" = "Hello ," && firstName & "."
()	Forces Director to execute enclosed operators first in a list of operators	5+(9/3+1)/4
*	Multiplies one value by another	235*29
+	Adds one value to another	356+25
/	Divides one value by another	956/18
<	Less than	85+1<92
<=	Less than or equal to	90+2<=92
<>	Not equal	85/2<>92
=	Equals	85+15=100
>	Greater than	85+20>100
>=	Greater than or equal to	85+15>=100
[]	Used to specify items in a special Lingo form called a *list*	["Sunday", "Monday", "Tuesday", "Wednesday", "Thursday", "Friday", "Saturday"]
¬	Use as a "continued on next line" character in a Lingo script, not read as a return character	IfmoneySpent>moneyEarned then¬set the text of cast "Financial Condition" = "God help us."

Commands

A *command* is a direction telling Director to accomplish a specific task during playback. All programming languages, including Lingo, have commands. In Director, the commands are listed alphabetically by initial letter under the Lingo menu after Operators, as shown in Figure 17-1. When you scroll to the initial letter of interest, a submenu appears and you can drag the mouse horizontally to choose one of the listed commands.

The go command is one of the most frequently used commands. When Director encounters a go command in the Script channel of the Score window, it executes the command like the stolid genie that it is. If you tell Director to go to Frame 15 with a line of Lingo that reads `go to frame 15` in the Script channel of Frame 10, the nanosecond Director lands on Frame 10 the playback head jumps straight to Frame 15, no questions asked — as long as you didn't leave behind any typos and your syntax is correct. Director's an uppity kind of genie, that's for sure. You know what they say, give a genie an inch, and he'll walk a mile for a camel.

Functions

A *function* tries to pass itself off as an ordinary old command but makes itself conspicuously different with a telltale giveaway. A function always returns a value. For example, the function `the date` returns the current date as recorded by your Mac's internal clock. Similarly, `the time` returns the current time. Commands are hyper; functions are mellow. They must have been developed in California.

You can use the Message window when you want to try out a function from the Lingo menu.

1. **Choose Window⇨Message to open the Message window.**

   Notice that the Lingo menu appears when you choose the Message window. Both the Script and the Message windows display the Lingo menu in Director's menu bar. If the Lingo menu is *disabled,* or grayed out, neither the Script or Message window is currently active. If that's the case, just click on either window to enable the Lingo menu.

   You need to use a Lingo command, often the put command, with a function to get a result in the Message window. Otherwise, Director doesn't know what to do, the dumb bunny.

2. **Choose** put **from the P submenu, as shown in Figure 17-2.**

   The phrase `put Athing` appears in the Message window on its own line. *Athing* is just a placeholder and appears selected because Director knows that you want to enter what to put after the put command. The put command finds some information and then places or "puts" it in the Message window.

3. **Choose a function from the Lingo menu.**

   For example, choose time from the T submenu and the phrase, `the time`, replaces the selected placeholder, `Athing`. By the way, *the* is another giveaway that *time* is a function; you'll find plenty of *the*s as you use functions — the time, the date, the key, et cetera. Ad nauseum. E pluribus unum.

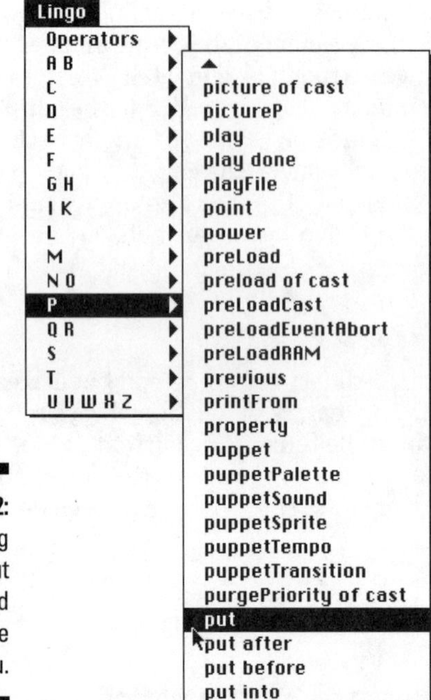

Figure 17-2: Choosing the put command from the Lingo menu.

4. **Press the Return key to execute the line of Lingo in the Message window.**

   If you chose the time function, Director displays, underneath the line of Lingo, the current time prefaced with two hyphens (the comment operator) to indicate the command was executed.

By the way, a function has one of two forms. For example, you'll see the date function as *the date* and *date()*. Same thing.

Handlers

A *handler* is at least two lines (but usually three or more lines) of Lingo that follow a very rigid format. A two-line handler basically doesn't do much of anything; Director doesn't object to one but doesn't get too choked up about it, either. A functioning handler has three or more lines, as in

```
on exitFrame
go to frame 15
end
```

Line 1 always consists of *on,* a space, and then the name of the handler. In this example, `exitFrame` is the name of a built-in handler you'll use often in the Script channel of the Score. An exitFrame handler activates as the playback head in the Score window leaves the frame that contains the exitFrame handler.

The name of the handler *must* always be one word. In other words, you can't have spaces in the handler's name. A well-established convention for scripting calls for starting the name of a handler with a lowercase letter. You can add words to the name of the handler by capitalizing the first letter of each additional word *without* adding spaces. For example, you can name a handler *on getARandomNumber.* Notice that the name of the handler is technically still one word even though you can read it as a phrase or sentence. You may also use an underline to add separation to words that make up the name of a handler. Director reads a handler name like *get_A_Random_Number* as one word, too.

Line 2 of a handler begins the list of Lingo commands used in the specific handler. In the earlier example, you find only the go command. In some complex handlers, the list of commands may be half a page or more in length.

The last line, line 3 in this case, is always `end`. It's that simple, folks.

Events

Director echoes the way your Mac works. Probably all that empty space inside your Mac. Seriously, your Mac is considered an event-driven computer, very different from that other type . . . what was its name? Anyway, your Mac is waiting to serve you and nervously checking whether you've pressed a key on the keyboard or clicked the mouse so that it can respond appropriately. Pressing a key on the keyboard or clicking the mouse are both *events.*

Director behaves the same way on playing back a movie; it constantly checks for ten types of events:

While a movie is playing, Director constantly checks for any event that is occurring. It constantly checks for ten types of events:

- *enterFrame event:* When the playback head enters a frame in the Score.
- *exitFrame event:* When the playback head leaves a frame in the Score.
- *idle event:* A non-event, when no event is occurring during playback.
- *keyDown event:* When you press a key on the keyboard.
- *keyUp event:* When you release a key on the keyboard.
- *mouseDown event:* When you press the mouse button down.

- *mouseUp event:* When you release the mouse button.
- *startMovie event:* When a movie begins to play back.
- *stopMovie event:* When a movie stops playing.
- *timeOut event:* Another kind of non-event, and anticipated event not occurring by an anticipated duration of time.

These are the only ten events you have to worry about, trust me. I could make up more, if that would make you happy. But out of the box, Director is stuck with ten events. Period. Over and out.

Messages

Each time one of the ten events occurs, Director sends out an alarm or message. With a keyDown event, Director releases a keyDown message. A mouseDown event gets a mouseDown message.

Message window

You can actually see these messages occur, and you don't even have to drink a six-pack with the Coneheads. Just call up the Message window from the Window menu, be sure to check the Trace check box, and play your movie. Figure 17-3 shows the Message window in action, displaying messages in a scrolling list as a movie plays.

Message

```
== Frame: 1 Script: 14 Handler: startMovie
--> set the mouseUpScript to "set the
foreColor of cast 13 = random(255)"
--> end
== Script: 15 Handler: exitFrame
--> go to the frame
--> end
--> go to the frame
--> end
== MouseDown Script
--> go to the frame
--> end
--> go to the frame
--> end
== Clickon Script for sprite: 1
== Script: 13 Handler: mouseUp
--> beep 2
--> end
== MouseUp Script
== Script: 0 Handler:
--> set the foreColor of cast 13 = random(255)
== Script: 15 Handler: exitFrame
--> go to the frame
--> end
--> go to the frame
--> end
```

☒ Trace

Figure 17-3: Messages passed and displayed in the Message window when you run the primary event handler demo.

Message passing

By now you must be asking yourself the burning question, "Self, where does Director send all these messages?" To understand how messages behave in Director, imagine a department store that gets more exclusive the higher up you go in the elevator. At the top floor you find only the most elegant, expensive, one-of-a-kind items imaginable. At the bottom, bargain basement time, the cheapest stuff with the broadest appeal possible. In between, items get more exclusive with every floor. If you buy something at the top floor, you don't bother visiting the floors below. Otherwise, you ride the elevator to the next floor down and find out if anything has your name on it. And so it goes until you wind up frantically flinging stuff out of giant bins in the basement.

Same thing with message passing. Messages flow from the highest to lowest level. If no handler exists in the button to "catch" the mouseDown or mouseUp message, the messages take the elevator and head for the next floor down, a handler in the Score channel. If a mouseDown or mouseUp handler in the Script channel of the current frame exists, the message activates the handler, or it's back on the elevator heading for bargain basement time. You find movie scripts in the basement, the most generic, all-purpose type of handler available in your movie. By making the analogy of movie scripts and bargain basements, I don't mean to imply movie scripts are unworthy. In fact, movie scripts contain some of the most important handlers in a movie precisely because of their broad availability. For more on movie scripts, see the "Movie scripts" section later in this chapter.

Variables

A *variable* is a little bit of memory you reserve and name to store a value. In a handler, you might enter the following line:

```
put 10 into theNum
```

That single statement accomplishes three things:

- Declares a variable. (Declare is programmerSpeak for "create.")
- Names the variable *theNum.*
- Stores the value 10, in the variable.

It's that simple; don't make it any more complicated.

You might decide to create another variable in the same handler with an additional line:

```
put "Lauren" into firstName
```

This line tells Director to put Lauren into firstName. Notice that when storing a value such as 10, no quote marks are required. To store words, such as *Lauren, cat,* or *dog,* quotes are required to tell Director the value is *literal,* which means that the value of the word stored is the word itself. You need to use quotes to differentiate a literal from the same word used as a variable.

For example, you might enter the following line in a handler:

```
put "Lauren" into cat
```

In this case, you *declare,* or create, a variable, name it *cat,* and store it in the variable. Remember, a variable is just an arbitrary name you give to a little bit of memory in your Mac's hardware.

Local variables

When you declare a variable named *cat* in a handler by entering a line such as the examples shown in the preceding section, you create a *local variable,* local because it's recognized only in that one handler. If you decide you want to add a line in another handler that takes the value of cat and puts it in a text sprite, Text Cast Member 1, you might enter something like the following:

```
set the text of cast 1 = cat
```

But Director objects, saying that you're trying to use a variable that doesn't exist. The only handler that knows that the variable *cat* exists is the original handler in which you created the variable. You need to use a special kind of handler called a *global variable.*

Global variables

Global variables are variables that may be called in any handler of your movie, ergo *global.* To make a global variable, simple type **global**, a space, and the name of the variable, usually in the second line of a handler. That's all there is to it. Staying with the example of using the variable *cat,* you might type a couple of lines to a handler as follows:

```
global cat
put "Lauren" into cat
```

Now, whenever you want another handler to access the value stored in the variable *cat,* just be sure to add **global cat** under the first line of the other handler, too, and any other handlers that might need the current value in cat. Cappice?

Scripts

A *script* is the text in a Script window that consists of one or more handlers. Say you have a button on the first frame of a movie. The Script window has a mouseUp handler and a custom handler named *getARandomNumber.* The mouseUp handler moves the playback head to a new frame. The *getARandomNumber* handler generates a random number with the random function that determines the number the mouseUp handler uses to move the playback head. These two handlers form a script in the Button Cast Member Script window. It's that simple and would look like Figure 17-4.

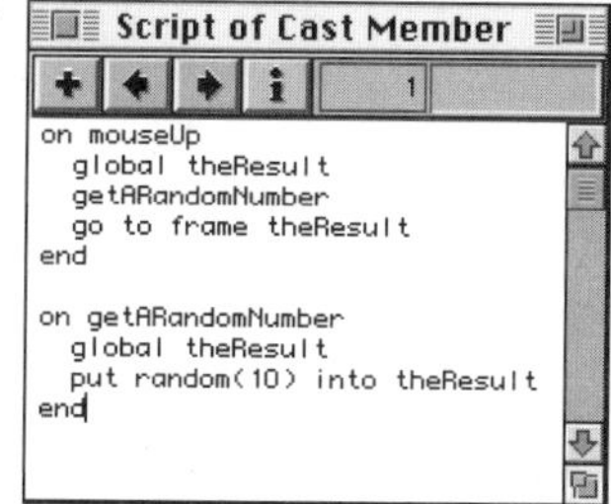

Script of Cast Member
1
on mouseUp
global theResult
getARandomNumber
go to frame theResult
end
on getARandomNumber
global theResult
put random(10) into theResult
end

Figure 17-4: Two handlers in the script of a Button Cast Member.

To briefly explain what this script accomplishes, the *getARandomNumber* handler declares a global variable, discussed in the previous section, named *theResult.* The handler uses the random function to pick a random number, in this case, a number from 1 to 10, and places the number into *theResult.* The mouseUp handler also declares the global variable so that it can use the number stored in *theResult.* The mouseUp handler calls on *getARandomNumber,* gets the random number from the global variable, and tells Director to move the playback head to the random frame number that is generated by *getARandomNumber.* You might have a different image on each frame so that the person viewing the movie may see a different image each time he presses the button.

Where a specific script resides in your movie determines the type of script and how "accessible" the script is or what floor it's on in our department store analogy. In a sense, some scripts, such as movie scripts, are listed in the Yellow

Pages so everyone knows about them and can call on them. Other scripts, such as button scripts, have unlisted numbers because they're intended to be used in very restricted situations. Types of scripts are discussed in the following sections.

Movie scripts

Most *movie scripts* are a set of initialization handlers that set primary event handlers, load values into memory, and generally set up the movie for playback. Using the startMovie message, a movie script might typically look like Figure 17-5.

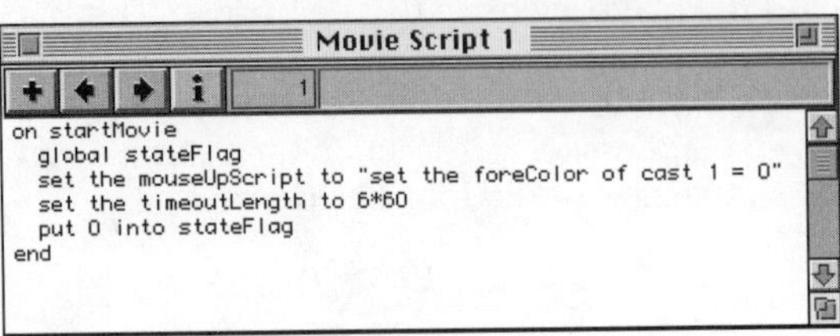

Movie Script 1
1
on startMovie
global stateFlag
set the mouseUpScript to "set the foreColor of cast 1 = 0"
set the timeoutLength to 6*60
put 0 into stateFlag
end

Figure 17-5: A typical movie script in a Movie Script window.

This initialization movie script in Figure 17-5 translates as follows:

- Line 1 says: Make a handler called *startMovie.*
- Line 2 says: When the movie starts, name a part of memory *stateFlag* and make it a global variable so that the value the variable holds is available to any other handler that declares *stageFlag.*
- Line 3 says: Set the color of text inside Button Cast Member 1 to white.
- Line 4 says: Start timing down from 360 ticks, or 6 seconds (and if nothing happens within 6 seconds, do the timeoutScript handler defined elsewhere in thc movic).
- Line 5 says: Put the starting value, 0, into a reserved part of memory you named *stateFlag,* telling Director whether a user has pressed the button since the movie began. Another handler in the button declares the global variable, *stateFlag,* and sets *stateFlag* to 1 the first time the person running the movie presses the mouse over the button.

Movie scripts want to be available to everyone, everywhere. Movie scripts and primary event handlers are the most accessible scripts in your movie. In my department store analogy, you find them in the bargain basement. They're the scripts that advertise in the Yellow Pages so that everyone knows about them.

To make a movie script, follow these steps:

1. **Choose Window⇨Script.**
2. **If not blank, click the New Script button (the + icon) in the upper-left corner of the Script window.**
3. **Click the Script Cast Member Info button (the i icon).**
4. **In the Script Cast Member Info dialog box, choose Movie from the Type pop-up menu.**
5. **Click OK to return to the blank Script window.**
6. **Enter your movie script handlers and commands.**

   For example, you might enter one or more of the following commands in a startUp handler:

   ```
   on startUp
   set the soundLevel to 7
   set the colorDepth to 8
   preloadCast 5
   end
   ```

   The soundLevel indicates the current setting for your Mac's built-in speakers from 0 for off to 7 for ouch, the highest sound level. Using the set command, you set the sound level to its highest setting, ouch.

   The colorDepth indicates how many colors your Mac monitor is currently displaying. In the second command line, you set color depth to 8 bits, giving you 256 different colors.

   PreloadCast is a Lingo command that copies designated Cast Members into RAM before they appear on the Stage for improved performance. The third command line copies Cast Member 5 into RAM; maybe it's a big QuickTime mooV.

7. **Press Command+P to play your movie and test the handler.**

By the way, you can have more than one movie script in a movie.

Primary event handler

Actions in Director are generally considered events. Director always knows when an event occurs. Four specific actions a user can do in Director are so basic they've been named *primary events.* The four primary events are

- *keyDown Event:* Whenever you press a key on the keyboard.
- *mouseDown Event:* Whenever you press the mouse button.

- *mouseUp Event:* Whenever you release the mouse button.
- *timeOut event:* Whenever a specific duration of time passes without an anticipated event occurring.

Director allows you to write a handler for each of these primary events. You can write a keyDownScript, a mouseDownScript, a mouseUpScript, and a timeOutScript for your movie. Had I designed Director, I'd have stuck with the term *handler.* But someone in his or her infinite wisdom named them *scripts;* don't let that confuse you — they're handlers. Usually, you'll write these special handlers as part of a *movie script,* explained in the following section.

Primary event handlers execute whenever a primary event occurs during your movie's playback. To help you understand the unique consequence of including a primary event handler in your movie, consider what occurs without a primary event handler in your movie. An example of a regular mouseDown handler in a button might be

```
on mouseDown
beep 2
end
```

Clicking the mouse over the button generates a mouseDown message. The mouseDown handler in the button acts like a trap, "catching" the mouseDown message. Director beeps twice because the command is activated. The mouseDown message ends there, echoing the meaning of the third line of the handler, `end`. No other handler gets triggered by that particular mouseDown event.

On the other hand, when you add a mouseDownScript to the movie, the mouseDown Script executes every time the mouse is pressed, even if the mouseDown event triggers a button that would normally trap the mouseDown message.

For example, you can write a mouseDownScript to randomly change the color of a button on-screen each time the user clicks the button. First, you'd add a script to a button so that it beeps when pressed.

1. **Select a button on the Stage you'd like to add a script to and double-click the heavy gray border of the selected button.**

   Director takes you to the Cast Member window for the button. If you need to create a button, page back to the section, "Checking out the Tools window tools," in Chapter 9.

2. **Click the Script button of the Button Cast Member window, highlighted in Figure 17-6.**

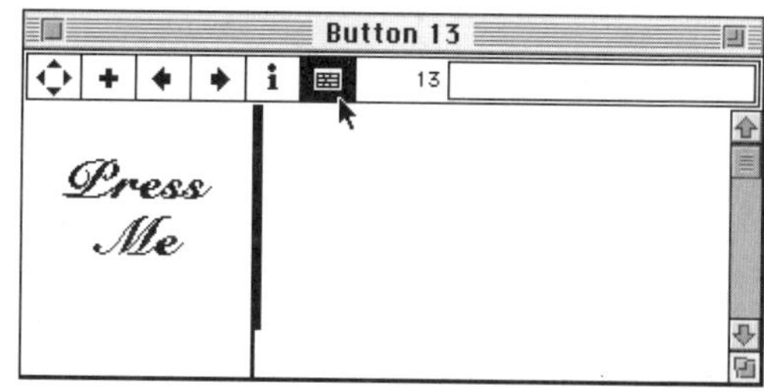

Figure 17-6: The Script button in the Cast Member window of a button.

The Script window for the button appears with the handler, "on mouseUp," already entered on line 1, a blank second line ready with the blinking insertion point, and "end" automatically entered on the third line.

3. **Enter your command line(s) at the blinking insertion point, in this case** beep 2, **then click the Close box.**

The following set of steps show you how to now add a script to the Score so that you remain in the same frame while the movie plays back.

1. **Choose Window⇨Score.**

   In Frame 1, notice the sprite representing the button on the Stage. The frame just above the sprite is the Script cell for Frame 1.

2. **Double-click the Script channel in Frame 1.**

   The Script window for Frame 1 appears with the handler, "on exitFrame," already entered on line 1, a blank second line ready with the blinking insertion point, and "end" entered on the third line.

3. **Enter** go to the frame.

   Go to the frame is a special version of the go command that keeps the user in the frame the command was called from, even though the movie is playing.

4. **Click the Close box of the Script window.**

Now that you've set up your button and Frame 1 with a couple of simple scripts, you can write a primary event handler that will kick in with a mouseDown message even if a button you click executes its handlers. Without a primary event handler, the mouseDown message would stop at the button and never reach a movie script.

Say you decide to make the primary event handler, to change a button's color when pressed, a startMovie type handler.

1. **Choose Window⇨Script.**
2. **Enter** on startMovie **for the first line.**
3. **For the second line, enter a mouseDownScript.**

   For example, `set the mouseDownScript to "set the foreColor of cast 1 = random(255)"` will change the color of the button's name to different colors each time the button's pressed.

   The first part of the line, `set the mouseDownScript to`, is what you just accomplished, establishing the current handler for a mouseDown event, one of four primary events in Director.

   The next part of the line, `"set the foreColor of cast 1`, uses the set command to change the foreground color of cast 1, referring to the button you made, Cast Member 1 in the Cast window. The foreground color of the button is the color of the text you typed in the button.

   The last part of the line, `= random(255)"`, is one of those functions I mentioned earlier in this section. You're telling Director, each time the user presses the mouse, to return, or pick, a random number from 1 to 255 and to change the foreground color of the button to that random number. In Lingo, colors are set by number.
4. **For the third and final line, enter** end.

Press Command+P to play back your movie; you can test your scripts by clicking the button several times. The button should beep and change color each time. If you click the background, the button should still change color without beeping, thanks to the mouseDownScript.

Cast Member scripts

A *Cast Member script* is exclusive to the Cast Member. Director executes handlers in a Cast Member script after you click the Cast Member's sprite on the Stage during playback.

To make a Cast Member script, follow these steps:

1. **Choose Window⇨Cast.**
2. **Select the Cast Member in the Cast window.**
3. **Click the Script button at the top of the Cast window.**

   Director takes you to the Cast Member Script window.
4. **Enter Lingo commands between** `on mouseUp` **and** `end`.

   Try playing with the *beep* command or, if you feel up to it, checking out the *set foreColor of cast* command in the preceding selection on primary event handlers.

5. **Click the Close box.**
6. **Press Command+P to play your movie and test the handler.**

Frame scripts

Frame scripts are scripts you enter in the Frame channel of the Score window. They execute when the playback head reaches the frame in which a frame script occurs.

To create a frame script, just double-click the Script channel cell for the intended frame. The Script window for the respective frame appears with `on exitFrame` entered for you on the first line, a blank second line ready to go with the blinking insertion point, and `end` entered for you in the third line. Simply enter a handler and click the Close box to create a frame script for the respective frame.

Sprite scripts

When you drag a Cast Member onto the Stage from the Cast window, you create a sprite of the Cast Member on the Stage and a sprite in the Score. A sprite script is a script for that particular sprite in that particular frame of the Score. Director can execute a sprite script when the person viewing the movie clicks on the sprite during playback or when the mouse pointer touches the sprite on the Stage.

Here's how to make a sprite script:

1. **Choose Window⇨Score.**
2. **Select the sprite in the Score.**
3. **Click the Script box at the top of the Score.**
4. **In the Script window that appears, add lines of Lingo between the first line, `on mouseUp`, and the last line, `end`.**
5. **Press Command+P to play your movie and test the handler.**

Why You Want to Write Lingo Scripts

As you can tell from my whirlwind tour of Lingo, just adding simple Lingo scripts to a movie elevates the Director experience to a dramatic new level, for you and for whoever is watching your movie. With Lingo, you can check the type of Mac running your movie, set the color depth of the monitor, fade in a sound, fade out a sound, adjust the volume of the sound, and at least two or three other things, actually hundreds, probably thousands.

Most important of all to you multimedia types out there in ReaderLand, you can add a level of interactivity to your movie only accessible through scripting with Lingo. When you learn to "make your movie make decisions" with conditional statements using "if-then" lines of Lingo to branch to one of several different possible options — at random, perhaps — and use repeat statements and a number of other advanced scripting techniques, you'll be well on your way to developing fully interactive products with Director 4 that'll make your Mother's eyes pop with pride. Bon voyage!

The 5th Wave By Rich Tennant

"The error messages on these multimedia applications are getting more interactive all the time."

Chapter 18

Showing Off Your 15 Minutes of Fame on Video

In This Chapter

- Using video with Director
- Creating projectors

One of the fantasies that draws people to multimedia is The Big Show. All your friends gathered round, anticipation etched in foreheads, necks straining forward, eyes glued in envious approbation to the Big Monitor, waiting dry-lipped for you to make the sign that The Big Show is about to begin. Your relatives, too, are there. Picketing the show, but they're there just the same. It's The Big Show, and you've got room in your heart for Charlie Manson tonight. You make your sign, the lights dim, and the Big Show begins.

Director makes *your* Big Show possible with its capability to display and edit digital video and export Director files as QuickTime mooVs. Knowing as much as you can about video and the Mac's capability to manipulate video information can't hurt. In that spirit, I offer a potpourri of topics to chew on. Just don't spit on the floor, OK?

What You Really Need to Know about Video

Wow, what a dream. But it's a dream that can come true with today's technology. This part of the book is intended as a primer on video — what you can and can't do without spending mucho moola. It's also meant as another inspirational speech with a very clear message, "Don't let anyone talk you out of your dreams."

Broadcast quality

Video people seem to talk endlessly about what broadcast video isn't. Everything I've read convinces me no one knows what broadcast video is. Judging by all the commercials and slick magazines, you'd think broadcast quality is the one determinate of a program's usefulness or a peripheral's lone measure of quality. Well, the plain fact is, it's not.

Unless you dream of doing state-of-the-art video, you don't need to concern yourself about reaching broadcast quality, whatever that is, or spend oodles of money on equipment trying to attain broadcast quality. In fact, you can do a lot with stuff you can buy at your local electronics store. And I'm talking professional level work. Plenty of professionals work with Hi-8 and Super-VHS equipment these days. I wouldn't drop below that level, but who doesn't have a camcorder these days?

It certainly doesn't hurt to have more professional equipment, but you shouldn't feel that you *must* wait until you can spend $500,000 on equipment. Don't listen to all the naysayers who tell you that "You can't do it," "You don't have enough equipment," and "You don't have enough experience."

By the way, there's always this thing called *renting*. If you can't or simply don't want to make heavy purchases, consider renting equipment on an as-needed basis. Plenty of camera operators don't own a camera; they rent. And don't forget service bureaus; they offer a lot of resources and services — including high-powered workstations, video digitizing, and other multimedia goodies — at reasonable rates.

Multimedia: kiosks, presentations, and CDs

Much of what multimedia types produce is not meant for broadcast in the first place. Most of the output is intended for intimate viewing conditions, including kiosks, event-type presentations, and CD-ROM publication. A *kiosk* is nothing but a monitor and computer tossed in a box. Who needs broadcast quality video for that?

Presentations are either displayed on giant 37-inch monitors (that are also great for getting an even tan) or projected onto a large screen with an LCD panel and an overhead projector. But we're not talking CinemaScope here; the experience is still relatively intimate.

As of this writing, a giant boon in CD-ROM publication is occurring. Good multimedia types of all persuasions are stoking the insatiable kiln of industry like so many briquettes. And talk about an intimate experience. In addition, the Internet is catching on; everyone now wants to publish and market on the Internet. That means that you can find plenty of multimedia productions, but not necessarily very much broadcast quality video.

When something's moving, it's hard to see

Funny thing about a moving object. When something's moving, it's hard to see. Actually, it's blurry. Ever see something filmed or taped in slow motion? What's the single most striking common denominator of all the images? Blur. They're all blurred. In fact, one of the telltale features of stop-motion animation has been — until recently — an absence of blur. Watch King Kong again. Wondrous as the animation work may be, we know it's stop-motion animation partly because the images of old Kong are *too* sharp. Even master animator of bygone days, Ray Harryhausen, working on his Sinbad epics, couldn't escape *this sharpness thing,* as a former president might say.

So, have animators slaved away to find a system producing sharper animation? No, they've developed techniques to blur their work. What I'm trying to say is that an image in motion must not be held to the same critical standards as a still image. What I'm *not* saying is, "Forget quality."

AV Macs

If you're careful and thoughtful, you can do professional work with AV Macs. Their built-in capabilities allow you to digitize incoming video and to output a real TV video signal you can copy to videotape — two very important features since television and computer video are two very different animals.

Your monitor uses a color scheme called RGB, for electronic "guns" in the picture tube that paint the image on your screen with red, green, and blue light, what's known as additive color. Real TV is known as NTSC TV, set for a number of technical reasons to a limited range of colors and level of quality. For more information on NTSC TV and related color issues, read the sidebar, "Free to be NTSC," in Chapter 10, as well as several sections in Chapter 21.

AV Power Macs are even more capable than their Quadra cohorts for working with digital video. If you are seriously interested in digital video, you should buy an AV Power Mac 8100 that runs at 100 MHz. Of course, any day now, the next generation of Power Macs should arrive sporting 604 *RISC* (Reduced Instruction Set Chip) chips several times faster than the 601 RISC processors in the current Power Mac models. In addition, Mac clones are now surfacing from various third-party vendors, from simple but powerful configurations to hefty workstation models just right for digital video. Chances are the information I'm recording now will be outdated by the publication date, the way things change these days; the info in this section is only meant to give you a reference point to help you consider your needs, what's in the marketplace, and what direction the technology is going.

Video production

This section contains some tips to help you produce and digitize video. You will also find some post-production tips. The tips in this section should help you maximize performance of an AV Mac and assist you in producing high-quality digital video.

Videotaping masters

When videotaping master tapes, be sure to think about the following:

- Shoot master video with at least Hi-8 or Super-VHS.
- Use the highest quality tape you can afford.
- Clean recording heads before taping.
- Use the best, most heavily shielded cables you can afford. Avoid cheap cables that degrade images.
- When videotaping, use *static* shots whenever possible and a tripod for steadiness.

  You should use static shots, shots where the camera doesn't move, because most compression schemes note the differences from frame to frame and only record the differences when turning video into QuickTime mooVs. In a panning shot, each frame changes completely, defeating compression technology. For more information on compression schemes, skim over the "Codecs" section in Chapter 11.
- Avoid close-ups of people to maximize compression. People tend to move, twitch, gyrate, and generally squirm, giving you the same kind of problem a panning shot presents.

Before digitizing video

Here are some things that you should do before you digitize video:

- Clean recording heads before playback.
- Install the best cables you can afford. Avoid cheap cables that degrade images.
- Use the S-video ports on both VCR and AV Mac for highest quality digital video.
- Turn off all INITs on your Mac. With System 7.5, press Shift and restart your Mac, holding the Shift key down until you come to the Desktop. Restarting also frees up more of your Mac's memory.
- Place a floppy disk in the floppy drive. Otherwise, your Mac will regularly check for floppies during digitization, slowing things down.

- Use the fastest and largest drive you have for saving digital video. You can compare hard drive speeds with a freeware program such as MacBench.

  Better yet, break down and buy an AV type drive — a Micropolis AV drive, for example. They are specially designed to handle the steady stream of data flow that video requires. Also, they have redesigned maintenance routines that tend to routinely stop data flow in regular hard drives in millisecond intervals.

- Install the latest drivers for your drive. Check with the manufacturer and get drivers compatible with System 7.5's new SCSI Manager 4.3, which increases performance of the drive.
- If possible, low-level format the storage drive.

The Format command in most commercial formatting programs like Drive 7 or SilverLining does a low-level format on the hard drive selected in the program. Choose the Initialize command in Apple HD SC Setup 7.2 to low-level format a hard drive.

Low-level formatting destroys all data on the disk. Be sure you have solid backups for everything on the disk before you low-level format it.

If low-level formatting isn't practical, optimize the drive with Speed Disk, Disk Express, or a similar optimizing program.

Optimizing eliminates file fragmentation. It also results in a large, contiguous block of disk space to write to, contributing to maximum hard drive performance.

Digitizing video

When you digitize video, be sure that you keep these things in mind:

- If possible, don't use compression while digitizing master tapes.
- If possible, digitize video separately from audio to help increase your AV Mac's performance.

  Chances are whatever program you use to digitize video offers commands somewhere in the menu bar to choose video, video and audio, or just audio. Eliminating one of the demands on your Mac's processor will achieve better performance all around.

- Consider smaller sizes for the digital video window. In Director you can use a still image for the background and a small Digital Video window for the QuickTime mooV with a matching background to "trick" the user into thinking the size of the video is full screen.
- Consider installing VideoSpigot AV to increase performance. With an AV 8100 Power Mac and the VideoSpigot AV card, you can record full-frame, 30 frame per second video.

Post production

During post production, pay attention to the following:

- If possible, refrain from compression until the final edit.
- Use Cinepak compression for digital video destined for CD-ROM. Try a setting of 90 kilobytes per second for older, single-speed CD-ROM machines and 150 kilobytes per second for double-speed CD-ROM machines.
- Consider a smaller Digital Video window using the trick explained in the preceding set of tips. Blend the video's background with the matching background of a still image to create the illusion of a screen-sized video window.

Taping your movies

With Director movies using "hand-made" art — made from bitmaps painted in the Paint window or in Photoshop or Fractal Painter and with artwork from 3-D modeling programs like StrataStudio Pro — your movie contains original art as sharp as a tack, as crisp as your Mac's configuration can handle. You don't need to concern yourself about signal loss and image degradation that inevitably occur when converting images from life to digital information. In this sense, you're leagues ahead of the game. The challenge is copying your pristine movie to video.

For Director movies destined for transfer to video, be sure to use the NTSC palette in the Color Palettes window. The NTSC palette is a collection of NTSC-safe, or *legal,* colors that will not tend to change when you transfer the movies to videotape. *Illegal* NTSC colors tend to change dramatically on video, turning muddy or becoming over-saturated and cause *blooming* — a condition in which the color spills over into the rest of the screen.

I'm making an assumption at this point. Either you have an AV Mac with a video out port or a video board from one of a number of vendors that supplies a video out port. Or you're planning to buy a video board that supplies a video out port in the very near future. You can't get around this hardware requirement because, ordinarily, computer video and NTSC video don't mix any better than oil and water. The video your Mac uses to display Director on-screen is vastly different from the NTSC signal needed to tape to video. Some hardware is needed to make the translation.

Video boards aside, basically, you have two options. You can tape your Director movie in "real" time, meaning as the movie actually plays back from your Mac, signals streaming from the S-Video out port of your Mac to the S-Video in port of your VCR or camcorder. Or you can tape your movie with more control one frame at a time, which requires a special VCR such as the Sony EVO-9650 that accepts control signals from one of Director's *XObjects* — a set of external routines you can load for extending Director's capabilities.

If you go with the real-time option, remember that Director is frame-based; it's designed to show every frame, and it slows down rather than drop even a single, precious frame. Better to export the movie as a QuickTime file and import it back as a Digital Video cast member because QuickTime is time-based and designed to play back at the right speed, giving the sound track priority over image to maintain sync. Take a gander at "Sync about It," in Chapter 19 for a detailed look at synchronization issues.

The problem *now* is that QuickTime drops frames running from a slow Mac to keep in step with the soundtrack. What's the expression — six of one, half a dozen of the other? You can't win for losing? Please, send me *your* favorite trite expression; I'll be happy to include it in my next book. The point is, you need to decide what's more important to you and the project, a few dropped frames or slowed animation on tape?

Making a Projector (and Why You'd Want To)

Director 4 adds the Create Projector command under the File menu. With this command you create a stand-alone application called a *projector* that incorporates selected movies and plays them so that the user doesn't need a copy of Director or the original files to view the movies. In addition, Director compresses the movies and turns lines of Lingo into assembly code, protecting your scripts from prying eyes.

Here's how to make a projector:

1. **After your movies are ready, choose File⇨Create Projector.**

   The Create Projector dialog box appears as shown in Figure 18-1.

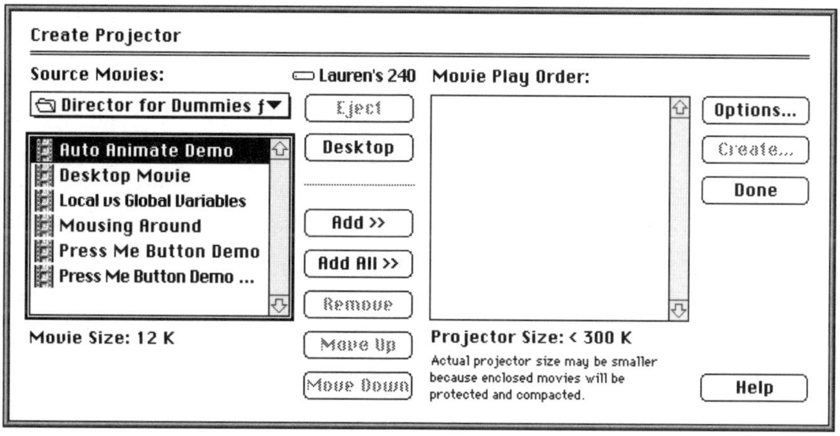

Figure 18-1: The Create Projector dialog box, where you decide which movies to include in a projector.

On the left is the directory where you locate movies to include in the projector.

2. **Highlight the movie you'd like to play first in the projector.**
3. **Click Add.**

   Director adds the movie to the Movie Play Order field on the right side of the Create Projector dialog box.
4. **If you want to add the entire list of movies displayed in the directory, click Add All.**

   Director adds all movie files currently displayed in the directory to the Movie Play Order field.
5. **If you want to change the position of a movie in the Movie Play Order field, highlight the movie and click Move Up or Move Down to move it to a new position.**
6. **Click Options.**

   The Projector Options dialog box appears as shown in Figure 18-2.

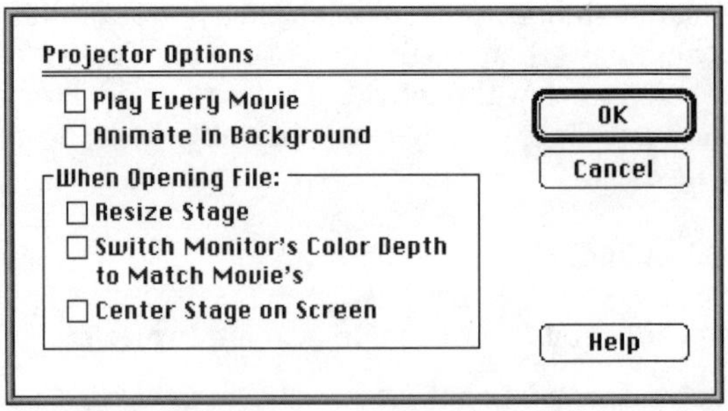

Figure 18-2: The Projector Options dialog box, where you can select five playback options for the projector.

Projector Options
Play Every Movie
Animate in Background
When Opening File:
Resize Stage
Switch Monitor's Color Depth to Match Movie's
Center Stage on Screen
OK
Cancel
Help

The Projector Options dialog box includes the following options:

- *Play Every Movie:* Checked, the projector plays every movie displayed in the list field of the Create Projector dialog box. Unchecked, the projector only plays the first movie listed in the Create Directory dialog box.

  TIP

  If a projector is playing a list of movies and you want to exit the movie currently playing to go to the next movie, press Command+. (period). To quit, use the old standby, Command+Q.

- *Animate in Background:* Checked, the projector continues playing even if you click on the Desktop to return to the Finder or open another application. Unchecked, the movie stops until you click on the movie's window again.

Some movies, especially interactive movies, are designed to continue playing until the user stops the movie with Command+. (period) or quits with Command+Q. Either keyboard shortcut exits you from the projector and returns you to the Desktop. Movies designed to stop at the last frame simply exit the projector and return you to the Desktop.

- *Resize Stage:* Checked, the projector resizes the Stage area for the Stage size set for each movie in the Preferences dialog box. Unchecked, the Stage remains the same size throughout playback.
- *Switch Monitor's Color Depth to Match Movie's:* Checked, the projector automatically sets the monitor's color depth to the color depth used when the movie was created in Director. Otherwise, the projector plays the movie in 256 grays, for example, if the monitor's color depth is set to 256 grays when you open a projector with a full-color movie.
- *Center Stage on Screen:* Checked, the projector plays each movie in the center of the screen. Otherwise, it plays each movie in locations set in the Preferences dialog box of Director when each movie was created.

7. **Click the desired options in the Projector Options dialog box and click OK.**
8. **Click Create.**

   The Save Projector as directory appears.
9. **Enter a custom name for the projector.**
10. **In the directory, navigate to where you'd like the projector saved and click OK.**
11. **At the Desktop, find the projector and double-click its icon to test playback.**

Remember to always test your work!

I'll give you another great reason for making a projector, even if you have no intention of letting someone else see it on a Mac. Make a projector to copy the movies to video. The projector application is minuscule compared to loading Director to play your movies and the movies themselves are compressed. Your chances of recording them to tape in real time is greatly increased. You're welcome — my pleasure.

Chapter 19

You Talking to Me? Adding Sound to Your Movie

In This Chapter

- Where you acquire sound
- Where you store sound files
- How to use smaller sound files
- All about sync, not including the kitchen kind

You may be asking yourself, "Self, add sound to my movie? OK, I'm all for that, but . . ."

Where Do I Get All This Stuff, Anyhow?

Sound? What am I, a producer? As a matter of fact, that's exactly what you become when you get involved in multimedia: a multimedia producer, a wild mix of Hollywood and Silicon Valley. So, knowing sources for audio becomes pretty important. With a little thought, a number of possibilities come to mind.

Sampling your own audio

With an AV Mac, you're all set to sample sounds. Sampling is using an ADC (Analog to Digital Converter) to translate the sound you'd like to add to your movie into digital information, meaning 0s and 1s, the only thing your dumb bunny of a Mac really understands. An AV Mac samples 16-bit sound at four different sampling rates; the higher the sampling rate, the better the sound. By the way, 16-bit sound offers near CD-quality results.

The right connections

The AV Macs, some Performas, and most PowerBooks have input for sound on the back; it's the connection with the Mic icon on top. You can get your audio from a number of sources: VCRs (most hi-fi VHS decks have terrific audio specs), CDs (including your Walkman, the well-known cassette player), and even your camcorder. Connect either the headphone output or RCA jack output of your audio source to your Mac. Be prepared with a slew of adapters. Radio Shack and most stereo shops have a wide selection of adapters, but remember this: Somewhere there's a Universal Rule of Adapters that states you never have the adapter you need. I'd relocate if I were you, cat and all, closer to a Radio Shack, just for the peace of mind.

Anyway, the AV Mac features stereo sound, but it sports a single mini-type stereo Sound-In port. So, skip to your handy electronics shop and get a stereo RCA plug-to-stereo mini-plug adapter. The RCA cables go into the adapter, the adapter goes into the Mac, and you're all set for sampling fun.

Double-check that you're using *line* output for records. If you have professional level audio equipment, you may have BNC ports. You can find an adapter for them, too. The main problem is signal loss, inevitable with analog-to-digital conversion, including audio sampling.

Be sure that you have the right to use someone else's audio professionally. You don't want to violate any copyright protection; it's not right, and it's against the law. Check whether the audio is in the public domain, that you've been granted *written* permission to use the material, or that purchasing the audio gives you the right to use it in a commercial product or public performance. Even then, did you pay for one-time only use (a so-called *drop needle fee*) or unlimited usage? Listen to your Uncle Lauren, be sure to check.

Sampling sound

But how do you actually sample or digitize sound once you're all connected? AV Macs come with a program called FusionRecorder, used for making QuickTime movies. You can use QuickTime technology to record audio only, and there's no law against a QuickTime mooV with only an audio track. In FusionRecorder, simply turn off its video capabilities. The only other decision to make is the sampling rate. The following lists various sample rates, and the acceptable uses for them. Remember, the higher the sample rate, the better the sound.

- *48 kHz*: The AV Mac's highest sample rate in kHz. KHz stands for kilohertz, or 1,000 hertz, a way of describing the number of sound waves that pass a fixed point, referred to as frequency and a determinant of pitch quality. Use for sampling music, especially from CDs, to obtain highest playback quality.
- *44 kHz:* Next highest sampling rate. Use for sampling music from non-CD sources.

- *24 kHz:* Use this sampling rate or higher for narration and sound effects. This special sampling rate is available mainly for the Geoport Telecom Adapter used with AV Macs for modem and fax features.
- *22.05 kHz:* Use this sampling rate or higher for sampling narration and sound effects.

Another common sampling rate is 11 kHz, not directly available when sampling with an AV Mac. Many utilities are available for "downsampling," to turn sound sampled at a high sampling rate, 44 kHz or 22 kHz, for example, into 11 kHz, which is considered acceptable for narration, although higher is always better. You'll also see 7.5 kHz listed in these downsampling utilities, but this sampling rate is for desperation time only: for example, if you *must* fit tons of audio in Director movies that *must* fit on a double-density floppy. I'd drop the client if I were you.

Why use lower sampling rates at all? The lower the sampling rate, the smaller the sound file. With extended narration and musical scores, sound can dramatically swell a movie's size. In the section, "Great Sound for the Price of Good," later in this chapter, I show you a way to get double the sound quality at half the file size.

AV Macless?

By the way, if you don't have an AV Mac and have no intention of buying an AV Mac, chances are your Quadra or PowerBook has built-in sound sampling technology. Otherwise, you can install a sound card, such as the Audiomedia card from DigiDesign, in the expansion slot of your Mac. Some sound cards offer features equivalent to an AV Mac's capabilities. Others add considerably more robust professional features, so that results are true CD-quality audio.

If you don't have an AV Mac or an expansion slot, or you don't want to make an investment in a sound card, you can sample sound with an external "box," such as Macromedia's MacRecorder digitizer bundled with SoundEdit 16, a capable sound-editing program. The MacRecorder plugs into the serial port of your Mac and allows you to sample audio from a built-in microphone, an external microphone, or line output. You can use two MacRecorders to sample stereo sound using both serial ports.

Disk-To-Disk

Disk-To-Disk is a great commercial program that allows you to "copy" sound directly from a CD, giving you the highest possible quality because it's a digital-to-digital data transfer, avoiding analog-to-digital signal loss that occurs when you send analog output from a CD (that's right, it's no longer digital by then) to your Mac with RCA type audio cables. Disk-To-Disk works through the SCSI bus, connecting your internal or external CD-ROM drive to your Mac. You do know that you can play audio CDs on your CD-ROM drive, don't you?

Make sure you've paid those royalties!

Freeware and shareware

Commercial on-line services, such as America Online, CompuServe, and Prodigy, have vast libraries of sampled sound to *download* (copy via a modem to your Mac). The Internet's the latest craze, and who knows the types of sound you can find there? Most freeware audio allows unlimited usage, but you'll want to double-check the privileges granted you by the owner and read all the fine print.

Commercial floppy and CD-ROM collections

Vast numbers of music and sound effect collections are on the market on floppies and CD-ROM disks. Of course, CD-ROM collections offer a number of advantages over floppies, including storage capacity, shelf life, and sound quality. Combined with the capabilities of Disk-To-Disk software, discussed earlier in this chapter, CD audio offers the highest quality transfer to your hard drive. Again, check and double-check usage rights before you purchase anything. My recommendation is to look for unlimited usage to get your full money's worth.

Where Sounds Go in Director

Just as you can import a PICT into your movie, you can import sound files. In the Import dialog box, you have an opportunity to import the sound as a linked file, referenced by a movie during playback but not actually incorporated into the movie file. Your other option is to add the sound to the movie file itself as a so-called *resource,* which is just a special module of code. Either way, the sound winds up as a Sound Cast Member in the Cast.

One way to determine which option to choose is to consider that incorporated sounds must load completely into memory before being played, and that they become the property of that one movie. A linked sound file, on the other hand, such as an AIFF sound file, plays from disk, reducing memory requirements and remaining available to be shared among several movies. A special advantage of an AIFF sound file is its portability, meaning you can use the same AIFF sound file for Mac and Windows Director movies.

Sounds incorporated into a Director movie become part of the so-called *resource fork* of the file, the place where sounds and other resources are stored. In MacLand, sounds are stored as resource type *snd* . By the way, the space after snd is correct. All resources are designated by type with a unique four-character code.

Great Sound for the Price of Good

Wouldn't it be great to play 44 kHz sound at a 22 kHz storage and memory price? Or 22 kHz sound, great for narration, at an 11 kHz price? You can achieve the impossible with a wonderful little shareware utility called Sound Mover, created by Riccardo Ettore. It's available for downloading to your Mac from most commercial on-line services and private bulletin boards.

If you remember Font/DA Mover from System 6.8, you're familiar with Sound Mover's interface, a window with a left and right scrolling directory field and a button underneath each field. Pressing Option and clicking the left Open button opens a pop-up menu that allows you to choose the type of sound file you want from your hard drive. When sounds are listed in the left directory, you may copy any sound to a file you find in the right directory. If you press Command, Option, and then Copy to copy a selected sound displayed in the left directory to a file on the right, Sound Mover cuts the size of the sound file in half without lowering the quality of playback.

How does Sound Mover achieve this miracle? Basically, the utility copies every other byte of sound information. Four out of five doctors claim they can't hear a difference between the original 44 KHz file and the 22 KHz file. Try it, you'll like it. Trust me.

Sync about It

Synchronizing sound to picture is every multimedia type's nightmare, although digital technology makes this task a lot easier. In addition, when you really think about it, much of the sound you hear around you and in movies and TV isn't synced sound at all. Background noise, most special effects, and musical scores aren't synched in the critical sense we expect of lip-synced sound. Even then, if someone's head is turned away from the camera, or if a figure is moving or in the distance, sync becomes a much less critical issue.

Playing a sound through

Before running, maybe you'd better learn to crawl. How do you play a complete sound file in Director? Adding a Sound Cast Member to one cell in the Score's Sound channel doesn't do it. You hear the narration, music, or sound effect for an instant, and as soon as the playback head moves on to the next frame, the sound dies.

To play a sound from beginning to end, you need to add the same Sound Cast Member to as many cells as needed in the Sound channel to play back the sound from beginning to end. Not enough cells and the sound dies before the end of the piece; too many cells and you waste valuable cells in your movie. Remember, Director sees a block of cells with the same Cast Member as one "performance" of the sound. To play the sound again, leave at least one cell blank between the first and second performance of the sound.

You can use the In-Between Linear command under the Score menu to fill a block of cells with a Sound Cast Member. Just copy the Sound Cast Member to a frame that is the number of frames forward from the original frame that you want, press Shift and select the range of frames, and choose In-Between Linear from the Score menu.

You can also play with different tempo settings for a selected block of sound cells. Changing tempo doesn't change the sound itself, but rather the number of frames needed to play the sound from beginning to end.

Remember, sync is one of those ticklish areas dependent on the speed of your Mac's processor. Slower machines will need different settings than fast Quadras and Power Macs.

Syncing sound to your movie

Following are some tips for synchronizing sound to sequences in your movie, be it music, be it narration, be it creepy sound effects.

- Make sure that your audio is clear and well recorded. You don't want to start with source audio that has lots of noise, pops, or other distractions. When you sample audio, something called *antialiasing* may occur, adding digital "noise" to the result (especially on lower-end sampling devices or settings). Also, pay attention to levels; digital audio is very sensitive to high recording levels, the settings you use for your VCR or cassette may sound very different when applied to digital.

  You want to record as *hot* (audiophileSpeak for loud) as possible without going into the danger zone of your sound-level meter. Find the loudest part of your audio track and set the levels to that segment, then record.

- Try changing tempo settings for various blocks of sounds in the Sound channel of the Score window. Select a block of cells in the Sound channel that contain the same Sound Cast Member. Double-click the Tempo channel in the first frame of the selected sound cells and set the Tempo with the slider control in the Set Tempo dialog box.

When using Tempo settings to sync sound to Director animation, use the slowest machine that you anticipate the movie will play on. Working the other way around, you'll lose sync as you move to slower machines and the frame rate drops while the sound plays on. Remember that Director is built to play every frame of your movie, and it slows down on slower Macs, rather than drops frames.

- If you've developed an animation sequence that you're syncing sound to with the In-Between Linear or In-Between Special commands under the Score menu, try redoing the *tweening* with a different number of frames between the key frames. To review the tweening technique and In-Between commands, jump back to Chapter 5.
- If you own a QuickTime editing application such as Premiere, export your Director movie with sound as a QuickTime mooV. In Premiere, picture and sound will be in separate tracks, and you can take advantage of special tricks that Premiere offers, such as shortening or lengthening audio passages, to sync sound to picture without distorting the sound. If you need to run the final mooV from Director, re-import it as a Digital Video Cast Member to play back in its own Digital Video window while maintaining the sync you established in Premiere. Remember, QuickTime was built from the beginning to maintain sync between audio and picture, even dropping frames if necessary to maintain sync.

Chapter 20

Ready to Wear All Those Hats?

In This Chapter

- Multimedia in real life
- Some of the roles you play
- Ever notice all those credits at the end of a movie?

The image of the lone wolf is very tempting to a lot of us. The maverick, the loose cannon, the independent producer, the radical, *The Man with No Name,* Newt Gingrich. As red-blooded, all-American types, we're drawn to the image. We see ourselves like Gary Cooper in *High Noon,* facing the enemy alone on a dusty street in some God-forsaken town. We hear Sinatra crooning in the background doing it "my way." We honor the entrepreneur and the athlete bucking all odds to become a winner.

When it comes to multimedia, we want our name and our name alone to be called when it's time to hand out the awards.

Multimedia in Real Life

At San Francisco State University, where I give a number of multimedia courses, I break up one class in one of the last meetings into groups of four or five students and have each group develop an idea for a kiosk, that is, a self-standing computer setup used to easily maneuver through a lot of information. To pass the class, they must work together as a *team,* producing a so-called *alpha version* of the kiosk by the end of the day.

An alpha version of a multimedia project is the equivalent of a traditional storyboard in the TV advertising world where a sequence of stills suggests the direction of a commercial's story line and how its images will flow. Sometimes, it *is* a storyboard. More often, the alpha version is a nonfunctioning placeholder, shown on-screen for graphics, text, sound, and animation to give your client a better idea of what she has in mind, that is, what you think she has in mind and what you have in mind, plus any suggestions you don't think she'd mind.

One student plays the part of creative director, giving the project a unique and consistent point of view. Another takes on the role of project manager, helping the team stay on track and meet deadlines. A third student provides graphics and production support, because multimedia is inevitably reliant on the visual, despite its broader appeal to all the senses. A fourth team member develops the *GUI* (graphical user interface) for the project.

Essentially, this classroom example is multimedia in real life. Aside from an occasional opportunity to develop a project alone, perhaps because of the modest size of the project or, more likely, the modest size of the budget, multimedia development requires a joint effort by a creative team with extraordinarily diverse backgrounds.

Even with a small project, the client may require such tight deadlines that one person — given all the required skills and services — can't possibly complete the assignment alone. In fact, the demands of the project may compel you to develop a team, against your desire to play all the parts. One of the resurrected images to come out of the growth of multimedia has been that of the renaissance person of the 21st century: artist, artisan, programmer, Mac guru, entrepreneur, good cook, able to leap tall buildings in a single bound. Every now and then, you see an article in one of the computer magazines about being a renaissance man or woman, and how you need to prepare yourself to handle any and all demands of a multimedia project.

Well, it certainly doesn't hurt to grasp the fundamentals of each of the pieces that make up the multimedia puzzle. As part of a team, you want to be able to communicate with the Lingo programmer, for example, and have a deep enough understanding of Director's built-in language to know what level of performance Lingo can and can't provide out of the box. Knowing what the client desires or whatever features you'd like to include in a project is possible only through developing a custom *XObject* or external command that helps you anticipate the effect on the project's assignment of resources, budget, and estimated time of completion.

It certainly doesn't hurt to be more than familiar with Apple's graphical user interface guidelines, published in a number of formats, including a CD-ROM disc version. Conforming to these guidelines is one of the more important decisions to be made on start-up of a multimedia venture, in addition to nightly flossing. Yes, you heard right. Staying with Apple's guidelines is a decision you *make*. There's no amendment to the U.S. Constitution, that I know of, dictating multimedia developers to conform to Apple's guidelines. Kai Krause's use of unique interfaces for his products, such as Power Tools Photoshop plug-ins, unlike any other Mac application interface known to humanity, serves as dramatic examples that you can depart from Apple's golden rules and still be wildly successful, critically and in the marketplace.

Some of the Roles You Play

Multimedia is a collaborative process, the melding of any number of areas of expertise to realize a successful product. Certainly, you want the client to consider the product a success measured in his own sometimes skewed terms. You look for critical and personal success, too. Part of the formula for success includes making the right decision for going it alone or putting together a team to complete the project. I've listed some of the supporting cast in a typical multimedia production team. By the way, multimedia offers plenty of parts for you readers out there who have little or no graphics background. (I've seen this concern expressed by many of my students at San Francisco State.)

Creative director

The creative director provides the main vision of the project, much like the director of a motion picture or the editor of a magazine. Having a background in film, video, computers, all three, or any two areas doesn't hurt. With two, you get egg roll.

Above all, the creative director communicates to all parties involved what needs to be done on a moment-to-moment, real-time basis to successfully complete the assignment. So there's a critical managerial aspect to the role of creative director, a leadership ability at least as important as specific skills in the areas mentioned in the preceding paragraph.

The creative director's vision holds the project together like superglue. She maintains continuity to the work from screen to screen and contributes to the project's ultimate look and feel. The creative director maintains a broader view of the project than the rest of the team working in their various, specialized areas.

Art director

A multimedia project may have an art director whose vision is as broad as the creative director's, but focuses on aesthetic issues on a real-time basis. In this sense, the art director has a significant impact on the visual outcome of the project, second only to the creative director.

The art director focuses on issues such as color schemes, typefaces used throughout the project, and the look and feel of illustrations, charts, and graphs displayed on-screen. He also contributes managerial skills to the project, overseeing artiste types who are contracted to provide screen illustrations, animation sequences, and specialized multimedia items such as custom icons and cursors for the project. The art director also often oversees photo shoots for quality and content.

Project manager

The success of a multimedia project is often due in large measure to the expertise of its project manager, who is contracted to help establish and meet milestones and other critical deadlines. Milestones include the beginning and ending dates of the project and due dates for *alpha, beta,* and *golden masters* of the production.

- An alpha version is like an on-screen storyboard for a project with little or no functionality, but useful for walking the client through the creative team's interpretation of the client's wishes. An alpha version is also important as a check that all important points are included in the production as planned.
- The beta version is near final quality with all essential functionality in place. Few, if any, placeholders stand in for animation sequences or screen art, though some other rough edges may show at this point.
- The final version, sometimes called the golden master, is ready for client approval and presentation.

The project manager manipulates the resources of the project through events that inevitably occur, such as technical stumbling blocks, loss of staff from illness, and shortage of supplies from vendors. She may use software tools such as Claris MacProject Pro to help reallocate resources and reset non-critical deadlines so that the team stays on track and meets milestone commitments.

GUI designer

A graphical user interface (GUI) designer is often hired to provide the interface for the project. An extremely critical aspect of a project, the interface can make or break a multimedia production. In general, the GUI designer is responsible for maintaining close adherence to Apple's graphical user interface guidelines. Otherwise, he is responsible for creating an interface that's consistent with the mission of the project.

Lingo programmer

In many, if not most, Director multimedia teams, you'll find at least one key Lingo programmer who has been contracted to implement scripting for a Director project. His background usually includes heavy experience in traditional programming languages such as C, Pascal, or Fortran. This kind of background ensures that the programmer can develop scripts that are optimized for speed and performance, which is not to say that someone without a

GUI GUIdelines

The heart of Apple's graphical user interface guidelines includes these ten general principles:

1. Real world metaphors: For example, use of controls such as buttons, sliders, and dials as part of the interface.
2. Direct manipulation: Giving the user control over the screen environment.
3. See-and-point: Designing the interface to exploit visual cues rather than asking the user to remember commands.
4. Consistency: Building on the user's expectations about how a Macintosh program is going to behave from previous experience with other programs.
5. WYSIWYG: *W*hat *Y*ou *S*ee *I*s *W*hat *Y*ou *G*et, giving the user an on-screen experience as close as possible to reality or to the experience in another medium; for example, a printout of the screen compared to the screen itself.
6. User control: Developing an interface that makes the user in control of actions; reinforcing the Macintosh as an *event-oriented* computer, waiting to respond to the user's wishes.
7. Feedback and dialogue: Maintaining communication to the user so that the Macintosh recognizes and responds to user actions; for example, a button that highlights when pressed by the user.
8. Forgiveness: Including "outs" for the user to change her mind *without penalty* and warning the user when an action is irreversible.
9. Perceived stability: Providing a comfort zone of predictability in the interface so that critical elements don't arbitrarily disappear or change location; for example, menu items graying out instead of vanishing when disabled.
10. Aesthetic integrity: Basically, the whole arsenal of design tools and techniques available for supporting the other nine principles to ensure user friendliness.

similar background is incapable of writing excellent scripts. The key word is *ensure,* that is, the probability of such a team member being stumped by a scripting challenge is greatly diminished, and the programmer can achieve the level of scripting required as quickly as possible.

In addition, a programmer with experience in other computer languages may be able to develop external commands, or XObjects, if needed, to supplement Director's built-in capabilities.

Instructional designer

Multimedia as an educational product, a self-running tutorial, for example, often means adding the services of an instructional designer to the project. The in-structional designer has a background in applied learning theory and experience in developing interfaces that maximizes the educational experience of a *CAI* (computer-aided instruction) or *CBT* (computer-based training) product. The instructional designer works in unison with the GUI designer, the art director, and the creative director.

Program tester

Testing is an extremely critical area for multimedia development. More often than not, a team member specializing in software testing is brought in to ensure the product runs on all intended platforms within the given minimum specifications established at the beginning of the project. Most recently, Disney's *Lion King* CD-ROM underscores the importance of solid testing for multimedia products so that embarrassing and unnecessary software failures don't occur.

Software is never perfect, but rigorous testing under a number of different conditions helps to alleviate most problems that might otherwise occur. Users are very creative, and the program tester tries to anticipate all the scenarios a user might play out while running the program in untraditional ways and builds in safeguards to protect the integrity of the program.

Ever Notice All Those Credits at the End of a Movie?

Was it beginning with *2001: A Space Odyssey* or earlier that the credits seemed to go on and on forever at the end of the movie? I don't really remember when I first realized that credits were getting longer than the movie itself, but one thing's for sure: These days, you expect credits to go by interminably. Directed by . . . Second Assistant Directed by . . . Best Boy . . . Best Boy's Third Cousin on His Mother's Side, Twice Removed . . . and on and on. At least they don't list Shoes by . . . anymore, as they used to in those old Italian movies about gladiators and the benefits of rubbing olive oil all over your pecs.

What I'm trying to say is, going it alone is pretty rough. I hope this chapter has given you an idea of how complex even a relatively small multimedia project can be, not to discourage you but to show you that recognizing you may need support is more typical than unusual in the wacky world of multimedia.

It's fun to fantasize about doing it all yourself, wearing all those hats and reaping all the credits. But when was the last time you saw only one name in the credits for a movie? Except for *Citizen Kane,* of course.

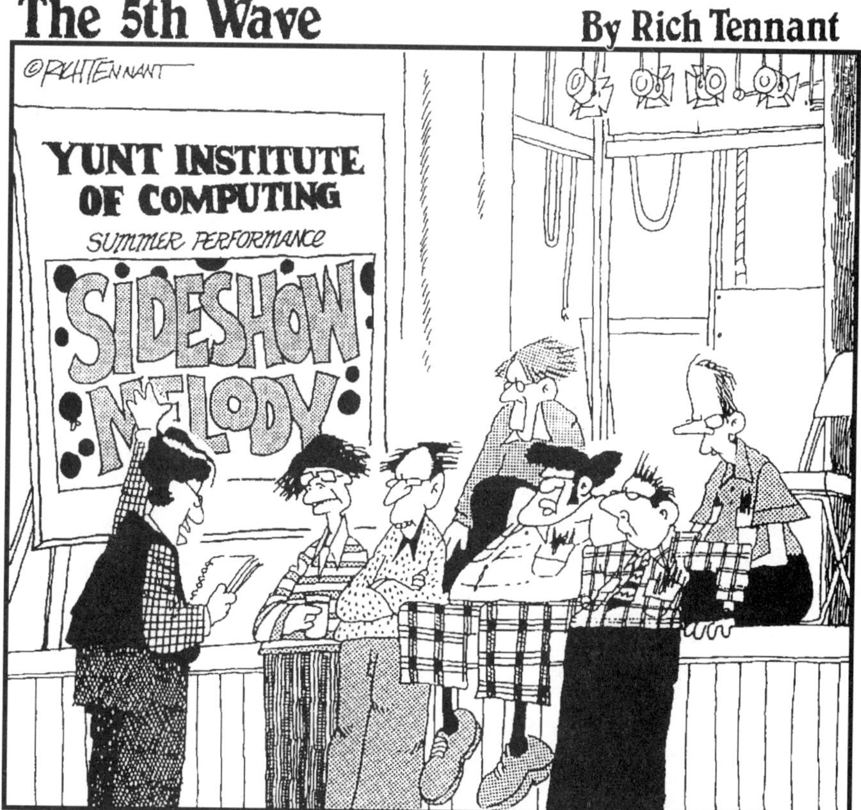

"ALL RIGHT, NOW, WE NEED SOMEONE TO PLAY THE PART OF THE GEEK."

Part V
The Part of Tens

"It's amazing how much more some people can get out of Director than others."

In this part...

If you know anything about the . . . *For Dummies* tradition, we like to leave you with a partful of chapters to peruse in sets of tens— really ten glorified bullet points. Charlton Heston would feel right at home here.

Anyway, relax and enjoy my collection of the top ten Director tips and tricks available in each chapter. Hey, it's Miller time.

Chapter 21

Ten Common Director Questions and Answers

In This Chapter

- How can I cut down the size of my movie?
- What can I do to make my movies play faster?
- What's the best way to speed up QuickTime mooVs in Director?
- How can I tape Director movies to my VCR?
- Why am I getting weird colors when I tape my Director movies?
- How can I improve the color of my movies on tape?
- Why do I keep losing part of my screen when I tape my movies?
- Can I set up my movie to play at the right speed on any Mac?
- I've never done any programming. How do I know my Lingo scripts are OK?
- Can I play my Mac movies on a PC?

Perfect strangers come up to me all the time entreating me to answer questions about Macromedia Director. Following are the ten most common questions they ask and my answers for your edutainment and amusecation.

How Can I Cut Down the Size of My Movie?

You can use a couple of techniques to cut down the size of a Director movie, which isn't a bad idea, by the way. Your movie will run faster on slower hard drives, older Macs, and CD-ROM drives should it be destined to star on a CD.

Rather than choosing File⇨Save, choose File⇨Save and Compact, especially after you complete an especially large Director movie. The Save and Compact command offers special features, including the following:

- *Trashing unneeded info from the Director movie:* Director is kind of a pack rat. As you develop a movie, Director tends to hang on to outdated info that it records along the way, causing bloating of the file and occasional jock itch. Running Save and Compact makes Director dump this digital flotsam and jetsam, effectively compacting the file.
- *Internally rearranging Cast Members:* Helps to further optimize the Director movie for playback. You won't necessarily see a change in the Cast window, but whatever Director does contributes to building the smallest and fastest running Director file possible.

Another way of trimming the fat from a Director movie is to move the Score to a new movie. Here's the scoop step-by-step:

1. **Choose Window⇨Score.**
2. **Choose Edit⇨Select All.**

   Selecting cells in the original Score by choosing Select All is very important. Choosing cells by dragging the mouse or by pressing Shift and clicking a range of cells won't include in the selection markers that are set in the Score and won't transfer to a new file with the Paste Cells command.
3. **Choose Edit⇨Copy Cells.**
4. **Choose File⇨New.**

   A new movie appears with the Score window open and active.
5. **Choose Edit⇨Paste Cells.**
6. **Choose File⇨Save As.**

   Choosing Save from the File menu only records changes to the Cast and Score windows in your movie since the last time you saved to your hard drive. Use Save As to create a new Director file as a different version of the same movie, or to save a movie to a different hard drive without leaving Director.
7. **Type a unique name and click OK.**

   If you want to replace the original movie, enter the original movie name in the Save As dialog box, click OK, and then click OK again when your Mac asks whether you really want to replace the file.

This second method actually has an advantage or two over the Save and Compact command. Copying selected cells from the Score of one movie and pasting the selection into the Score window of a new Director file fills the new

Cast window with only the Cast Members used in the Score. Just be sure that you don't mind losing all those deadbeat Cast Members too lazy to make an appearance in the original movie's Score or Stage. Deleting unused Cast Members in this way makes an even smaller file than using the Save and Compact command. In addition, Director eliminates any empty pockets of cells that may have been present in the original movie's Cast window, because it fills consecutive cells of the new Cast window with Cast Members for the new movie.

If you're tight on memory, you can achieve the same benefits of the second method, without leaving the original movie, by choosing Find Cast Members under the Cast menu and clicking the "that are not used in the Score" radio button. Director highlights all the unused Cast Members; you can delete them by choosing Edit⇨Clear Cast Members, and then you can choose File⇨Save and Compact for a Director pick-me-up. Or try pouring Clamato down the floppy port. (Just kidding.)

Command+Option+S is the keyboard shortcut to save and compact your movie.

What Can I Do to Make My Movies Play Faster?

Use a bouquet of strategies to make your movies play faster.

- Compact your movie with one of the methods discussed in the preceding section.
- Change single-color Cast Members to 1-bit Cast Members using Director's Transform Bitmap command under the Cast menu. Then apply a color to the bitmap selected on the Stage with the Foreground Color selector in the Tools window.
- Change 16-bit and 24-bit Cast Members to dithered 8-bit Cast Members using Director's Transform Bitmap command under the Cast menu. A 16-bit Cast Member asks your Mac to process roughly 32,000 colors at one time. A 24-bit Cast Member tasks your processor even further, with over 16 million colors. Dithering to 8-bit cuts down the number of colors to a mere 256, along with a special trick reminiscent of what some of the impressionists accomplished with dabs of different colors of oil paint. Up close, all you see in their paintings is dabs of color, but from a normal viewing distance, the spots of color blend into new color combinations. That's the idea behind dithering, creating the illusion of seeing more than 256 colors by placing the right colored pixels next to each other in an unobtrusive pattern.

- Take advantage of Director's memory management features. If you have tons of RAM, select all Cast Members from the Cast window and choose Purge Priority 0 from the Cast Member Info dialog box so that they all stay in memory. Anything in memory is about 1,000 times faster to access than having Director find a Cast Member on disk and load the object into RAM. In limited RAM situations, choose Purge Priority 3 for your most important Cast Members and Purge Priority 2 for secondary Cast Members whenever possible so that Cast Members not used frequently are quickly trashed from memory. Cast members with Purge Priority 2 are released from memory before Cast Members assigned Purge Priority 3. See Chapter 4 for more on prioritizing your cast.
- Apply the Copy ink effect to all sprites whenever possible. With a white background, assign white background ink to non-rectangular sprites that must pass in front of other sprites on the Stage; otherwise, choose Matte ink for these sprites. Choose Mask ink if you must have a doughnut hole effect, but *avoid* all other ink effects unless absolutely required.

What's the Best Way to Speed Up QuickTime MooVs in Director?

To speed up QuickTime mooVs in Director, use Director's Direct To Stage feature, which optimizes playback of digital video in a movie. Just follow these steps:

1. **Choose Window⇨Cast.**
2. **Select the desired *Digital Video Cast Member* (Director's name for a QuickTime mooV) in the Cast window.**
3. **Click the Cast Member Info button at the top of the Cast window, as shown in Figure 21-1.**

   The Digital Video Cast Member Info dialog box appears.
4. **Check the Direct To Stage check box, as shown in Figure 21-2.**

Figure 21-1: The Cast Member Info button in the Cast window.

When you apply Direct To Stage to a QuickTime mooV, you must conform to *The Rules.* The Rules state: No other object may be placed in a higher channel than the QuickTime mooV; no other object may animate across the QuickTime mooV; and no special inks may be applied to the QuickTime mooV. For more info on Direct To Stage, peruse the section, "Setting up your digital video," in Chapter 11.

Digital Video Cast Member Info
Cast Member: 1 HD Platters.mooV
Length: 2 seconds
OK
Cancel
Script...
Loop Paused at Start
Video Crop
Sound Center
Enable Preload into RAM
Direct To Stage
Show Controller
Play Every Frame
Play at Normal Rate
Play as Fast as Possible
Play at Fixed Rate: 10 fps
Purge Priority: 3 - Normal
Memory Size: 75.3 K
File Name: Lauren's 24...:HD
Help

Figure 21-2: The Direct To Stage check box in the Digital Video Cast Member Info dialog box.

How Can I Tape Director Movies to My VCR?

Taping a Director movie to your VCR is a technological stunt. In other words, the video being driven by your Mac is so radically different from the video you watch on real TV, you're asking your Mac to do hand sprints and cartwheels when you decide you want to tape your movie to a VCR.

Unless you own an AV Mac, there's really no effective way to put your Director movies on videotape. If you insist on trying, the simplest technique involves your Mac's monitor and a camcorder.

Simple, cheap, but not terribly impressive

The simplest, most inexpensive, but least effective way of videotaping a Director movie is to tape the Mac's monitor itself with your camcorder. You lose a lot of definition, color, and quality along the way. You also get weird, shimmering patterns and vertically rolling bars in the image because of the difference in synchronization signals between the video camera and the computer monitor.

But you can minimize many of these pitfalls with a few tricks:

- If your camcorder features a variable shutter, visually adjust the shutter until vertical roll disappears from the image on the monitor or is minimized. Many high-end consumers camcorders, especially Hi-8 and Super-VHS models, feature a variable shutter these days. Check your manual.
- To reduce distortion, shoot from a distance using the longest telephoto setting your camcorder has to offer.
- Soften the screen's pixels by shooting the slightest bit out of focus. Better yet, shoot through a Hasselblad diffusion filter to minimize screen pixels on tape. Nikon diffusion filters are the next best choice.
- Adjust your Mac monitor's settings to reduce contrast, and shoot in a darkened room to avoid glare.
- If at all possible, use a color PowerBook that features an active matrix LCD (Liquid Crystal Display) screen. How do you know if your PowerBook has an active matrix screen? Break down and read the manual. Because LCD screens work differently than conventional computer monitors, they don't display rolling bars or annoying distortions when videotaped. LCD panels are flat, too, minimizing distortion.

AV Macs

If you're the proud owner of an AV-type Centris, Quadra, or Power Mac, you're all set to copy your Director movies to videotape. For highest quality, use the S-Video Video Out port from your AV Mac to the S-Video Video In port available on Hi-8 or Super-VHS camcorder and VCR models. Otherwise, use premium quality, shielded RCA-type video cables for the connection.

You'll need to purchase an adapter at your friendly electronics shop to convert the stereo miniplug Audio Out port on the AV Mac to left and right audio cables, most likely RCA-type cables unless your VCR features more professional BNC-type ports. Either way, use the best shielded cables and highest quality videotape you can afford, and be sure to clean the recording heads of your VCR before taping.

You'll be recording in real time, the way your movie plays back on your monitor, so be sure to take precautions before taping. Choose About Director from the Apple menu and click Purge Memory. And remember to follow the suggestions for optimizing playback speed found earlier in this chapter.

Video boards

Without an AV Mac, you need to turn to a relatively inexpensive video board, such as Radius's VideoSpigot, to do the job of converting computer video into real TV signals compatible with your camcorder or VCR. A more expensive but elegant solution is to purchase a video board such as Radius's VideoVision board, with the added benefit of creating full-screen digital video running at 30 *fps* (frames per second) from incoming video.

After installing a hardware solution, be sure to follow the prep work and other tips discussed earlier to ensure highest quality input to your camcorder or VCR.

Why Am I Getting Weird Colors When I Tape My Director Movies?

One of the biggest differences between real TV, the stuff we watch at home with our shoes off, and so-called RGB computer video is the *gamut,* or range, of colors available on each system. (By the way, it is technically possible to watch real TV with your shoes on.) If you're fortunate enough to be working with 24-bit color, you're playing with 16 million plus colors on your Mac monitor. With the monitor properly adjusted, any one of these colors displays relatively purely on-screen, although your monitor does have limitations of its own that I won't get into here (thunderous applause).

Real TV color, in comparison, is atrocious. It's atrocious compared to just about anything, but especially compared to the beautiful images beaming off your pristine, perfectly adjusted RGB monitor. Real TV's gamut of colors is extremely limited; only a small portion of the spectrum of colors displays at all. And of these colors, only a percentage of them displays acceptably for viewing purposes. These are the so-called NTSC, or "legal," colors. "Illegal" colors that may display beautifully on your RGB monitor are said to *bloom* on real TV, meaning that the colors spill over the borders of the object that owns them and, in motion, smear across the rest of the television image. They may look DayGlo-ish and psychedelic, the way colors look on your TV when you crank up the color control. Generally, these are colors above 70 percent of their saturation point (saturation being a measure of how blue a blue is, for example).

So the answer to the question is, you're getting weird colors because so few of the colors that look fine and dandy on your Mac monitor translate into NTSC colors on your Ray-O-Vision TV set at home. If you're interested in how to overcome this seemingly impossible technological hurdle, read my answer to the next question that perfect strangers come up and ask me all the time.

How Can I Improve the Color of My Movies on Tape?

OK, you've just installed your high-definition, surround-sound, wide-screen, 80-foot, monster Ray-O-Vision television set and anti-aircraft radar detector, settled back to enjoy watching your Director *pièce de résistance* you've transferred to tape, and . . . . Lo — bad color, all that work for bad color. What's a videophile to do?

NTSC palette

The easiest, least technologically challenging, and least costly method to improve colors when you print to video, as multimedia types are wont to say, is to use Director's NTSC palette, one of the special collection of colors included with Director out of the box. No extra charge.

To set an entire Director movie to NTSC-legal colors, do the following:

1. **Choose Window⇨Score from the menu bar.**
2. **In frame 1, double-click the cell in the Palette channel, as shown in Figure 21-3.**

   Director displays the Set Palette dialog box.

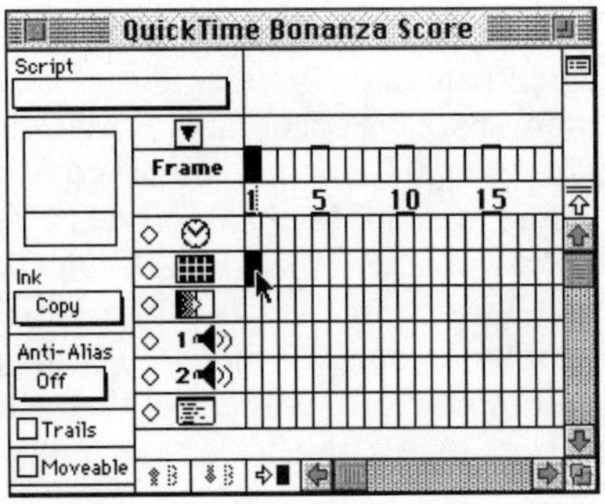

Figure 21-3: The Palette channel in frame 1 of the Score window.

3. **Choose NTSC from the Palette pop-up menu, as shown in Figure 21-4.**

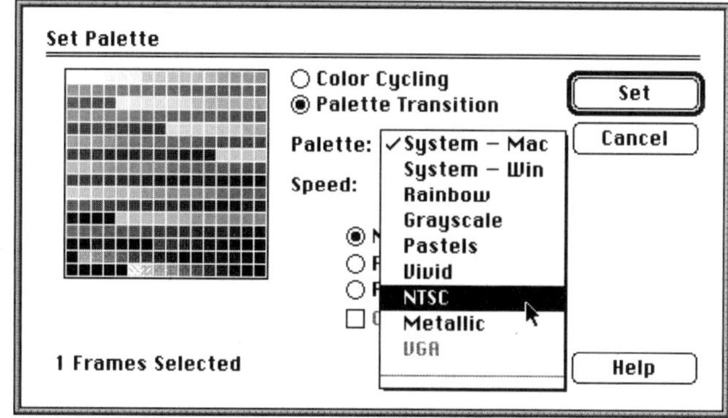

Figure 21-4: The Palette pop-up menu in the Set Palette dialog box.

4. **Be sure that the Palette Transition radio button is on and click OK.**

Until you change palettes again, all screen images will be built on the NTSC collection of "legal" colors.

The best strategy is to anticipate printing to video at the beginning of a project and to use an NTSC palette at all times. You'll find NTSC colors as an option in programs such as Photoshop too, where you have the opportunity to create bitmaps exclusively with "legal" colors *before* importing them into Director, which is the preferred method.

When you add a bitmap created with the default System palette in some other program, be sure to choose Remap Colors and Dither from the alert that appears after you import the graphic. The basic scenario plays something like the following:

1. **Choose File⇨Import.**

   The Import dialog box appears.

2. **Locate and select the bitmap to import in the directory and click Import.**

   A special Director alert appears as in Figure 21-5.

3. **Click the Remap Colors and Dither radio button.**
4. **Click OK.**

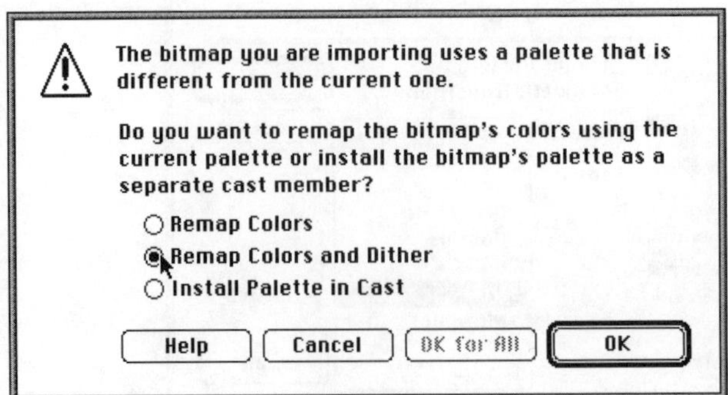
The bitmap you are importing uses a palette that is different from the current one.
Do you want to remap the bitmap's colors using the current palette or install the bitmap's palette as a separate cast member?
Remap Colors
Remap Colors and Dither
Install Palette in Cast
Help
Cancel
OK for All
OK

Figure 21-5: When an imported bitmap's palette differs from the current movie palette, a Director alert gives you a chance to remap the bitmap's colors.

With a Bitmap cast member built on the System palette already in the Cast, try the following to remap the cast member to the NTSC palette:

1. **Highlight the Cast Member in the Cast window and choose Cast⇨Transform Bitmap.**

   The Transform Bitmap dialog box appears, shown in Figure 21-6.

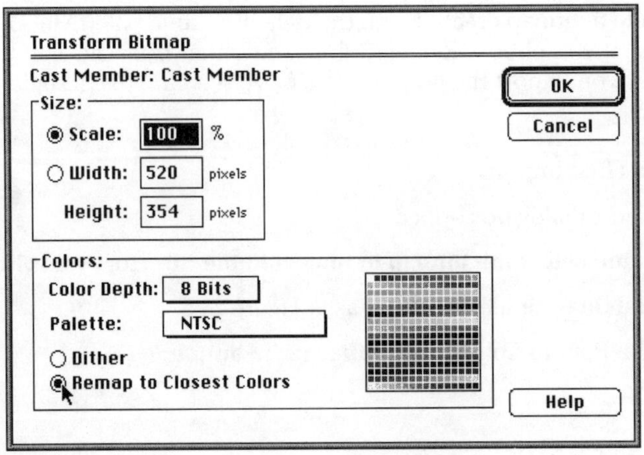

Figure 21-6: The Transform Bitmap dialog box, where you can remap a Bitmap Cast Member's palette.

Transform Bitmap
Cast Member: Cast Member
Size:
Scale: 100 %
Width: 520 pixels
Height: 354 pixels
Colors:
Color Depth: 8 Bits
Palette: NTSC
Dither
Remap to Closest Colors
OK
Cancel
Help

2. **Choose NTSC from the Palette pop-up menu.**
3. **Click the Remap to Closest Colors radio button and click OK.**

A better way to be NTSC safe

Working with an NTSC screen is the best way to prepare a Director movie for printing to video. If you have an AV Mac, you can switch to your real TV with the Monitors control panel.

1. **Choose Apple⇨Control Panels⇨Monitors.**
2. **Click the Options button.**

   The Monitors dialog box appears as in Figure 21-7.

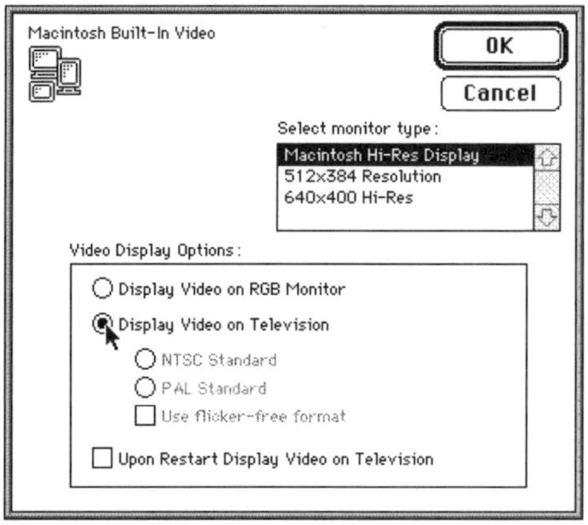

Figure 21-7: The Monitor Options dialog box, where you can switch output from an AV Mac to an NTSC TV.

3. **Click the Display Video on Television radio button.**

   If your monitor is set to 256 colors or less, your Mac allows you the option of checking the Use flicker-free format check box so that all images are free of annoying flicker (the annoying technical problem, not the annoying horse). With your monitor set to thousands or millions of colors, the check box is automatically checked and disabled.

4. **Click OK.**

   An alert appears asking whether you really want to switch monitors.

5. **Click Switch in the alert box.**

Your monitor will go black as your Mac begins sending an NTSC signal to your real TV set. When you want to return to your RGB monitor, select the Display Video on RGB Monitor radio button from the Options window of the Monitors control panel.

Now you can work using your real TV as your computer monitor. You have instant feedback to the colors you decide to use and can instantly note the effect on your NTSC "monitor." The only problem with this setup is that the resolution is so poor on a real TV compared to the crisp pixels of a good RGB monitor, you may begin suffering eye strain and headaches in a very short time.

The best of all worlds is running both an NTSC television and an RGB monitor at the same time, using the NTSC screen to check regularly on the progress of your work, especially colors and patterns. Unfortunately, AV Macs don't offer this feature but some other high-end video boards do offer support for running your RGB monitor and an NTSC television concurrently. Using this setup along with Director's NTSC palette is the ultimate print to video configuration. You can always create a custom color within the NTSC palette and save the new palette as a new custom palette. Just be sure to avoid raising the saturation level of the color above 70 to 75 percent.

Why Do I Keep Losing Part of My Screen When I Tape My Movies?

The differing makeup between RGB video and NTSC video reveals itself again when you tape a Director movie or print to video. You'll find that the beautiful image you carefully composed on your Mac monitor partially disappears. Some of the title may be missing, resting in the nether regions beyond the border of the TV screen, along with other lost details you worked so hard to perfect.

The cause of all this trouble is overscan. NTSC video is designed to create an image larger than the picture area of the television monitor so that it fills the screen, bordered only by the physical, plastic frame of the Ray-O-Vision TV set, itself. This phenomenon is called *overscan* by broadcasting types. The same thing happens to your Director movie when its video signals are converted to NTSC-compatible signals as you print to video. The image is blown up, and you lose a good inch or more of picture all the way around.

The solution is to anticipate overscan when you're planning a Director project for taping and to designate a safe title area that is 512 x 384 pixels and centered in the Stage. Don't let titles, other copy, or important objects extend beyond this area. Keep borders well within an inch of this safe area, too. If you set up a multiple monitor configuration as described in the previous section, you can visually adjust areas on the RGB display so that they don't get cut off on real TV.

Can I Set Up My Movie to Play at the Right Speed on Any Mac?

The trick to producing your Director movie so that it plays at the right speed on any Mac is twofold. First, you need to decide on the minimally acceptable configuration for playing back your movie, and then reproduce the configuration in your studio. If you decide you want anyone with a Mac SE, 4 megabytes of RAM, and a stick of bubble gum to run your movie off a high-density floppy, that's the platform you must design the movie on. For the sake of speed, you'll work in other programs and do some of the tinkering in Director on a high-powered Mac, but you'll want to do the serious tempo settings and playback on the dusty, old SE when you start timing and syncing stuff for the final production.

When you've got everything timed down to the nanosecond on the sluggish SE, the second ploy comes into play: locking the tempo. To prepare for locking the tempo, do the following steps with Director running on the target platform; in this example, that's the SE:

1. **Choose Edit⇨Disable Lingo so that the Disable Lingo command is *checked*.**
2. **Choose Edit⇨Loop so that the Loop command is *unchecked*.**
3. **Press Command+R to rewind the movie.**
4. **Press Command+P to play back the movie once on the target Mac.**

Now you're ready to lock your movie's tempo. Choose Edit⇨Lock Frame Durations, or bring up the Control Panel and click the Lock Frame Durations icon so that the lock appears, well, locked, as in Figure 21-8.

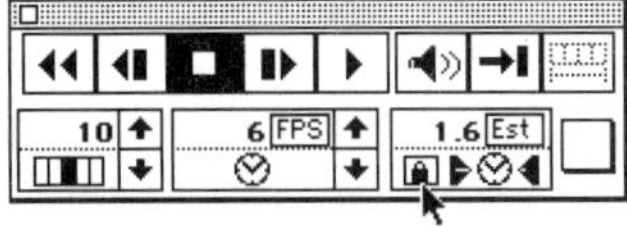

Figure 21-8: Clicking the Lock Frame Durations icon on the Control Panel.

Remember, this technique doesn't ensure *optimal* playback. Locking the movie's tempo ensures *consistent* playback from Mac to Mac by designing with the lowest common denominator in mind. Sigh, this is the stuff that makes multimedia great.

I've Never Done Any Programming. How Do I Know My Lingo Scripts Are OK?

First, go slowly with the scripting. Then, the best way to check your first Lingo scripts is to test them line by line in the Message window as you include them in your Director movie. For each line of Lingo you want to test, enter it in the Message window, and then press Return. You don't want to wait until you've amassed hundreds of lines of scripts and then discover errors you need to trace back to who knows which object. As you add scripts to your movie, include plenty of comments to yourself, explaining why the line of Lingo is needed and what it's going to cause to happen. Contrary to any stories you may have heard, comments don't slow down scripts; use plenty of them. Director simply ignores them. Remember, choose Text⇨Comment or use the keyboard shortcut, Command+>, for each line in a script you want to mark as a comment.

When you think you're finished with your movie, display the Message window, check the Trace check box, and play back your movie. Don't be surprised if Director stops your movie and slaps a script error on the screen. Go to the script and find out whether you can find the problem in the line with the blinking insertion point. Remember, odds are the problem's either a simple typo or a syntax problem. Sometimes, a script doesn't work because of a memory problem; check that you're allocating the best Purge Priorities to your Cast Members. Review the Lingo material in this book again (see Chapters 12, 17, and 23), and don't forget Director's on-line help.

Can I Play My Mac Movies on a PC?

You can create a projector using the new Windows version of Director 4, which is nearly identical to the Mac version. It's a simple matter of choosing the Create Projector command from the File menu and selecting the Mac movies to be incorporated into the Windows projector.

The real trick is prepping Mac movies intended for playback in a Windows projector on a PC monitor (VGA, Super VGA). Take the following precautions to avoid nasty surprises:

- *Use Windows file naming rules:* Begins with a letter; up to eight characters long, not including the period and the extension that Windows tacks on to the end of a filename; no spaces or punctuation characters, including a period, which is reserved for the filename's extension.

- *Use the VGA palette included with Director:* Jump back to the section, "How Can I Improve the Color of My Movies on Tape?" in this same chapter to review how to set up a custom palette for your movie. Also, you'll need to run a VGA monitor on your Mac to enable the VGA palette option in the Palette pop-up menu. Many of the recent Mac models have built-in capabilities to drive a VGA monitor. Otherwise, you'll need to check into the availability of an adapter.
- *Prepare for font wars:* PC fonts are dramatically different from the Mac fonts we've grown to cherish. The easiest way to avoid problems is to turn text into bitmaps while in Director. If you must use editable text, meaning text in a text box, stick with boring, old Helvetica and Times.
- *Prep your QuickTime mooVs:* QuickTime mooVs may be included in a Director file destined for a Windows projector, but each mooV must be prepped in a utility program such as MoviePlayer 2.0. Open each QuickTime mooV in MoviePlayer 2.0, then choose File⇨Save As. Click the Make movie self-contained radio button and check the Playable on non-Apple computers check box, as shown in Figure 21-9, and then click Save. Repeat with each QuickTime mooV featured in your Director movie.

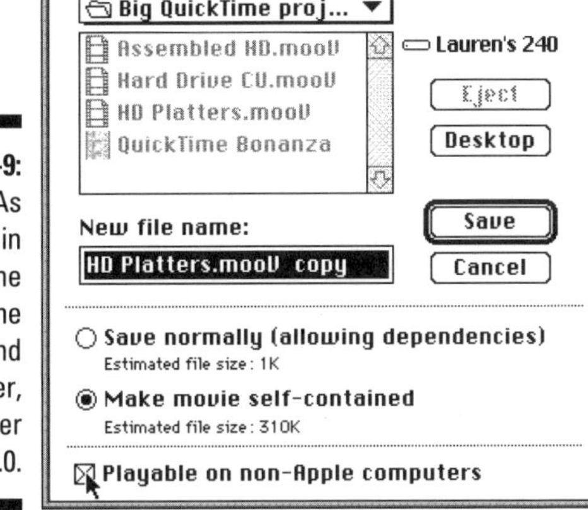

Figure 21-9: The Save As dialog box in the QuickTime utility and player, MoviePlayer 2.0.

Chapter 22

Ten Ways to Add Animation to Your Movies

In This Chapter

- Use Auto Animate's built-in special effects
- Remember the In-Between commands
- Try color cycling
- Buy good clip animation
- Turn Cast Members into moveable sprites
- Import QuickTime mooVs
- Import PICS files from non-QuickTime applications
- Record real-time animations
- Use film loops
- Switch color palettes

Director offers a number of techniques for adding animation to your movies, some with near push-button ease, many others only slightly more complex. Use the following list-o-techniques as a useful reference for yourself. When you're stumped, just say, "Self, let's take a look at that useful list Lauren put together just for me."

Use Auto Animate's Built-In Special Effects

Consider using Director's Auto Animate feature, especially helpful for creating presentations on a super tight deadline. Review the material in Chapter 16 and create impressive animation sequences with little more than a couple of clicks of the mouse and a few keystrokes to enter a title and a little bit of copy.

If you missed Chapter 16 altogether, the following is a summary of Auto Animate's features for your perusal:

- *Banner:* Text scrolls across the screen horizontally, bringing to mind Times Square and crackly old MovieTone newsreels of winning World War II and the like.
- *Bar Chart:* An animated bar chart with up to six bars that rise to their respective values, and five choices for bar style: solid, concrete, coins, bullion, and hands.
- *Bullet Chart:* An animated bullet chart with flying type and bullets.
- *Credits:* Classic Hollywood-style film credits scrolling vertically on the screen.
- *Text Effects:* Choose one of three special effects applied to your text: Sparkle, Letter Slide, and Typewriter.
- *Zoom Text:* Choose one of three options for creating the effect of a zoom lens, placing you closer and closer to the subject with a Zoom in, Zoom out, or Zoom in, then out effect.

Remember the In-Between Commands

In Chapter 5, I discuss the dark art of *tweening,* not for the faint of heart. In prehistoric days, human beans were actually hired, by people with funny names like Walt Disney, to tween twixt sunup and sundown. And what is tweening, you may well ask? It's the art of breaking up an animation sequence into *key frames* and then developing intermediate frames from key frame to key frame. In other words, tweening develops all the in-be*tween* frames, which is where the term tweening comes from.

Using In-Between Linear

For example, say you wanted to start your movie with a car driving across the Stage from left to right in a half second. I'll describe the steps in very general terms, and you can apply the formula to whatever you like.

1. **Create a bitmap in the Paint window.**

   In this example, you whip up a bitmap of a car in Director's Paint window with your eyes closed, automatically adding the Bitmap Cast Member to the Cast window. Actually, this happens even with your eyes open.

2. **Select the bitmap in the Paint window by double-clicking the Selection tool, and drag the bitmap on the Stage.**

   Director automatically adds the bitmap sprite to Frame 1 of the Score. It's usually Frame 1, unless you couldn't resist and clicked some other frame in the Score window before attending to Step 2.

3. **Drag the sprite on the Stage to the far left of the Stage so that it's half hidden.**
4. **Select the sprite in the Score and choose Edit⇨Copy Cells.**
5. **Click on Frame 15 in the same channel as the original sprite and choose Edit⇨Paste Cells.**

   A copy of the sprite appears in Frame 15 of the Score and on the Stage in exactly the same location as the original sprite.

6. **While in Frame 15, press Shift and drag the copy of the sprite to the far right of the Stage, exposing the first sprite in its original location.**
7. **Back in the Score, click the sprite in Frame 1, and then press Shift and click the sprite in Frame 15 to select the range of frames from Frames 1 to 15.**
8. **Choose Score⇨In-Between Linear.**

Director *tweens* the frames between Frame 1 and Frame 15 of your movie. When you rewind the movie and play it back, the bitmap appears to move across the Stage. In this example, the toy car scoots across the screen.

Using In-Between Special

The In-Between Special command adds additional animation opportunities by creating a curved path that a bitmap follows after tweening is completed. To use In-Between Special to create a curved path, follow these steps:

1. **Click on a frame near the middle of the group of frames you intend to select, Frame 8, for example, and drag the sprite on the Stage to a point near the top of the screen.**
2. **Click the sprite in Frame 1, and then press Shift and click the sprite in Frame 15 to select the range of frames from Frames 1 to 15.**
3. **Choose Score⇨In-Between Special.**

   The In-Between Special dialog box appears, as in Figure 22-1.

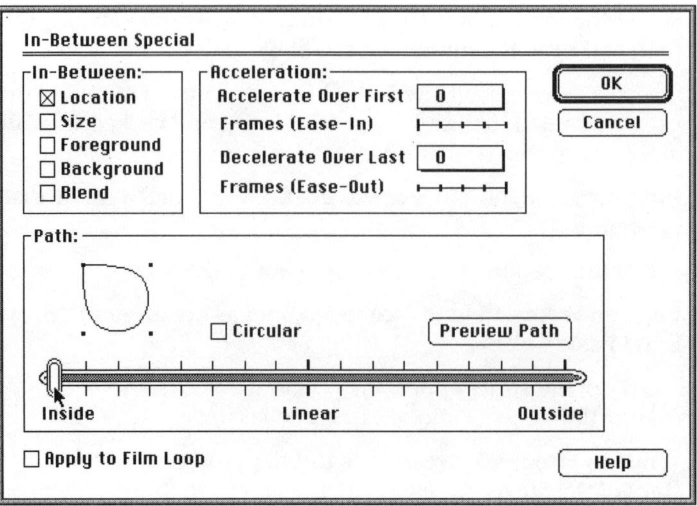

Figure 22-1: The In-Between Special dialog box, where you can set up a curved path for a sprite to follow.

4. **Check the Location check box in the In-Between panel.**
5. **Drag the Path sliding control to the left side as in Figure 22-1 and click OK.**

Director incorporates the upper movement of the sprite in frame 8 with the In-Between Special command. In this example, when the movie is played back, the little car appears to drive in a curved path, up to the top of the screen by frame 8, and back down as it completes its trip across the Stage. Try experimenting with Acceleration options in the In-Between Special dialog box, too.

Try Color Cycling

Ever notice the animation happening behind your favorite weather reporter's back? You know, the little, icon-like animations indicating snowfall over a particular region of the country, rain pouring here, or the sun beaming down there with radiant energy streaming from its little happy face?

All these animations were probably created with the same kind of color cycling you can use in Director to add animation to your movie. Color cycling is especially well suited to repetitive movement, like the weather map examples above, and is very efficient because you set the whole sequence up in one custom palette placed in the Palette channel of the Score.

Say you want to create an animation that features repetitive action, such as a fire crackling and popping in a beautiful brick fireplace. First, you'd create a custom palette based on the System palette, and then you'd import or paint your Bitmap Cast Members.

Creating a custom palette

To create a custom palette, follow these steps:

1. **Check that your monitor is set to 256 colors with the Monitors control panel.**

   Color cycling only works in 256-color mode.

2. **Choose Window⇨Color Palettes and check that System — Mac is the current palette.**
3. **Choose Palette⇨Duplicate Palette.**
4. **Enter a meaningful name for the new palette, such as Cycling Palette, and click OK.**

   Your new palette becomes the current palette in the Color Palettes window. Now you'll create a special blend of colors for the fire.

5. **Click the color chip that you've selected to start the special color blend, or gradient.**
6. **Press Shift and click the color chip that you want as the ending color in your custom gradient.**

   Make sure that the second color is at least ten to twelve chips away from the first color. The more colors between the first and last selected color chips, the smoother the gradient.

7. **Choose Palette⇨Blend Colors.**

   Using the first and last colors in the selected range of color chips, Director creates a smooth color gradient for a custom palette.

Painting color-cycling artwork

While the color chips making up the gradient are still selected in the Color Palettes window, you can invert the selection and reserve the colors not in the gradient, effectively disabling them so that the only colors available in the Paint window are the color-cycling colors of your custom palette.

1. **Choose Palette⇨Invert Selection to select the colors not in the gradient.**
2. **Choose Palette⇨Reserve Colors.**
3. **In the Reserve Colors dialog box that appears, click the Reserve Currently Selected Colors radio button, as shown in Figure 22-2.**

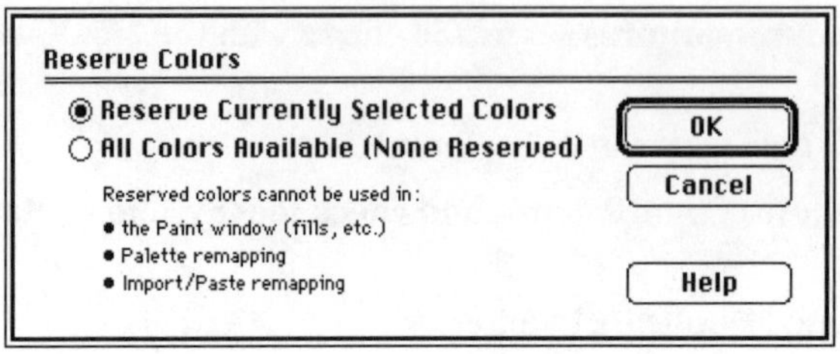

Reserve Colors
Reserve Currently Selected Colors
All Colors Available (None Reserved)
Reserved colors cannot be used in:
• the Paint window (fills, etc.)
• Palette remapping
• Import/Paste remapping
OK
Cancel
Help

Figure 22-2: With the Reserve Colors dialog box, you can disable selected colors in the Color Palettes window.

The colors you used to create a special gradient are now the only colors available for painting in the Paint window. Until you turn off Reserve Colors, all imported bitmaps are remapped without including the reserved colors.

While the colors in the custom blend are the only available colors in the Paint window, paint the artwork you want to display color-cycling. For example, if you're painting a fireplace scene and intend to apply color cycling to tongues of fire in a fireplace, now would be the time to import a bitmap for the fire or to paint the fire in the Paint window as a Bitmap Cast Member.

For the lowdown on importing graphics, check out the section, "Calling All Cast Members," in Chapter 4. Chapter 6 gives you the scoop on using Director's Paint tools to whip up glorious digital graphics for the amusement of family and friends.

Painting support graphics

With artwork for color cycling completed, you can now set up your custom palette for painting support graphics.

1. **Choose Window⇨Color Palettes.**

2. **Choose Window⇨Reserve Colors.**
3. **Click the All Colors Available (None Reserved) radio button in the Reserve Colors dialog box and click OK.**

   When you return to the Color Palettes window, the previously reserved colors are now selected.
4. **Choose Window⇨Invert Selection, selecting the color-cycling colors in the Color Palettes window.**
5. **Choose Window⇨Reserve Colors.**
6. **Click the Reserve Currently Selected Colors radio button in the Reserve Colors dialog box and click OK to disable the color-cycling colors in the custom palette.**

Now you can import or create the graphics you need to complete your color-cycling sequence. However, beware the following caveats. If you import a bitmap, its colors will be remapped to your modified System palette, minus the reserved colors. For non-people pictures, the result will probably be acceptable. If people appear in your imported graphic, you may need to do some serious retouching in the Paint window to make skin tones look hunky-dory. No, I have no idea where that expression came from.

If you decide to create a bitmap from scratch in the Paint window, remember the following two points:

- You need to stay with your custom palette if you want to incorporate color-cycling animation in the sequence.
- You'll be able to select all but the reserved colors for your Paint tools from the custom palette. This limitation may strain your creativity to the max, leading to surprise migraines and unexpected urges to impersonate Lola Montez. (Who's that? Look it up, Jack.)

Setting up for color cycling

It's time to set up your custom palette for color-cycling.

1. **Choose Window⇨Score and double-click the Palette channel in the frame where you want color-cycling to begin.**

   The Set Palette dialog box appears, shown in Figure 22-3.
2. **From the Palette pop-up menu, choose the custom palette you created in the last section.**

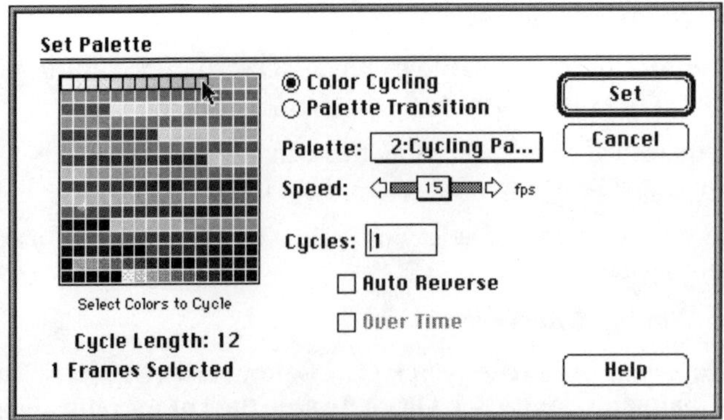

Figure 22-3: The Set Palette dialog box, where you set up color cycling.

3. **Drag the Speed slider control to set the frame speed.**

   Try 15 fps for starters.

4. **Click the Color Cycling radio button.**

5. **Drag the mouse to select the colors you created for the special blend and click Set.**

   Clicking the Color Cycling radio button and the Set button in the Set Palette dialog box tells Director to cycle through the highlighted colors, provided the custom palette is the current palette, and color-cycling colors appear in bitmap sprites on the Stage. The effect will continue until you change the palette or turn off color-cycling manually or with advanced Lingo scripting.

6. **Place support graphics on the Stage by dragging their Cast Members from the Cast window.**

7. **Place the artwork with color-cycling colors on the Stage.**

8. **Press Command and select the color-cycling sprite on the Stage so that the Ink pop-up menu appears and choose Bkgnd Transparent.**

   Any white background surrounding the color-cycling sprite becomes transparent with Bkgnd Transparent ink.

Adding a line of Lingo

Back in the Score, add a line of Lingo to pause the playback head where your color-cycling sequence begins.

1. **Double-click the Script channel in the same frame you added the color-cycling Palette.**

2. **In the Script window, enter**

```
go to the frame
```

3. **Click the Close box of the Script window.**
4. **Choose Window⇨Control Panel and click the Loop button.**
5. **Press Command+1 to hide all windows and Command+P to play back your movie.**

As you admire your color-cycling animation, you may find you need to speed up or slow down the frame rate from the Control Panel for optimal effect, or return to the Set Palette dialog box and try a different value in the Cycles entry field.

Buy Good Clip Animation

It's not cheating to use good clip animation. The operative word is *good.* Many packages are now available on floppies and CDs and can save a lot of development time, or bring in a project with an extremely tight deadline that otherwise couldn't be met.

The rule of reading all the fine print applies to using clip art to ensure that you're using royalty-free material or, if not, that you understand the conditions you agreed to upon opening the package. Even if you modify the artwork substantially, you may be violating the agreement with the use of clip animation that's not completely royalty-free or in the public domain.

Turn Cast Members into Moveable Sprites

You can easily add real-time animation to your Director movie by turning Cast Members into *moveable* sprites, meaning sprites that are given the moveable property so that the person viewing the movie may drag the sprite to different locations on the Stage while the movie is playing. For example, in some of my courses, I demonstrate what I call simulations, real-time animations that illustrate how to disassemble various Macintosh models. During playback, I interact with the movie, moving various components of the Mac model aside as if I were actually disassembling the machine before my students' eyes.

This bit of digital wizardry is accomplished by making each component a separate Bitmap Cast Member, and then "assembling" the computer component by component from back to front in a frame's channels. The final step is to select all the sprites in the frame and check the Moveable check box in the lower-left corner of the Score window. By the way, to keep the playback head in the same frame, double-click the Script channel for the frame and enter `go to the frame`, a variation of the go command that basically means, "Stay in this frame." Don't ask me why there isn't a *Stay in this Frame* command, please.

Import QuickTime MooVs

In Chapter 11, I discuss what QuickTime is and how you can add QuickTime files, so-called mooVs, as Digital Video Cast Members to your Director movies. If you've played with QuickTime in Premiere or a similar application, you may be able to salvage some of your work as self-made clip art.

As I suggested in an earlier part of this chapter, tons of commercial clip art, including QuickTime mooVs, exist in the marketplace, as well as on commercial and private bulletin boards for your use. As long as you thoroughly understand your rights for using the material, you should be able to find a QuickTime mooV to satisfy any basic need of yours.

Director automatically imports a QuickTime mooV as a *linked* file, meaning that the mooV is not incorporated directly into the Director file; only a *reference* to the QuickTime mooV is established, linking the external mooV to the Director file, thus the term *link*. The QuickTime mooV remains an independent, external file that needs to be present in the same folder as the Director file referring to the mooV.

Import PICS Files from Non-QuickTime Applications

Some animation and 3-D applications don't offer QuickTime as a file format when saving the document. This may be the case if you have an older version of a program and haven't upgraded. If QuickTime is unavailable, saving the file in PICS format is probably an option. PICS is a special format that contains a series of PICTs glued together into one file.

Director is one of the programs that can read and import PICS files. Each PICT in the PICS file becomes a separate Bitmap Cast Member in the Cast window. The new Cast Members are automatically *cast to time* in the Score window. Cast to time places Cast Members in the Cast window into separate frames of the Score starting with the first free frame in the Score Director can find.

In the case of an imported PICS file, Director places the row of PICTs in the Score, beginning with the current channel of the current frame, *eliminating* any unsuspecting sprites in its path. For example, say you have Channel 3 of Frame 5 selected with sprites in Frames 11 to 15 when you import a PICS file containing ten images. Director places the first image of the PICS file in Channel 3 of Frame 5, happily deleting the sprites in Frames 11 to 15 as it adds the rest of the ten images from the PICS file. If you don't want this sad melodrama to happen you, listen to your Uncle Lauren. *Before* importing a PICS file, check that the currently selected channel in the Score allows enough free cells to hold each image of an imported PICS file.

In the Import dialog box, be sure to choose PICS from the Type pop-up menu, as in Figure 22-4; otherwise PICS files won't appear in the directory.

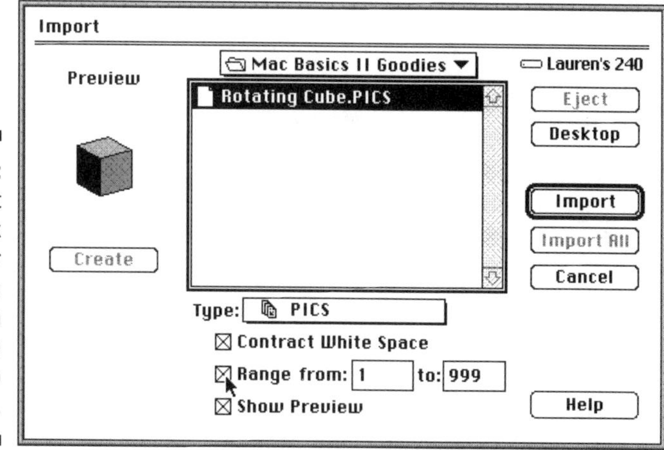

Figure 22-4: The Import dialog box after choosing PICS from the Type pop-up menu.

When you choose PICS, two new check boxes appear under the directory, Contract White Space and Range, as shown in Figure 22-4.

Highlight a PICS file in the directory *before* checking the Range check box; otherwise Director may quit unexpectedly back to the Finder, what I'd call a slight bug in the program. That's like saying World War II was a slight inconvenience in the early '40s.

After highlighting a PICS file in the directory, check Contract White Space if you want Director to crop each PICT in the PICS file down to its smallest *bounding box.* An image's bounding box is the rectangular frame enclosing the graphic, defined by the image's maximum width and height. Contract White Space results in a smaller Director file that runs faster than a file containing PICTs with large borders of white space surrounding them.

On the downside, since the PICTs are now probably different sizes, they're no longer aligned as an animation sequence and will tend to jump around on playback. The best solution is to anticipate the problem and to settle on a minimal file height and width in the original application that creates the PICS file without cutting off any of the images. Barring this, in Director's Paint window, locate the first PICT in the PICS sequence, choose the Registration tool (to the left of the Eyedropper tool), press anywhere in the easel, and drag the Registration Point to the extreme upper-left corner of the easel. Repeat with each of the remaining PICTs to realign the sequence.

As for the Range check box back in the Import dialog box, after highlighting a PICS file in the directory, you can click Range and enter a set of range values, for example, **5 to 9**, directing Director to import only images 5 through 9 of the PICS file. Of course, you would need to know in advance that these are the images of interest to you.

Record Real-Time Animations

One of the most fun things you can do without taking off your clothes is record real-time animations in Director. With a Bitmap Cast Member in the Cast window, follow these directions to make those long winter nights just melt away.

1. **Choose Window⇨Control Panel and check the Loop icon.**
2. **Choose Window⇨Cast and move the Cast window to the upper-left corner of the screen to give a clear view of the Stage.**
3. **Choose Window⇨Score and move the Score window to the lower-right corner of the screen to give a clear view of the Stage.**
4. **Highlight an empty cell in the Score.**

   Check that the cell's channel has enough free space to contain the animation you intend to create.
5. **Press a sprite in the Cast window and drag it to its beginning location on the Stage.**

   Notice that Director adds the Cast Member's sprite to the Score in the selected cell. Now for the special keyboard command . . .
6. **Press Control and then the spacebar.**

   Notice in the Score that Director places a special bulls-eye icon to the right of a seemingly arbitrary channel number, designating real-time recording is in progress, and how Director sets the currently selected cell to that channel.

7. **With the Control key and spacebar still held down, click the sprite in the Score window, notice that the real-time recording icon jumps to the sprite's channel, and then click the Close box of the Score and Cast window to view the entire Stage.**

8. **With the Control key and spacebar *still* held down, press the mouse on the sprite and begin dragging the sprite around.**

   Director records your movements in the Score window as successive frames until you release the mouse button.

9. **When you're finished mousing around, release the mouse button.**

   If your movie is set to loop (as in Step 1), Director automatically replays all the movements of the sprite. Instant déja-vu!

Use Film Loops

Making film loops is the second-most fun you can have with your clothes on. Actually, it's a toss-up between real-time recording, making film loops, and drinking a steaming mug of Ovaltine. Anyway, using film loops is good. For sequences of repetitive movement, film loops are invaluable and very economical because you can extend an animation sequence simply by running the film loop longer.

A classic example of applying a film loop to animation is "the flying dove." Imagine you're taping a dove in flight and following its movement in the sky. If you followed it perfectly, the dove's body wouldn't really seem to move at all; the only movement you'd see and record is its wings flapping up and down. This kind of movement is perfect for making a film loop. Another example of repetitive movement is "the walking man." Once you have the stride captured in several frames, you're ready to make your film loop.

Say you've drawn or scanned in ten frames of the flying dove, ranging from its wings positioned above to below its body, and the frames are represented as Cast Members 1 to 10. To make your film loop, whether or not it's with flying doves, follow these steps:

1. **Press Shift and select Cast Members 1 to 10 in the Cast window.**

2. **Choose Cast⇨Cast to Time.**

   Director places the Cast Members as sprites in Frames 1 to 10 of the Score window. If you played your movie, you'd see the dove flap its wings once, from above to below its body. You want to complete the cycle of movement by adding the frames that make the dove move its wings from below to above its body, which is simply a copy of the ten frames in reverse sequence.

3. **Press Shift and select the ten sprites in the Score window.**
4. **Press Option and drag the selection to the right, making a copy of the frames, and place the first frame of the selection in Frame 11.**
5. **Choose Score➪Reverse Sequence.**

   Notice the 20 frames you now have in the Score. You have a couple of extra frames you'll want to delete. Currently Frames 10 and 11 and Frames 1 and 20 are identical and unnecessary pairs.

6. **Click on the sprite in Frame 11 and choose Score➪Delete Frame.**
7. **Click on the sprite in Frame 19 and choose Score➪Delete Frame.**

   Now you have a complete sequence of the dove flapping its wings up and down recorded in Frames 1 to 18 of the Score. You're all set to actually create the film loop.

8. **Press Shift and select the 18 sprites in the Score.**
9. **Drag the selection to the first empty cell in the Cast window.**

   Director displays the Please name this Film Loop dialog box, as in Figure 22-5.

Please name this Film Loop:
The Flying Dove
OK
Cancel

Figure 22-5: The Please name this Film Loop dialog box.

10. **Enter a name for the film loop and click OK.**
11. **Delete the sprites in the Score and drag the film loop on the Stage.**
12. **Press Command+P to play back your film loop.**

A really great thing to do with your film loop is to combine it with real-time recording. Using the example of the film loop of the flying dove, you can make it sail across the Stage, flapping its wings along the way.

1. **Press Control and then the spacebar and click the film loop sprite in the Score window.**
2. **Still holding down Control and the spacebar, press the film loop sprite on the Stage and drag the mouse across the Stage.**
3. **When your dove finishes flying across the Stage, release the mouse button.**

Rewind the movie with Command+R and press Command+P to play back and admire your sequence.

If you set your movie to loop in the Control Panel window, Director automatically plays back the animation sequence when you release the mouse. Otherwise, rewind the movie and press Command+P to play back and admire your sequence.

Switch Color Palettes

In the "Try Color Cycling" section earlier in this chapter, I walk you through setting up a custom palette in the Set Palette dialog box to cycle through a selected range of colors for relatively easy animation effects. Another option in the Set Palette dialog box allows you to create a different kind of animation by setting up a *palette transition.* This kind of animation is especially effective for situations where color changes globally on the Stage. The classic example crying out for a palette transition is "the sunset" or the clever variation, "the sunrise."

Say you have a beautiful desert day scene as a Bitmap Cast Member, featuring the ever popular System palette. The image presents us with the bleached, white sand of the desert, bright green cacti hither and yon, a brilliant azure sky specked with creamy fluffs of cloud. But you want this gorgeous image to change to a nighttime scene filled with blues and grays, *using the same bitmap.* Here's how, beginning with creating a custom palette from boring, old System palette:

1. **Choose Window⇨Color Palettes and choose Palette⇨Duplicate Palette.**
2. **In the Please name this Palette dialog box that appears, name the palette something meaningful, such as Sunset Palette, and click OK.**
3. **Back in the Color Palettes window, click the Zoom box in the upper-right corner so that the window zooms to full-screen size, making the color chips easier to work with.**
4. **Double-click the second color chip from the upper-left corner of the palette to display the Apple Color Wheel.**
5. **Click a deep blue on the wheel, deepen the color more by dragging the scroll bar elevator down about halfway, and click OK.**
6. **At the bottom right of the palette, notice the gray scale from light gray to black and double-click the color just to the left of the light gray chip.**
7. **In the Apple Color Wheel, slide the scroll bar elevator up to the top.**
8. **Click on a medium blue chip in the wheel and click OK.**

Now you're going to make a blend:

1. **With the medium blue chip (of step 8 in the preceding set of steps) still selected, press Shift and click the deep blue chip you first created to add the set of chips between these two color chips to the selection.**
2. **Choose Palette⇨Blend Colors to create a custom blend from deep blue to medium blue in your custom palette.**
3. **Click the Zoom box to reduce the Color Palette window's size.**

Now you're going to set up the Score for the palette transition:

1. **Choose Window⇨Cast.**
2. **Choose Window⇨Score.**
3. **Drag the Bitmap Cast Member, desert scene, from the Cast window to Frame 1 in the Score.**

   The desert scene now appears centered on the Stage.
4. **In the Score, press Option and drag the desert scene sprite to the next cell to the right, duplicating the sprite into Frame 2.**
5. **Double-click the Palette channel in Frame 2 to open the Set Palette dialog box.**
6. **Choose Sunset Palette from the Palette pop-up menu.**
7. **Click the Palette Transition radio button so that it's on.**
8. **Slide the Speed control to 6 fps and click OK.**

   Generally, you don't want this kind of effect to loop so make sure that Loop is turned off.
9. **Choose Window⇨Control Panel and turn off the Loop button.**
10. **Press Command+1 to hide all open windows.**

All that's left to do is to rewind the movie and play back your Director animation to thunderous applause.

Chapter 23

Ten Most Important Lingo Words

In This Chapter

- Go command
- Play command
- Pause command
- Continue command
- Set command
- UpdateStage command
- DirectToStage property
- & and && concatenation operators
- Repeat while and repeat with control structures
- If-then control structures

Attempting to sum up Lingo with just ten of its most important words may strike some in the know as quixotic at best, foolhardy at worst. On the other hand, I believe the ten terms I've chosen to review in this chapter form a foundation that new scripters can reference to write most of their scripts and to build upon as they find the need for the more esoteric of Lingo's commands. May this be the beginning of a grand adventure for you.

Go Command

Probably the most frequently used Lingo command, you can use the go command to skip from one frame to another, as well as to go to another Director movie.

To skip to another frame, double-click the Script channel in the frame from which you want to leave and enter

```
go to frame
```

followed by a space and the number of the frame: for example, `go to frame 10`.

To go to another movie, double-click the Script channel in the frame from which you want to leave and enter

```
go to movie
```

followed by a space, a quote character, the name of the movie to go to, and another quote character: for example, `go to movie "What We Can Do For You"`.

To keep the playback head in the same frame, without actually stopping playback of the movie, double-click the Script channel in the frame where you want to stay and enter

```
go to the frame
```

Play Command

The play command is most likely the second-hardest working command in Lingo. Use the play command to go to another movie and play the movie.

To go to another movie and play the movie from frame 1, double-click the Script channel in the frame from which you want to leave and enter

```
play movie
```

followed by a space, a quote character, the name of the movie to go to, and another quote character: for example, `play movie "An Offer You Can't Refuse"`.

To go to another movie and play the movie from a frame other than frame 1, double-click the Script channel in the frame from which you want to leave and enter

```
play frame
```

followed by a space, the number of the frame from which you want to start playing the movie, and a space. Then add

```
of movie
```

followed by a space, a quote character, the name of the movie to go to, and another quote character: for example, `play frame 10 of movie "An Offer You Can't Refuse"`.

To return to the original movie after playing the second movie, double-click the Script channel in the last frame of the *second* movie and enter

```
play done
```

Pause Command

Pause is another common command, used when you want to freeze the movie's playback, allowing the user to decide when to continue the movie. As you may have guessed, the pause command is typically used in league with the command that follows: continue.

To pause a movie at a particular frame, double-click the Script channel in the frame where you want the pause to occur and enter

```
pause
```

between the lines `on enterFrame` and `end`.

Continue Command

The continue command allows a movie that has been suspended with the pause command discussed in the preceding section to play back, again. Continue is typically placed in a button object created with the Button tool in the Tools window so that the user may click the button to continue playback.

To continue a suspended movie, create a button on the Stage in the frame where the movie is paused. Double-click the heavy, gray border of the selected button to go to the Button window. Click the Script button and enter

```
continue
```

between the lines `on mouseUp` and `end`.

Set Command

Set is an extremely useful, multipurpose command you'll use often in Director. In the example script for the UpdateStage command later in this chapter, the set command is used to change the color of Cast Member 13, referring to the Cast Member residing in cell 13 of the Cast window.

Set is also used to place text in a text sprite on the Stage created with the Text tool from the Tools window. To put the text, "All the world's a Stage . . ." in a Text Cast Member named "Today's Quote," you might enter the following in a button that a user may click:

```
on mouseUp
  set the text of cast "Today's Quote" = "All the world's a
              Stage…"
end
```

UpdateStage Command

Normally, Director refreshes the screen automatically as a movie plays back from frame to frame. Occasionally, you need to give Director a little nudge with the updateStage command, especially after you alter conditions on Stage with various Lingo commands, such as changing a sprite's color. After the line of Lingo that performs the change, simply add updateStage as the next line. An example might look like the following:

```
on changeMyColor
set the foreColor of cast 13 = 200
updateStage
end
```

Colors in Director are referred to by number from the set of 256 colors in the current palette. In MacLand, the first color in a palette is color 0, not 1, and always white, color 255 is always black, and the numbers in-between refer to specific colors depending on the current palette and their positions.

DirectToStage Property

In strictest terms, directToStage isn't a command but a property, that is, a contributing description of a QuickTime file in Director. A QuickTime mooV, as multimedia types are wont to call a QuickTime file, either has the directToStage property enabled or disabled. Turning on the directToStage property of a QuickTime mooV allows it to play at its fastest speed on the Stage, which is why the directToStage property is so important to multimedia types like you and me.

Set a QuickTime's directToStage property one of two ways:

- Highlight the Digital Video Cast Member in the Cast window, click the "i" button at the top of the window and check the Direct To Stage check box in the Digital Video Cast Member Info dialog box.
- Using Lingo, enter `set the directToStage of cast 1 = true` in the Script channel in the frame where the respective QuickTime mooV appears in the Score. This line assumes that the QuickTime mooV is in cell 1 of the Cast window. Substitute 1 after "cast" for the number reflecting the real position of your QuickTime mooV in the Cast window.

& and && Concatenation Operators

Remember the first item under the Lingo menu, those operators such as +, -, *, and /, many of which are arithmetic operators? A few of the operators are special, such as & and &&, so-called concatenation operators you only find in programming languages. When you use concatenation operators, you're basically doing addition with words, gluing words and phrases together with & and &&. Here's how concatenation works.

Say you have three Text Cast Members on the Stage. And say for some reason, who knows why, you simply can't have the entire phrase, "All the world's a Stage," in the third Text Cast Member at the beginning of the movie. You must piece together, or concatenate, the phrase from the first two Text Cast Members when your movie begins to play back. Again, who knows why. The first Text Cast Member contains half of the phrase, "All the world's"; the second Text Cast Member contains the other half, "a Stage." To glue a phrase together as in this example, you need to use the concatenation operators, along with the Set command discussed earlier in this chapter. In the Script channel of frame 1, you'd enter the following:

```
set the text of cast 3 = the text of cast 1 && the text of
         cast 2
```

Now I'll go through step by step why this line makes Director do what you want it to do:

- With `set the text of cast 3 =`, you're telling Director to make the contents of Text Cast Member 3 equal to the rest of the line of script coming up.
- The next part of the script, `the text of cast 1`, refers to the contents of Text Cast Member 1 in the Cast window which, in this example, contains the first half of the phrase: "All the world's."
- The last part of the script, `&& the text of cast 2`, tells Director to glue the first part of the phrase from Text Cast Member 1 together with the contents of Text Cast Member 2 which, in this example, contains the second part of the phrase: "a Stage." The script also says to add a space character between the two parts of the phrase. && means to add a space in-between. & means to glue the parts of the phrase together without a space character in-between.

Concatenation is that simple. Don't let the multisyllabic nature of the term put you off. You're just gluing bits and pieces of info together to form a whole.

Repeat While and Repeat With Control Structures

Sometimes you want Director to repeat a command as long as a certain condition is true. Other times you want Director to repeat a set of commands a certain number of times. That's when a repeat control structure comes in handy.

Say you want to hear when the user presses the mouse on a button you created with Director. The condition you want to test for is pressing the mouse. You decide on the System beep as the sound or cue that lets you hear when mouse pressing occurs. You decide to use the *repeat while* control structure in the script of the button, which winds up looking like this:

```
on mouseDown
repeat while the mouseDown
beep
end repeat
end
```

I'll go over this handler line by line.

- `on mouseDown` tells Director to carry out the commands that follow when the mouse is pressed, that is, when the mouse button is down.
- `repeat while the mouseDown` tells Director that you want it to carry out the line that follows as long as the mouse button remains down.
- `beep` is the command you want Director to carry out as long as the mouse button is pressed.
- `end repeat` is simply a convention for how to end a repeat statement such as the one above. Director must see this line after each repeat statement or it'll slap an error message up on-screen.
- `end` is another convention that must be followed when using Lingo. All so-called handlers like this one must end with the line `end`.

Another form of the repeat control structure, *repeat with,* is useful for repeating a command or set of commands a certain number of times. Say you want the color of a button to change from white to a rainbow of colors when a user presses it. (Remember that Director calls colors by number.) Using the repeat with control structure allows you to change a number over time, such as the color of a button. The lines of Lingo in the button for this example would look something like the following:

```
on mouseDown
  repeat with n = 1 to 150
    set the backColor of cast 2 to n
    delay 100
  end repeat
end

on mouseUp
  set the backColor of cast 2 to 0
end
```

Again, I'll go over the lines step by step.

- `on mouseDown` tells Director that you want something to happen when the mouse button is pressed. What you want to have happen comes in the next lines of Lingo.
- `repeat with n = 1 to 150` tells Director that, as long as the mouse button remains pressed down, you want Director to substitute the generic value, *n,* for numbers from 1 to 150. The next line tells Director what to do with each of these numbers. Remember, the number 150 means that the commands within the repeat statement will be repeated 150 times.
- `set the backColor of cast 2` tells Director to change the button color, called the *backcolor* in Director, of Button Cast Member 2 of the Cast window. You tell Director which color to use in the rest of this line.
- `to n` tells Director to set the button to the current value of *n.* `set the backColor of cast 2 to n` is going to be repeated 150 times. The first time Director substitutes 1 for the generic value *n* so that the real meaning of the line becomes `set the backColor of cast 2 to 1`, telling Director to set the color to color chip 1 in the current palette. The repeat statement makes Director repeat the `set` line again. The next time around, Director substitutes 2 for the generic value *n* so that the real meaning of the line becomes `set the backColor of cast 2 to 2`, in other words, to color 2 of the palette. As long as the user presses the mouse button down, this process is repeated until the last, or 150th in this case, repetition.
- `delay 100` is simply a way to slow down the process using the Delay command, since Director executes the commands so quickly on a fast Mac, so that you can detect the color changes without slowing everything down. The number 100 in the line stands for 100 *ticks.* Director measures time in ticks; one tick equals $^1/_{60}$ of a second.
- The last two lines, `end repeat` and `end` are those conventions that must be followed when using a repeat statement and a mouseDown handler, as discussed earlier in this section.

The second handler, the mouseUp handler, simply sets the color of the button to 0, which is DirectorSpeak for the color white, when the user releases the mouse button.

If-Then Control Structures

One of the most powerful ways to add real interactivity to your Director movies is with if-then control structures. Basically, you're building alternate scenarios into your movie that depend on choices made by the user, or perhaps made arbitrarily by Director itself.

Remember the three Text Cast Members in the concatenation section earlier in this chapter? I showed how you can use Director to piece together a phrase so that when your movie begins, it's placed in a third text box. What if the third text box sometimes contains text when the movie begins and is empty at other times? But you only want Director to piece the phrase together and place it in Text Cast Member 3 if the third text box is empty. Somehow you need to have Director check whether the text box is empty or not. That's when an if-then structure comes in so handy. The script in the movie would look something like the following:

```
on startMovie
  if the text of cast 3 = empty then
    set the text of cast 3 = the text of cast 1 && the text
            of cast 2
  else beep
end
```

Basically, you give Director a choice. If Text Cast Member 3 is empty, you tell Director to piece together the two halves of the phrase in Text Cast Members 1 and 2 and enter it in Text Cast Member 3. If Director finds some text in Text Cast Member 3, you don't want to lose the text by replacing it with the phrase divided up between Text Cast Members 1 and 2. Instead, you simply instruct Director to beep harmlessly.

Again, I'll go over those lines one by one.

- `on startMovie` means that this kind of handler is a movie script that executes the moment your Director file begins to play back.
- `if the text of cast 3 = empty then` instructs Director to check whether there's anything in Text Cast Member 3 and, if empty, to execute the next line.

- `set the text of cast 3 = the text of cast 1 && the text of cast 2` is explained earlier in this chapter in the concatenation section. Basically, you're giving Director the go-ahead to glue the phrase together and place it whole in the third text box.
- `else beep` gives Director the alternate scenario to play should it find that some text does exist in Text Cast Member 3 that you don't want Director to overwrite with the glued-together phrase. In fact, you don't let Director glue the phrase together at all, as this script is written.

In more complicated if-then statements, you'd include an `end if` line for each if-then statement. But that's basically all you need to know — not exactly rocket science, eh? If you have the slightest handle on the stuff in this chapter, you're well on your way to becoming a Director master.

The 5th Wave

Appendix A

I'm Ready for My Install, Mr. DeMille

If Director is your first install, the whole process may seem overwhelming. Let me assure you, it is. Remember those wisdom tooth extractions? Well . . .

Just kidding. Installing Director is a breeze. If you can insert a floppy disk into the floppy drive, you've got a lifetime career set in stone.

System Requirements

The following is the minimum configuration required to get Director 4 up and running:

- A 68030 or 68040 CPU (central processing unit) Mac, including PowerBooks (other than the PowerBook 100 that features a 68000 CPU like the original Mac 128K), or a Power Mac.
- 4 MB of RAM (random access memory).
- Hard drive storage device, internal or external, with 32.4 MB of free space for a complete install.
- System 7, or Copland, if you sneaked a copy (just kidding, Apple).

Now here is my real-world minimum recommended configuration:

- A 68040 CPU Mac, including a Color PowerBook, or a Power Mac.
- 12 MB or more of RAM.
- 80 MB hard drive storage device or better with 32.4 MB of free space for a complete install.
- 13-inch RGB monitor or better.
- System 7.5.1 (with System 7.5 Update, the latest update as this is being written).

Installing Macromedia Director 4

Believe it or not, installing a program — even Director — is pretty straightforward. The most difficult part of a Director install comes at the very beginning, lifting the stack of floppy disks without causing serious bodily injury to your person. From then on, it's a piece of cake.

I'm going to assume that you've never used Director before and, even more, you've never done an install before. You'll want the full install, even though it adds up to a monstrous 32.4 MB, so that you get all the goodies and extras. You can always trash later what you decide you don't need.

Before installing Director, *back up all master disks*:

1. **Beg, borrow, or steal a copy of DiskCopy 4.2 and launch it.**

   DiskCopy is a free disk-copying utility from Apple Computer that is usually included somewhere on your hard drive when you purchase a Mac. At the Desktop, search for DiskCopy with the Find command; or you can find DiskCopy on-line on America Online, CompuServe, or a user's group such as BMUG (listed in Appendix B). Either way, launch the DiskCopy.

2. **Click the introductory screen to arrive at the main interface, as in Figure A-1.**

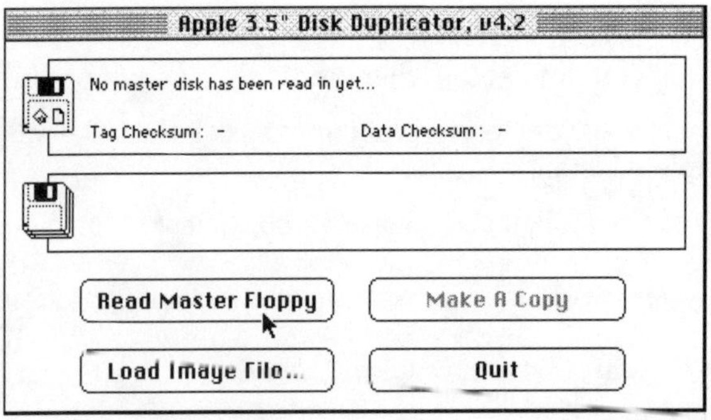

Figure A-1: The main interface screen of Apple's disk-copying utility, DiskCopy.

3. **Insert Disk #1 in the floppy drive.**

   The Read Master Floppy button becomes enabled.

4. **Click Read Master Floppy.**

5. **After DiskCopy finishes reading the disk into memory and ejects the floppy disk, insert a blank high-density disk.**

6. **After an alert box appears, click Duplicate.**

   After DiskCopy completes its duplication of Disk #1, it ejects the disk.

7. **Repeat Steps 3 through 6 for each of the remaining installation disks.**

To install Director 4, follow these steps:

1. **Find Disk #1 among the set of master disks and insert it in the floppy drive.**

2. **Double-click the Disk #1 icon on the Desktop.**

3. **Double-click the installer application named *Install Macromedia Director.***

4. **In the dialog box that appears, choose the standard installation.**

5. **In the standard directory that appears, navigate to where you want Director installed and click Install.**

   After the Installer program finishes with Disk #1, it ejects the disk and asks for the next disk in the install sequence.

6. **Insert Disk #2 to continue the install and follow instructions until the install is complete and you return to the Desktop.**

7. **Be ready with your registration number, find Director on your hard drive, and double-click the Director application icon to begin using the program.**

That's it. Pretty painless, huh. By the way, if Macromedia introduces a CD install by the time this book rolls hot off the press, installation is just the same. Double-click the CD icon on the Desktop, find *Install Macromedia Director,* and you're off and running.

In Director's Extras folder, you'll find two so-called FKey utilities, ScreenClip and the Scrapbook FKey to make a "screen shot," or a PICT image, of how your screen looks at a particular moment in time. Add the FKey utilities to your system by dragging them over your System folder. To save a screen shot to the Clipboard, press Command+Shift+6. To save a screen shot to the Scrapbook, press Command+Shift+8.

Appendix B

The Mother of All Resources

Books

Bove, Tony and Cheryl Rhodes, *Official Macromedia Director Studio*, Random House/New Media Series, 1994

Burger, Jeff, *The Desktop Multimedia Bible*, Addison-Wesley Publishing Company, 1993

Clark, Cathy and Lee Swearingen, *Macromedia Director Design Guide*, Hayden Books, 1994

Holsinger, Erik, *MacWEEK Guide to Desktop Video*, Ziff-Davis Press, 1993

Laurel, Brenda, *The Art of Human-Computer Interface Design*, Addison-Wesley Publishing Company, 1990

Thomas, Frank and Ollie Johnston, *Disney Animation: The Illusion of Life*, Abbeville Press, 1981

Vaughan, Tay, *Multimedia: Making It Work*, Osborne McGraw-Hill, 1994

Training

American Film Institute
Advanced Technology Programs
2021 North Western Avenue
Los Angeles, CA 90027
213-856-7600

Center for Creative Imaging
Camden, ME
207-236-7490

Nothing But Lingo training videos
2-Lane Media
1575 Westwood Boulevard
Suite 301
Los Angeles, CA 90024
301-473-3706

San Francisco State University
Multimedia Studies Program
The New Downtown Center
425 Market Street
San Francisco, CA 94105
415-904-7700

Vendors

Adobe Systems, Incorporated
Adobe Photoshop, Adobe Premiere
1585 Charleston Road
Mountain View, CA 94039
415-961-4400

America Online
Customer Service
800-827-6364

Apple Computer
20525 Mariani Avenue
Cupertino, CA 95014
408-996-1010

Apple Customer Assistance Center
800-776-2333
800-786-7777 for System 7 customers
Monday through Friday, 6 am–5 pm PST

Apple Direct
(Apple mail order purchases)
800-795-1000

BMUG
Berkeley Macintosh Users Group
1442A Walnut Street #62
Berkeley, CA 94709
510-849-BMUG

CompuServe
Customer Service
800-524-3388

Illusion Art
Clip animation
P.O. Box 21398
Oakland, CA 94611

Macromedia, Incorporated
MacRecorder audio digitizer, Macromedia Director 4.0 animation program, MacroMind Three-D 3-D program, MacroModel 3-D program, SoundEdit Pro audio editing program, Swivel Art 3-D clip art
600 Townsend Street
San Francisco, CA 94103
415-442-0200

Radius, Incorporated
Video Spigot AV video digitizer, VideoVision video digitizer
1710 Fortune Drive
San Jose, CA 95131
408-434-1010

Ray Dream, Incorporated
Ray Dream Designer 3-D program
1804 North Shoreline Boulevard
Mountain View, CA 94043
415-960-0768

Specular International
Infini-D 2.6 3-D program
233 North Pleasant Street
P.O. Box 888
Amherst, MA 01004
413-549-7600

Strata, Incorporated
StrataVision Pro 3-D program
2 West
St. George Boulevard
Suite 2100
Saint George, UT 84770
800-869-6855

User Group Locator
(finds local user groups)
800-538-9696

Visual Magic
Animation clip art
620 C. Street #201
San Diego, CA 92101
800-367-6240

The 5th Wave **By Rich Tennant**

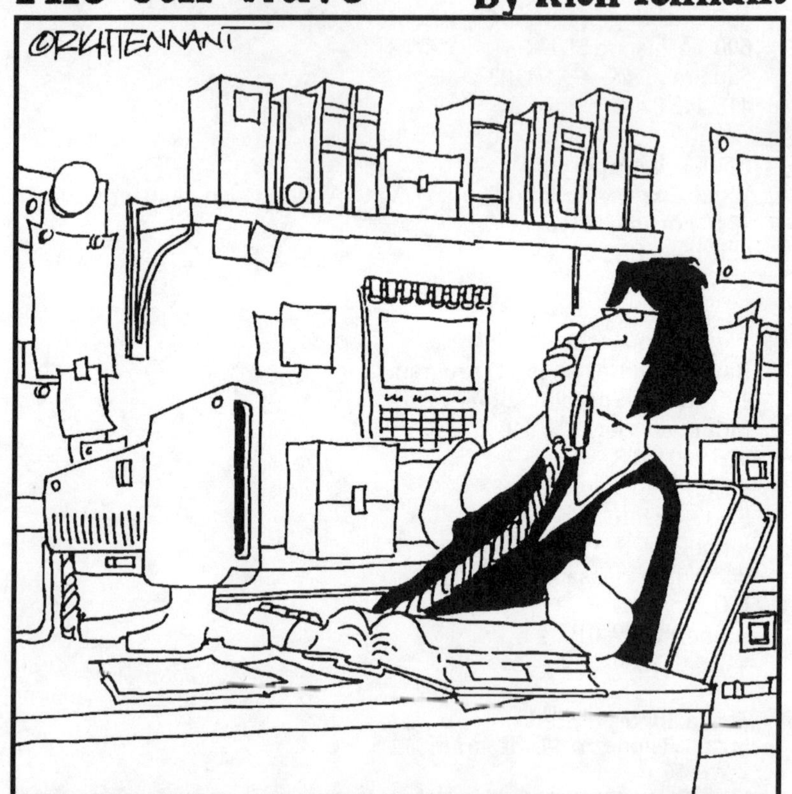

"FOR ADDITIONAL SOFTWARE SUPPORT, DIAL "9", "POUND" THE EXTENSION NUMBER DIVIDED BY YOUR ACCOUNT NUMBER, HIT "STAR", YOUR DOG, BLOW INTO THE RECEIVER TWICE, PUNCH IN YOUR HAT SIZE, PUNCH OUT YOUR LANDLORD,..."

Index

• Symbols •

• A •

(continued)

• B •

• C •

(continued)

• D •

• E •

• G •

• H •

• I •

• K •

• L •

• N •

• O •

• P •

• Q •

• R •

• S •

• T •

• U •

• V •

• W •

• Z •

IDG BOOKS WORLDWIDE REGISTRATION CARD

RETURN THIS REGISTRATION CARD FOR FREE CATALOG

Title of this book: Macromedia Director 4 For Macs For Dummies

My overall rating of this book: ❑ Very good [1] ❑ Good [2] ❑ Satisfactory [3] ❑ Fair [4] ❑ Poor [5]

How I first heard about this book:

❑ Found in bookstore; name: [6] ❑ Book review: [7]

❑ Advertisement: [8] ❑ Catalog: [9]

❑ Word of mouth; heard about book from friend, co-worker, etc.: [10] ❑ Other: [11]

What I liked most about this book:

What I would change, add, delete, etc., in future editions of this book:

Other comments:

Number of computer books I purchase in a year: ❑ 1 [12] ❑ 2-5 [13] ❑ 6-10 [14] ❑ More than 10 [15]

I would characterize my computer skills as: ❑ Beginner [16] ❑ Intermediate [17] ❑ Advanced [18] ❑ Professional [19]

I use ❑ DOS [20] ❑ Windows [21] ❑ OS/2 [22] ❑ Unix [23] ❑ Macintosh [24] ❑ Other: [25] ______ (please specify)

I would be interested in new books on the following subjects:
(please check all that apply, and use the spaces provided to identify specific software)

❑ Word processing: [26] ❑ Spreadsheets: [27]

❑ Data bases: [28] ❑ Desktop publishing: [29]

❑ File Utilities: [30] ❑ Money management: [31]

❑ Networking: [32] ❑ Programming languages: [33]

❑ Other: [34]

I use a PC at (please check all that apply): ❑ home [35] ❑ work [36] ❑ school [37] ❑ other: [38] ______

The disks I prefer to use are ❑ 5.25 [39] ❑ 3.5 [40] ❑ other: [41] ______

I have a CD ROM: ❑ yes [42] ❑ no [43]

I plan to buy or upgrade computer hardware this year: ❑ yes [44] ❑ no [45]

I plan to buy or upgrade computer software this year: ❑ yes [46] ❑ no [47]

Name: Business title: [48] Type of Business: [49]

Address (❑ home [50] ❑ work [51]/Company name:)

Street/Suite#

City [52]/State [53]/Zipcode [54]: Country [55]

❑ **I liked this book!** You may quote me by name in future IDG Books Worldwide promotional materials.

My daytime phone number is ______

IDG BOOKS

THE WORLD OF COMPUTER KNOWLEDGE

YES!

Please keep me informed about IDG's World of Computer Knowledge. Send me the latest IDG Books catalog.

NO POSTAGE NECESSARY IF MAILED IN THE UNITED STATES

BUSINESS REPLY MAIL

FIRST CLASS MAIL PERMIT NO. 2605 FOSTER CITY, CALIFORNIA

IDG Books Worldwide
919 E Hillsdale Blvd, STE 400
Foster City, CA 94404-9691